Working Americans
1880-2005

Volume VI: Women at Work

WORKING AMERICANS
1880-2005

Volume VI: Women at Work

by
Scott Derks

A UNIVERSAL REFERENCE BOOK

Grey House
Publishing

PUBLISHER:	Leslie Mackenzie
EDITORIAL DIRECTOR:	Laura Mars-Proietti
EDITORIAL COORDINATOR:	Neil O'Connor
MARKETING DIRECTOR:	Jessica Moody
AUTHOR:	Scott Derks
COPYEDITOR:	Elaine Alibrandi
COMPOSITION:	Q2A Solutions

A Universal Reference Book
Grey House Publishing, Inc.
185 Millerton Road
Millerton, NY 12546
518.789.8700
FAX 518.789.0545
www.greyhouse.com
e-mail: books @greyhouse.com

First edition 2005

Publisher's Cataloging-in-Publication Data
(Prepared by The Donohue Group, Inc.)
Derks, Scott.
   Working Americans, 1880-2005 / by Scott Derks.
     v. cm.
   Includes bibliographical references and indexes.
   Contents: v. 1. The working class -- v. 2. The middle class -- v. 3. The upper class -- v. 4. Their children. -- v. 5. At war. – v. 6. Women at Work
   ISBN: 1-891-48281-5 (v. 1)
   ISBN: 1-891-48272-6 (v. 2)
   ISBN: 1-930-95638-X (v. 3)
   ISBN: 1-930-95635-5 (v. 4)
   ISBN: 1-592-37024-1 (v. 5)
   ISBN: 1-592-37063-2 (v. 6)
1. Working class--United States--History--19th century. 2. Working class--United States--History--20th century. 3. Labor--United States--History--19th century. 4. Labor--United States--History--20th century. 5. Occupations--United States--History--19th century. 6. Occupations--United States--History--20th century. 7. Social classes--United States--History--19th century. 8. Social classes--United States--History--20th century. 9. United States--Economic conditions. I. Title.

HD8066 .D47
305.5'0973'0904—-dc21
ISBN 1-59237-063-2   hardcover

TABLE OF CONTENTS

1920-1929 INTRODUCTION 127

1930-1939 INTRODUCTION 155

INTRODUCTION

Working Americans 1880-2005 Volume VI: Women At Work, is the sixth volume in an open-ended series. Like its predecessors, *The Working Class, The Middle Class, The Upper Class, Their Children*, and *At War, Women At Work* observes the lives of Americans, decade by decade. Unlike its predecessors, *Volume VI* focuses on women and includes material through 2005.

The book is arranged in 12 decade-long chapters. Most include three individual **Profiles** sectioned into work, home and community; several **Historical Snapshots** that chronicle major milestones; and a handful of **News Features** from a variety of magazines and newspapers. These common elements, as well as specialized data such as **Selected Prices** and **Average Pay**, punctuate each chapter and act as statistical comparisons between decades, as well as between Americans of different socioeconomic backgrounds. The 33 women profiled in this volume represent wide ranges of: ages (12 to 88 years); social backgrounds (farmer's daughter to Los Angeles actress); ethnic backgrounds (Armenian to African American); and professions (artist to molecular research scientist). Some careers focus on fortune, some on fame, some on a regular paycheck and some on no paycheck at all. The goal of this volume is to illustrate how women's work has evolved from 1880-2005.

A Man May Work from Sun to Sun but a Women's Work is Never Done…

By the very nature of their gender, women's working environment is often intertwined with their social environment. A woman's choice of her life work – much more then a man's – can result from societal restraints or specific family situations; hence you'll find suppressed women gravitating toward creative outlets and childless women caring for the world's impoverished children. There are women whose work is not about choice, such as the farmer's wife, and the "juggler" balancing her roles as minister's wife, mother of two, teacher and full time student. Then there are women whose career rival's that of any successful man, such as our surgeon, judge, or successful publisher.

Like the other five titles in this series, *Working Americans VI: Women At Work* is a compilation of original research -- personal diaries, school files, family histories – combined with government statistics, commercial advertisements and news features. To the brand new material we have added some carefully chosen elements from the preceding five volumes to achieve the widest range of women's working situations. Together, this material provides an outstanding look of the working woman from the late 19th century to the present.

The text is presented in bulleted format. There are hundreds of supportive graphics -- photographs, advertisements, magazine covers, even campaign buttons. Like the earlier volumes in this *Working Americans* series, *Volume VI* is a "point in time" book, designed to illustrate the reality of that particular time. Some women grew up in less than ideal situations, which are portrayed as accurately as possible. We again asked previous purchasers, primarily high school and public librarians who own and find *Volumes I – V* valuable, if they objected to such content, as we did before publishing the graphic descriptions in *Volume V: At War*. And they again responded "Don't change a thing!" They all confirmed that the point of primary source material is to show others how it was . . . that it is crucial to show others how it was . . . and that the *Working Americans* series does just that.

This title was requested by previous purchasers of earlier volumes who asked us to use this engaging format to chronicle women. The next title in this series, *Working Americans 1880-2005: Social Protests*, is due out early in 2006.

The Editors

Praise for earlier volumes –

"The volume 'promises to enhance our understanding of the growth and development of the working class over more than a century.' It capably fulfills this promise... recommended for all types of libraries. "

ARBA

"[the author] adds to the genre of social history known as 'history from the bottom up,' which examines the lives of ordinary people...Recommended for all colleges and university library collections."

Choice

"this volume engages and informs, contributing significantly and meaningfully to the historiography of the working class in America...a compelling and well-organized contribution for those interested in social history and the complexities of working Americans."

Library Journal

"these interesting, unique compilations of economic and social facts, figures, and graphs will support multiple research needs. They will engage and enlighten patrons in high school, public, and academic library collections."

Booklist

This in no dull statistical compilation of economic history. It is a very interesting, readable account of life in the United States for the worker or laborer. It would be very useful for undergraduate students researching laborers or working and social conditions.
Journal of Business & Finance Librarianship

PREFACE

Welcome to the sixth book in a series examining the social and economic lives of working Americans. At the suggestion of a Virginia high school librarian, this volume focuses exclusively on working women and their lives. Another volume was planned, but because one of our primary users took the time to explore, question and assist, we struck out in a new direction. Like its predecessor volumes, *Working Americans VI: Women at Work* is about regular people meeting the unvarnished challenges that life perennially presents. Several chapters are drawn from profiles completed earlier in this series, marrying the story of the Chicago-based chocolate dipper, who first appeared in Volume I, with new stories about a New York judge and a New Mexico surgeon, to create a complete work about working women.

The first volume, *Working Americans 1880-1999: The Working Class*, launched this series, exploring the struggles of working class Americans through the eyes and wallets of three dozen families. With pictures, stories, statistics and advertisements of the period, it studied their jobs, wages, family life, expenditures and hobbies throughout the decades. The second volume, *The Middle Class,* captured the struggles—and joys—in a similar but sometimes subtly different way, profiling the lives of everyday families who played an incremental role in building the economy of America. Few were heroes, all felt the pressures of life, and most wanted to create a better life for themselves and for their children. The third volume, *The Upper Class*, studied the fascinating and often complex world of America's upper class. Through hard work, grit, good luck or inheritance, these families were elevated to the highest pinnacle of economic prosperity. All were wealthy, though not all were well off. The fourth volume built on the concepts and social issues explored in the previous three volumes by examining the lives of children of working Americans throughout the entire spectrum of economic status. In this way, *Working Americans IV: Their Children* looked at issues of growing up: parents, homework, child labor, education, peer pressure, food, fads and fun with friends. The fifth volume extended these examinations to an often life-changing event: war. Decade by decade, *Working Americans V: At War* explored the ways that officers, enlisted personnel and civilians handled the stress, boredom and brutality of war, involving declared conflicts, one-time military actions, protests or preparations for future wars.

Working Americans VI: Women at Work celebrates the contributions of women, chronicling both the progress they have made and the roadblocks that have been placed in their way. The study of history offers all of us the opportunity to view change over the sweep of time. In a detailed fashion, these profiles and articles help the reader reflect on the transformation of female independence and transition into the workplace. Although the author is a lifelong member of the male persuasion, the publisher, copy editor, editorial director and more than half the contributors are female. It is a trend represented in a variety of ways within this volume, well-illustrated by the gender composition of today's graduate schools. In the early 1970s, when the magazine *Ms.* was in its infancy, women received approximately 10 percent of the nation's graduate degrees in medicine, law and veterinary medicine. Today women represent half of all law students, 40 percent of medical students and two-thirds of the graduate degrees awarded in veterinary medicine and pharmacy. The actions and contributions of one generation are rarely lost on the next.

As in the previous volumes, each story is unique, as each of us is unique: the North Carolina widow who continues to enjoy farming without her husband; the Armenian woman who finds a safe refuge by moving to America; the Ohio teen eager to test the boundaries of 1920s society by playing the saxophone in a boy-dominated band. The story of a young woman judge expresses the joy of her profession and the sorrow in the death of a husband. We meet a grandmother still living without indoor plumbing in the 1950s, a hairdresser in Seattle and a surgeon in New Mexico. Each has a story to tell.

All of the profiles are modeled on real people and events, although, as in the previous books of this series, the names have been changed and some details added based on statistics, the then-current popularity of an idea, or writings of the time. Otherwise, every effort has been made to profile accurately the individual's early and family life, education, and work experiences. To ensure that each profile reflects the feelings of its subject, diaries, letters, biographies, interviews and magazine articles were consulted and used. In some cases, the featured individuals represent national trends and feelings, but mostly, they represent only themselves. Ultimately, it is the people, events and actions of working Americans—along with their investments, spending decisions, time commitments, jobs and passions—that shape society and the economy.

Working Americans: Women at Work is dedicated to my mother,
Martha Hope Derks, and my wife Ellen's mother,
Ruth Farmer Hanckel, with love and gratitude.
Raising us could only be defined as work.

ACKNOWLEDGEMENTS

As I review the list of acknowledgements for this book, the sixth in the *Working American* series, the names are like family now. Elaine Alibrandi has been an ever diligent and resourceful editing partner since the beginning, even though in this age of computers, we have never met. The work of Greg Flowers once again graces these pages with his detailed research into lives past. Special thanks also must go to Erika DePaz for two contributions, Caroline Gottlieb for her second appearance in the *Working American* series, as well as Sally Gaillard, Austin and Carol Watson, and Dr. Books of Columbia, SC, for their suggestions and pictures. Once again, praise goes to my son Marshall Derks for the research and writing of a profile, his third appearance in the series, and to my daughters Elizabeth Derks and Lucia Derks for their library research. Hal Stallworth, who has done research in the past, makes his first appearance as a contributor. Finally, thanks must go to the unsung hero of this series, Grey House Publishing's Editorial Director Laura Mars-Proietti, who has guided me through more than 175 profiles consuming more than 3,300 printed pages of this ongoing saga about the lives of working Americans.

1880–1899

The final two decades of the nineteenth century danced in the reflected glow of the Gilded Age, when the wealth of a tiny percentage of Americans knew no bounds. The role of women was still strictly defined and most women were forced to choose between a profession and marriage. Few were encouraged to attend college; still fewer attended. Women teachers who married were expected to surrender their jobs as an accepted part of the nuptials. Those who rubbed against the edges of these restrictive rules were derisively branded "mannish" or "new women." At the same time, women were beginning to play a more visible role in recreational sports, international travel and the emerging field of journalism. During this age, children of the working class routinely left school in their teens to work, the middle class was small and college was largely reserved for the elite and wealthy men of America. It was also a time marked by an abundance of emerging technology and changing opportunities, symbolizing the restless spirit of the American people. The highly popular children's books featuring Horatio Alger reinforced the notion that opportunity and wealth lured around every corner.

The rapid expansion of railroads opened up the nation to new industries, new markets and the formation of monopolistic trusts that catapulted a handful of corporations into positions of unprecedented power and wealth. This expanding technology also triggered the movement of workers from farm to factory, the rapid expansion of wage labor, and the explosive growth of cities. Farmers, merchants and small-town artisans found themselves increasingly dependent on regional and national market forces. The shift in the concentrations of power was unprecedented in American history. At the same time, professionally trained workers were reshaping America's economy alongside business managers or entrepreneurs eager to capture their piece of the American pie. It was an economy on a roll with few rudders or regulations.

Across America the economy—along with its work force—was running away from the land. Before the Civil War, the United States was overwhelmingly an agricultural nation. By the end of the century, non-agricultural occupations employed nearly two thirds of the workers. As important, two of every three Americans came to rely on wages instead of self-employment as farmers or artisans. At the same time, industrial growth began to center around cities, where wealth accumulated for a few who understood how to harness and use railroads, create new consumer markets, and manage a ready supply of cheap, trainable labor. Jobs, offering steady wages and the promise of a better life for workers' children, drew people from the farms into the cities, which grew at twice the rate of the nation as a whole. A modern, industrially-based work force emerged from the traditional farmlands, led by men skilled at managing others and the complicated flow of materials required to keep a factory operating. This led to an increasing demand for attorneys, bankers, and physicians to handle the complexity of the emerging urban economy. In 1890, newspaper editor Horace Greeley remarked, "We cannot all live in cities, yet nearly all seem determined to do so."

The new cities of America were home to great wealth and poverty—both produced by the massive migrations and influx of immigrants willing to work at any price. It was a time symbolized by Andrew Carnegie's steel mills, John D. Rockefeller's organization of the Standard Oil monopoly, and the manufacture of Alexander Graham Bell's wonderful invention, the telephone. By 1894, the United States had become the world's leading industrial power, producing more than England, France, and Germany—its three largest competitors—combined. For much of this period, the nation's industrial energy focused on the need for railroads requiring large quantities of labor, iron, steel, stone, and lumber. In 1883, nine tenths of the nation's entire production of steel went into rails. The most important invention of the period—in an era of tremendous change and innovation—may have been the Bessemer converter, which transformed pig iron into steel at a relatively low cost, increasing steel output 10 times from 1877 to 1892.

The greatest economic event during the last two decades of the nineteenth century was the great wave of immigration that swept America. It is believed to be the largest worldwide population movement in human history, bringing more than 10 million people to the United States to fill the expanding need for workers. In the 1880s alone, 5.25 million immigrants arrived, more than in the first six decades of the nineteenth century. This wave was dominated by Irish, German, and English workers. Scandinavia, Italy, and China sent scores of eager workers, normally men, to fill the expanding labor needs of the United States. To attract this much-needed labor force, railroad and steamship companies advertised throughout Europe and China the glories of American life. To an economically depressed world, it was a welcome call.

Despite all the signs of economic growth and prosperity, America's late-nineteenth-century economy was profoundly unstable. Industrial expansion was undercut by a depression from 1882 to 1885, followed in 1893 by a five-year-long economic collapse that devastated rural and urban communities across America. As a result, job security for workers just climbing onto the industrial stage was often fleeting. Few wage-earners found full-time work for the entire year. The unevenness in the economy was caused both by the level of change under way and irresponsible speculation, but more generally to the stubborn adherence of the federal government to a highly inflexible gold standard as the basis of value for currency.

Between the very wealthy and the very poor emerged a new middle stratum, whose appearance was one of the distinctive features of late-nineteenth-century America. The new middle class fueled the purchase of one million light bulbs a year by 1890, even though the first electric light was only 11 years old. It was the middle class also that flocked to buy Royal Baking Powder, (which was easier to use and faster than yeast) and supported the emergence and spread of department stores that were sprouting up across the nation.

1890 Profile

Twenty-six-year-old Mabel Vandergrift is fascinated by photography, travel, world events, and the "Indian problem" out West; her mother is convinced that Mabel's love of knowledge and fixation on photography have doomed her chances of a respectable marriage.

Life at Home

- Mabel Vandergrift is an unmarried woman at 26, past the traditional marrying age of women of her class; this fact has begun to worry her mother.
- Talk among her friends is that Mabel believes herself to be better than all of the boys who wish to take her out.
- An only child, she was raised by her mother and grandparents in a rambling seventeenth-century home overlooking the bay from the north end of Staten Island.
- Her grandfather purchased the house in 1844.
- The family home has a sullied history that includes a loyalist of the American Revolution who hanged himself for unrequited love and a previous owner's daughter who declined Cornelius Vanderbilt's proposal of marriage because she believed his financial prospects to be poor.
- Although Mabel's family is not wealthy, Staten Island is a very fashionable place during the summer season for the rich, including the Vanderbilts, Cunards and the Roosevelts.
- Mabel is very athletic and has won many trophies for golf, bowling, and a new game just brought over from Bermuda called tennis.

Mabel Vandergrift sees herself as a photographic pioneer.

- Mabel loves playing tennis at the Cricket Club, but is convinced it would be more sporting if played in something less confining than floor-length dresses and tight corsets.
- When she complains, her mother invariably reminds her, "A woman must conduct herself properly at all times."
- The manor in which she lives is situated on rolling hills that flow on to the sea; large manicured gardens cover the area.

- She acquired a sparse education at a private school for young girls set up by two English women.
- Her real education has come from her opportunities to sail, travel to Europe, and from her uncle, a sea captain who encouraged her pursuit of her principal hobby, photography.
- He taught her the proper way to maintain the large glass plates that are the medium for negatives and how to mix the chemicals in order to prepare the plates.
- Right outside the house is the home's primary source of water, a pump where Mabel washes their photographic plates, even in the dead of winter.
- Some plates require 25 separate washings to obtain a perfect negative.
- The manor has dormer windows and a porch with a hammock, a bird cage, and a spyglass that Mabel uses to watch the ships that pass by.
- Inside the house, the rooms are furnished with an abundance of art, clocks, and candlesticks taking up every inch of free space on the mantle.

Photographic negatives are washed at the pump.

Mabel uses a spyglass to watch the ships that pass by.

- In Mabel's room, elaborate whicker chairs stand next to bookshelves crammed with religious books, travels in Europe, and articles about the proper development of photographic negatives.
- The room, like those of her best friends, is inundated with knick-knacks collected from around the world and carefully arranged on every flat surface.
- Mabel especially cherishes seashells, large butterflies, carved objects from the South Pacific islands, and colorful Asian fans brought back to Staten Island by her seagoing uncle.
- Collections of foreign natural history objects are widely regarded as a sign of sophistication.
- She and the other women of the family are expected to decorate the house, and they do so with both subtlety and volume.

"The whole island is like a garden, and affords very fine scenery."

—Henry David Thoreau, Staten Island, 1843

Mabel wishes to shoot photographs of Indian chiefs and warriors.

Life at Work

- Mabel Vandergrift enjoys telling her friends and parents that it is her ambition to travel West to shoot photographs of Indian chiefs and their warriors.
- She loves to see the expressions of shock and fear this dream evinces.
- When her tales of meeting an Indian chief fail to shock, she likes to say she wants to answer Susan B. Anthony's call for missionary women suffragists willing to be sent to Southern fields to open the eyes of the daughters of Dixie to the error of their ways.
- She has also caused a lot of talk in the community by telling friends, including eligible men, that she would not be afraid to dress like a man so she could fight in the next war.
- She knows for a fact it is possible; at least one woman is now fighting for a pension from the Union Army, where she fought and was wounded in the leg, leading to the discovery of her deception.
- Some of her friends are amused by the suggestion; most don't think Mabel's fine features would pass for a man's even if she were dressed in men's clothing.
- A woman of high energy and prodigious mechanical skill, she likes to think of herself as a female pioneer in the world of photography.
- Despite her boasts of exotic travel, most of her photography reveals the private life of the island; many of the pictures are self-portraits, and images of her friends, parties, and her home.
- Before she was 10, Mabel's uncle showed her how to use a dry plate camera of British manufacture.
- Another uncle, a professor at Rutgers University, taught her enough chemistry to handle the complex, messy job of developing the large glass plates.

"The Mannish Girl," *New York Truth*, January 21, 1893:

"...So she falls out of sympathy with her sex. She loses its delicacy; she is reckless of its conventions. That is always the peril of the mannish girl. But the fact that she is a woman in body, but tries to be a man in mind, exposes her to the animadversions of the ribald. As she mingles with the world, she feeds a kind of vanity by being mannish. To talk slang, to smoke cigarettes, to ride hounds, commend, in a measure, to her male companions. They declare her to be jolly, fetching, stunning.... But they rarely marry her."

- Together, the uncles and Mabel built a tiny darkroom in a storage closet, where she spends hours developing plates, and toning and fixing prints.
- Alone in the dark room with a good negative and fresh chemicals, watching a picture develop, she feels alive and in control of her world.
- The dry plate method works when emulsion is formed using light-sensitive silver bromide in a viscous gelatin solution, processed from cattle bones and hides.
- The dry plates eliminate the need for immediate processing and allow for commercial production of the plates.
- Mabel buys her plates in a New York City photography store, which also supplies the numerous chemicals required to develop the exposed plates and to print pictures.
- For almost a decade, she rarely has gone anywhere without her photographic equipment—all 50 pounds of it.
- She has even ventured into New York City to photograph "types" of the city: immigrants, beggars, slum dwellers, and oystermen.
- Always, her pictures are in focus and fun to view.
- Sometimes, hours are spent setting up the perfect picture, often with Mabel in the center of the frame activating a remote cable to trigger the camera.
- Some photographic setups have become so elaborate, friends refuse to be involved with the meticulous details required for one of Mabel's photographs.
- Blessed by her home's sweeping view of New York harbor, she has observed and photographed a wide range of ships: square riggers, coasting schooners, racing yachts, tugboats, excursion steamers, immigrant ships, and ocean liners.
- She also spends hours photographing animals in the Central Park Zoo, patiently waiting for the perfect expression from a prize chimpanzee or a vexed elephant.
- The dry plate method still requires that her subjects remain relatively still, although the long 10- and 20-second exposures of the past are gone, thanks to modern techniques.
- Mabel and her friends consider themselves "new women" and have formed a females-only organization known as the "Darned Club."

Mabel and her friends consider themselves to be "new women."

- Recently, Mabel saw that inventor George Eastman is planning to introduce a new type of film that is more flexible, unbreakable, and can be rolled.
- Photographers would buy a wooden, light-tight camera with the film already inside; once the 100-frame film was used up, the photographer could mail the film and camera to the Kodak factory, where the film would be removed from the camera, processed, and printed.
- The camera would then be reloaded with film and mailed back.
- Mabel wants to see the camera operate, but knows she wants to continue developing her own negatives.
- Some on the island say she is too "mannish" and believe her to be a foolish, wild woman who is throwing away any chance of marriage and happiness.
- In defiance, Mabel and two friends recently dressed as men for a self-portrait, declaring, "Maybe we look better as men than women."

Mabel and her friends dress as men for a self-portrait, to mock changes they see as too "mannish."

"Fell Dead in Her Cage, The Lady Chimpanzee in Central Park Has Passed Away," *The Washington Post*, March 2, 1890:

Miss Kittie, the former fiancée of Crowley, the Central Park chimpanzee, died in her cage in the old arsenal building, Central Park, this morning of consumption.

Yesterday Jake Cook, her keeper, noticed that her appetite was beginning to fail. She had been in the habit of eating a pound of grapes every day, but yesterday she ate only half a pound, and that with evident difficulty.

At 6 o'clock last evening, when Mr. Cook was going home to dinner, Kittie did not look as bright as usual. When he returned he saw that her eyes were sunken and that she breathed with difficulty.

All night long Jake watched by the bedside of his charge, holding her hand and trying to soothe her. She suffered greatly, and frequently tried to expand her chest, while she looked beseechingly at her faithful friend as if begging him to relieve her.

At 2:40 o'clock she suddenly turned away from her keeper and fell to the floor gasping for breath. Jake quickly raised her head, but saw in a moment that she was dead.

When Miss Kittie arrived she was but two years old. In accordance with the traditions of the Chimpanzee families, marriages between members of that family must not take place until each of the contracting parties are four years old. A courtship of two years was therefore in prospect for Mr. Crowley, who immediately started in upon the labor of love. From that time dates the romantic story of the Crowley engagement.

Everything seemed to be progressing as happily as the proverbial marriage bell and apparently the hopes of both the chimpanzee lovers were to be sealed within a few short months, when about August 1, 1888, Mr. Crowley had an attack of indigestion, which weakened him, and when he caught cold a few days afterward, pneumonia set in. His lungs had always been weak, and on August 31 he succumbed to the variable climate of the metropolis. Thus was the prospective joy of Miss Kittie turned to grief.

Miss Kittie has been accustomed to holding daily public receptions in front of her cage from 9:30 a.m. to 4:30 p.m., and thousands of nurse girls and children besides a good sized quota of the Empire City's population have each month stood in front of her big iron-barred cage, and delightedly watched her antics.

"Surely this country is the Paradise of the world... the inhabitants of this Island are tall, thin, narrow shouldered people, very simple in their manners, know neither Poverty nor Riches, each house has a good farm, and every man a trade, they know no distinction of Persons, and I am sure must have lived very happily till these troubles."

—A British officer stationed on Staten Island, 1776

Life in the Community: Staten Island

- Staten Island is a select upper-middle-class community across New York Bay from Manhattan.

- The first bridge from the island to New Jersey opened last year; the railroad bridge links Howland Hook to Elizabeth, New Jersey.
- On the island, the quality of one's horse carriage reveals one's station in life.
- Plain people drive buggies, farmer's wagons, or buckboards, while the well-to-do sport custom-made carriages.

"Amateur Photography," by Nathan Haskell Dole, *The New York Times*, August 17, 1890:

I fell in love with Phyllis Brown;
She was the nicest girl in town.
Her father had a bank account
Of a superfluous amount;
And so the more I thought of it
The clearer seemed the benefit
That such a union would confer
At least on me—perhaps on her.
For she was pretty. Such a nose!
Such grace of curves! Such a tint of rose!
Such sylph-like elegance of pose!
Such sunny eyes of heavenly blue,
With little cherubs peeping through!
Such golden bangs! Oh, every such
Was the superlative of much!
And educated? She could speak
Italian, Spanish, Volapuk, French,
Russian, Swedish, Danish, Dutch,
And every language born of Babel—
To read and speak them she was able.
So learned, pretty—rich besides;
Yes, she would be the gem of brides!
And I, though poor, had every taste,
The wealth of Kroisos would have graced;
So I resolved to risk my fate

In winning such an equal mate.
At first my chances promised fair:
She met me halfway everywhere;
Accepted my civilities;
And sometimes made me ill at ease
When I on parting held her hand
And felt that mute "you understand,"
Expressed by just the faintest squeeze.
(I cannot think she was a flirt,
And yet she did to my hurt!)
One day I crossed the Rubicon:
I knew her father would have gone;
I rang her door-bell inly bent
On knowing she would consent.
She sent me down a little note,
The coolest that she ever wrote:
"Excuse me, please, from seeing you,
I've something else I must do;
I'll see you later if we live."
I asked the footman if he knew
Why such an answer she should give;
The servant shrewdly shook his head;
"She's busy, Sir," he gravely said,
"Developing a negative!"

- The brighter the varnish, the nattier the coachman's livery, the more beautiful the construction of the coach, the prouder a Staten Island lady is to set forth on a round of calls.
- It is widely believed that women must be the guardians of culture and morality; it is their role to regulate everything from family church attendance to the proper use of finger bowls.
- Many local residents are very upset that year-round ferry service to the island has been reduced to only the summer months.
- Officials claim that the ferries were set up primarily for the summer season, and that they were never intended to be used by year-round residents.
- When discovered by Giovanni da Verrazano in 1524, Staten Island was occupied by the Aquehonga Indians, a branch of the Raritans.
- In 1609, Henry Hudson established Dutch trade in the area and named the island Staaten Eylandt after the Dutch parliament, Staaten Generaal der Vereenigde Nederlanden.
- Although the first Dutch settlement of the New Netherlands colony was made on Manhattan in 1620, Staten Island remained uncolonized by the Dutch for many decades.
- In 1630, the Dutch West India Company granted the island to Michael Pauw, and it was bought at this time from the Indians for some "duffels, kettles, axes, hoes, wampum, drilling awls, jews harps, and divers other small wares."
- In 1641, the settlement at Oude Dorp Old Town was established near South Beach by a small group of Dutch Walloon and Huguenot families.
- It was destroyed by the Indians in the same year, was immediately rebuilt, was again destroyed in 1642 and was again rebuilt, but was abandoned after its destruction for the third time in 1655.
- At the end of the Second Anglo-Dutch War in 1667, the New Netherlands colony was ceded to England; Staten Island became part of the new English colony of New York.

"Photography News," *The New York Times*, April 21, 1890:

The fact is that an amateur photographic outfit is not necessarily expensive and that, as in fishing tackle, the prices cover along on the sliding scale. Five dollars to two thousand is the record on finely made trout rods. In amateur photography the start is about the same and the end not far distant. For $7 the amateur may make his beginning. This will include a small camera and a developer of the old-fashioned pyro type; not old-fashioned from disuse, but because so many new developers have been offered to the picture makers that they have firm adherents. The seven-dollar camera often proves a little prize and pictures turned out from it are the peers of specimens from the seventy-five-dollar instrument. This cheap camera is of standard tripod stamp. Passing a little further up to the fifteen-dollar mark, the detectives and hand camera can be obtained. Twenty and twenty-five dollars will secure to the novice in the art an excellent outfit and reliable apparatus. There are many of these in use and some excellent work is being done with them. Perhaps it is wiser for the amateur to commence with, say, a twenty-five dollar outfit. If he tires of the work, he has not wasted much money, for his always bring something if not misused.

Fashions of To-Day.

- In 1671, in order to encourage an expansion of the Dutch settlements, the English resurveyed Oude Dorp, which became known as Old Town, and expanded the lots along the shore to the south.
- These lots were settled primarily by Dutch and became known as Nieuwe Dorp meaning "New Town," which later became Anglicized as New Dorp.
- Staten Island played a significant role in the American Revolution when the British forces under William Howe evacuated Boston in the summer of 1776 and prepared to attack New York City.
- Howe used the strategic location of Staten Island as a staging ground for the attack.
- He established his headquarters in New Dorp; it is here that the representatives of the British government reportedly received their first notification of the Declaration of Independence.

"The Apache Prisoners: General Miles Strongly Opposes Sending Them to Fort Sill; They Would Stir Up the Other Redskins, and the Settlers to Arizona Would Again Suffer a Reign of Terror. North Carolina Suggested as a Settlement," *The Washington Post*, March 10, 1890:

Another Apache outbreak has been quieted by the troops in Arizona. The Indians who murdered George Herbert a week ago were overtaken by troops and two killed. They were chased over 300 miles over the toughest country in the Territory. Had the Indians been in force it would have taken a campaign to subdue them. In connection with this outbreak, the views of General Miles as to the advisability of sending the Apaches at Mount Vernon, Ala., to the Fort Sill reservation are of interest. General Miles is strongly opposed to the proposed transfer.

He believes that the return of Indians to that country would stir up further outbreaks, and would be prejudicial to the safety of the people in Arizona. He believes that the prisoners should be kept far from that country, and suggests North Carolina as a suitable place. In recent hearings before the House Committee on Foreign Affairs, he gave his views at length, and described the circumstances connected with the last Apache war, which have not been generally known. In describing the difficulties of the chase of the Apaches in 1886 by the troops, he said:

"To give you an idea of the difficulty encountered by the troops, not only in climbing those mountains, but the heat was so intense that the soldiers could not put their hands on their gun-barrels, or on the rocks, as shown in this report of Assistant Surgeon Wood, who was present. While this was being done, which lasted about four months, I became satisfied that there could be no permanent peace in that country until the Indian camp at Apache, which was the recruiting station and camp of supplies from which all these raids have been made, and to which they have oftentimes finally returned, was broken up and cleared out of that country."

The Apaches were finally forced to beg for terms. General Miles promised protection, but said that they should be sent from the country. After sketching the campaign against the Apaches and its successful conclusion, he says:

"That, in brief, gives the history of my connection with those Indians. As far as their confinement in Florida is concerned, I had nothing whatever to do with it. I have, however, always believed that it was a mistake to send them there, because they are accustomed to the high altitude of the mountains."

- The following month, in August, the British forces crossed the Narrow to Brooklyn and routed the American forces under George Washington at the Battle of Long Island, resulting in the British capture of New York.
- Three weeks later, on September 11, 1776, the British received a delegation of Americans represented by Benjamin Franklin, Edward Rutledge, and John Adams; the Americans refused the peace offer from the British in exchange for the withdrawal of the Declaration of Independence.
- British forces remained on Staten Island throughout the war.
- Although local sentiment was predominantly Tory, the islanders found the demands of supporting the troops to be onerous; many buildings and churches were destroyed, and the military demand for resources resulted in an extensive deforestation of the island by the end of the war.
- The British again used the island as a staging ground for their final evacuation of New York City on December 5, 1783.
- After the war, the wealthiest Tory landowners fled to Canada and their estates were subdivided and sold.

"The New Woman," *Pick-Me-Up* magazine, October 10, 1891:

The woman of the future will not trifle with our hearts,
She will find more time to study into sciences and arts;
She will not be too disdainful, irreverent, and proud,
But with the highest virtues and attainments be endowed.
The woman of the future will be modest in her looks;
She will sing the sweetest ballads and peruse the choicest books;
Her sympathies will widen, her goodness will expand,
Until the poor shall bless her, and the weak will call her friend.

"Fashions in Ribbons, What the Manufacturers Are Doing to Capture Woman's Fancy," *The New York Times*, April 16, 1890:

Every week shows more plainly the great efforts which are being made by ribbon manufacturers to keep this article in front and make it as attractive as possible. This, of course, is the only way of capturing a woman's fancy, and we must say that foreign and domestic manufacturers know how to do it.

There is a ribbon with straw effect which is splendidly adapted for ornamenting straw hats. The body is double-faced satin and the border hemp interwoven with small satin stripes in different colors. The fabric can be had in all colors which assimilate with any straw shade.

Another new material conveys the idea of two ribbons, and is called the two-ribbon effect. One side is a gross grain with a satin edge, while the other side shows a plain satin effect. The color combinations are numerous, but we find that in this fancy fabric, all ribbons of dark colors are prettier than those of delicate shades.

HISTORICAL SNAPSHOT
1890

- Jane Addams set up Hull House in Chicago, the first of many settlement houses to aid the poor
- Two hundred Sioux were killed by soldiers at Wounded Knee, South Dakota
- Lightweight aluminum cooking pans, which were easier to care for than iron pots, were invented in Ohio
- Two-thirds of the nation's 62.9 million people still lived in rural areas; 32.7 percent were immigrants or the children of at least one immigrant parent
- American women began wearing knickerbockers instead of skirts while riding bicycles
- All members of a women's baseball club were arrested following a game against the Danville, Illinois Browns before 2,000 fans on Sunday, June 8; they were fined a total of $100 for disturbing the peace by playing baseball on Sunday in violation of the local "Blue Laws"
- *New York World* reporter Nellie Bly (Elizabeth Cochran Seaman) became the first woman to travel around the world; she did it in just 72 days
- Fay Fuller climbed the 14,410-foot Mt. Rainier in Washington
- The *San Francisco Examiner* reporter Winifred Sweet Black became the first woman to report on a prize fight
- The Daughters of the American Revolution was founded
- The first commercial dry cell battery was invented
- Three percent of Americans, age 18 to 21, attended college
- Elizabeth Cady Stanton became the president of the National Woman Suffrage Association
- The first full-service advertising agency was established in New York City
- Ceresota flour was introduced by the Northwest Consolidated Milling Company
- Alice Sanger became the first female staffer for the U.S. White House
- The United Mine Workers of America was founded
- Because of the demand for domestic servants, more women than men were emigrating from Ireland to America
- Thousands of Kansas farmers were bankrupted by tight money conditions
- Yosemite Park was created by an Act of Congress
- Idaho was admitted as the forty-third state, and Wyoming as the forty-fourth
- The census showed that 53.5 percent of the farms in the United States comprised fewer than 100 acres
- Dr. Ida Gray became the first African-American woman dentist in the United States

Selected Prices

Child's Suit	$2.00
China, 130 Pieces	$30.00
Flour, Half Barrel	$2.50
Folding Bed	$15.00
Fountain Pen	$3.50
Hair Curler	$1.00
Man's Shirt	$1.50
Music Box	$2.50
Parasol, Satin	$3.90
Piano Lessons, 24	$8.00
Tooth Extraction	$0.25
Woman's Bicycle Costume	$7.50

The History of Photography

1727: Professor J. Schulze creates the first photosensitive compound when he mixes chalk, nitric acid, and silver in a flask; he notices darkening on the side of the flask exposed to sunlight.

1800: Thomas Wedgwood makes "sun pictures" by placing opaque objects on leather treated with silver nitrate; the resulting images deteriorated rapidly, however, if displayed under light stronger than that of candles.

1816: Joseph-Nicéphore Niepce combines the camera obscura with photosensitive paper and creates a permanent image.

1834: Henry Fox Talbot creates permanent (negative) images using paper soaked in silver chloride and fixed with a salt solution.

1837: Louis Daguerre creates images on silver-plated copper coated with silver iodide and "developed" with warmed mercury; Daguerre is awarded a state pension by the French government in exchange for publication of methods and the rights by other French citizens to use the daguerreotype process.

1841: Talbot patents his process under the name "calotype."

1851: Frederick Scott Archer, a sculptor in London, improves photographic resolution by spreading a mixture of collodion (nitrated cotton dissolved in ether and alcohol) and chemicals on sheets of glass. Wet plate collodion photography was much cheaper than daguerreotypes; the negative/positive process permitted unlimited reproductions, and the process was published but not patented.

1853: Nada (Felix Toumachon) opens his portrait studio in Paris.

1854: Adolphe Disderi develops carte-de-visite photography in Paris, leading to a worldwide boom in portrait studios for the next decade.

1855: Direct positive images on glass (ambrotypes) and metal (tintypes or ferrotypes) become popular in the United States.

1861: Scottish physicist James Clerk-Maxwell demonstrates a color photography system involving three black-and-white photographs, each taken through a red, green, or blue filter. The photos are turned into lantern slides and projected in registration with the same color filters. This is the "color separation" method.

1861-65: Mathew Brady and (mostly) staff covers the American Civil War, exposing 7,000 negatives.

1868:	Ducas de Hauron publishes a book proposing a variety of methods for color photography.
1870:	The U.S. Congress sends photographers out to the West; the most famous images are taken by William Jackson and Tim O'Sullivan.
1871:	Richard Leach Maddox, an English doctor, proposes the use of an emulsion of gelatin and silver bromide on a glass plate, the "dry plate" process.
1877:	Eadweard Muybridge, born in England as Edward Muggridge, settles the "do a horse's four hooves ever leave the ground at once" bet among rich San Franciscans using time-sequenced photography of Leland Stanford's horse.
1878:	Dry plates are manufactured commercially.
1880:	George Eastman, age 24, sets up Eastman Dry Plate Company in Rochester, New York. The first half-tone photograph appears in a daily newspaper, the *New York Graphic*.
1888:	The first Kodak camera appears, containing a 20-foot roll of paper, enough for 100 2.5-inch-diameter circular pictures.
1889:	Kodak introduces an improved camera that uses a roll of film instead of paper.
1890:	Jacob Riis publishes *How the Other Half Lives*, images of tenement life in New York City.

1892 Profile

Upper Class

Seventeen-year-old Clarissa Strobel has found great freedom and friendship at Miss Porter's, a private girls' school in Farmington, Connecticut, known for developing women of character and intellect.

Life at Home

- For the past two years, Clarissa has been summering with her mother, attending Miss Porter's School, and thinking about her future.
- Her mother is often mystified by Clarissa's serious thoughts, mingled with a mischievous nature.
- Secretly she is happy that she doesn't know everything her daughter, the last of three, is up to.
- Clarissa and her mother summered in York Harbor, renting one of the Twin Dominick Cottages, where they were able to play tennis in bright sunshine, "while our friends on the ocean are in a damp fog," her mother liked to say.
- In addition to tennis, Clarissa has learned to swim, mastering various strokes with the help of a friend and a new book on swimming.
- Her father, a major industrialist, has earned millions since the end of the Civil War; her mother is talking about building a place of her own.
- Clarissa loves taking pictures, which everyone calls Kodaks; she believes that the modern camera is so easy to use, anyone can do it, but her mother seems reluctant to try.
- The film is loaded into the camera at the factory, and after taking 12 pictures, the photographer sends the entire camera straight to Kodak, where

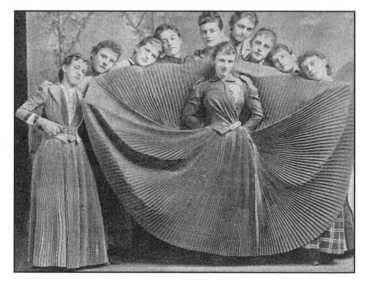

Clarissa Strobel enjoys the companionship at Miss Porter's School.

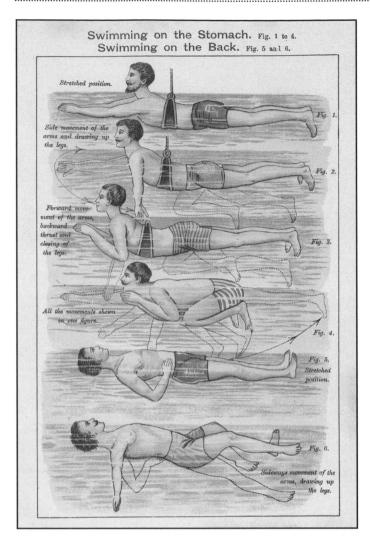

Swimming on the Stomach. Fig. 1 to 4.
Swimming on the Back. Fig. 5 and 6.

Stretched position.

Side movement of the arms and drawing up the legs.

Fig. 1.

Fig. 2.

Forward movement of the arms, backward thrust and closing of the legs.

Fig. 3.

All the movements shewn in one figure.

Fig. 4.

Fig. 5.
Stretched position.

Fig. 6.

Sideways movement of the arms, drawing up the legs.

the pictures are developed, printed and returned by mail along with the camera, newly loaded with film.

- Recently, Clarissa took pictures of her friend Mary Sprague and was most upset that a young man who admires Mary took one of the Kodaks without her permission.

- She is not only angry about the theft, but also feels bad that the boy now has a picture of her friend, which is not proper in the least unless Mary gives her consent; it might give the wrong impression.

- In addition to her camera, one of Clarissa's prize possessions is a delicate doll with a bisque head known as Miss Elizabeth, which she dresses in a white silk gown.

- When she returned to Miss Porter's School last fall, the doll was carefully boxed and wrapped, but her head was broken during the trip; after several trips to Hartford, her father was able to locate a new head so that Miss Elizabeth could be put whole again.

- In Farmington, where fashion is always important, the girls are now wearing sweaters.

- Clarissa has discovered that sweaters can be found in red, white and black, but chiefly in dark blue.

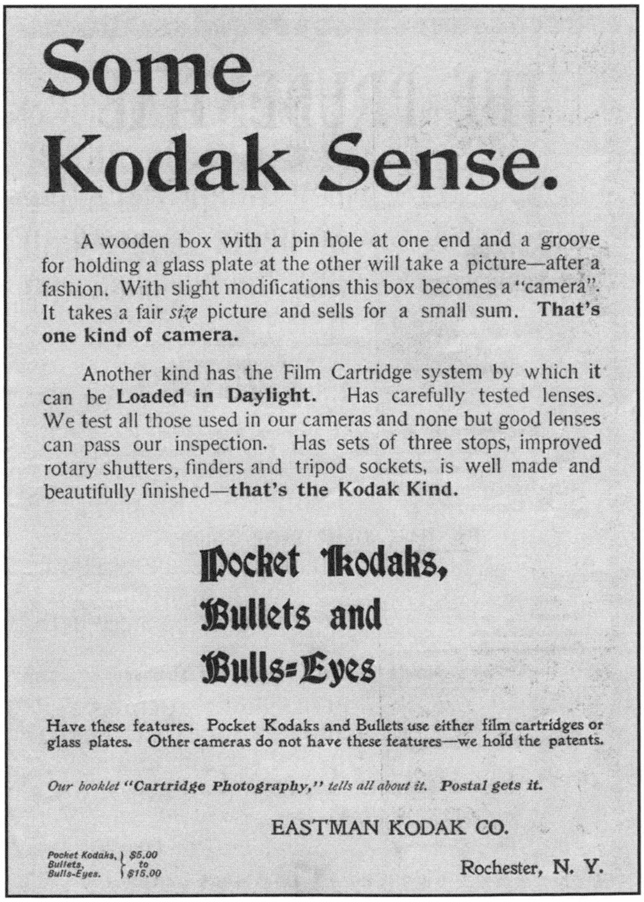

- Most of the sweaters were originally made for small men, she believes, but at least one girl at school enjoys the distinction of owning a sweater that was made to order and obtained through Harvard by a friend on the varsity team.
- It is dark red, with an extremely wide double collar, which is open with lacing a few inches from the throat.
- In addition to her many skills, Clarissa is an accomplished palmist, and is believed by many to be capable of telling fortunes.
- During visits home, on more than one occasion, she has been called upon during gatherings to tell someone's fortune and character by looking at the shapes, lines and suppleness of the person's hands, which she firmly believes are a window to the soul.

Spring Costumes.
JACINTHA WAIST. OPRA DRAPERY.
ERNESTA JACKET. (BACK.)—HERMIONE WAIST. FREDA DRAPERY.

Life at School

- Clarissa's room at Miss Porter's School is decorated with great care; she is using a Spanish theme, dominated by Spanish shawls and pictures taken by a cousin while traveling in Spain.
- She hopes to include Spain on her traveling itinerary when she takes her grand tour of Europe next year.
- For most of last semester, she used an elaborate assortment of Japanese fans to spark up the room, but that grew boring.
- Her room is also filled with fresh flowers, which she buys almost daily.
- Flowers, she and her roommates agree, make life more pleasant and the room a joy.

What Your Hand Means, *New York Sun*, 1892:

A soft hand, said Mr. Heron-Allen, in his lecture, indicated a fervent but fickle lover, while a hard hand denoted a long, enduring, though possibly smothering, love. A spatula hand, wherein the tips of the fingers are broad and flat, denoted inconstancy, desire for change and love of locomotion. It was found in jockeys and colonists. A hand with conically tipped fingers indicated inspiration, instinct, Bohemianism and generosity.

A hand with squarely built fingertips showed order and arrangement, particularly when the joints throughout were prominent. A scientific hand was irregular to a marked degree, the joints lumpy and highly developed—altogether a malformed conglomeration of knots and twists. This sort of hand is invariably small, while the analytic hand is large. The hand of the idealist is the most symmetrical of all and the most useless in every sense.

A supple hand indicates generosity. A hand, the fingers of which, when placed together and held to the light, exhibit transparency, and between which no rays of light penetrate, shows avarice or, in other words, closeness. Fingers submitted to the same test which will not fit alongside each other without openings and which are denser, indicate curiosity and loquacity. People with hands that are always white are egotistical and have no sympathy.

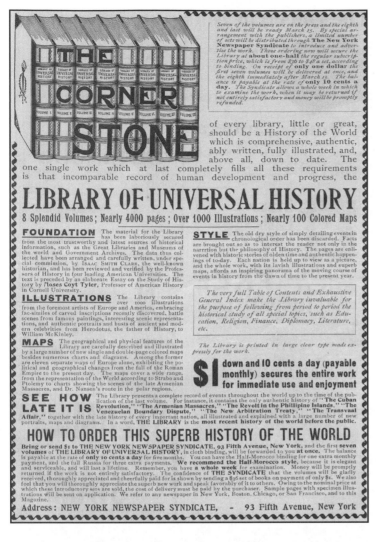

Clarissa is currently helping to select a new reading for her book club.

- Currently, she is attempting to help select a new reading for her book club, which she and several friends started last term, and which now consists of six members.
- Others are asking to join the group, but she believes that restricting the size of the club is important.
- For pleasure, they read *The Dancer's Jewels, The Witch of Prague* and *Laut Plario*.
- They are now reading *Villette*, but it will be finished soon.
- With the onset of winter snow in Connecticut, she and her friend Louise were able to go coasting, or sledding, on the hills near the school.
- Directly after dinner, they donned leggings and undertights, and went straight away to the stable for a sled.
- Unfortunately, only two were available, both rather high and long, which made them more suitable for gentle slopes than daunting hills; Clarissa, who had not been on a sled in seven years, was timid at first.
- Louise offered to take her along on her sled for the first trip, but she declined; she likes to learn quickly and by experience.
- When Louise prepared herself to go down the hill, Clarissa watched carefully as her friend gathered the rope in one hand, rested a hand on either side of the sled, then ran a step or two before throwing herself full-length on the clipper for the trip down the slope.
- She thought Louise's legs looked comical sticking up in the air as she zoomed down the hill.
  - When Clarissa took her turn, she found it easy and exhilarating, discovering how quickly she could gain more speed, and left the slopes feeling quite proud of herself.
  - Although her height is five feet, four inches, she is often considered small at Miss Porter's because her three roommates are all five feet, eight inches tall.
  - She does not like to be compared to them, and sometimes gets so angry that she does not even like to hear compliments about her many good features, such as her voice.

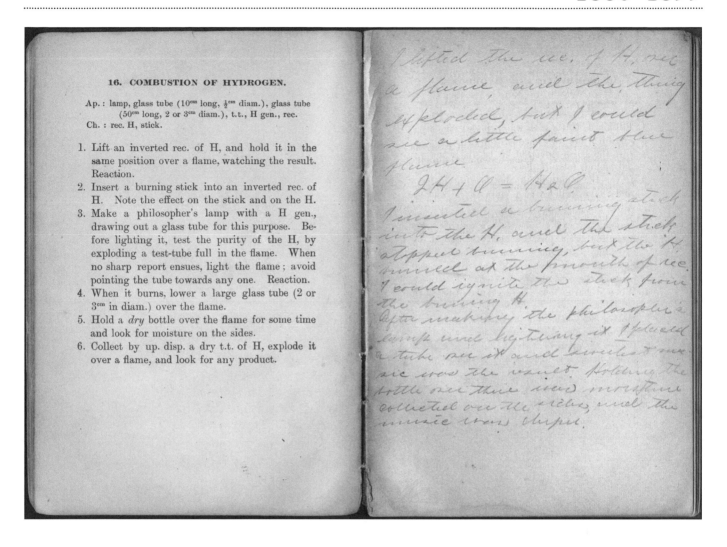

- She loves pink ribbons, placing them on every possible article of clothing she owns; during a recent round of goodnight calls within the dormitory, she wore a very dainty pink jacket with long pink ribbons.
- She planned for the calls to take only a moment, but found her friend Lucy busily sewing and in need of help; Lucy's brother has written her asking for a gown to wear to a dance given at Williams College.
- He also asked for gloves, a fan and a handkerchief; both girls agree that he will look quite amusing in white muslin.
- Although Miss Sarah Porter is still involved with the school, occasionally conducting a class when a teacher falls ill, the day-to-day leadership of the school falls to Mrs. Mary E. Dow, Miss Porter's trusted associate of many years.
- In recent years, critics have said Miss Porter's School has paid small heed to the requirements of a modern education.
- Instead the school has endured by ensuring that its students carried away the ideals of the meaning of life, appreciation of culture, love for the place and the traditions that are found in a natural home.
- Approximately 125 girls attend the school, many of them daughters and relatives of the "ancients" or graduates who came before.
- Because of demand and limited space, admission is a privilege extended to few outside the immediate family circle.

The "AHS" in a Girls' School, John Chinaman Illustrates a Lecture, *New York Semi-Weekly Tribune*, June 18, 1892:

FARMINGTON, CONN., JUNE 18—Everyone knows about the prosperous school for young ladies which is so conspicuous a feature of the life of this New England village. At least everyone who knows of Farmington must know the school, for the school is Farmington. Without it, the village would be quiet and staid enough. Having it, the village possesses an animation and spirit which seems to fire even the woods and mountains with purpose. It lies back in the hills a few miles from the railroad station, secluded among great groves of elms and maples and oaks, where the bracing air bears no other freight than the perfumes of flowers and the songs and birds, and where nothing interferes with the spirit of education and refinement which this school has cultivated during half a century.

Its proprietress, Miss Porter, the sister of the former president of Yale College, is a progressive woman. She utilizes everything and everybody that can serve to improve the minds of her pupils or to throw light upon their studies. Perhaps nothing better illustrates this fact than the lectures on music which her musical director, Mr. Boekelman, has instituted. The last of these, delivered on Tuesday evening by Mr. H. E. Krohbiel, was on the subject of Chinese music, a theme that, at first sight, scarcely looks suggestive of much that could assist the study of the musical art in its present stage, and yet before he was done, the lecturer made it clear that the lowly Wings and Hos and Kiangs and Tiems of the Celestial Empire, the home of His August Mightiness, the Son of Heaven, know a good deal about music.

- Clarissa writes daily in her diary, taking care to detail her day so that later she can enjoy it all over again; several of her roommates envy her discipline and have discouraged her from working in her theme book so frequently.
- For her, writing is a task and a joy; her thoughts flow fluidly from her pen no matter how tired she might be, and the writing process itself seems to give her new energy and many personal insights.
- Recently a young woman entered Miss Porter's from Ohio, arriving at the school with her entire family.
- Clarissa realized quickly that the new girl was not accustomed to restraint and did not understand that her actions must be more circumspect in a town such as Farmington.
- The new girl is 16 and thinks men useful only as dancing partners, but make poor substitutes when feminine society can be found.
- She was quickly and clearly informed by the girls that men are the only enjoyment in life; a girl who could not boast of at least two or three admirers was considered a "stick" by her girlfriends and other men.

- On George Washington's birthday, Clarissa was assigned the task of writing about the celebration, but she has grown discouraged.
- Even though there is a flag in the hall downstairs and the homes in the village are decorated, she finds most people rather unpatriotic, or at least undemonstrative of their loyalty to the Stars and Stripes.
- As the spring grew warmer and the flowers bloomed, she and her roommates organized a daisy party; for an entire afternoon they picked fresh daisies in a field, decorated hats, ate lunch and even made a daisy banner with a large "92" crafted in flowers.

Life in the Community: Farmington, Connecticut

- Farmington, located only nine miles from the center of Hartford, is considered one of the mother towns of Connecticut because it formerly included land that has been divided into nine other towns.
- Land for the settlement was purchased from the Tunxis Indians in 1640; by 1645, enough people lived in the area to apply for incorporation and the name designation of Farmington.
- In the summer of 1841, the 37 freed slaves of the ship Amistad lived in the village, awaiting return to Africa.
- A school was maintained for them, and seats provided at church services, which they attended as a group.
- For most of the century, Farmington has been renowned for the quality of its private schools, including Miss Porter's.
- The village is also known for its historic sites, including the Elm Tree Inn, erected around a seventeenth-century house in 1865 by Philip Lewis, and the Congregational Church, built in 1771, with its tall steeple topped with an open-belfry spire.
- Until recently, a free library started by a public-spirited lady was housed in an old building on one end of town; two years ago it was consolidated with the village library.
- Efforts are under way to revitalize some parts of Farmington; running water has been introduced, sewers are being constructed, and highways have been graded and, in part, macadamized.
- When attempts were made to cut trees in the village to make way for a trolley line through Main Street, the people rose almost en masse and halted the project.

Current fashion emphasizes a tiny waist.

HISTORICAL SNAPSHOT
1892

- To meet the needs of the automotive industry, an improved carburetor was invented
- Violence erupted during a steelworker's strike at Carnegie-Phipps Mill in Homestead, Pennsylvania
- The General Electric Company was created through a merger of Edison General Electric Company and Thomson-Houston Electric Company
- The $1 Ingersoll pocketwatch was introduced
- Chicago's first elevated railway went into operation to begin the famous Loop
- The first U.S. motorcar was produced in Springfield, Massachusetts, by Duryea Brothers
- The Hamilton Watch Company was founded
- The United States boasted 4,000 millionaires
- New York's 13-story Waldorf Hotel was under construction
- The first successful gasoline tractor was produced by a farmer in Waterloo, Iowa
- Thousands of Kansas farmers were bankrupted by tight money conditions
- The first full-service advertising agency was established in New York City
- "Gentleman Jim" Corbett defeated John L. Sullivan for the heavyweight boxing title
- William Ewart Gladstone became prime minister of Great Britain, Prince Ito was made premier of Japan, and Grover Cleveland was elected president of the United States
- America's first automatic telephone switchboard was introduced

1896 NEWS PROFILE

**"Women in the Professions, Law," by Mrs. Theodore Sutro, *The Delineator*,
A Journal of Fashion, Culture and Fine Arts, April 1896:**

"Why should women embrace the profession of law as a means of livelihood? For
the same reason that men embrace it, for the same reason that has induced women
to become physicians, artists, scientists, ministers, educators, financiers, editors,
and to engage in almost all pursuits which a few generations ago were considered
the exclusive property of men. Because we have arrived at a point in our civiliza-
tions when their mental subordination, merely because they are women, has become
almost inconceivable.

Why should women not study law? This question could be answered far more readily.
The reason women have so long been debarred from this particular profession may be
partly explained because precedent more than anything else holds sway over the minds
of judges and lawyers, and it has become almost a matter of tradition that a woman
should not become a lawyer.

It may also be partly explained through a misconception on the part of the public
of the character of the profession. Among the laity the lawyer is pictured as a person
who must be constantly engaged in the strife and turmoil of the forum, whose stento-
rian voice must terrorize witnesses and impress juries, and who must move about in all
the highways and byways of life like a whirlwind in order to ferret out and discover
material which he may use in the trial of a case. No one knows better than members
of the profession how remote such an idea is from the facts. The main business of a
lawyer, insofar as his time is occupied at all in litigation, is performed in the seclusion
of his private office in the careful analysis of the facts of his case and the study of law
bearing upon it. Especially in our generation, however, the main portion of his work
consists in advising and counselling, [sic] and in performing such labor as rather tends
to prevent and avoid litigation than to conduct it when it is unavoidable. Surely in this
branch of the profession it is a question of intellect and training solely, and not one of
sex, as to whether the person pursuing it is fitted to be successful or not.

Actual experience has proved that in the classes which have now been opened to
women for the study of law (as since time immemorial they have been to men) women
take as high rank as men, if not higher. There are a hundred avenues in the profession

outside of actual court practice in which women, provided they have the necessary qualifications and training, may be equally successful with men.

To succeed in certain legal fields woman is no doubt particularly fitted and adapted by Nature. There is many a subject which a sensitive woman would shrink from revealing to a lawyer of the sterner sex, and therefore, rather bears her cross in silence, which she would only be too glad to confide to a woman lawyer upon whose womanly sympathy, instincts, and comprehension she could rely. Certainly in everything that pertains to office advice and counsel, the preparations for trial and laying out of plans for conducting litigations where the interests of women or young children are involved, woman is especially qualified so far as natural abilities go.

There surely can be no nobler study than that of law. Ages ago Aristotle said: 'Jurisprudence is the principal and most perfect branch of ethics.' Blackstone calls it 'a science which distinguishes the criterions of right and wrong; which tends to establish the one and prevent, punish, or redress the other; which employs in its theory the noblest faculties of the soul, and exercises in its practices the cardinal virtues of the heart; a science which is universal in its use and extent, accommodated to each individual, yet comprehending the whole community.'

At all events, women are now entitled to admission to the bar in New York as well as in several other states. Paragraph 56 of the Code of Civil Procedure of New York provides that 'Race or sex shall constitute no cause for refusing any person examination or admission to practice.'

The chief drawback to the study of the profession of law by women as compared with men is their greater lack of general educational training, a lack proportionate to the small number of colleges for women in comparison with those open to young men. While exceptional brilliant examples exist of success in almost every profession without ample preliminary general training, there can be no doubt that, as a rule, such training is necessary in law. I would not advise any young woman to undertake the study of law with a view of making a means of livelihood unless she has at least a thorough high school education; properly it should be a college education. The profession being for women as a novelty, many of them are tempted to think they must be adapted for it simply because so many men are engaged in it. These young women, however, forget that while, as Daniel Webster said, 'There is always room in the upper story,' the upper story nevertheless has its limits, and of the thousands of men who undertake to practice law the percentage of those who actually succeed is almost insignificant. Not only does the practice of this profession require thorough preliminary mental training, but also the possession of that peculiar type of intellect known as the 'legal mind.'

Moreover, the exactions of the profession are enormous, and unless able to bear an almost unlimited amount of work and possessing a constitution which can surmount the wear and tear of incessant mental anxiety, no man can succeed in this pursuit; how much less, then, a woman! While I fully believe in throwing open the avenues of every profession to my sex, I think it is also proper to point out to its members the danger of spending years and large sums of money in pursuing a mere fad. Let a young woman pause and well consider whether she has the educational and physical qualifications required for the pursuit of this exacting profession, and, over and above these, whether she has the peculiar mental traits which adapt her to make a success of it. . . .

Up to 1882, 56 women had been admitted to the practice as attorneys-at-law in the United States. There must be at least four times this number at the present time. In New York City there are now probably not more than half a dozen women against about 5,000 men admitted to the bar—a small enough proportion to encourage other women to endeavor to join the ranks of their professional sisters."

1898 PROFILE

Working Class

Gwen Shanklin, a 16-year-old Welsh girl, works as a maid for a wealthy Philadelphia family that is trying hard to copy many of the manners, patterns and routines of the English.

Life at Home

- Originally from Bethesda, Wales, a region known for the quality of its quarries, Gwen Shanklin loves working in America, where there is plenty of food to eat and the homes are heated.
- In Wales, her father often treated her like a servant, demanding that she care for him, especially after her mother died when she was 13 years old.
- Finally, convinced that she was too lazy to be of any use to him, he sent her to London when she was 14, where she was employed as a servant girl to a wealthy family.
- In London she learned the rules of a grand house and how to handle the needs of a large crowd.
- Answering a newspaper advertisement, she came to Philadelphia a year ago to escape the dampness of London for the promise of America.
- She found Philadelphia to have a pervasive brownness, thanks to innumerable furnaces burning the soft coal of Pennsylvania.
- In this wealthy American household, being a child is paradise: her employer's five daughters seem to get whatever they ask for from their father, Mr. Pfannebake—from new dresses to a carriage ride.
- Permission for the girls to travel or attend social functions and parties, however, is left entirely to Mrs. Pfannebake.

Gwen Shanklin loves working in America.

Mr. Pfannebake loves to indulge his five daughters.

- When Gwen first took the job, she found the smells of the kitchen so incredible, she felt she could eat the air.
- Like most large Philadelphia homes, this house is constructed of dark red brick with white marble steps, and accented with white mantels and shutters on the first floor and green on the second.
- Even though the house is massive, comprising 24 bedrooms, she now feels comfortable, as long as she sticks to a routine.
- Like many homes of wealthy Philadelphians, it is the interior quality, not the exterior appearance of the house, that is most prized.
- The house contains many beautiful objects—many made in England; a matching pair of china doorstops in the main living room particularly fascinates Gwen.
- One doorstop features a cat dressed as a woman holding a parasol and wearing a fancy hat with a red band tied under the chin and a frilly blue dress and apron; the second doorstop depicts a dog dressed as a man carrying a walking stick in one paw and wearing a tan suit with green waistcoat, watch chain and gold buttons, and sporting a tall hat on his head.
- Seeing them in the early morning light always gives Gwen a smile.
- The head of the household, Mr. Pfannebake, is very different from her father; when possible and appropriate, she watches him closely.
- He is a rich, staunch Republican, and not nearly so mean as the newspapers report.
- In addition, he is German and a mill owner, both characteristics about which she has been warned, yet he is kind to his daughters and does not molest the servants.
- The second daughter, Louise, who is the same age as Gwen, owns a beautiful music box bearing 12 musicians who dance along with the music while they stroke the violin, bang the drum or blow a horn.

Before coming to America, Gwen worked for a family in London.

- Gwen loves to watch the musicians dance to the music; it is so romantic!
- Each of the daughters is different: Louise is a bookworm, and her father loves to brag that her memory is colossal and her brains are the best in the family; he tells everyone that she takes after him.
- The third daughter has the style in the family; she cares about clothes, and her sashes and hair ribbons are always tied better and are more chic than those of her sisters.
- The youngest child goes from mother to father to sisters until she gets what she wants; Gwen thinks she is terribly spoiled, but says nothing, even to the other servants, some of whom can be terrible gossips.

Life at Work

- Having worked for a time in London, Gwen is grateful that American houses are well-heated, and has few regrets about leaving the cold-water discipline of the English upper classes.
- The most difficult part of her 17-hour day is the morning.
- As a maid, her workday begins at 5:30 a.m., when she must clean the kitchen floors and heat water.
- By 6:30 a.m. she wakes the more senior staff and helps lay and relight the fires in the 12 fireplaces located throughout the house.

> **"Household Helps and New Ideas,"**
> ***Ladies' Home Journal*, April 1898:**
>
> The deep cutting in fine glass requires special care to keep it clean and brilliant. A brush is now sold for polishing and drying cut glass. It is made of the finest Russian bristles and does the work speedily and well.

- Afterward, she helps start the other servants' breakfast and deliver breakfast to the upstairs maid, who works in the nursery.
- At 7:30 a.m., dressed in a print dress, she goes upstairs with jugs of fresh water and tea trays to wake the five girls; at the same time, she takes away the chamber pots and empties the contents that have accumulated during the night.
- The chamber pots will be emptied and replaced three or four times during the day; in addition, some of the senior servants have their own chamber pots, but most relieve themselves at an outhouse located 28 steps from the back kitchen.
- Currently, the only flushing water closet in the house is off the master's bedroom.
- The servants' breakfast is at 7:45 a.m.
- Three days a week, the woman of the house insists that everyone, including servants, participate in morning prayer services in the parlor, followed by the family breakfast and then cleanup.
- At noon the servants eat lunch, and at 1 p.m. Gwen helps to serve lunch, having changed into a black dress with white lace cap and white apron.
- She makes the dresses herself and always ensures they are clean and well-starched.
- By 2:30 lunch ends and she often takes a nap before the 4:30 p.m. tea time for the household.
- Before Mrs. Pfannebake toured England, the family rarely observed afternoon tea; now, convinced that high tea is the epitome of civilization, she insists that all work cease at 4:30 p.m. for tea.
- By 6 p.m. Gwen helps set the banquet table for dinner and helps in the kitchen until 7 p.m., when the meal begins.
- As part of her preparation for dinner, she and one other maid must arrange the table linen, which is very heavy and beautifully monogrammed.
- At each plate, she carefully lays oversized table napkins that measure 30 inches square; afterward she helps serve or assist in the kitchen until the meal ends.
- Most nights the family dresses formally for the multicourse dinner.
- Once it is over, cleanup normally takes until 9 p.m., when she and the rest of the servants eat dinner before retiring at 10 p.m.
- She is frequently delighted by the foods available to the servants, once the household has been served.
- She has dined often on a combination of chicken salad and fried oysters (one of Mr. Pfannebake's favorites), oyster croquettes, fresh shad, soft-shell crabs, Philadelphia ice cream, cream cheese, terrapin and snapper soup.
- European wines are often served with dinner, but are rarely included in the servants' meals.

> The things that truly last when men and times have passed, they are all in Pennsylvania this morning!
> —Rudyard Kipling

> ### "Bacteria, the Progress of Science,"
> ### by Bertha Gerneaux Davis, *The Cosmopolitan*, March 1897:
>
> Zoologists and botanists alike laid claim to the bacteria until comparatively recent years, but the zoologists were forced to yield to their botanical brethren, and the curious little organisms popularly known as "microbes" are now classified, almost without question, among the simplest of the plant forms, and as near relatives of algae. The common form of bacteria is rod-shaped, though others are spiral, spherical and egg-shaped. In size they vary considerably. Some of the larger forms are 20/25,000 of an inch in length, while one of the smallest is about 1/50,000 of an inch. To give a rather more definite idea of the minuteness of some of these organisms, imagine 1,500 placed end to end, hardly reaching across a pinhead. Extremely powerful lenses must consequently be brought to bear upon them before they will yield up the secret of their life history and workings; and, as the little bodies are almost transparent, the microscopist is obliged to stain them with some dye to render them anything but shadowy and indistinct.

- Despite all the good food, she is cautious about what she eats.
- She knows for a fact that swallowing grape seeds will cause appendicitis, which actually happened to a friend of hers.
- Some foods are restricted in the house; Mrs. Pfannebake has banned all soft drinks, declaring them to be "common" —despite the pleas of her daughters.

A stereoscopic view of fine dining in an affluent household.

Every guest is offered a piece of butterscotch candy purchased in England.

- Until recently, maids had no days off; now Gwen is allowed most Sunday afternoons free unless guests are expected at the home.
- Her biggest breaks take place in the summer when the family takes the rail to their country estate a few miles outside the city.
- While the family is away, they only need 10 servants, so Gwen takes on different duties such as washing the walk each Saturday, polishing silver or receiving supplies for the kitchen.
- At these times she is allowed to take long walks, since the demands of the house are fewer.
- On one such trip, she discovered Fairmount Park, which looks like a 12-mile-long valley in the center of the city.
- While out, she often buys shaved ice at the numerous apothecary stores and goes window-shopping at the many fine stores.
- While on a recent trip, a handsome young man spoke to her favorably; she often thinks about that encounter, but has not seen him since, even though she often walks the same route.
- For most of her life, Gwen has worn her hair free around her shoulders; upon employment she was instructed always to have her hair braided while at work.
- Another maid, who came from Scotland, helped her fix her hair in braids and pin them to the back of her head.

Letter written by Lafcadio Hearn

Philadelphia is a city very peculiar, isolated by custom, antique, but having a good, solid morality, and much peace. It has its own dry, drab newspapers which are not like any other newspapers in the world, and contain nothing not immediately concerning Philadelphia. Consequently, no echo from New York enters here—not any from anywhere else . . . . But it's the best old city in the whole world all the same.

"Risks of Modern Life,"
The Youth's Companion, February 17, 1898:

Most of the appliances of modern civilization bring risks as well as advantages. The people who lived a hundred years ago could not travel so rapidly nor communicate with each other across great distances so conveniently as we do; but on the other hand, they were strangers to some perils which are familiar nowadays.

Their journeys were slow and serious affairs; but they were in no danger of being blown up on a steamboat, or tumbled over a railway embankment, or even of being run over by a trolley car or a "scorching" wheelman. Their houses were not lighted by electricity or by gas; but they were not burned up by reason of badly insulated wires or asphyxiated in their beds. They knew nothing of 15-story buildings, but they also knew nothing of elevator accidents.

Nevertheless, it is doubtful if more lives are lost by accident in travel, in proportion to the number of people travelling, than was the case a century ago.

Hundreds of people travel by water now than did so then; but ocean travel has been made relatively more safe, as well as more swift and comfortable, by modern appliances. There are still possibilities of collision or of striking a reef in a fog, but it almost never happens that a modern, seaworthy vessel founders through stress of weather. One steamship company which has sent its steamers back and forth across the Atlantic for more than 50 years is able to boast that it has never lost the life of a passenger in the service.

As to the railways, in 1896, 181 passengers were killed on the railways of the United States, and nearly 2,900 were injured. When these figures are compared with the amount of passenger traffic, it appears that the railways carried nearly three million passengers for every one who was killed and about 180,000 passengers for every passenger injured.

A famous humorist once compared the number of people killed in railway accidents with the number dying in their beds, and reached the conclusion that it was several thousand times more risky to lie in bed than to travel on a railway. It was a playful exaggeration; but it is true that, if modern discovery and invention have resulted in new hazards to human life, they have also supplied new safeguards and preventives.

- Recently, she decided to have her hair cut short in preparation for a studio picture of herself.
- She loves the new look, and wants to send the picture home to show everyone that she is doing well.
- The madam of the house insists that the household follows English customs, and for that reason only hires servants from the Isles.
- Following Mrs. Pfannebake's most recent trip to Britain, the madam's friends whispered, "She is more English than the English."
- Her fascination with England does not end with work routines and observing afternoon tea; she also loves to serve English foods.
- It is now obligatory that every guest be offered a piece of Callard & Bowser's Butter-Scotch Candy out of the tin box she bought in England.
- The box features a hen and her chicks, and Gwen has taken great care never to mention that normally in Britain, this particular design is reserved for the nursery or the sickroom, nor does she snicker when the madam talks about the aristocracy of Philadelphia, meaning the very rich—not the titled, as in Europe.

"Fruits as Foods and Fruits as Poisons," by S. T. Rorer, *Ladies' Home Journal*, June 1898:

Fruits Which I Allow on My Table

It may be interesting to know that the fruits allowed on my table are fresh figs, dried ones carefully cooked, guavas canned without sugar, guava jelly, orange marmalade made by special home recipe, dates both raw and cooked with almonds, persimmons, bananas cooked, and an occasional dish of prunes with the skins removed, blackberries and dewberries, slightly cooked, strained and made into flummery. The objection to the latter [sic] fruit, however, is the addition of starch and sugar, which is prone to fermentation. All fruits, whether cooked or raw, should be used without sugar. It must be remembered that sugar in no way neutralizes an acid; for this an alkali must be used. Sugar sprinkled over an acid fruit masks the objectionable and severe acid until it slips by the "guard-keeper," the palate. Once in the stomach, however, it regains its own position and grants the same to the irritating acid.

Acid Fruits Have No Food Value

Acid fruits are used by the great majority to stimulate the appetite, that they must eat what is called "breakfast," miscalled, however, for really there is no fast to break. It is well to observe that the person who eats a heavy luncheon at or near midnight is the same who eats one or two good-sized oranges or a dish of strawberries to give him an appetite the next morning.

Another fact of no small importance is that starches are digested and sugars converted only in an alkaline medium. What, then, becomes of the bowl of cereals taken immediately after these acid fruits for breakfast, taking no account of the sugar that is usually sprinkled over it? The intestinal tract must sooner or later become irritated by these fermenting foods. The blood loses its alkalinity, and a train of diseases, already only too well-established in the system, follows such a diet.

Fruits and bread and butter are very common mixtures for those who have at the end of the day a supper. One can see at a glance that such combinations are not wise.

- Coffee comes to the house in large straw and canvas sacks, one sack of mocha, the other of Java, a blend being made according to quarter measure, after which the beans are parched in the kitchen, one panful at a time.
- The beans are then ground in a hand coffee mill, a day's supply at a grinding.
- Recently, a merchant brought around a mandarin orange, which he called "the kid glove orange" because it could be peeled without removing one's gloves.
- Last Christmas, the fruiterer who supplies the house year 'round sent a handsome basket of fruit as a gift, including oranges, both red and yellow apples, bananas, assorted nuts and Malaga grapes.
- The whole basket was dripping with gold and silver tinsel, and tucked in the corners were firecrackers, a box of candy and balloons for the children.
- On Christmas Day, Gwen received a gift of cloth for a new dress from the family, and then joined the entire staff for an afternoon of singing Christmas carols in the parlor.
- Currently, the household is buzzing about a new invention that could protect them from illness; Mr. Pfannebake purchased a Ralston new-process water-still that sterilizes water with heat to destroy the bacteria, then re-aerates the water with sterilized air.

- Everyone in the house feels safer from invading microbes now, though the fear of yellow fever and other diseases always lingers in Philadelphia; this is one of the reasons the family maintains its own garden, especially for the cultivation of healthful vegetables.
- Work in the massive garden is often done by three men and a mule; the tools used include small steel plows, hand tools and a horse-driven Zephanian Breed Weeder, which has proven invaluable in improving crop production.
- Recently, most of the staff was allowed to stop work for the afternoon to watch a balloon ascension.
- Gwen joined the five sisters on the third-floor balcony, where they could see the balloon being inflated with gas, then witness a man climb into a large, woven basket.
- As the ropes were untied, he waved his hands wildly to the crowd and slowly floated upward into the air and out of sight.
- The other joy of city life is the ice cream cart; several times a week the ice cream vendors peddle ice cream blocks in push carts.
- Ringing a large dinner bell, they wend their way down the streets selling vanilla, chocolate, pineapple and lemon, each wrapped in wax paper; the price is $0.05.
- Gwen looks forward to a lemon ice cream break, especially in the afternoons.

The household is now protected from microbes by the Ralston water-still.

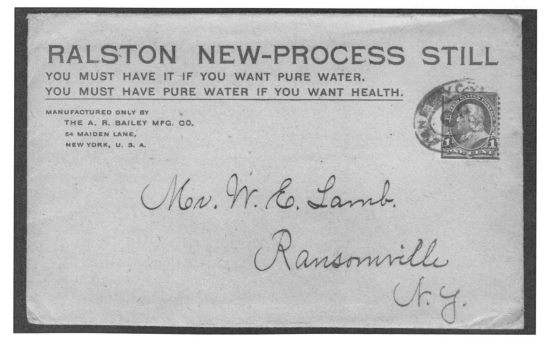

WATER-DRINKING.

WHEN it is considered that the body is made up very largely of water it can readily be understood how important to health is a constant supply of this fluid. Many people have a notion that the drinking of water in any amount beyond that actually necessary to quench thirst is injurious, and acting on this belief they endeavor to drink as little as possible. The notion, however, is wide of the truth. Drinking freely of pure water is a most efficacious means not only of preserving health, but often of restoring it when failing.

All the tissues of the body need water, and water in abundance is necessary also for the proper performance of every vital function. Cleanliness of the tissues within the body is as necessary to health and comfort as cleanliness of the skin, and water tends to insure the one as truly as it does the other. It dissolves the waste material, which would otherwise collect in the body, and removes it in the various excretions.

These waste materials are often actual poisons, and many a headache, many rheumatic pains and aches, many sleepless nights and listless days, and many attacks of the "blues" are due solely to the circulation in the blood or deposit in the tissues of these waste materials, which cannot be got rid of because of an insufficient supply of water.

Water is accused of making fat, and people with a tendency to corpulence avoid it for that reason. But this is not strictly true. It does undoubtedly often increase the weight, but it does so because it improves the digestion and therefore more of the food eaten is utilized and turned into fat and flesh. But excessive fat, what we call corpulence, is not a sign of health but of faulty digestion and assimilation, and systematic water-drinking is often employed as a means of reducing the superfluous fat—which it sometimes does with astonishing rapidity.

It is impossible to recount in a few words all the benefits which may result from the taking of pure water in sufficient quantity, but the discussion of this subject will be resumed in a future number of the *Companion*.

Life in the Community: Philadelphia, Pennsylvania

- The city's principal boulevards are wide; Broad Street, especially its northern portion, is wider than the great boulevards of Paris or the Ringstrassen of Central Europe.
- Philadelphia has about 1.3 million residents, making it the third-largest American city and one of the 10 largest cities in the world.
- In all, it encompasses 130 square miles—more than London—thanks to the Consolidation Act of 1854.
- Because so much property was included in the city limits under this Act, people still go fox hunting within the city's municipal boundaries.
- Although Philadelphia has experienced significant growth during the past decade, the percentage of foreign-born residents at 23 percent is lower than New York's 38 percent and Boston's 35 percent.
- Currently, the Jewish population, many who are immigrants from Russia and Rumania, is growing rapidly.
- Unlike New York, whose streets appear to be constantly in motion, Philadelphia is slower-moving, without the fierce rhythms of other American cities.
- Philadelphia has few landmarks that it can boast are recognizable to people who are not from the city, and even fewer renowned vistas.
- The solitary exception is City Hall, with an enormous statue of William Penn topping its tower.
- There, 547 feet above the street, visitors can obtain a view of the city, and even use a Kodak camera to capture the scene.
- Some consider the statue, constructed by Alexander Milne Calder in 1894, a Philadelphian Statue of Liberty.
- Real-estate prices are reasonable, compared with other urban areas; a middle-class house containing seven rooms can be rented for $15 a month.
- Between 1886 and 1893, 50,000 houses were built in west and northern Philadelphia, most of them financed by the 450 neighborhood savings and loan associations.
- Currently, more people own their houses in Philadelphia than in any other city in the world.
- The city also enjoys a sense of spaciousness; typically, 100 houses in Philadelphia accommodate an average of 550 people, while in New York, the same number of homes harbor 1,650 inhabitants, according to census figures.
- Philadelphia is known for its shops and local wares: Dexter's for cakes, Margerum's for beef, Fluke's for dainties, Dreka's for stationery, Sautter's for ice cream, Jones's for oysters and Leary's for books.
- Leary's, owned by Mayor Edwin S. Stuart, is considered one of the finest bookshops in the United States.
- A cherished tradition of the city, especially among the more élite families, is for the men to be involved in cooking special dishes; wealthy businessmen are often seen at the market selecting meat, and many take great pride in their ability to make mayonnaise.

HISTORICAL SNAPSHOT
1898–1899

- The first shots of the Spanish-American War were fired
- The Louisiana "grandfather clause" restricted most blacks from voting
- The Union Carbide Company was founded
- Motorcar production reached 1,000 vehicles per year in 1898; production topped 2,500 in 1899
- Goodyear Tire and Rubber Company was founded
- The New York Times dropped its price from $0.03 daily to $0.01; as a result, circulation tripled
- Pepsi-Cola was introduced by pharmacist Caleb D. "Doc" Bradham in New Bern, North Carolina
- Uneeda Biscuits was created
- J. P. Stevens & Company was founded in New York
- Shiga Kiyoshi, a Japanese bacteriologist, discovered the Shigella bacillus, responsible for dysentery and named after him
- Trolley cars replaced horse cars in Boston
- Wesson Oil was developed
- The United Mine Workers of America was founded
- The first concrete grain elevator was erected near Minneapolis
- A very destructive insect, the boll weevil, began spreading across cotton-growing Southern states

1899 News Feature

"A Soldier's Wife in the Philippines," by Eda Blankart Funston,
Cosmopolitan, **May 1900:**

Never shall I forget my first glimpse of Manila. General Miller and staff, the 1st Battalion of 20th Kansas Infantry, a detachment of California Heavy Artillery and 14 ladies had arrived in Manila Bay on the Newport on the evening of December 5, 1898. All but two of the ladies had come to meet their husbands. Three of us were brides who had been speculating deeply as to which one would see her husband first. Need I tell how happy I was, and how victorious, when my husband proved to be the first one on board? After having paid his respects to General Miller, my husband declared himself ready to move, and we went at once by rowboat to the Indiana. In consequence of lack of quarters, the two battalions of the 20th Kansas which had come on the Indiana had been obliged to stay on board ship. Naturally, the officers had to remain. In addition, my husband had been unable to secure a house, for good houses had become scarce by that time.

Thus it was that I got the first glimpse of Manila early on the morning after my arrival in the bay. The bright tin and tile roofs, so almost entirely prevalent in Manila, surmounted now and then by a church dome or tower, reflected the rays of the sun, which even at that early hour blazed unmercifully. The bright, rich green of the trees and foliage seemed in remarkable contrast with this baking heat, for the sun was apparently hot enough to dry up the very waters of the bay. In spite of the heat, I was most anxious to get a closer view of this remarkable city, of which we had all heard and read so much within the last six or seven months; so when the next launch came alongside, Major and Mrs. Whitman, my husband and I, boarded it and were soon approaching the Pasig.

Our little launch puffed its way up the river among the most varied and remarkable craft, from cascoes 50 to 75 feet long to little canopy-topped dugouts six to eight feet long. These boats and both banks of the river seemed literally alive with men, women and children in all stages of dress and undress. After pursuing our way about a quarter of a mile up the river, we arrived at the landing. I was surprised to see the fine stone quay and splendidly paved street, and was intensely interested in and amused at the remarkable kinds of vehicles. Large, small, open and closed, one-seater, more-seated, and from brand-new down to the most dilapidated imaginable. But the horses attached to these remarkable equipages were more remarkable still— little more than dogs, and so thin and sore that I hated the idea of riding behind them. Perhaps you have seen pictures of the typical Manila equipages. In case you have not, let me attempt to describe the one in which we drove that day. It was square, much like a gurney cab, but very light. It was higher than a gurney, was open and had but two wheels. Such a time we had getting seated for our trip to town! We drove through a number of narrow, dirty streets, over a bridge, and through another street before we reached the Escolta—a narrow street with a single car-track down the middle and just space enough on each side for a carriage. The sidewalks in some places were wide enough for two persons to walk side-by-side very comfortably, and in others barely wide enough for one. Some of the buildings, though not masterpieces of architecture, were by no means bad, and, as we soon discovered, there were at least a dozen stores in the place, where after talking for an hour you could manage to get many desired articles.

We hunted up a house-agent, an enterprising American, and late arrival, and after an hour's driving discovered a very good house. It was the district called Ermita. From a corner window we looked over the Lunetta toward the bay, the most beautiful view imaginable. We were altogether delighted with our discovery and good fortune, in spite of the fact that we should be obliged to wait at least a week before we could occupy the house. We returned to the ship that evening more than pleased with our day's doings, and counting the hours until we could take possession of our home, for the Whitmans and the Funstons were to occupy the house together. The next three days

were spent aboard ship. Shall I ever forget those days? I cannot imagine anything warmer, and we suffered accordingly. By Sunday, Major Whitman and my husband devised a scheme by which we could go ashore, even though our house was not ready for us. Regimental headquarters were in the Second Battalion barracks, where my husband had an office. This was quite a large room, and here we put up two cot-beds, which Mrs. Whitman and I occupied, while our husbands bunked with two of the officers. The three days we spent there were dreary enough. Major Whitman and Colonel Funston were extremely busy and left their wives to take care of themselves. We did not go out on the streets alone (though at that time it was safe to do so), and we thought, as we really had no right in the building, it would be wrong toward the men, embarrassing, to say the least, to have us about, so we stayed in our room—prisoners. But we could look out of the windows, the view from which almost repaid us for our imprisonment. The barracks were on Calle Analoague and in the Binondo District—one of the worst—thickly populated with Chinese. Calle Analoague was a very busy street, so that from morning until night it was most interesting to watch the numberless passersby. The men of the better classes appeared with their spotless white suits and patent-leather boots, and those of the lower classes with trousers of "any old kind" rolled up to the knees or above, and an ordinary undershirt which was always worn outside the trousers. The women were there with their odd and rather picturesque costume, consisting of a bright-colored skirt which just escaped the ground in front and in the back was made en train in the oddest imaginable shape about a yard or more in length. The train very much resembles the bowl of a spoon in shape, though, of course, it is flat. Over the skirt is worn a garment which looks like an apron. This for ordinary use is almost always made of a black material closely resembling our cashmere. For dress occasions, the tapis, as it is called, is made of a fine lacy material

called husi, and richly embroidered about the edges. The waist, or pina, is always loose and low-necked, showing the shoulders, and the large loose sleeves, very like those of a Japanese kimono except that they are gathered in at the armholes, are very much starched and stand out, leaving the arm bare. The ordinary children sometimes wear clothes and sometimes nature is entirely unadorned. When they do dress, their clothes are exactly like those of the grown-up people, the effect being most picturesque.

Finally, after three days of this imprisonment, we moved to our home on Calle San Luis, and now the fun of furnishing began. I shall never forget our first experience in shopping. We started out quite early in a hired victoria (worth $0.20 an hour)—not without a little trepidation, it must be confessed, for furniture-shops were conducted by the Chinese, and the streets in which they were situated were anything but inviting, being hot, dirty and full of odors. Our desire was to keep as far away from the crowd as possible, but at that time, there were so few American women in Manila that we were quite a curiosity. When we entered one of the tiny shops almost on the street, we were followed by 15 or 20 wretched specimens of humanity and stared at until it became distressing. Our purchases were all made as soon as possible, and when finally we got away and out into the more open part of the city, we marveled that we had escaped without trouble, for some of the men had been most surly. A few days after this, word came from headquarters that the officers were too far away from the regiment and must move into town. It was fully a week before a suitable house could be found in the required locality, and in the meantime, the men of the household were obliged to sleep at the barracks, coming home only to lunch and dinner. This arrangement, however, did not last very long, for we soon found a house quite close to the barracks—three blocks below and on the same street. The house being altogether too large for the four of us, we asked Major Metcalf, Mr. Walker, the adjutant,

and Mr. Hull, the quartermaster, to occupy it with us, which they were only too glad to do, and we made a very merry, happy family.

This was in the latter part of December 1898, and from the time that we got fairly settled in our new quarters until the outbreak on the night of February 4, our experience was a very pleasant and agreeable one. Though the insurgents had forgotten to smile upon us and were getting more surly and sullen in their demeanor toward us every day, we continued to have the best of good times. The navy did all in its power to make things agreeable for us, and hardly a week passed without some pleasant entertainment being prepared on one or another of the warships.

Driving was our chief recreation. Many a pleasant trip we had behind our dear little white ponies; in fact, I don't know how we could have done without them. The heat between the hours of nine in the morning and four in the afternoon is so intense that one cannot do anything but lounge in the most negligée of garments, but by five it grows cooler, and then the whole city turns out on the Lunetta. The Lunetta, by the way, is a large plaza, elliptical in shape, about 600 feet in length and situated in the western part of Manila on the bay, just outside the walled city. In the middle of this pleasant expanse is the bandstand, and around it a broad driveway which on the side nearest the bay extends along the beach to the Pasig. Every evening one or another of the regimental bands gave a concert here, which began at six and lasted an hour, and here every evening were to be seen the élite of Manila city, taking their daily airing. We

Americans soon fell into their ways, for not only did we find it necessary to benefit by the fresh ocean breezes, but we were attracted by the superb sunsets which were an everyday occurrence. Thus, the time was most delightfully spent, in spite of heat and discomforts, until that historic night of the 4th of February.

After a pleasant evening spent quietly in reading, my husband and I had just retired, when we were startled by a banging at the door. At the same time we heard the boom of cannon, and Major Metcalf shouted through the door, "Colonel, Colonel, the ball has begun!" Both my husband and I were on our feet in an instant, and in a few moments he was gone.

Then, gathering up the few valuables I had brought with me, I packed them with my toilet articles in a "telescope" which for some weeks past I had kept prepared—for we had been expecting an outbreak. By this time the soldiers who had been sent to take us to the barracks had arrived, and after having given our two Chinamen all necessary instructions we left the house. The night was quiet, save for the distant crackling of rifles and the heavy boom of the "Monadnock's" big guns. Halfway to the barracks we were met by the 2nd Battalion on its way to the front. With what mingled feelings of hope and fear we watched them as quickly they marched past us! Arrived at the barracks, we were shown into a little room belonging to three noncommissioned officers. Here we were told to make ourselves comfortable.

Of course, sleep for us was out of the question. The hours dragged on with only now and then an interruption by some noisy little cochero forced to give up his carromato, or an unusually loud report of the navy's guns. The next morning matters were a little more interesting. Men began to come in from the line with such long and interesting tales to tell. With what eagerness we drank in the news as each man came in during the day! By this time we had been joined by the other Kansas ladies, making our party five in all, and this made our room more crowded than ever, for we were naturally obliged to bring in more beds. This did not last long, for two of the ladies soon left us. In spite of our anxiety, we managed to make things a little lively. Mrs. Haussermann had her piano put into what we used as a parlor and sitting room. I had my violin, and together we managed to while away many a weary hour.

On the morning of the 7th, an orderly came in from the lines. I rushed to meet him, anxious for news, and received a note from my husband asking me to come to see him that day.

By the time the orderly had attended to his numerous errands, I was ready for the start. A little quelis awaited me in the court. One soldier acted as cochero, another rode on horseback in front of us, while another rode in back. Each carried his rifle. Just as we were starting, one of the ladies gave me a small pistol.

Our trip was a most interesting one, for we passed the ground which our regiment and the artillery had so bravely fought over. Ever and anon, my escort would point out a particular place where the fighting had been the hottest, or where the limbs of trees had been literally torn off by the cannon of the Utah Artillery. On either side of the road were houses fairly riddled with bullets. At length we arrived at the camp, where the officers were most kind and did everything to make me comfortable until my husband's return, which they assured me would be soon. Just then we heard a shot, and then another, and soon the bullets were falling about us. In the shortest time imaginable I was hurried off behind a large embankment, and there I stayed, with my pistol clasped tightly in my hand and feeling like a fool. The shooting lasted but a few minutes, and soon my husband put in an appearance. Then we learned that it was at him and his party that the insurgents had been firing. Almost the first thing he did, after greetings had been exchanged, was to beg of me to put my pistol away. Having safely deposited it in a carromato near at hand, we started off toward brigade headquarters, where after a few minutes' walk I was introduced to Brigadier-General Otis and his staff. After a few minutes' chat, we retraced our steps and called on the officers of the 3rd Artillery, among whom I had several friends. From this camp, which was situated on a slight eminence, we had an excellent view of the enemy, of course with the aid of field glasses. I now thought it about time for me to return to the barracks, and immediately upon reaching our camp set off. I afterward learned that I had not been gone more than half an hour when one of the fiercest battles was fought.

1900–1909

The first decade of the twentieth century was not only marked by dramatic innovation, but also by the changing economic roles of women, especially the working class. The crush of immigration resulted in entire families—women and children included—taking jobs as seamstresses, factory workers or peddlers in a desperate search for the elusive American dream. Although a majority of Americans still lived in rural areas and maintained farms, America's men and women were gaining a sense of the country's potential on the world stage. After decades of living in the shadow of Europe, Americans saw themselves as the progenitors of the future, whether the topic was the fastest automobile, the perfect soft drink or the latest fashion.

At the same time, the number of inventions and changes spawned by the power of electricity was nothing short of revolutionary. Factories converted to the new energy force, staying open longer and employing entire families, including children as young as 10. A bottle-making machine patented in 1903 virtually eliminated the hand-blowing of glass bottles; another innovation mechanized the production of window glass. A rotating kiln manufactured in 1899 supplied large quantities of cheap, standardized cement, just in time for a nation ready to leave behind the bicycle fad and fall madly in love with the automobile. Thanks to this spirit of innovation and experimentation, the United States led the world in productivity, exceeding the vast empires of France and Britain combined.

In the eyes of the world, America was the land of opportunity. Millions of immigrants flooded to the United States, often finding work in the new factories of the New World—many managed by the men who came two generations before from countries like England or Germany or Wales. When Theodore Roosevelt proudly proclaimed in 1902, "The typical American is accumulating money more rapidly than any other man on earth," he described accurately both the joy of newcomers and the prosperity of the emerging middle class. Elevated by their education, profession, inventiveness, or capital, the managerial class found numerous opportunities to flourish in the rapidly changing world of a new economy.

At the beginning of the century, the 1900 U.S. population, comprising 45 states, stood at 76 million, an increase of 21 percent since 1890; 10.6 million residents were foreign-born and more were coming every day. The number of immigrants in the first decade of the twentieth century was double the number for the previous decade, exceeding one million annually in four of the 10 years, the highest level in U.S. history. Business and industry were convinced that unrestricted immigration was the fuel that drove the growth of American industry. Labor was equally certain that the influx of foreigners continually undermined the economic status of native workers and kept wages low.

The change in productivity and consumerism came with a price: the character of American life. Manufacturing plants drew people from the country into the cities. The traditional farm patterns were disrupted by the lure of urban life. Ministers complained that lifelong churchgoers who moved to the city often found less time and fewer social pressures to attend worship regularly. Between 1900 and 1920, urban population increased by 80 percent compared to just over 12 percent for rural areas. During the same time, the non-farming work force went from 783,000 to 2.2 million. Unlike farmers, these workers drew a regular paycheck, and spent it.

With this movement of people, technology, and ideas, nationalism took on a new meaning in America. Railroad expansion in the middle of the nineteenth century had made it possible to move goods quickly and efficiently throughout the country. As a result, commerce, which had been based largely on local production of goods for local consumption, found new markets. Ambitious merchants expanded their businesses by appealing to broader markets.

In 1900, America claimed 58 businesses with more than one retail outlet called "chain stores"; by 1910, that number had more than tripled, and by 1920, the total had risen to 808. The number of clothing chains alone rose from seven to 125 during the period. Department stores such as R. H. Macy in New York and Marshall Field in Chicago offered vast arrays of merchandise along with free services and the opportunity to "shop" without purchasing. Ready-made clothing drove down prices, but also promoted fashion booms that reduced the class distinctions of dress. In rural America the mail order catalogs of Sears, Roebuck and Company reached deep into the pocket of the common man and made dreaming and consuming more feasible.

All was not well, however. A brew of labor struggles, political unrest, and tragic factory accidents demonstrated the excesses of industrial capitalism so worshipped in the Gilded Age. The labor-reform movements of the 1880s and 1890s culminated in the newly formed American Federation of Labor as the chief labor advocate. By 1904, 18 years after it was founded, the AFL claimed 1.676 million of 2.07 million total union members nationwide. The reforms of the labor movement called for an eight-hour workday, child-labor regulation, and cooperatives of owners and workers. The progressive bent of the times also focused attention on factory safety, tainted food and drugs, political corruption, and unchecked economic monopolies. At the same time, progress was not being made by all. For black Americans, many of the gains of reconstruction were being wiped away by regressive Jim Crow laws, particularly in the South. Cherished voting privileges were being systematically taken away. When President Roosevelt asked renowned black educator Booker T. Washington to dine at the White House, the invitation sparked deadly riots. Although less visible, the systematic repression of the Chinese was well under way on the West Coast.

1902 FAMILY PROFILE

Mary Kennealy, a single Irish woman, works as a clerk in a downtown department store in Boston, Massachusetts. Like many young working women, she is a boarder in a home that consists of a man and his wife and their three children, two girls and a boy. They rent a five-room furnished home. The man is a loom fixer and one of his children is also employed.

Annual Woman's Income: $364.00

Annual Budget

Clothing	$55.00
Food	$78.00
Miscellaneous	$23.00
Room and Board	$208.00
Total	$364.00

Life at Home

- Mary makes approximately $7.00 per week, depending upon sales commissions and the time of the year. Her room and board is approximately $16.00 a month, or $4.00 a week, more than half of her regular pay. She eats most of her meals with the family with whom she lives, who may be relatives, reducing her food costs.
- The family of seven, plus boarder, lives in a five-room house that has no bathroom. According to the survey, the house is well-furnished. The family can also boast some savings. The head of the household makes $12.37 per week.
- This woman shares a bedroom with one of the family's children.

Mary works in a Boston, Massachusetts department store.

"The Irish American Family Album." Encouraged by his brother Frank, who had immigrated to New York City, Paul O'Dwyer decided to leave his home in County Mayo, Ireland:

"There was a custom, which must have grown up in the famine of 1848, that was known as the 'American Wake.' It occurred on the eve of an Irish emigrant's departure for the United States. In those days most emigrants never returned, hence the term 'wake.' My relatives and neighbors gathered in the house, stood around, and encouraged me. They said such things as, 'Well, you're going to be with your brothers, so it will be just like home.' I knew that was not true, but I smiled just the same. The older people were saddened, and I had mixed emotions. I feared going to America, but I knew there was nothing for me in Mayo. The neighbors left about midnight. Each one pressed a coin into my hand. The sum came to $7.00 in all, a tremendous amount for the poor of our parish to part with. My mother had purchased a new suit for me, tightly fitted and in keeping with the latest Irish style. It was a blue serge suit and the bottom of the jacket barely came to my hips. The next morning my mother and sisters accompanied me on the trip to the railroad station by pony and trap (cart). There were periods of silence when we faltered in making the best of it. At the station my sisters cried, and my mother didn't. It wasn't manly to cry, so I didn't either until the train left the station. Then I did. I felt bereft and terrified."

- The house has no electricity, no running water, and no indoor toilet facilities.
- Mary is unmarried and is probably a first-generation Irish immigrant.

The Family Finances

Annual income for the family with whom Mary stays is $1,071. This family of seven is a second-generation Irish family. The father earns $612.00 a year, or $12.37 a week. His 16-year-old son earns $258.00 annually. The woman, as a boarder, pays the family $195.00 a year, which includes meals. The family is composed of three adults, three children under the age of 14, and one child over the age of 16. The father is employed as a loom fixer in a textile mill.

Annual Family Budget

Amusements and Travel $20.00
Clothing $115.00
Education $15.00
Fuel and Light $57.00
Furniture $20.00
Groceries $286.00
Insurance $9.00
Meat, Fish, and Ice $182.00
Milk $44.00
Newspaper $12.00
Personal Expenditures $52.00

Religion and Charity $18.00
Sickness and Funeral $30.00
Societies and Unions $15.00
  Total $875.00

Life at Work: Retail

- Mary works as a department store clerk.
- She starts work at 8 a.m. Business starts to build at 11 a.m. and she works until 6:30 p.m.; she is allowed 30 minutes for supper during her 10-hour day.
- Sitting while at work or "unnecessary conversations" can lead to dismissal.
- In some stores, sales clerks earning $7.00 per week are routinely fined $0.30 for 10 minutes' tardiness.
- Typically, department store employment pays $2.00 a week during the two-week Christmas rush, plus five percent commission. The woman is often asked to work 12 to 16 hours a day during the holiday season.
- Supper costs $0.15. She reports, "We were fed in droves and hurried away before the last mouthful was swallowed. The meal oyster stew, which was left over from the previous day, consisting of hot milk and three oysters."
- Generally, room and board provided to working women under the age of 30 years costs $2.50 a week, if they are willing to occupy a single bed in a dormitory.
- The dorms accommodate 10 to 15 women each, most of whom are saleswomen. Our family's tenant once lived in a boarding house and prefers living with a family.
- From the beginning of department stores, female clerks dominate the sales force, but not management; some stores boast 80 percent female clerks at the turn of the century.
- One manager reports, "I've been a manager for 13 years, and we never had but four dishonest girls, and we've had to discharge over 40 boys in the same time.

"The Irish American Family Album," by Dorothy and Thomas Hoobler:

Michael Donohue, the son of immigrant parents who settled in New York around 1905, describes how he decided to take a civil service test for city employment: "I wanted to be an artist, but I didn't feel that it was in the cards right then. It was too insecure for someone from my background. I was concerned about finding a gainful occupation. The only great desire I had was to become a civil servant and I zeroed in on that. It was the only idea I got encouragement for. And essentially, for the typical Irishman, it required very little in the way of education." (Donohue passed the civil service test for a fireman's job.)

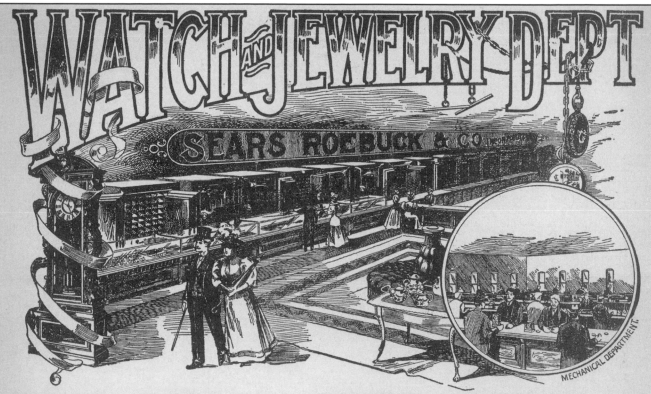

WATCH, DIAMOND AND JEWELRY DEPARTMENT.

WE CALL SPECIAL ATTENTION to our very complete lines of Watches, Diamonds and Jewelry, goods that will appeal to the most refined taste. There is perhaps no other merchandise in which so much reliance must be placed upon the dealer. Confidence must be had when buying watches and jewelry, and to inspire that degree of confidence in us we guarantee every item as represented or we will cheerfully refund your money.

IN WATCHES ESPECIALLY we acknowledge no competition. Our watch department is the largest and most complete in the world, and our prices by reason of our purchasing power are the lowest of any, quality considered.

SEARS, ROEBUCK & CO.'S Special Watch Movements are the perfection of mechanical skill, made especially for us after our own original design and in such large quantities that we get them at a price which enables us to sell them to you at what other dealers very often ask for cheap and unreliable watches.

WE WANT YOUR ORDERS FOR EVERYTHING IN THE WATCH, DIAMOND AND JEWELRY LINE.

OUR GUARANTEE With every gold filled, silver or solid gold watch we give a certificate of guarantee. With gold filled watches the certificate guarantees the case to wear and keep its color for two, five, twenty or twenty-five years, and the movement to be an accurate timekeeper for five years. This guarantee is given in addition to the guarantee which is fitted in the back of the watch case. As to the value of our guaranty, we will refer you to the first page of this book under the head of OUR RELIABILITY.

TERMS Our only terms are cash with the order. While in the interests of economical business methods we require the full amount of cash with the order, as explained in the introductory pages of this catalogue, we stand ready to immediately refund the money including transportation charges for anything that does not prove entirely satisfactory and fully as represented. You run no risk whatever in sending cash with your order.

OUR PRICES In Watches and Jewelry we buy EVERYTHING direct from the manufacturers in large quantities for spot cash. As we sell for cash, having no bad debts, we are satisfied to sell at prices which the retailer pays, and, on a large per cent of goods, for much less money.

MAIL SHIPMENTS We recommend sending Jewelry, Watches, etc., by mail, as it is perfectly safe and far the cheapest. Postage is 1 cent per ounce. A watch packed for shipment weighs from 6 to 8 ounces; chains, rings and other small articles of jewelry about 2 ounces. Packages amounting to $1.00 or over should be registered, which costs 8 cents extra. We guarantee the safe delivery of all registered mail packages. Be sure to send enough for postage, and if any balance remains we will return it to you.

ENGRAVING We charge for engraving in script on jewelry, watches, etc., 2½ cents per letter; in old English, small, 5 cents per letter; small script monograms on jewelry, etc., from 25 to 75 cents. In writing orders when goods are to be engraved, write or draw plain letters, so as to avoid mistakes. We cannot exchange goods after they have been engraved.

REGARDING ENGRAVINGS ON WATCH CASES It sometimes happens that we are out of the exact engraving on watch case ordered, but we aim to carry exact designs. When the exact engraving cannot be had, we always have a very similar one, which we will take the liberty of sending rather than delay your order. It being understood, you can return same if not perfectly satisfied.

WATCH REPAIRING We have a thoroughly equipped mechanical department, which is fitted with all of the latest tools and appliances for the repairing of all kinds of watches. We have a large force of thoroughly skilled watchmakers under the supervision of a very competent foreman, and any watch sent to us for repairs will receive very careful and prompt attention. We do not solicit for watch repair work, but are willing to accommodate our customers who wish to have work done in a thoroughly first class manner. Our charges are about one-half what is usually charged by the retail dealers, but the work will be done in a very superior manner. We cannot give an accurate estimate of the cost of repairs without a thorough examination. Our charges are merely enough to cover cost of manufacture and labor. None but a thoroughly competent watchmaker should ever take a watch to pieces, for the chances are that he will ruin it.

YOU CAN MAKE MONEY SELLING WATCHES, ETC.

For when you can buy them for the same, or less money than the retail dealer who sells on from 30 to 100 per cent profit and has large expenses in the way of rent, clerk hire, fuel, light, etc., you can readily see that you could undersell him and still make a handsome profit for yourself.

Boys smoke and lose at cards, and do a hundred things that women don't and they get worse instead of better. I go in for women."

- Other stores like women because of their sales skills, their ability to be "a queen behind her throne," and others simply liked the fact that women are willing to work cheaper.
- Of the 153 families in this survey, 32 show women working. Their income contributions equal five percent of the family total.
- Women typically leave the work force after marriage; 85 percent of all working women are unmarried.
- In Massachusetts at this time, only six percent of all saleswomen are married although approximately one-third are living independently of their parents, similar to Mary Kennealy.

Labor Department Testimony before a Congressional Commission, 1901:

"The front doorbell and the bay window have become boons to the social condition of the tenement dweller. The early tenements never had private entrances. When the individual began to build his own house, he had a doorbell and a private entrance, even though a family lived on the floor above him. He also has a bay window on his house, and everything also has to be in keeping with that bay window – better furnishing and belongings of all types."

Life in the Community: Boston, Massachusetts

- Boston is experiencing heavy immigration and competition for jobs. The principal immigrants now include Slavs, Greeks, and Sicilians. Many American workers believe these immigrants are keeping wages low and hampering union efforts.

- Over the next 10 years immigration increases, but many of the men come without families, intent on earning their fortune and returning to their homeland.

- Among Italian immigrants 78 percent are male and among Greeks, 95 percent. Many migrate to America in spring, stay until autumn, and return to their home country during winter.

- The North and West ends of Boston become predominantly areas of tenements and lodging houses by the turn of the century to include Mary and the family she lives with.

- Millions of immigrants flood the city after the cost of steerage passage from Bremen, Germany, is lowered to $33.50 in the 1890s.

- Most transportation within Boston is provided by electric trolley cars.

- The country's first subway opens in Boston in 1898, and an estimated 50 million people use the line in its first 11 months. By 1901 Boston is operating a unified streetcar and rapid transit system servicing most of the Boston metropolitan area on 300 miles of track. For a nickel fare, more than 222 million passengers annually ride its rails.

- Boston is taking a leadership role nationally in the development of city parks for all its citizens. Since 1898, the city has spent more than $200,000 a year to develop parks. By 1915, the city would boast 26 playgrounds for full-time operation. Nationwide, in 1903 only 18 cities have public playgrounds of any description. By 1923 there are 6,601 playgrounds in 680 cities.

- The new concept of newspaper comic strips is expanding rapidly. Richard Outcault, who in 1894 invented the popular strip, "The Yellow Kid," introduced "Buster Brown" in 1902, based on members of his family.

- Sports become popular and newspapers are starting to carry sports scores, reflecting the popularity of professional sports nationwide.

- A group of aggressive $0.10 and $0.15 popular magazines are gaining widespread popularity, notably McClure's, Cosmopolitan, and Collier's

WHAT THEY DID TO THE DOG-CATCHER IN HOGAN'S ALLEY.

The Ladies' Home Journal, January 1901, "Housekeeping in a Millionaire's Family," by M.E. Carter:

"The laundry department is an interesting quarter. Here again only skilled hands can find employment. Three or four women are busy from early in the morning until evening. Sometimes nine o'clock finds them hard at work. Fortunately they have Sunday to themselves or they would soon give out, the tension is so continuous."

with "muckraking" stories of the poor and corruption in the big cities of America.

- Quality bicycles sell for $100 each, although cheaper models are available; however, the cycling craze is coming to an end.

- The typical phone connection across the city takes a minimum of 40 seconds; the installation of the home phone is considered a luxury. Most people go to the nearest hotel or neighborhood store at the invitation of the proprietor to use the phone.

- Most brownstones are illuminated by gas. The wealthy use electricity to operate revolving electric fans. It is predicted that cooking can be done with gas in the future.

- A musical sensation at the turn of the century is the autoharp, which becomes widely available thanks to the Sears and Roebuck Catalogue. It can be played "without instruction."

- Minstrel shows are going strong, highly stylized with black-faced men, white-voiced tenors, ballad-singing baritones, clog-dancing, banjos, and trumpets. The Eagle Minstrels Show costs $0.25, $0.50, or $0.75 depending on the seat.

Roxy Theatre violinist.

Boston Daily Advertiser, "Well-to-Do Farmer Seeks Divorce," July 14, 1902:

"John Haskins, a well-to-do farmer of Secaucus, is seeking separation from his wife Marthat because she is a 'new woman.' Haskins says she spends nearly all her time 'attending club meetings and reading trashy literature on the enfranchisement of her sex.' He married her 18 months ago as a help mate, he says, but she proved to be an incumbrance too expensive for a farmer, refusing to milk cows, feed chickens, make butter or perform 'any of the duties normally expected of one of her station.'"

HISTORICAL SNAPSHOT
1902–1903

- The Brownie Box camera was introduced by Eastman Kodak Company with a sales price of $1.00
- The hamburger was introduced by Louis Lassen in New Haven, Connecticut
- Firestone Tire and Rubber Company began operations based on a patent for attaching tires to rims
- 30,000 trolley cars operated on 15,000 miles of track in American cities
- U.S. railroads now charged an average $0.75 per ton-mile, down from $1.22 in 1883
- The first modern submarine, the Holland, was purchased by the navy
- Uneeda Biscuits achieved sales of more than 10 million packages per month
- Life expectancy nationwide in 1900 was estimated to be 47 years
- The census determined that the U.S. population was 76 million; over the next 20 years it would grow 40 percent to 106 million, pushed by a steady influx of immigrants
- Membership in the American Federation of Labor reached the million-person mark
- The National Association of Manufacturers launched an anti-union campaign that promoted the right of Americans to work when and where they pleased, depicting labor organizers as agitators and socialists
- The price of coal in New York went from $5.00 to $30.00 a ton during a five-month strike of anthracite coal workers
- Rayon was patented by U.S. Chemist A.D. Little
- Russian American Morris Michtom and his wife introduced the teddy bear with movable arms, legs, and head
- Philip Morris Corporation was founded
- Charles Lewis Tiffany, founder of Tiffany and Co., died, leaving an estate of $35 million
- The first automat restaurant was opened by Horn & Hardart Baking company in Philadelphia
- The Wright Brothers made the first sustained manned flights in a controlled gasoline-powered aircraft
- The 24-horsepower Chadwick motorcar was introduced; it was capable of going 60 mph. Price: $4,000
- Massachusetts created the first automobile license plate
- Bottle-blowing machines cut the cost of manufacturing electric light bulbs
- The Harley-Davidson motorcycle was introduced
- An automatic machine to clean a salmon and remove its head and tail was devised by A.K. Smith, speeding processing and cutting costs
- Sanka Coffee was introduced by German coffee importer Ludwig Roselius

1904 Profile

Iris Clinton and her recently deceased husband Robert spent a lifetime raising three children—all girls—on their 112-acre farm outside Raleigh, North Carolina, where they cultivated cotton, corn, cattle, tobacco and many neighborly friendships. Today, Iris lives within a buggy ride of her seven granddaughters and still actively manages the farm. Her annual income amounts to approximately $150 a year.

Iris Clinton and her husband, Robert, raised three children on their 112-acre farm near Raleigh, North Carolina.

Life at Home

- Farming is a 24-hour-a-day occupation for 54-year-old Iris Clinton.
- It has been an all-consuming fight for survival throughout her youth during and immediately following the Civil War.
- When plowing was completed, there were always animals to tend, machinery to repair, food to fix, mouths to feed and clothes to make or mend.
- And Iris Clinton has loved every minute of farm work, except the time hail killed the chickens or disease caused a 400-pound hog to unceremoniously die in the middle of the family drinking-water stream.

- Iris started getting up at 5:30 a.m. to tend cows when she was little; today, she wakes up at the same time even though she has fewer head to tend.
- Iris quits outside work when the sun goes down and works by lamplight at night inside the house.

- She has seen an electric light working inside an office building during a trip to Raleigh, but is sure anything related to lightning can't be fully trusted.
- No home in her community has electricity, running water or an indoor bathroom.
- For Iris, the past 54 years have been a good, Christian life with not a drop of liquor ever passing her porch; menfolk in the area simply knew better.
- Iris has always enjoyed the rhythm of the land, the smell of pork on the stove and wearing old boots that fit like a glove.

"Candy Pulling," *Aunt Kate, 100 Years Dear, The Life and Times of an Early Dutch Fork Family*, by Elberta Sease, 1979:

"We made an effort to give our girls as much pleasure as possible at home as they grew up. They had a candy pulling right often. All the neighborhood boys and girls would gather at our house. We'd put pans of home-made syrup on the stove to boil. When it was almost ready I'd add baking soda and a little vinegar, boil it over a minute longer and pour it up on big platters to cool. As soon as it could be handled, the children buttered their freshly washed hands and each picked up a batch of candy and started to work. Out it was pulled, then folded back, out again, back again until the candy was creamy white and almost cold. Often three narrow strips were held by one child while another child braided it into a nice flat braid. Whether plain or fancy, just before it was stone cold but still pliable, I helped the children cut it in small pieces and place it on buttered tins to harden. Out into the yard, then, they went to play games until the candy was ready to be devoured with all the appetite of a bunch of happy, healthy youngsters.

On other days a crowd of them would gather in the afternoon and go fishing in the creek in our pasture. Up the hill they'd come about five o'clock with a nice string of perch and cat fish strung on a muscadine vine. I'd help them dress the fish, then build a fire in the stove and fry them, adding to their refreshments a platter of corn meal dodgers fried in the fish fat. To them it was a genuine party. Those children had a good time and I did too, for it always delighted me to see children made happy.

"Letter to the Editor," by Martin Long, *The (Raleigh, N.C.) News and Observer*, November 19, 1903:

I notice that these Americans seem to think the raising of crops to be quite unnecessary; and they are applying their remarkable intelligence to the task of depopulating their rural regions. They have acuteness to see that if they want to drive people out of the country, they cannot begin with the adult population. Life in the open country is so alluring and so natural that even when it has not been made as complete as it might be, it holds people fast. So these far-reaching Americans, in order to crowd people back into the cities, where they obviously want them to be, have devised a campaign of education directed at our children. They have planned all their rural schools on city models.

Even in such details as arithmetic problems, they see to it that the children's minds should be directed toward urban life . . . . How can a child born and reared in the country respect the life of the farmer when the community in which he lives does not regard the farmer's occupation worthy of study? How can he be expected to look with ambition toward agriculture as a vocation when he finds that training for it is regarded as less important than preparation for a clerkship? How can he think of village and rural life as anything more than a makeshift when he finds that in the schools he attends there is not a word taught concerning crops or cattle or roads?

- For all of her married life, the kitchen and its wood-burning stove have been 15 steps from the back porch—a safe distance in case of fire.
- Of course, it is closer than the outhouse, which was carefully placed downwind from the house, almost 25 feet away.
- Before his death a year ago, Robert, with the help of his three sons-in-law, moved the kitchen next to the house.
- Advances in the safety of stoves allowed the kitchen to be closer; no plans are being made to move the outhouse nearer to the Clinton home.
- As interesting as life is on the farm, nothing approaches the joy of having children, Iris believes.
- Maggie was born two years after Iris and Robert married.
- Iris went to her mother's for the coming and stayed five weeks.
- At this important time, only a decade past the Civil War, Iris wanted her mother to show her how to start off a family right, and she knew her aging mother couldn't come to the Clinton house.
- Maggie was delivered at her mother's home without incident; the doctor's charge was $2, which the Clintons paid with several bushels of corn when the crop came in.
- Robert made a cradle of red cedar boards that were planed and mortised; eventually, all the girls got their start in the same cradle.
- Maggie was three when Martha was born.
- Martha was eight when Bessie was born.
- The same week that Bessie arrived, Grandpa Monts, Robert's father, already old and feeble and ill for months, died of a kidney complication.
- Grandpa Monts was buried on Tuesday afternoon; Bessie was born on Wednesday night.

- "Everyone was scared for me and kept telling me what not to do, but I just kept right on in my regular way," Iris recalls.
- Middle child Martha cried when the newcomer arrived: "Now I'll be thrown away because I'm not the baby anymore!"
- Iris's one financial indulgence, after Martha was born, was a helper for the children.
- Despite the added expense, Iris employed Little Della, daughter of a former slave, to help care for the girls: "I don't believe in turning little children over to other children in the family."
- Recently, the grown-up girls, their husbands and children gathered at the farm for a candy pull—an all-afternoon activity that reminded all the adults of their growing up days.
- With a yard full of giggling, laughing little girls, all eager for a taste of the finished candy, Iris could easily remember the days when her girls were little, Robert had a head full of hair and all 112 acres were under regular cultivation of cotton, corn or tobacco.

Iris loves the picture of her grandchildren in rocking horses made by Robert.

- That was also the day that Martha took a Kodak of her girls riding the rocking horses that Robert made.
- Many a year when corn prices were down, tobacco kept the family going; for the past 10 years, tobacco has been the crop the Clintons could count on.
- Iris still attends church regularly, despite the 20-minute buggy ride; she sits with the other widows on the women's side of the church.
- All her life, the women have sat on the left side of the church, apart from their husbands, who sat on the right side.
- The children sat with either their mother or father, occasionally switching places during the middle of the service, but never during the sermon.
- Sometimes Iris wishes she could hear someone else preach; Pastor Long has led the church for 22 years, but the next-closest Baptist church is 50 minutes by buggy, two hours by oxen.

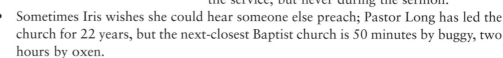
Oxen and horses serve as the primary source of transportation.

- That's a lot of traveling on unpaved roads every Sunday morning.
- Iris's most recent purchase is a New Queen sewing machine ordered from the Sears, Roebuck & Co. catalogue, which advertises itself as the "Cheapest Supply House on Earth."
- It cost $10.45 and came with a 20-year guarantee, which is more than Iris thinks she will need.
- However, she is pleased that she can sew worry-free until she is 74 years old.

- When the notice arrived that the sewing machine was at the train depot, Iris hitched up the wagon and went for it herself.
- When she uncrated her new machine in the front yard, using Robert's old claw hammer, she was so pleased with her purchase she sat down, pumped the peddle a few times, and then sewed the first seam of a dress without even carrying the machine indoors.
- The next creation was a white sea-island apron for granddaughter Dorothy, made exactly like the apron Iris had made for her own daughters dozens of times.
- When the sewing machine was inside the house, Iris kept the fancy address label that read Sears, Roebuck & Company, Chicago, Illinois.

- She only knew of one person who had ever traveled that far by taking a train.
- Iris has never traveled more than 30 miles from the farm since birth, but has little desire to go far.
- Going to Raleigh, the state capital of North Carolina, makes her nervous enough; Chicago would just be out of the question at her age.

Fayetteville Street looking north in Raleigh, N.C.

"Learning by Doing for the Farmer Boy," by School Superintendent O.J. Kern, Winnebago, Illinois, 1903:

It is not the belief of the writer that we should educate country boys to be farmers merely, any more than that we should educate boys to be blacksmiths, carpenters, or electricians. We should train boys to be men in the highest sense of the term. But why not a course of training in the country school for the country boy which shall teach him more about life around him? Along with his study of the kangaroo, the bamboo, and the cockatoo, why not study the animals on the farm and a proper feeding-standard for them, the care and composition of the soil on the farm, the improvement of types of grains and vegetables, and protection of birds beneficial to the farmer? Instead of all the boys' arithmetic being devoted to problems, more or less theoretical, on banking, stock, exchange, brokerage, allegation, and partnership, why not some practical problems with reference to farm economics? For the boys who will remain on the farm (and 85 percent perhaps will), the course of instruction should be such as will be an inspiration and a help in their future life work.

"Why She Didn't Marry," *The (Raleigh, N.C.) News and Observer,* March 10, 1904:

An antique maiden was asked why she did not marry.

"There's no need of it," she answered. "I have a parrot that swears, a cat that stays out all night and a monkey that chews tobacco and spits all over the house. I am satisfied."

Life at Work

- The Clintons are always prepared for the vagaries of the weather; farming provides few guarantees—the corn crop can fail, cotton become flooded or pigs die.
- Iris Clinton's favorite farming chore is tending tobacco.
- Cotton has been good to the Clintons, always producing a little coin when nothing else would.
- But cotton, Iris believes, is a vengeful mistress that is demanding, fickle and hard to manage.
- Besides, Iris cannot count the number of mornings she has awoken powerfully sore from the back-bending work of hoeing cotton, knowing that another full day lay ahead.
- Tobacco, on the other hand, is a handsome prince who is always whispering about the promise of tomorrow.
- Growing tobacco is like an annual courtship that follows a predictable pattern of flirtation, engagement, marriage and then rebirth, yet, like most relationships, the outcome remains uncertain until the auctioneer hollers out the final buying price.
- The first phase, Iris likes to tell her girls, is playing hard to get; for tobacco to make good roots, the plant must be starved before it goes into the ground so it will be more eager to produce.
  - Next is timing the engagement phase—plant too early and frost will kill off all potential; plant too late and the relationship will require too much work and watering.
  - But when it all works and the top leaves begin to grow strong and beautiful in the morning sun, all the uncertainty is rewarded, the courtship fulfilled.
  - Corn also holds a special place for Iris, thanks to a little contest.
  - In spring, the local Farm Alliance voted to give a cash prize of $10 to the member who raised the most corn on one acre of ground.
  - Robert and Iris chose a field of good bottom land on the creek and planted there.

"Tobacco Puffs," *The (Raleigh, N.C.) News and Observer*, March 11, 1904:

In an interview with several of Lenoir's most successful farmers today, the reporter learned that it is the consensus of opinion of those farmers that the acreage of tobacco planted in the county this year will not be over one-fourth what it was last year. One said that in this neighborhood, where nearly every farmer raised tobacco last year, not a single tobacco bed was to be found. On the other hand, there will be considerable increase in the acreage of cotton, a number of farmers having sold their crops already at eleven cents.

A carload of chewing tobacco arrived in Monroe, N.C., last week from a tobacco company of Winston, consigned to the Heath-Morrow Company, wholesale grocers. This is noteworthy because of the fact that it is the first carload of chewing tobacco consigned to any jobber in North Carolina. The value of the car of tobacco is $10,000.

- A committee of three men came around at the end of the season and pronounced it "50 bushels of very fine corn."
- The Reverend himself, one of the judges, declared the patch to be the winner.
- After that, the Clintons always called that land by a new name: Prize Bottoms.
- Another critical time on the Clinton farm is hog-killing day, made more special because of the participation of neighbors, longstanding ritual and lots of preparation.
- Iris has never liked for the hogs to get too large; 300 to 350 pounds is about right.
- In her experience, 500- to 600-pound hogs yield coarse meat and poor flavor.
- With neighbors to help, the day-long event is a celebration.
- The regular butchering dinner, enjoyed in the middle of the day, is sauerkraut to cut the grease, baked potatoes, rice, pork steak, pickles, fresh bread, stewed dried peaches and coffee.

"Change in Prices," *The (Raleigh, N.C.) News and Observer*, March 11, 1904:

Comparisons of 1904 with 1896 show an increase of from 25 to 33.3 percent in the cost of living. This means that persons who are getting the same salary or wages now as in 1896 can buy only two-thirds or three-fourths as much of the necessaries of life now as then.

Suggestions for Clothing for School Girls, Clothing for One Year, Hampton Institute, Hampton, Virginia:

6 undervests (summer)	$0.60	1 pair low shoes	2.50
4 undervests (winter)	1.00	1 pair high shoes	3.00
4 pairs drawers, homemade	0.80	1 pair corsets	0.50
2 white petticoats	1.00	1 hat	2.00
3 nightgowns, homemade	1.65	1 wool skirt	3.00
4 underwaists, homemade	1.00	1 suit	12.50
1 gingham petticoat, homemade	0.40	1 raincoat	3.00
2 short flannel petticoats, homemade	0.70	1 pair rubbers	0.60
6 shirtwaists, homemade	2.40	1 umbrella	1.00
1 white percale dress skirt, homemade	0.55	4 collars	0.40
1 gingham dress, homemade	1.00	12 handkerchiefs	1.20
1 muslin dress, homemade	1.50	1 pair gloves, lisle	0.25
4 gingham aprons, homemade	0.72	1 pair gloves, wool	0.25
2 white aprons, homemade	0.60	Belts, neckties	1.50
4 pairs stockings	1.00	**Total**	**$46.62**

Life in the Community: Norris, North Carolina

- The Norris community outside Raleigh has never appeared on the county map, but it exists nonetheless in the minds of six families.
- The center of Norris, population 21, is Bill Norris's store, built in 1841 and in continuous operation ever since, despite being burned once by the invading Yankee Army in 1864 and once by teenagers playing with imported Chinese firecrackers in 1894.
- For Iris, Norris's has always been a second home, especially on rainy or snowy days when field work is impossible or housework simply unbearable.
- At Norris's, Iris could finger new bolts of cloth and dream about the dresses she would make if time permitted and occasion demanded.
- It was there she had her first fresh orange when she was 17—a gift to each child in the neighborhood from old man Norris, Bill's grandfather.
- What a thrill it was to peel each slice and savor the sweet juice!
- After that it became a grand, annual tradition for Norris to buy a crate of oranges each year to be sold to the community for $0.10 an orange.
- To make the treat even more delectable, Iris, after she had children, made her girls contribute their own money to buy an orange, the cost of which sometimes consumed half a year's savings.
- One year, when middle child Martha was 11, she decided to spend her dime on hard rock candy instead of an orange, only to live in deep regret for weeks.
- Iris also buys Ivory Soap there because it works so well and its name comes from the Forty-fifth Psalm of the Bible: "All thy garments smell of myrrh, aloes, and cassia; out of the ivory palaces, whereby they have made thee glad."
- She also gets to try different foods, thanks to the nearby store.
- Recently, Iris has switched from regular coffee to a new drink called Grain-o.
- Made of roasted cereal grains, Grain-o is designed to protect all who drink it from the "dreadful consequences" of coffee drinking.
- She is sure she will get accustomed to the taste soon.
- Norris's is also where husband Robert kept a liquor bottle for occasional late afternoon sips—a fact Iris was never told and pretended not to know about during their 34-year marriage.
- Even though Robert has passed, the men of the area still include Iris in the beef club.
- For 30 years, 16 farm men have worked to help each other's families put meat on the table.
- By tradition, every Friday night for 16 weeks, one man kills a beef cow; by Saturday at sun-up, the other men are at his house.
- The beef is cut up and each man puts his share in a cloth bag, called a beef wallet, then gallops home to a family anticipating steak for breakfast and liver dumplings for dinner.
- The beef is divided such that after 16 weeks, every family receives an entire calf.
- Recently, the newspapers and magazines have been populated with articles about rural schools and their efforts to destroy agriculture by depopulating the farms.
- Other articles are calling for an educational system that emphasizes farm economics and practicality over lessons on the kangaroo and bamboo.
- Three years ago, North Carolina Governor Charles B. Aycock introduced a far-reaching program of education throughout the state; Iris believes reform is critical to her granddaughters and the men they will eventually marry.

"Hog Killing Day," *Aunt Kate, 100 Years Dear, The Life and Times of an Early Dutch Fork Family*, **by Elberta Sease, 1979:**

Hog killing time was a big day! We'd decide the day before to butcher and go out and invite Charlie and Emma Shealy to come help us. Then we'd walk over the hill and invite John and Lizzie Monts to come. Late in the afternoon, we'd set up three big, black iron pots and fill them with water. Next came laying the fire with lightwood, and some pine and plenty of oak to hold the heat and make good coals. Everything was ready for the shovel of red hot coals to be brought from the kitchen fireplace and thrown on the lightwood kindling before day the next morning. Then the scalding barrel was set at an angle in the ground and a platform of thick planks laid across scantlings was fixed in front of the barrel so there'd be a nice place ready to scrape the scalded hog. Next, the hanging place must be readied. A nearby oak tree had thrust a limb out at just the right place and height. It was used for every hog we killed. A heavy chain was thrown across the limb and the single tree, brought from the harness room and fastened to the chain. The bucks were placed nearby with thick heavy boards across them to make the chopping block on which the hog would be cut. Such a time it took to get ready! The heavy work was over now but there were still a few things to do. [Husband] Mike would gather up all the knives and go to the grindstone and make them as sharp as razor blades. I'd see that the lard jars were clean and ready, stack the pans and great wooden trays where they'd be handy and our preparation for butchering morning was about complete. We didn't feed the hog we were going to kill any supper, of course, and usually he was put in a pen by himself. Sometimes we killed two hogs the same day, but not often, as one gave us all the fresh and little meat we needed at one time.

Before day the next morning, the fires were started and when the neighbors arrived, the water was boiling. While the men killed, scalded and hung up the hog, we women ground black pepper in the little pepper mill, rubbed up sweet basil, coriander and sage and cut up onions for seasoning the sausage and puddings. We always seasoned a-plenty . . . . Our next work came when the men had the hog hung up by his hind legs on that single tree, washed down and opened. The entrails, liver, melt, etc., were caught in a huge wooden tray and we set to work separating everything. Into a pot where the head, already cleaned and cut up, was beginning to boil, we put the parts which go into the pudding. Then Emma Shealy riddled the guts. She could do that faster than anybody . . . . That means she plucked all the fatty tissue from the entrails. Straightened them out, and got them ready for us to scrape and prepare for sausage and pudding cases. By the time the cases were ready and soaking in warm water, to which a small handful of borax had been added, the men had the sausage meat ground and ready for us to mix and stuff. After the sausages were hung across the stick in the meat house, we turned our attention to the pudding. We ground up the well-cooked jowl, snout, tongue, liver, etc., mixed it with a pot of cooked rice, seasoned it with onions and herbs, stuffed it in the big cases and tied the ends together with strings. Then we gently laid the puddings back in the pot and boiled them very slowly in the pudding broth, hoping that none would burst open. However, one or two always burst. That was lucky, for then there was always some good "bottom" to our scrapple or pudding mush as some people call it. That was made by slowly stirring corn meal into the pudding broth and cooking it gently for a long time. Poured into the pan, it was set aside to harden. Cut out in strips or blocks, it was browned in the oven or on top of the stove in an iron skillet . . . .

By two o'clock everything was finished and put away. Some people took all day to butcher one hog, but we always said that was because they didn't get ready the afternoon before. Our neighbors went home by mid-afternoon carrying sausage, pudding, back-bones, ribs, crackling, and a pan of scrapple with them.

HISTORICAL SNAPSHOT
1904

- Ida Tarbell published *The History of Standard Oil*, an indictment of the company's practices
- The Supreme Court ruled that citizens of Puerto Rico could not be denied entry to the continental U.S.
- Hit songs included "Give My Regards to Broadway," "Meet Me in St. Louis, Louis," and "I Can't Take My Eyes Off You"
- Lydia Scott Howell won three gold medals in archery, an unofficial Olympic sport at the St. Louis games
- The teddy bear made its first appearance, named after President Theodore Roosevelt
- Hats ranged from summer straw in sailor shape, trimmed in satin, to handmade silk styles with a lacy braid
- Construction of the Panama Canal began; malaria and yellow fever were brought under control in the Canal Zone after Army Surgeon William Gorgas developed successful disease control
- During the Olympic games, staged in St. Louis, the U.S. dominated in basketball
- Sixteen-year-old Amanda Clement became the first female umpire to officiate a men's baseball game in Iowa for pay
- Nonfiction books for the year included *The Shame of the Cities* by Lincoln Steffens, *The Theory of Business Enterprise* by Thorstein Veblen, *The Toy and the Man* by Upton Sinclair and *The Negro: The Southerner's Problem* by Thomas Nelson Page
- The first photoelectric cell was developed
- Popular movies included *The Land Beyond the Sunset*, about slum children taken on an outing, *A Love Story and Meet Me at the Fountain*
- Bertha Kapernick became the first woman to give bronco riding exhibitions at the Cheyenne Frontier Days rodeo
- Vaudeville star Eva Tanguay debuted at Hammerstein's Victoria Theater in New York; she was paid $3,500 a week
- Refusing to wear tight shoes or restrictive ballet costumes, Isadora Duncan introduced the world to non-traditional dance
- Helen Keller graduated cum laude from Radcliffe College
- Foreign companies cut their steerage rates to the U.S. to $10 to compete with British lines
- Colgate Ribbon dental cream, Post Toasties, Campbell's Pork and Beans and tea bags all made their first appearance

eapest Supply House on Earth, Chicago. CATALOGUE No. III. 679

Acme Walking Gang Plow.

RIGHT HAND ONLY.

In the Acme Walking Gang Plow we have the best plow ever offered for anything like what we ask for it. It is a well made, practical plow, warranted to do good work. We claim this plow will skin sod from 1½ to 3 inches deep. Will plow corn land or oat stubble from 2 to 7 inches deep. Will cut and turn under all June grass on summer fallow, and do better work than any other plow on the market. Will prepare wheat and oat stubble for winter wheat in less than half the time required by a single plow or cultivator. While this plow will do good work in most parts of the country, we do not recommend it as a prairie breaker or on corn land where the stalks have not been cut. Compare the price with a single plow and you will see you are getting three plows for less than the price of two. Has three 9-inch plows, cutting 27 inches. Weight, 300 pounds. Shipped direct from factory in Western Michigan. Gangs with chilled shares are furnished with one extra set of shares.

No. 32R422	With chilled moldboard, landside and chilled shares. Price	$16.25
No. 32R423	With soft center steel moldboard, chilled landside and chilled shares. Price	18.00
No. 32R424	With soft center steel moldboard, chilled landside and cast steel shares. Price	18.90
No. 32R425	With soft center steel moldboard, landside and shares. Price	23.40
No. 32R426	Chilled shares. Price, each	.24
No. 32R427	Cast steel shares. Price, each	1.08
No. 32R428	Soft center steel shares. Price, each	1.43

Kenwood Steel Frame Two-Horse Corn Planter.

Constructed entirely of steel and wrought iron, malleable and charcoal iron castings, and will outwear any other two-horse corn planter made. It is a full hill combination planter. Can be used either as a hand drop drill planter, or a check rower planter by only changing the plates. The drill is adjusted to different positions by changing the chain on different size sprocket wheels on the axle without changing plates; it will drop regularly one grain every 12, 16 or 20 inches apart. The frame is coupled close, giving the driver full and easy control. The forcing lever is attached to the two hounds which are placed at an equal distance from the runners, so that both runners are forced into the soil at equal depth. The drop is simple and sure. The succeeding hills drop down separate channels and are held at the heel of the runner for prompt deposit when check rower is operated. Combination hand and foot lever is furnished so that the planter can be rigidly set to the desired depth, or can be run flexible and under easy control of the driver's feet, allowing him the full use of his hands for taking care of team. The check rower is one of few parts, not complicated. One side always at rest. Stroke positive every time button passes through fork. Forks are made of soft center steel, carefully hardened, and are wide enough apart to prevent kinks in wire from making a stroke. Has automatic winding reel for laying out the wire and for rewinding when field is complete. The wire can be released by the driver pulling a cord without leaving seat. The wire is of the finest quality, and with ordinary care will last many years. Standard width, adjustable for 3-foot 6-inch and 3-foot 8-inch. Price includes three sets of hill plates and three sets of drill plates. Does not include eveners or neckyoke. Furnished regularly with concave wheels, but will furnish with flat wheels at same price, if so ordered. Open wheels will be furnished at 75 cents extra. Shipped direct from factory in Southwestern Ohio.

No. 32R500	Corn Planter without check rower. Weight, 400 pounds. Price	$21.60
No. 32R501	Corn Planter with check rower, automatic reel and 80 rods of wire, complete, Weight, 500 pounds	$29.70
No. 32R502	Corn Planter with fertilizer attachment, but without check rower. Weight, 450 pounds. Price	$33.60
No. 32R503	Corn Planter with fertilizer attachment, check rower, automatic reel and 80 rods of wire, complete. Weight, 550 pounds. Price	$40.90
No. 32R504	Extra check rower wire, per rod	.05
No. 32R505	Extra plates, per pair	.42
No. 32R506	Clod Fenders and Covering Hoes. Price, per set	2.55

Kenwood Steel Frame One-Horse Corn Drill, Cotton Planter and Fertilizer Distributor.

In the construction of this planter we use steel frame, wrought iron wheel, high grade steel seed box, iron hopper for fertilizer—all finished throughout in a first class manner. For planting field corn or for ensilage corn, as also for planting peas, beans or other small seeds, the Kenwood is unequaled. It drops 12, 15, 18 and up to 24 inches apart, the distance being governed by number of holes in seed plates. The lever for throwing in and out of gear is near the operator; it can be changed without stopping horse. All wearing parts are large and true; there is no complicated machinery about the machine. Price includes three regular plates and one blank plate, also the marker, but does not include whiffletree or marker rope. Extra plates can be furnished to drop from 2 inches to 4 feet apart, and thick plates to drop more than one kernel at a time. Can also furnish extra plates to plant broom corn, pop corn, beans, peas, beet seed, sorghum, millet, etc.

The Fertilizer Distributor is simple and positive, no delicate gears to get out of order; there are no slides or wheels to gum or clog. Fertilizer attachment is a drill drop, not a hill drop. Must be ordered with the drill as it cannot be attached except at factory. It is the most simple and perfect planter made. Shipped direct from factory in Southwestern Ohio.

No. 32R508 Corn Drill only. Weight, 100 pounds. Price $8.75
No. 32R509 Corn Drill with fertilizer attachment. Weight, 125 pounds. Price $11.00
No. 32R510 Extra plates. Price, each .24
We can furnish this drill with our pick feed cotton planting attachment, if ordered with the drill. Cannot be attached except at factory.

Our $4.35 Cotton Planter.

This is a perfect, reliable and very desirable cotton planter, and one which has had a tremendous sale in the great cotton belt of the south. It is made of first class materials throughout, has a large hopper, a splendid agitator and a perfect feed regulating device. Center shovel is strong and cannot break. Driving wheel is made of wood, 16 inches in diameter, 3 inches thick and beveled to run in the trench made by the shovel. The coverer is supported by steel springs, which allows it to adjust itself to the condition of the ground and relieves the hands of all jarring. This machine is also a first class fertilizer distributor as well as a cotton planter, requiring no extra parts, and by adding the corn planting attachment it makes a splendid corn drill, dropping the kernels about 24 inches apart. Shipped direct from factory in Southwestern Ohio.
No. 32R512 Cotton Planter only. Weight, 65 pounds. Price $4.35
No. 32R513 Corn Planting Attachment extra. Weight, 5 pounds. Price 80c

We can always furnish repairs for our implements at any time at the lowest prices. See notice on first page of this department.

Selected Prices

Buggy	$59.75
Camera, Delmar Folding	$3.75
Coffee, One Pound	$0.30
Cooking Stove	$4.85
Fertilizer, 100 Pounds	$2.00
Handkerchiefs, Dozen	$3.00
Hat, Child's Straw	$0.49
Ice Box	$27.50
Pony Plow	$2.39
Range, Steel	$20.55
Vaudeville Show	$0.25
Water Closet	$19.75

E LADY FROM PHILADELPHIA

pose we ask the Lady from Philadelphia what is best to be done."—The Peterkin Papers.

DRAWINGS BY KATHARINE N. RICHARDSON

What I Am Asked

MAID MARIAN. Under the cover of your incognito I may speak the more frankly, especially as you desire the answer published for the benefit of other girls. If a young man insists upon holding your hand when calling upon you, in spite of your protestations, it must be only because he does not believe you

Highland Linen

rules of the each inquirer according to

THE tea service is on the luncheon table except when many guests are present, and the lady of the house makes the tea; the water

Highland Linen Writing Paper

1904 NEWS PROFILE

"The Lady from Philadelphia," *The Ladies' Home Journal*, May 1904:

" 'Suppose we ask the Lady from Philadelphia what is best to be done': *The Peterkin Papers*

Many requests have come to me for information on the subject of the conventional setting and serving of the table. I will give the rules of the present usage, leaving each inquirer to make the adaptation according to the means, needs, and circumstances of her household.

The first rule of all is not to attempt more than one can do easily and well. Anything conspicuously out of harmony with one's circumstances is in bad taste. It is, however, quite possible to combine simplicity with a pleasing presentation of food, and the accepted standards have been made with a view to minimizing the difficulties.

For instance, the placing of glasses, spoons, and knives on the right of the plate and the forks at the left is not an arbitrary regulation, but because the forks are used by the left hand and the other things by the right.

That each dish passed around the table by the servant is offered at the left of a person and all plates removed from the right, does not come from any fashionable precedent, but from the greater ease in helping one's self and convenience to the person serving the table, who may thus use the right hand in drawing the plates.

Besides the convenience, the eye is also to be pleased. In setting a table, therefore, the dishes should be placed with careful regularity, the plates at each side opposite each other. The room must be freshly aired, shaded in summer, and every possible sunbeam encouraged to enter in winter.

The modern breakfast table is dainty in appearance, the linen, whatever its quality, immaculate. The dish of fruit or a few growing ferns occupies the centre. The tray with the coffee service, cups—each standing in its saucer if there be room, not piled up— and the plate of the lady of the house is at one end. A teaspoon in each saucer does away with the old-fashioned spoon-holder.

At each place or 'cover' is a plate, dessertspoon, knife, and the forks that will be required, a freshly-filled glass of iced water, but without ice, and a small saltcellar at the left—unless large ones are at the four corners of the table.

If bread-and-butter plates are used they are placed, with small silver knives upon them, at the left of the breakfast plate. Upon this the napkin is laid, simply folded. Napkin-rings are out of fashion. As fruit often forms the first course, sometimes finger bowls are placed at the beginning of the meal—grapefruit or unhulled strawberries make their presence to be desired—otherwise they are used only at its close.

As each soiled plate is removed with one hand a clean one is substituted by the other. When the hot plates have replaced those used for the fruit, the lady of the house will have poured the coffee. A cereal is usually served next, followed perhaps by eggs, fish, kidneys, or mince.

No hot dishes are placed upon the tables of fashionable folk these days; everything is passed around. Those, however, who like old-time ways adhere to the custom of having the principal dishes placed before the master of the house to serve; others wait upon themselves, summoning assistance by a bell when needed. In winter steaming food upon the table has a suggestion of homely comfort, but in warm weather the newer way has its advantages.

Dry toast is hidden in the folds of a napkin to keep it hot, as are also boiled eggs if eggcups are at each cover, or they are passed on a tray in the small eggcups. Dessertspoons are used for grapefruit, berries, and cereals. Smaller napkins are used for breakfast and luncheons.

At luncheons the custom of using a bare table has been revived. Doilies which match the centerpiece are placed under the plates and principal dishes. Many, however, prefer to use a tablecloth over a cover of thick canton flannel.

The tea service is placed on the luncheon table except when many guests are present, and the lady of the house makes the tea; the water is supplied from a kettle over an alcohol lamp.

If the 'good old-fashioned way' be followed, the bread, butter, cake, preserves, or fruit are placed on the table before the summons of the meal is given. A folded doily is interposed between the bread, cake, etc., and the plates containing them. The caster is relegated to the side table, its furnishings being less used than formerly.

As has been said, it is the fashion to have no food on the table, but four small dishes of pretty china, glass, or silver are placed around the formal centerpiece (a foot from it) containing small dainties, as, for instance, cakes or wafers, peppermints, prunes, maple sugar, preserved ginger, almonds, and raisins, etc. Smaller dishes of olives and radishes give a pretty touch to the table.

Though we may prefer the old way when the family is alone, it has been found not only more attractive but also far easier to serve a meal in the newer mode; and when we have guests we welcome all that helps to make the service move smoothly. Each dish is passed around in turn, beginning at the right and left of the hostess alternately, and placed on the side table when not in use. No broken food or half-filled dishes are in sight. That which well-bred people accept today as the most ordinary and commonplace was once an innovation, challenged and demurred at by those who like accustomed ways.

With this fashion has come that of providing little more than just enough—a hint from the frugal French, who deprecate anything that seems wasteful.

A luncheon may begin with fruit and end with some simple sweet, or begin with bouillon (served in cups) and conclude with fruit—the intermediate courses being eggs or fish, one hot meat with a single vegetable, or a cold meat with a salad. The provision of fewer courses is allowable.

Afternoon tea is usually served at five o-clock, but the arrival of callers between the hours of four and six is the signal for offering, whether accepted or not.

Some persons have their tea tables ready, set in their drawing or living rooms, requiring only to have the kettle filled and the cream and cakes or tiny cress, olive, or cucumber sandwiches brought in. Others follow the English custom and have everything brought in on a large tray and deposited upon the tea table.

An informal assemblage of a few congenial spirits asked to meet and chat over a cup of tea is the simplest of feminine functions."

1907 NEWS FEATURE

"A Better Chance for Children of the Slums," by Charles W. Eliot, President of Harvard University, *The Outlook*, August 10, 1907:

Well-to-do people, having found it very difficult to bring up their children satisfactorily in closely built towns and cities, have invented two different means of securing a healthy life for them while at school. One means is the patronage of academies or schools situated in the country, but conducted by accomplished teachers who know how to provide for the intellectual and moral, as well as the physical, needs of children in their charge; hence the prosperity of the partially endowed academies of New England, and of the more recent private country schools which provide board and lodging as well as instruction. The second means is the provision of day schools well-situated in the country, within easy reach of the city, so that the children can easily come out of their city homes to the country every morning, and return near the close of the afternoon. This is a comparatively recent invention used with satisfaction by parents who do not wish their children to be wholly separated from them. The families who use one or other of these two means are well-to-do, live in the cleanest and most wholesome parts of the crowded cities, and can provide their children at home with such facilities for out-of-door exercises as cities afford.

The children of the slums need the fresh air and light of large open spaces much more than the well-to-do children, but the noisy, obscure and dirty streets of the poorest quarters of the city are their only resort.

In the interest of these poor children, a Boston architect, Mr. J. Randolph Coolidge, has lately made to the Boston School Committee a new proposal with regard to the location of public school buildings. He suggests that grammar schoolhouses for the children who live in congested districts be placed on the edge of one or more of the city parks, and that the pupils be carried out to the schoolhouses so situated in the morning and brought home again at night in streetcars, at the public expense, five days in the week, so that on school days the children shall no longer play in the streets or study at home.

There can be no doubt that this arrangement would be highly advantageous to the children who should be thus brought out from the slums five days in the week, and kept under supervision nine or 10 hours a day. They would have the adjoining park to play in, and each schoolhouse could be provided with a large yard and plenty of light and air.

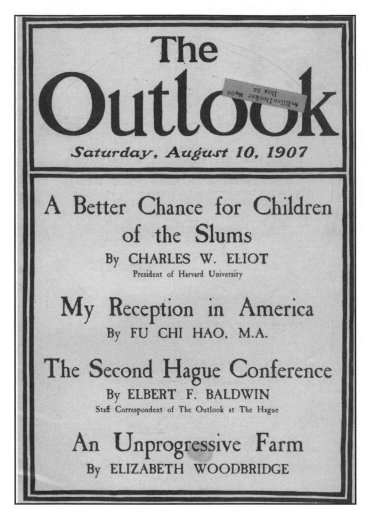

The Outlook

Saturday, August 10, 1907

A Better Chance for Children of the Slums

By CHARLES W. ELIOT
President of Harvard University

My Reception in America

By FU CHI HAO, M.A.

The Second Hague Conference

By ELBERT F. BALDWIN
Staff Correspondent of The Outlook at The Hague

An Unprogressive Farm

By ELIZABETH WOODBRIDGE

If it be assumed that the fathers and mothers in the slums will be willing, or more than willing, to have their children treated in this way, the only objection to this excellent proposal is that it would cost the city something more than the city now spends on these children. There would be two new items of expense: (1) the transportation of the children, and (2) the supervision of the children's play hours. If cars could be used running the opposite direction from that of the greatest traffic during the busiest hours, the transportation companies might make the children's fare very low and yet lose no money. The supervision of the play and study hours of the children would be a clear additional expense which would be different in different localities, but might easily cost $5,000 a year for each school of 1,000 children. These extra charges would be partially met by the interest on the difference in cost between a schoolhouse site in the heart of the city and a schoolhouse site taken on the comparatively cheap land of the suburb adjoining a large country park. This difference in cost would be very considerable in many American cities. About 40,000 square feet is the least suitable area for a schoolhouse to accommodate 1,000 children. Such an area might easily cost in Boston, for example, $50,000, whereas the same area opposite one of the large Boston or metropolitan parks might be procured for $5,000. The park sites would also have the advantage of being permanent, as well as thoroughly suitable in all respects. In the closely built parts of a city, the shifting of population so infrequently makes it necessary to sell an old site and procure at great cost a new one.

This plan is not applicable to young or delicate children, or to children whose services at home for part of the day are absolutely required. It is proposed for healthy children, not less than 10 years old, who are not required to work for their families in the afternoon. These country public schools should have facilities for exercise, occupation or games under cover in stormy weather; in good weather the children's games and exercise should take place in the open air, partly in the park and partly in the large schoolyard. It is not proposed to give away any food at the country schoolhouse. Food brought from home would be warmed, and food would be sold over a counter at cost.

This proposal is certainly very attractive to the humanitarian, the sanitarian and the economist, for it would give the children of the slums a far better chance for a healthy and happy childhood, and for the future serviceableness at adult age. The general plan would have to be adapted in its details to each locality which should determine to try it, for the transportation problem would be different in different cities, and the cost of adequate supervision would vary in different localities. The amount of money to be saved on the difference of cost between schoolhouse sites in the congested districts and sites near the parks would also vary widely in the different localities. It is an advantage of the plan that it can be tried with one schoolhouse at a time. That the method is strictly analogous to the methods being adopted by well-to-do people for the benefit of their children should additionally commend it to the democracy for trial.

1909 FAMILY PROFILE

Rosi Knaust, a 23-year-old single, German woman, is employed as a chocolate dipper, where she works a 92½-hour week during the busy Christmas season. She lives by herself in Chicago, Illinois, a city coping with the crush of immigration during the past two decades. She is considered lucky to be such a skilled worker.

Annual Income: $738.00

Annual Budget
The Chicago study provides no personal information about this worker. As a reference, the average per capita consumer expenditure in 1909 of all workers nationwide is:

Auto Parts $0.59
Auto Purchases $1.85
Clothing $30.00
Dentists $0.91
Food $81.43
Furniture $3.25
Gas and Oil $1.36
Health Insurance . . . . .NR
Housing $61.48
Intercity Transport $2.97
Local Transportation $5.12
Personal Business $9.61
Personal Care $2.88
Physicians $3.24
Private Education and Research $4.59
Recreation $9.49
Religion/Welfare Activities $9.05

Telephone and Telegraph $1.00
Tobacco $6.33
Utilities $4.00
Average Per Capita Consumption $318.42

Life at Home

- Rosi lives by herself in a tenement and shares a bathroom with four others.
- Groceries she is likely to purchase include the following:

Bread, homemade, per loaf $0.04
Columbia family soap, 10 bars $0.40
Crystal domino sugar, Two-Pound box $0.18
Fancy dry picked turkeys, per Pound $0.19
Fancy soft shell almonds, One Pound $0.21
Florida head lettuce, three for $0.25
Granulated yellow cornmeal, 10 Pounds . . .$0.19
Hawaii sliced pineapple, 2 1/2-Pound can . .$0.23
Honey washed figs, One-Pound box $0.25
Jersey sweet potatoes, 10 Pounds $0.23
Large black cherries, in syrup, per can $0.23
Oranges, per Dozen $0.18
Old-fashioned Japan tea, per Pound $0.37
Wilbur's breakfast cocoa, One-Pound can . .$0.35
Wisconsin June pears, per can $0.12

Life at Work: The Chocolate Factory

- A general depression nationwide exists in 1907–1908 that disappears by 1909, increasing the demand for candy production during the Christmas season.
- During the Christmas rush, normally from October 15 to December 15, Rosi works 92 1/2 hours per week dipping cherries into chocolate.
- According to her foreman, "The 1909 rush season began October 15 and from that time until Christmas it was necessary to make 40 days, or 360 hours, extra time."
- During the rush season, the factory opens at 6:30 a.m., with an unpaid half-hour for lunch at noon and one half-hour for supper, closing at 9:00 p.m. for a work day of 13 1/2 hours.
- When the foreman is asked if it is difficult to get the girls to begin work at 6:30 a.m., he says, "No, they like it; but it is hard to keep them at work Wednesday and Saturday nights."
- On Wednesday nights, this working woman often brings her own lunch and then works through the supper half-hour so she can stop work early—by

8:30 p.m. rather than 9:00 p.m. Wednesday is the traditional night for workers to seek entertainment.

- The remainder of the year she works a 68- to 72-hour week, normally working six days a week. Unlike many workers of her day, she works year-round. She receives no paid vacations or paid sick leave.

- During the Christmas season, she makes $23.12 a week, or approximately $0.25 per hour. During the remainder of the year, she makes an average of $14.21 a week. Her pay is near the top of the scale among fellow workers; chocolate dipping is a prestigious position.

The elevated rail system linked the factory worker to the factory.

- Her wages are based on her piece rate production, not hours. At the time of the survey, she has worked in the candy factory for approximately eight years, since she was 15 years old.

- In 1909, 944 women work in eight Chicago candy factories, concentrated on the west side of the city. Approximately 194 of the women are younger than 16 years old.

- The candy factories operate year-round, six days a week, during the normal season. Workers average a 68-hour work week.

- The largest of the factories employs 293 women, including 83 women under the age of 16. The smallest of the factories employs 35 women.

- The prevailing system of payment is a piece-rate basis which encourages long hours. "During the summer months business is very dull," the foreman says. "The girls work at times only three or four days a week. They have always counted upon making up this summer's loss during the Christmas rush."

- Rosi's factory is sanitary, although it only has two toilets for 200 female workers. It is not recorded how often the bathrooms are cleaned. The majority of the chocolate dipper's work can be done while sitting and sometimes standing.

- The per capita consumption of candy in 1880 was 2.2 pounds; by 1914 the per capita consumption is 5.6 pounds.

- Types of candy produced in the candy factories include stick and hard candies, cough drops, lozenges, licorice, gumdrops, caramels, popcorn, and fancy novelties.

- Other jobs in the candy making industry and representative average weekly pay during the normal season are: packer, $7.00; bonbon roller, $5.50; lozenge cutter, $8.00; cornball maker, $4.50.

- The candy industry started on the East Coast but quickly fans out across the country. Since the basic ingredients are dairy products, Chicago becomes a natural hub for candy making and candy bars in particular.

- Chicago has 1,000 Greek-owned candy stores in 1906. The candy industry is a mainstay of the large Greek community. From 1904 to 1909 the number of Greeks in Chicago doubles from 7,500 to 15,000—"12,000 of whom came and went according to their work in the city or on the railroad lines in states further west. As the Greeks became more numerous on the West Side, they invaded the Italian section, gradually displacing Italians from the area."

- The factories are primarily located on the West Side of Chicago. According to an early observer of Greek immigration to the United States, the district becomes more typically Greek than some sections of Athens. "Practically all stores bear signs in both Greek and English, cook houses flourish on every corner, in the dark little

grocery stores one sees black olives, dried ink-fish, tomato paste, and all the queer, nameless roots and condiments which are so familiar in Greece."

- Rigid tradition forbids Greek women from entrance into the labor market, especially after marriage. If they work it is usually in industries which also employ Polish, Bohemian, Russian, and Italian women. To be a domestic is frowned upon. Greek men consider it a disgrace to have a wife or a sister working outside the home.

- In 1908, the Russell Sage Foundation surveys the confectionery manufacturing industry in Pittsburgh to determine the conditions for workers. They find that candy must be protected from the smoke which makes the city picturesque to a non-resident.

- Yet the means adopted to protect the product from outside impurities involve serious harm to the workers. The atmosphere is cloudy from boiling kettles and cooling candies; the need for fresh air is urgent. Some of the small workrooms are well kept and well aired, it is true, but the type of room most in evidence is steamy, dark, and narrow, with windows tightly closed.

"Conversation with German Workers in Chicago," by Alfred Kolb, 1909:

"Whoever isn't just a bag of rags will make something of himself here. That's why I came over (from Germany). You say that wages are better here. You might just be right. But what're you worrying about wages for: you've got to become your own boss if you want to get on. But those days are over in America. I tried it myself a couple of times. The last time as an innkeeper. Me and my late wife, we'd saved ourselves a nice little sum. Within a year everything was gone. No, you can forget it nowadays; for everyone who gets rich, there are ten who go broke. And it's getting worse every year. For the Yankees who were present, this sort of thing was grist for their mills. 'And whose fault is it, anyway that it's getting worse and worse?' They shouted, 'Who else if not the quarter million European starvelings who come over every year and take up all the jobs. High time for some sort of law against this rabble. Stay home, why don't you, we don't need you. You work like snails anyway.'"

- The survey says, "It has long been declared that men make the best cooks. In recurring instances, when cooking is for a critical public, and not for an indulgent home, some rule of survival selects the undomestic sex to do the work." The wholesale making of candy is no exception. Men are the cooks, the makers.

- Men preside over the open furnaces where the chocolate is melted and the caramel is prepared. They are responsible for baking the peanuts; they have entire charge of the hard candy making, with all its wonderful possible variations of peppermint canes, round kisses with red stars in the middle, suckers, and chips in green, white, and red.

- The wrappers twine waxed paper around the peppermint canes, and twist the peanut kisses with a little rosette at each end. There are nine girls to handle the output of three furnaces; they work here by the week, because the kinds of candy change so frequently that at piece rates they would not be able to make anything. Half of them are laid off in February, but in March the sudden popularity of peanut kisses brings in so many orders that the wrappers have to work overtime every night for three weeks.

- Separated by piles of boxes and cases of stock are six chocolate dippers, two of them experts. Their work is more nearly a trade than that of the other girls, and they are respected accordingly.

- One woman, who has been employed at teaching new girls in factories from Boston to Denver, says, "You can't just teach a dipper. A girl's got to have a natural talent for it or she'll never succeed. It's like millinery, an art that you're born with."

- The chocolate dippers sit at a table with pans of hot melted stuff in front of them. Each girl has a mixing board, beside her a square of waxed paper, indicating where the chips are to be put, and how many each paper is to hold. Taking the chip in her left hand, she dips first the top and then the bottom of the chocolate, and with her right hand puts it on the waxed paper and finishes by a ridge or other decoration. She is paid by the hundred pounds.

- The packer takes the waxed sheets of chips from the table, and puts up the candy in half-pound boxes, crediting each dipper with her amount. The two expert dippers can usually turn out 100 pounds a day, which means a total pay of $9.00 a week.

- Cleanliness in candy factories is recognized as axiomatic. But sufficient air, pure air, circulation of air, are essentials to health which are not axiomatic, and the absence of which is met with at every hand.

- In the dipping department the air is changed at frequent intervals and artificially cooled to about 60 degrees, so the chocolate will be kept at the right heat.

- The emphasis is on quality of output. There are neither fines for bad work, nor rate cutting if the girls make too much. Instead, the rates are in many cases a little better than those of the other factories, the attitude of the managers is a little more liberal, and the result is the retention of the best candy makers in the Pittsburgh trade.

- Concerning wages in the candy industry, the Pittsburgh study finds "The wage basis for both the packers and the miscellaneous hands is on the whole the same, and that same is extremely low. Of the 526 girls in the two departments, only 21 are earning $7.00 a week; the majority earn about $4.00 to $5.00."

"Pessimism and the Labor Movement," 1908:

"Complaints concerning the human resources at our disposal are, when considered reasonably, completely unfounded. Whoever shares our view of the world must know that the people living today, coming out of society utterly consumed by egoism and ground up, as it were, between the grindstones of master and slave, have no choice but to be the way they are."

> ### *Chicago Tribune*, December 1, 1909:
>
> "More than 100 additional women tailors yesterday joined the strikers of that craft making a total of 500 men and women involved. At a meeting of strikers at 10 South Clark Street, officers of the Union charged the employers with breaking contracts made with the employees six weeks ago. The contracts called for an eight-hour day and pay at the rate of time and a half of overtime. A joint committee of the Chicago Federation of Labor, including billposters, stage employees, scene painters, and musicians, will deliver an ultimatum to Chicago theater managers on Thursday unless a favorable answer is received by the time relative to the demands of the striking billposters."

- Among the dippers, however, we may expect to find a different situation. Here, we have seen that real skill is needed, or if not skill, a knack that everyone does not possess. Sometimes a girl can learn to dip in two weeks; for others, it will take six months, and there are some who never learn. The chocolate curls, hearts, and bands on top of creams are marks of hand-dipped work, and it is the prize of a good dipper to make exact decorations on piece after piece, gauging each time the right amount of chocolate.
- If the chocolate itself is either too hot or too cold, it cannot be used, and if when dipped, one hot streak will be left on the outside of the chocolate, it will not dry and the piece will be worthless. The dipper must keep adding hot chocolate to her board from the steam-heated pan on the table to keep it at the right working temperature; moreover, she must see to it that the air in the workroom is dry, or the chocolate will be sticky and cannot be worked easily. The responsibility is on the dippers themselves to keep their windows closed most of the time.

Life in the Community: Chicago, Illinois
- The population of Chicago stands at three million people in 1910, over 70 percent of whom are foreign-born or the children of foreign-born parents. "It is a veritable babel of languages," a Frenchman observes. "It would seem as if all the millions of human beings disembarking year by year upon the shores of the United States are unconsciously drawn to make this place their headquarters."
- Chicago attracts worldwide attention as the nation's leading railroad center. The elevated rail system efficiently links the working class to factories in different parts of the city.
- The commercial center buildings are particularly remarkable because they are all brick, stone, and concrete, the consequence of a city ordinance passed in the wake of the great Chicago fire of 1871.
- The rise of activity—professional and recreational—among women drives the demand in 1909 for simplified clothes. Working women, particularly in cities, are a prominent part of the consumer culture fostered by women's magazines and those who advertise in them. This growing work force hopes to use their earnings to create lives for themselves that resemble those they read about in magazines and books.

- In the nineteenth century there was a marked difference between the dress of working class women and that of women in the upper class. By the 1910s, however, the key difference between the clothing of the well off and that of the working class was quality, not design. Mass-produced versions of the latest styles in clothing and dress are increasingly available and affordable. Where a middle-class woman could wear

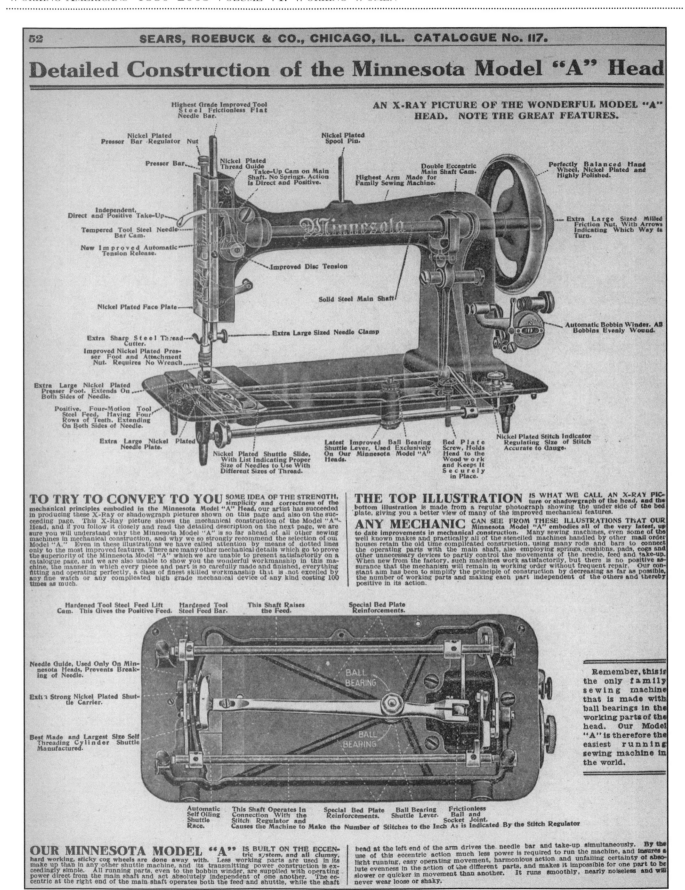

a fancy dress made of white linen with lace inserts, a working class woman could afford a simpler cotton version that, to the casual observer, looked much the same.

- The empire line is incorporated into the S-curve silhouette in women's dresses, which are still one piece but now have slightly raised waistlines and long, sweeping trains.

- The American Ladies Tailors Association exhibition in New York highlights the "suffragette suit," designed in protest against heavy, impractical skirts. It features a jacket with many pockets and a separated skirt with creases and cuffs like those of men's trousers.

- Marshall Fields, Chicago's leading department store, encourages workers of all ethnic and economic stations to visit the store. Store rules distributed to the store's salespeople stipulate that they be "polite and attentive to rich and poor alike."

- Despite this egalitarian attitude, department stores reinforce the notions of bourgeois good taste and propriety, emphasizing the correct clothes for each occasion.

- By 1909, silent movies become a mass medium and exhibition sites spring up everywhere. There are 10,000 "nickelodeon" or moving picture theatres in America this year, most of which are basically converted street-front stores.

- Early movie houses display an atmosphere of warm informality. Audiences often take part in the show, applauding and making comments about the actions or characters on-screen. Most films are often less than 10 minutes and often accompanied by music or sound effects, and sometimes a running commentary to help explain the lots.

- Among working class workers, activities such as amusement parks, movie theatres, dance halls, fraternal orders, skating rinks, and spectator sports become popular in the first decade of the 1900s.

HISTORICAL SNAPSHOT
1909

- D.W. Griffith featured 16-year-old Mary Pickford in his films; the former Gladys Smith made $40.00 a week starring in silent movies
- 20,000 members of Ladies Waist Maker's Union staged a three-month strike; they won most of their demands
- A tobacconist convention that year protested the automobile; they were concerned that it would lure people away from homes and clubs and smoking would be diminished
- The Sixteenth Amendment to the Constitution, authorizing income taxes, was passed by Congress
- More than 25 miners were killed in an explosion at the Saint Paul Mine in Cherry, Illinois
- Chicago's Jane Addams, founder of Hull House, ended her term as appointed member of the Chicago Board of Education, where she had lobbied for compulsory education and laws to end child labor
- By 1911, Milton Hershey, the father of the modern candy industry, had sales of $5 million a year making almond bars, kisses, and chocolate cigars
- The National Association for the Advancement of Colored People was founded by W.E.B. DuBois, Chicago reformer Jane Addams, Mary W. Ovington, and others
- The International Ladies' Garment Worker's Union called a strike to protest poor working conditions and low wages
- The Kansas attorney general rules that women may wear trousers
- Western women began to wear V-neck shirts, which some condemned as immoral
- The U.S. Congress passed the Mann White Slave Traffic Act to prohibit interstate and foreign transport of females for immoral purposes
- The U.S. Senate heard a resolution to abolish sex discrimination in the Constitution

1910–1919

The second decade of the century marked a dramatically changed role for women. In the early days of the decade, energized middle-class women set out to right the wrongs of America, calling to the nation's attention the need for better hygiene, public parks, safe working conditions for children and a better education system. By the end of the decade, women were accepting traditionally male jobs in business, factories, farms and industry so that America's men could fight in "the war to end all wars." As a result, million of dollars were poured into libraries, parks and literacy classes designed to uplift the immigrant masses flooding American shores. Laws supported by women were passed to limit child labor. Welfare leagues were created. Across America, women began to gain a sense of power and place as they gathered to fight for the right to vote or campaign against the drinking of liquor. The decade spawned new discussions about the role of women in law, medicine and academia, although only a few were allowed through those doors.

Immigration continued at a pace of one million annually in the first four years of the decade. Between 1910 and 1913, some 11 million immigrants—an all-time record—entered the United States. The wages of unskilled workers fell, but the number of jobs expanded dramatically. Manufacturing employment rose by 3.3 million, or close to six percent in a year during the period. At the same time, earnings of skilled workers rose substantially and resulted in a backlash focused on protecting American workers' jobs. As a result, a series of anti-immigration laws was passed culminating in 1917 with permanent bars to the free flow of immigrants into the United States. From the beginning of World War I until 1919, the number of new immigrants fell sharply while the war effort was demanding more and more workers. As a result, wages for low-skilled work rose rapidly, forcing the managerial class—often represented by the middle class—to find new and more streamlined ways to get the jobs done—often by employing less labor or more technology.

In the midst of these dynamics, the Progressive Movement, largely a product of the rising middle class, began to shape the decade, raising questions about work safety, the rights of individuals, the need for clean air and fewer work hours. It was a people's movement that grasped the immediate impact of linking the media to its cause. The results were significant and widespread. South Carolina prohibited the employment of children under 12 in mines, factories, and textile mills; Delaware began to frame employer's liability laws; the direct election of U.S. senators was approved; and nationwide communities argued loudly over the right and ability of women to vote and the need and lawfulness of alcohol consumption.

During the decade, motorized tractors changed the lives of farmers, and electricity extended the day of urban dwellers. Powered trolley cars, vacuum cleaners, hair dryers, and electric ranges moved onto the modern scene. Wireless communications bridged San Francisco to New York and New York to Paris; in 1915, the Bell system alone operated six million telephones, which were considered essential in most middle class homes as the decade drew to a close. As the sale of parlor pianos hit a new high, more than two billion copies of sheet music were sold as ragtime neared its peak. Thousands of Bibles were placed in hotel bedrooms by the Gideon Organization of Christian Commercial Travelers, reflecting both the emerging role of the traveling "drummer" or salesman and the evangelical nature of the Progressive Movement.

Yet in the midst of blazing prosperity, the nation was changing too rapidly for many—demographically, economically, and morally. Divorce was on the rise. One in 12 marriages ended in divorce in 1911, compared with one in 85 only six years earlier. The discovery of a quick treatment for syphilis was hailed as both a miracle and an enticement to sin. As the technology and sophistication of silent movies improved yearly, the Missouri Christian Endeavor Society tried to ban films that included any kissing. At the same time, the rapidly expanding economy, largely without government regulation, began producing marked inequities of wealth—affluence for the few and hardship for the many. The average salary of $750 a year was rising, but not fast enough for many.

But one of the biggest stories was America's unabashed love affair with the automobile. By 1916, the Model T cost less than half its 1908 price, and nearly everyone dreamed of owning a car. Movies were also maturing during the period, growing rapidly as an essential entertainment for the poor. Some 25 percent of the population, including many newly arrived immigrants, went weekly to the nickelodeon to marvel at the exploits of Charlie Chaplin, Mary Pickford, and Douglas Fairbanks, Sr.—each drawing big salaries in the silent days of movies.

The second half of the decade was marked by the Great War, later to be known as the First World War. Worldwide, it cost more than nine million lives and swept away four empires—the German, the Austro-Hungarian, the Russian, and the Ottoman—and with them the traditional aristocratic style of leadership in Europe. It bled the treasuries of Europe dry and brought the United States forward as the richest country in the world.

When the war broke out in Europe, American exports were required to support the Allied war effort, driving the well-oiled American industrial engine into high gear. Then, when America's intervention in 1917 required the drafting of two million men, women were given their first taste of economic independence. Millions stepped forward to produce the materials needed by a nation. As a result, when the men came back from Europe, America was a changed place for both the well-traveled soldier and the newly trained female worker. Each had acquired an expanded view of the world. Yet women possessed full suffrage in only Wyoming, Colorado, Utah, and Idaho.

The war forced Americans to confront one more important transformation. The United States had become a full participant in the world economy; tariffs on imported goods were reduced and exports reached all-time highs in 1919, further stimulating the American economy.

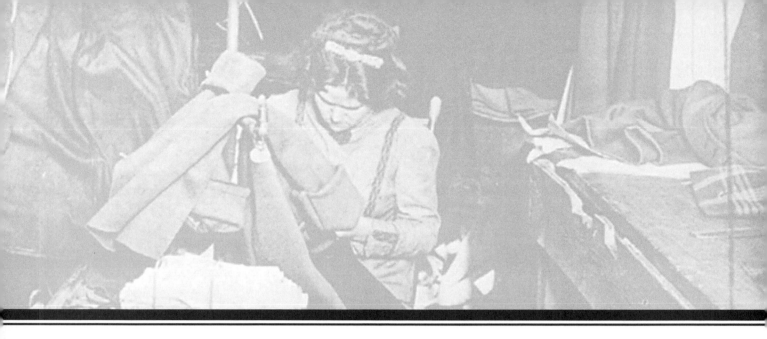

1910 NEWS FEATURE

"Born and Reared in Battle: The Impact of the Ladies' Shirtwaist Makers' Strike of 1909 and the Ladies' 'Cloakmakers' Strike of 1910," by B. Hoffman, *New Post*, 1929:

At the time the ladies' waistmakers went out on strike (in 1909), the International Ladies' Garment Workers Union actually existed in name only. But when the strike of the cloakmakers was declared (in 1910), the ILGWU had not only an office, but members. When the strike of the ladies' waistmakers ended, the ILGWU could boast of some twenty thousand members.

But while giving the ladies full credit for having laid the foundation of the ILGWU, it must be stated that the ILGWU became great and famous only after it had brought to a close the long and difficult strike of the cloakmakers in 1910.

The difference between the two strikes, though their causes were the same, was very great. The strike of the girls in the waist and dress industry was not regarded by the public as an ordinary conflict between capital and labor. In the strike of the girls, a great part was played by what may be called the social conscience. Ladies of the highest social circles threw themselves into the strike; the League for Woman's Suffrage was active in it, and the press, at least a considerable part of it, was outspokenly in sympathy with the girl strikers. Even newspapers who in case of a strike were wont to be on the side of capital and against labor, were, in the strike of the ladies' waistmakers, not so openly hostile to the strikers.

It was quite otherwise in the case of the cloakmakers' strike. In this case the conflict took on harsher forms. The "social conscience," apparently, had been appeased by the victory of the striking girls in the ladies' waist industry and resumed its peaceful slumber. The benevolent and philanthropic ladies of high society withdrew to their mansions during the cloakmakers' strike, while the press abandoned the friendly tone it had assumed toward the strike of the waistmakers. The cloakmakers' strike was a pure conflict between capital and labor. The line was sharply drawn, and the battle was one of considerable magnitude. Fifty thousand cloakmakers—some say sixty thousand—went out on strike.

What were the causes of that great revolt of the cloakmakers? There were causes aplenty. Long hours of work—65, 70, and often even 80 and 90 hours a week; the

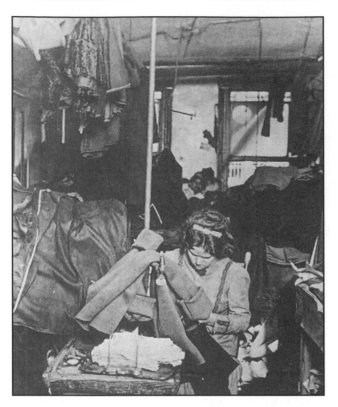

cloakmakers would come to the shops at five o'clock in the morning and work till midnight. A starvation wage of fifteen dollars a week, of ten dollars and even less; twenty dollars a week was considered a whole lot. Operators had to supply their own machines, their own cotton, their own needles, and had to pay various fines. I do not want to paint here a picture of how the cloakmakers then worked, lived, and were treated by their bosses. Suffice it to say that the sweatshop in the worst imaginable reigned supreme.

And it does not matter whether the shop was located in a small and rear bedroom or in a large, spacious front room. It is the conditions of work, the enormously long hours, the starvation wages, the brutal treatment, that mark the sweatshop. A wage worker does not even need a rich imagination to realize the hell in which the waistmakers, the cloakmakers, and the other garment workers then lived. And when they could stand it no longer, they revolted. The only question is: How were they able to endure it so long? Why did they not revolt sooner? This question calls for an answer.

The workers of the garment industry at the time were with few exceptions immigrants, most of whom had not been long in this country. A large number of them had not been workmen in the old country. They became workmen only after their arrival in America. And even those who had been workers back in the old country had for the most part been artisans who either worked for themselves or even employed help. Their psychology was not that of a factory worker. It was very easy occasionally to get them to strike for higher wages and shorter hours, but it was impossible to keep them organized in a union. There was not yet developed in them that sense of collective effort which is essential to maintain a union.

But this state of affairs began to change for the better with the great stream of immigration which poured into this country from Russia, Poland, and Lithuania during and following the Russian Revolution of 1905. A great many of these newcomers had already belonged to labor organizations in the old country. These organizations had at first been secret and illegal; afterward they became public and semilegal.

In this respect, the famous Jewish organization known as the "Bund" of Russia, Poland, and Lithuania exerted an enormously great educational influence. A considerable number of the newcomers had received from the "Bund" a certain training, both political and trade-unionist, and all of them were of a revolutionary bent. (At that time every decent person in Russia was more or less in a revolutionary frame of mind.) Now this element constituted excellent material not only for strikes, but also for the organization of unions. It had one great defect, however. In their first years in America, these immigrants felt wholly alien and for the most part looked upon themselves as temporary sojourners, as mere visitors.

At this juncture, there suddenly broke out the great economic crisis of 1907 with its disastrous consequences. Everything we tried to build up till then was wiped out by the panic. Only after the crisis passed away did it become possible to build anew, and then everything progressed swiftly. In the course of two or three years there arose an excellent fighting army among the waistmakers and cloakmakers, and the great revolution in the ladies' garment industry was effected.

1911 Profile

Sirvat Keghi, a 23-year-old Armenian woman, came to America a year ago to escape Turkish oppression; she works 10 hours a day, six days week at Ferris Industries in Madison, New York, as a core maker in a metal fabricating foundry. Her annual income is $422.50.

Life at Home

- Two years ago, Armenian Sirvat Keghi fled Turkey, which was part of the Ottoman Empire, to escape the Muslim-led purges and killings that were erupting across Turkey against Christians and Jews.
- The widespread attacks on the Armenians started in the 1870s during the Russo-Turkish war and sporadically continued ever since.
- Sirvat lived in Adana, Turkey, before fleeing first to Greece and then to America, with the financial help of her uncle.
- Her mother was a strong, energetic, and powerful country woman, her father a successful merchant skilled at harvesting and selling the gum used in making opium.

Sirvat fled Turkey in 1909 to escape Turkish oppression.

- Sirvat's mother was gifted with her hands and known for her ability to make a traditional Armenian poppy seed butter known as khashkash.
- When home from his travels, Sirvat's father loved to be with his two daughters and play a small instrument called the saz.
- Along with thousands of Armenians, Sirvat's parents hoped that the Russian Revolution of 1905 would allow them to finally gain their freedom.
- When they, along with Sirvat's sister, were murdered by the Turks, all hope of peace vanished; Sirvat felt that her only choice was to go to America.
- A revolution in Turkey led by the Young Turks allowed many Armenians the chance to emigrate when the travel ban was lifted.
- Sirvat took the opportunity to emigrate to Greece.
- As she was leaving the country—frantic to board a ship to Greece—she accidentally bumped into a Turkish man, whose only words were, "Hurrying comes from the devil, patience comes from Allah."

- The phrase frightened her, and was a further sign that she must leave immediately.
- Just after she escaped, another massacre was unleashed which killed nearly 20,000 Armenians, including the rest of her extended family in Turkey.
- In Greece, one of the countries willing to accept Armenian refugees, she found work in a shoe factory.
- To get the job, she had to deny that she was Armenian and pretend to be Greek.
- For months, she spoke little to anyone, especially her coworkers, until she had mastered the new language.
- While in Greece, much emphasis was placed on the need to be married; twice, her aunt attempted to arrange a marriage for her.
- Fifteen or sixteen is the traditional age of marriage; nearly always, the parents are involved in selecting their child's marriage partner.
- Her aunt—now that Sirvat was an orphan—felt it her duty to make proper arrangements.
- Because both of the prospective grooms were Greek, not Armenian, Sirvat was allowed to say "no" —a freedom she would not have been allowed if her mother were alive.
- An uncle who worked at Ferris Industries in Madison County, New York, came to the rescue; there were jobs available for women in the core room of his factory, he wrote.
- To make emigration possible, he bought steamship passage for Sirvat for $26.00.
- Over half of all immigrants in the early 1900s came to the United States with pre-paid tickets supplied by relatives already in America.
- Across Europe, steamship companies competed for immigrant business.
- The Hamburg-Amerika Line alone employed 3,200 American agencies throughout Europe.
- Currently, 96 percent of American immigrants arrive by steamship.
- The steamship took 10 days to traverse the Atlantic, down from the six weeks of constant seasickness-plagued travel that Sirvat's uncle suffered during his flight to America in the 1890s.
- Her uncle had always planned to return someday, but the memory of the seasickness and the humiliation at Ellis Island have kept him in the United States; moreover, there is no one left in his family to visit.
- "Sirvat," her uncle warned in a letter, "the streets of America are not only not paved with gold, many are unpaved and looking for Armenians to cover them in poor grade gravel!"

Full Page Newspaper Advertisement by the St. Raphael Society for the protection of Ruthenian emigrants from Galicia and Bukovyna, 1911:

Dear Countrymen! Do not forsake your homeland for always! When fate forces you to emigrate, at least, don't sell your lands, so that you will leave something to come back to. Go for the sake of making money. Be thrifty and don't lose your savings on drinking. Return with the money earned and use it to improve your farms/households."

"What Girls Ask, an Attempt to Unravel Some of the Perplexities That Come to Girls in Their Relation to the Other Sex," by Laura Hathaway, *The Ladies' Home Journal*, April 15, 1911:

Misunderstandings are always likely to occur, and in love affairs—as in other conditions of life—the only way to handle them is to make them right as soon as possible.

The Way an Older Woman Can Help

Dear Mrs. Hathaway:
Please answer this question as soon as you can, as it is a most important crisis in my life and I don't want to do anything now which I will regret afterward.

I have had a misunderstanding with one who is very dear to me, but he does not know it. We have been going together for about a year, and I feel sure he would have soon spoken if it were not for people who have come between us. Someone has misrepresented me to him, and now he is sailing for Europe very soon. Unless I see him, all will be over between us. I cannot make up my mind to go to him, and yet, if he sails away so far without understanding me rightly, it will break my heart. Please advise me.
—Alice M.

I see your point and appreciate the situation. It is quite true that people have been parted forever unnecessarily, and that possible happy marriages have been prevented by just such an accident as you describe. Of course, if you had been his promised wife, the right thing for you to do would have been to write him a special letter suggesting an interview. But since he has never revealed his feelings to you, definitely it would be the worst move on your part to take them for granted. There is nothing, if you ask me, that you can do personally. But that is not to say that nothing can be done by someone else to straighten out this unhappy tangle. Young people in our country are apt to ignore the fact that there are older people who can help them. They forget that every girl's love affair only repeats, in a way, her mother's love affair.

I am afraid that some mothers forget it, too, and do not preserve the confidence of their daughters in these close-to-the-heart matters. Your mother, if you have one, can act in this case with the most perfect propriety. Indeed, she has the right to. No young man could resent a call from a woman at whose house he had been received on a friendly footing. She can find what the difficulty is; she can instinctively reach his state of mind.

If you have no mother, then it should be an aunt, an older sister or a friend much older than yourself.

High-School Boys and Girls

I select this letter from more nearly like it, and in answering it I wish to write strongly what is in my mind upon this subject. I hope I shall not be prosy because I want every girl who reads this page to know what I, as well as many other persons whose opinions she would value, think about it.

Dear Mrs. Hathaway:
The boys that go to our high school are, most of them, rather common, not the kind a nice girl wants to go with. There are a few that we could have such a good time with if they were the sort that care for a good time. But these don't seem to care anything about girls' society. We ask them to call but they don't come. The girls of our set think you might write to us and tell us what you think of it. Please don't give my name.
—M.F.R.

(*continued*)

(*continued*)

This situation is one which is often found in the high schools all over the country. It is one thing which makes people object to coeducational schools.

To begin with, I want to call your attention to that side of it which most strongly concerns a girl personally. You and your friends are right. I certainly have a good many thoughts on the matter, but I am not sure you would hear them explicitly. You see, you have not written as fully as you might and thus I am forced into guessing. If I guess wrong, do not blame me.

One of the things which my intimate knowledge of boys and boy nature has taught me is that they hold in unspeakable scorn the girl who "makes up to them." If any girl who has ever made advances toward a boy could hear the tone in which he tells his mother, as he says, "Oh, she makes me so tired!" she would resolve that never, never as long as she lived would she do it again. Moreover, the remembrance of what she has done will trouble her when she is an old woman, so clear-cut do these problems become

in later life. Conversely, that same listening girl would learn another valuable lesson to add to her first one, could she hear the reverent tone with which that same young man speaks of a girl of whom he is beginning to think seriously, when he says: "I tell you, Mother, the fellows have to stand back from her! She won't have any nonsense. You don't get things out of her without asking pretty hard."

Believe me, there is nothing gained by the tactics you have referred to. Not only that, but everything you most wish for is also lost.

Girls underestimate the intrinsic attraction they have for the other sex. A pretty girl—no, let me modify that, for all girls are not pretty—a bright girl who dresses becomingly, does her hair well, makes the most of her good points, has nice manners and is frankly in for a good time, is attractive whether she knows it or not. But if she spoils it all by reaching out for what should come to her naturally, who can wonder if men say, "I don't care to be very much in that girl's society"?

- Twenty-two-year-old Sirvat arrived in Madison in 1910 in time for the expansion of Ferris Industries, a maker of farm equipment.
- Except for her uncle, she knows no one; she speaks no English, writes Armenian poorly and is still in mourning that her family—and virtually her entire town in Turkey—has been eliminated.
- She can no longer remember the faces of friends or the last sermon she heard before she fled, only the sorrow in the priest's voice that he was unable to suppress.
- Sirvat and her uncle are both hoping to save enough money and wait for conditions to improve in Turkey so they may return; in the meantime, he is also considering opening a grocery store so he can stop working for others and be his own boss.
- They live very frugally and have a one-room apartment; Sirvat saves about two dollars a week of her salary.
- She knows that at 23 she needs to marry, but she wants to experience the schooling she lost during the fighting and be a modern, educated woman.
- Since arriving, Sirvat has dreamed of taking classes at nearby Cazenovia Seminary, which graduates two or three women every year.
- A community of Armenians is growing in the area; maybe, she prays, one day things will be right.

"The Immigrant and the Farm, An experiment showing why the immigrant does not move from the crowded city into the open country, and suggesting some ways of remedying the conditions which hem him in," by Nan Mashek, *The World To-Day*, February 1911:

Every year nearly 800,000 immigrants come to America. We have no accurate figures to show their distribution over the country, but one has only to see the growing foreign population in our larger communities to realize that the trend is enormously toward the city. The question is often impatiently asked of us, why will these foreigners flock to the city to trouble us with their clamor for work when they might live in peace and plenty in the country? Why do they leave their own country at all if they cannot, when they come here, go where their labor is needed?

The solution of this problem by the sending of men into the country has become a tenet of our national belief. It has so simple and elemental an air that it naturally invites confidence. But the proof of a remedy being, after all, in the application of it, we look for some test upon which to rest our belief.

The experiment with which this article deals is offered as a small but practical test, a contribution to the greater remedies which it is to be hoped will be applied as the country becomes more and more sympathetically aware of the immigrant and more and more interested in our agricultural progress. It was made at the University of Chicago Settlement in the Polish-Slovak neighborhood in back of the stockyards, and had for its open fields the farms of Wisconsin and Illinois.

The packing industries of Chicago employ a large number of men taken on in the yards, and the length of their working day depends on the number of cattle and hogs and sheep to be killed on that day. The men taken on thus irregularly often earn less than $6 a week, working at the rate of from $0.15 to $0.20 an hour.

With board and room at from $12 to $16 a month, this is not a living wage even for a single man, though many families are compelled to exist on it. It was these casual laborers, dissatisfied with their wages and searching during their enforced leisure for better pay, that the experiment attempted to test as to their response to the farm idea.

That a scarcity of labor existed in the country was well-known, but in order to have a working basis, it was necessary to secure the offer of definite jobs on definite farms. To this end advertisements, stating that young Polish men wished work as farm hands, were placed in two Wisconsin farm journals. The advertisements were allowed to run for six issues, bringing at the end of two months 144 answers of inquiry. Reply was made to 100 of these inquiries, explaining the men were too poorly paid to have saved money and that it would therefore be necessary to advance railroad fare. Of the 100 farmers, thus appealed to, 44 responded enclosing the amount necessary.

In the meantime the settlement residents, through their natural entrance into the neighborhood homes, were able to make known that there were farm jobs to be had at good wages. One thousand dodgers in Polish were distributed among the men, advertising farm work in Wisconsin and Illinois at $25 a month . . . . To these various methods of advertising there were 89 responses. Of the 89, 28 accepted the jobs offered and were sent to 28 of the 44 farmers who had advanced fare.

(continued)

(*continued*)

Now what deductions can safely be made from these figures? They show unquestionably that the farmer needs help and is on the alert for any means of supplying it. They show a surprising response on the part of the foreigner. They show that this response falls short of its original intention, and point to the fact that there are forces working against the farm which we must control if we would direct the immigrant tide.

Theoretically, the problem of connecting this demand with its supply is simple. There is work to do and men to do it. It remains only to let the two find each other. Actually, the situation, interrelated as it is with human and economic problems, has a much more difficult solution. As a basic factor in this situation, we may lay down the truth that labor travels along beaten paths. New paths of labor are as hard to establish as new tracks of commerce . . . .

There are many objections to farm life itself, which it would still be difficult for the immigrant to overlook. Chief among these is the absolute change in the mode of life. Granting that the great mass of our immigration comes from the rural districts of Europe and therefore adapts itself readily to the open country, there are still a great many differences between foreign and American farm life. European farmers live in villages, each village having its school, its church and its well-established social life, so that the isolated American farm is inexpressibly lonely for the foreign farm hand. Then, too, our food is different and unsatisfying for that reason. The wages are unquestionably better and the life more healthful, but after all, many people care more for each other than they do for themselves, and those would rather get along socially on $5 a week than prosper lonesome on $10.

With regard to the sending of whole families into the country, there are almost insurmount-able difficulties. Where the families are large, it is difficult to find farmers who are willing or able to house them, or if occasionally a position is open, there remains the question of "What to do with the things." It is a large undertaking to move a family intact, and I doubt if any effort, unless undertaken immediately upon arrival from Europe, would bring any great measure of success.

Where there are no children or only one or two, the wife of the casual laborer usually helps earn the living. She enters industry as a regular wage-earner and is able often to bring home as much or more than her husband. As a result, she gains a position of definite economic value in the household, which she was never able to command as a mother and housekeeper. She may always have helped to pay the rent by saving money and by taking care of the children, but these duties do not bring her the recognition as a wage-earner. Her pejda (weekly wage) does bring her recognition. It gives a new opinion of the worth of her work and a standard to live up to. Naturally, she is unwilling to give it up for lower wage and the lower standard which she would find on the farm.

The highest wages offered for women's work on the farms with which this experiment has to deal were $10 a month. More often $8 was proposed as a fair wage. One farmer offered "$0.50 a day when she worked"; another naively expressed his idea of the status of women in industry as follows: "I would not care to pay highest wages, as there are only two of us, and if she washed, cooked or ironed, she would be doing one-third of the work for herself." With these obsolete ideas of women's wages still rampant on the farm, it is a small wonder that women refuse to be moved and cling to their city work, however disagreeable or difficult it may be.

THE WORLD TO-DAY

Victor
The record of quality

Victor Records are works of art—musical masterpieces.

They embody the very best music and entertainment of every kind, sung and played in the very best way by the very best artists, and reproduced absolutely true to life by the very best process—the new and improved Victor process of recording that results in a tone quality sweeter and clearer than was ever heard before.

Hearing is believing. Go today to the nearest Victor dealer's and he will gladly play any Victor music you want to hear.

Victor Talking Machine Co.
Camden, N. J., U. S. A.

Berliner Gramophone Co., Montreal
Canadian Distributors

The new Victor Record catalog lists more than 3000 selections—both single- and double-faced records. Same high quality—only difference is in price.

Victor Single-faced Records, 10-inch 60 cts; 12-inch $1.
Victor Double-faced Records, 10-inch 75 cts; 12-inch $1.25.
Victor Purple Label Records, 10-inch 75 cts; 12-inch $1.25.
Victor Red Seal Records, 10- and 12-inch, $1 to $7.

To get best results, use only Victor Needles on Victor Records

New Victor Records are on sale at all dealers on the 28th of each month

"HIS MASTER'S VOICE"
REG. U.S. PAT. OFF.

When writing to Advertisers kindly mention "THE WORLD TO-DAY."

Life at Work

- Based on the good reputation of her uncle, Sirvat Keghi was hired as a core maker at Ferris Industries in New York.
- To secure her job, her uncle paid the foreman a bribe of $7.00, a common practice in many factories.
- Ten hours a day, six days a week, Sirvat makes cores; metal fabrication is considered men's work, while core making is deemed suitable for women.
- A core is a baked internal mold, generally made of sand and silica, that is used to shape the internal features of forged goods such as engine blocks.
- A tray of cores might weigh between 10 and 50 pounds.
- Women are coveted because they can be paid much less than men.
- Women are not allowed in the labor union, which uses collective bargaining to negotiate the hourly wages of men.
- Generally, women are paid by the piece—according to how many cores they can make.
- Sirvat's average wage is about $1.15 a day; non-unionized men working the same job average about $2.50 a day.
- Sirvat makes 1,000 to 1,500 cores a day at an average pay of $0.10 per 100, depending on the needed core.
- When she is assigned to make finger-shaped cores with vents, the piece rate is $0.07 per 100; when she makes couplers that have a vent and spike, her piece rate is $0.12 per 100.
- The women who have worked there more than two years have the expertise to work faster; they sometimes manufacture up to 10,000 cores a day, or about three a minute.
- Recent gains by the unions have affected Sirvat, even though she is disenfranchised.
- Her hours have been shortened from 11 to 10 each day because the union negotiated fewer hours for its workers, impacting the entire factory.
- The foundry is able to close at 5:30 p.m. most days because it has shortened the lunch break to 15 minutes.

Sirvat Keghi works at a fabricating plant as an industrial core maker.

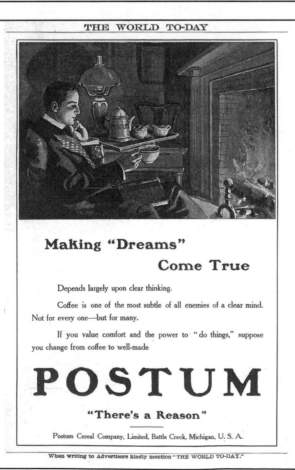

- Overtime is uncommon; the foundry works on an order basis, and because it is impossible to stock cores, they have to be made specifically for the job.
- Sirvat works overtime about three months out of the year, a day here, a week there.
- Besides, most core work requires daylight, and working after dark is not productive for workers who are paid by the piece.
- The area in which they work is off to the side of the foundry; core making is considered secondary to all other operations when laying out a factory.
- Sirvat and other Armenian workers are sometimes regarded suspiciously by management because of their reputation as potential strike breakers, commonly called scabs.
- Across America, only seven percent of native-born families report that a female earns an income within the family; for Armenians in America, 26 percent of families show a woman at work.

Life in the Community: New York

- Sirvat Keghi's met her uncle in New York City immediately after she passed through immigration at Ellis Island.
- She saw little of the city that day and has not been back since she arrived in America.
- In 1882, 87 percent of the 788,000 immigrants came to America from northern and western Europe; by 1907, only 19.3 percent were from those regions, while 80.7 percent came from southern and eastern Europe.
- Currently, the newspapers are filled with stories denouncing the "assault of our shores by immigrants, whose proudest possession appears to be their incomprehensible language."
- Some writers of the recent letters to the editor are convinced that "English is destined to disappear overnight under the assault of these mongrel languages."
- Others question why the immigrants all settle in big cities and factories, ignoring the opportunities of farm life; some politicians claim the new influx of immigrants will only create permanent slums and perpetuate poverty.
- This talk scares Sirvat, who fears the Armenians will be singled out for punishment; her uncle keeps telling her that what happened in Turkey cannot happen in America.

- Since her birth, Sirvat has been forced to survive multiple massacres and crackdowns on the Armenian communities in the Ottoman Empire.
- During the massacres in 1894, Kurdish and Turkish troops killed about 10,000 Armenians in retaliation for an insurrection.
- During the massacres in August of 1895, every major Armenian town was subjected to premeditated killings.
- By late 1896, the time of the last call for Jihad, nearly 100,000 Armenians had been killed and half a million had been left homeless.
- Before this, many of her male relatives, including her uncle in 1892, had fled Armenia for New York.
- Travel restrictions enacted in 1893 made further escape for the family impossible, although some Armenians were able to flee into Russia and from there emigrated to America.
- J. Rendel Harris, a professor at Oxford University and one of the first Europeans allowed to see the scope of the massacre in 1896, found refugees eating grass in order to survive.
- He heard "that . . . the Armenians have petitioned the Sultan either to give them the means of retilling their fields, or to let them leave the country, or to send his soldiers back again to put them out of their misery."
- Madison County is in the heart of New York State; Sirvat finds it very beautiful, but most unlike Turkey or Greece.
- She does not like being so cold for so long in the winter.
- Her first winter, when she was earning little, was so chilling she was forced buy a new winter coat.
- Sirvat makes nearly all of her other clothes, even though some of the stores in town now feature factory-made dresses in many beautiful colors.
- Most families in the area still farm for a living, and there is excellent hunting, an activity her uncle enjoys on Sundays.
- Oneida Lake forms the northern border of Madison County, which also boasts 14 other lakes and the Erie Canal.
- The population of the county is 40,000, the same as it was in 1840.

Photograph by Harris & Ewing, Washington
MRS. A. BARTON MILLER

Feminine Influence in Remaking Rivers and Harbors

PROBABLY those of us who are mere men suppose that the agitation in favor of developing our rivers and harbors is being carried on by such persons as governors and congressmen and journalists and lobbyists, but such belief shows not only our ignorance but our provincialism. There is a Women's National Rivers and Harbors Congress, with state sub-organizations as well. Mrs. A. Barton Miller of Charleston, South Carolina, the wife of a prominent business man of that city, has been elected president of this national congress after having served a year as state president. The time is past when such organizations as these provoke a smile. We count on women's clubs as among the great uplifting forces of the day, and it can not be doubted that the "Women's National Rivers and Harbors Congress" will have great influence in bringing about needed legislation.

Selected Prices

Baby Bottle, 12-Ounce	$0.50
Baker's Sweet Chocolate, Package	$0.10
Bed, Mahogany	$39.50
Coat, Man's Sheepskin-lined Corduroy	$4.95
Corset	$2.00
Flashlight, Ever Ready	$0.98
Muff, Opposum	$8.25
Nightgown, Child's	$0.22
Petticoat, Cotton	$1.48
Toilet Paper, Six Rolls, 1,000 Sheets each	$0.27
Trunk	$16.95
Whiskey, per Quart	$0.80

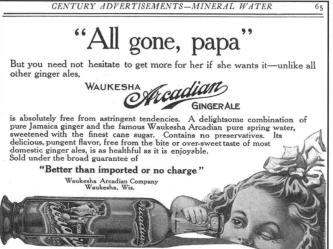

HISTORICAL SNAPSHOT
1911

- Crisco was introduced by Procter & Gamble to provide an economical alternative to animal fats and butter
- Women began to wear V-neck shirts, which were quickly condemned as immoral
- The use of fingerprints in crime fighting was becoming popular
- Harriet Quimby became the first woman to receive a pilot's license from the Aero Club of America
- The gyroscope and the self-starter for the automobile were invented
- The California and Illinois Senates approved bills granting suffrage to women
- The Triangle Shirtwaist Company fire killed 146 workers, mostly women and children; 80,000 people marched down Fifth Avenue in New York to attend the funeral
- Sixty-thousand Bibles were placed in hotel bedrooms by the Gideon Organization of Christian Commercial Travelers
- Domino brand sugar, Lee denim work clothes, Skidmore and Connecticut colleges for women and a white line down the middle of the road all made their first appearances
- *The Rosary* by Florence Barclay, *The Long Roll* by Mary Johnson and *Molly Make-Believe* by Eleanor Abbott were all bestsellers
- The United States Supreme Court upheld a woman's right, recognized under civil law, to her husband's property
- Marie Curie received her second Nobel Prize for chemistry, this time for the discovery of radium and polonium; suffragettes worldwide protested when she was refused admission to the French Academy of Science
- Massive European immigration continued; on a single day, 17,000 immigrants passed through Ellis Island
- The slang word "phone" for telephone came into popular use, thanks to the hit song, "A Ring on the Finger Is Worth Two on the Phone"
- The rising divorce rate, now one in 12 marriages up from one in 85 in 1905, was causing alarm
- New York State prohibited the representation of Jesus Christ on stage
- Fashion embraced youthful, thinner figures; huge breakfasts filled with meats and fish were replaced by lighter fare, featuring eggs and toast
- Demand rose for a cost-effective public parcel post system, especially in rural areas
- An estimated 40 million people attended summer Chautauquas which featured yodelers, opera singers, American Indians, magicians, Hawaiian crooners and inspirational lecturers

A CHANCE FOR OUR BABIES
By Della MacLeod

1915 News Profile
Working Children Study

In 1915, a study was conducted on the working children of Chelsea, Massachusetts, a suburb of Boston, who took out work permits when they were 14 years of age. The study attempted to survey children who quit school to work, and why. The researcher then followed the progress of each worker over a four-year period to measure the relationships of their goals to reality.

Study Number One

Peter is native-born of English parents. He became 14 years old on May 18, 1914. He left school June 16, 1914. Education: completed eighth grade; additional school training included an electrical course for 13 months. In addition, after going to work, he completed at Evening High School a commercial course, which took nine months, and a chemistry course that took four months. His first job, acquired through the Free Employment Bureau, was at a manufacturing facility that made dental plates; his occupation: running errands. According to the survey he worked eight hours per day, 49 hours per week and was employed for seven months. He started at $4.00 a week and moved to $4.50 a week.

His second job, as an office boy in a law firm, was acquired through a friend. He stayed employed seven months at $5.00 a week.

Comments: Has always intended to be electric wireman; when 16 will get a place in electrical shop. Is studying chemistry now and when 16 will enter Franklin Institute for a four-year course. Considers jobs so far as only temporary; has no special preference in either.

Four years later Peter is in the United States Navy with a rating of electrician.

Study Number Two

Joseph is native-born of Italian parents. He became 14 years old on December 20, 1913, and left school March 12, 1914. He took his first regular position March 13, 1914. Education: completed first year of high school; continuation school training—printing six months; other school after going to work—Technical High School, printing, and woodworking for five months. He got his first job through his brother in the leather industry. He worked nine hours per day, or 49 hours per week. He worked for six months at $4.50 to $5.00 a week, which was more than allowed by law. The inspector required him to stop working more than eight hours per day; he did not want to accept a position in the cutting room, where he could work legal hours.

His second position was as a baker in his father's business. He stayed two months and earned home support. At the same time he managed a Sunday newspaper route, from which he made $2.20 per week.

His third job was in the printing industry running errands, where he was employed three months. He preferred the first position because it was in the line of business which he wanted to follow. He was angry when he had to leave because of the illegal hours. In the third position he became dissatisfied with running errands, so he asked for a change of work and was made an apprentice. He did not like printing because he thought it was bad for his eyes, which were weak, and the pay was poor.

After he is 16 he wishes to enter the shipping department of a leather concern and work up, later going into the business with his father and brother. "I'm that kind of boy; I have to work every minute or I'm sick."

In a 1918 follow-up, he was employed as a salesman and chemist at a weekly wage of $25.00, working 50 hours per week.

Study Number Three

Anna is native-born of Russian-Jewish parents. She became 14 on October 22, 1914, and left school on October 22, 1914. She took her first regular position on November 23, 1914. Education: Completed eighth grade, continuation of school training—bookkeeping, 14 months. Her first job was offered to her by her father, who was a custom tailor. Her job was office work. She worked only five hours per day, which was illegal; (the law required a minimum of six hours daily if a child left school to go to work). At the time of the survey she had been employed one year and three months. Her pay was described as "support."

Her comments: Undecided as to future but likes bookkeeping and office work. Is about to go to work in a hosiery mill as a topper, but does not know what her chances are. Does not care to learn tailoring, her father's trade.

In December, 1918, she was employed as a clerk in a hospital office at a weekly wage of $10.00, working 48 hours per week.

Study Number Four

Maria is native-born of German parents. She became 14 years old on December 13, 1913, and left school June 21, 1914. Education: She completed the seventh grade; continuation of school training—bookkeeping, three months. Before leaving school she was employed for about 2½ years as nursemaid for her sister-in-law, working two hours a day after school and receiving $0.50 cents per week.

Her first job, which she got through a friend, was in garter and suspender manufacturing. Her job was putting buttonhole slips on suspenders. She made a weekly wage of $3.50. She quit because the wages were too low.

Her second job was in shoe manufacturing, a job she got through her sister. Her job varied from tagger, trimming pumper, stripper, and stayer. Her weekly wage ranged from $4.00 to $5.50.

Her comments: Knows relation of her occupation to other occupations in the factory where she is employed at present, but does not know opportunities for advancement or how long she will stay at the work. The survey said she was "fairly indifferent to work." She said, "My interest is taking care of children. It has always been my longing."

In December, 1918, she was employed as a stayer in the shoe factory at a weekly wage of $10.00, working 50 hours per week.

Findings of the Study

* Approximately one-third of the children of Chelsea took out employment certificates when they became 14 years old, a step required if they were to work before they were 16 years old.
* Among foreign-born children, nearly 60 percent went to work before they were 16 years old. Girls became regular workers at twice the rate of boys.
* Italians were more likely than children of other nationality groups to leave school to go to work.
* In Cambridge, 36 percent of the children born in Portugal took out work certificates, a larger proportion than of any other foreign-born group.

Our New Immigration Policy, by Professor Robert De Courcy Ward:

"It is significant that in the period 1871–1880 the 'old' immigration from northern and western Europe amounted to slightly over two million persons, while the new immigration from southern and eastern Europe and near Asia, numbered only 180,000. In the years 1874–1914, the period immediately preceding the war, the 'old' contributed about three million while the 'new' contributed over 10 million."

- Only one-fifth of the working children were foreign-born, while 72 percent had foreign-born fathers.
- Where the fathers were native, girls furnished only 37 percent of the working children. In families where the father was foreign-born, the proportion of girl workers rose to 45 percent.
- Many of the foreign-born children had barely completely the fourth grade when they went to work.
- Approximately 70 percent of the children who went to work came from families with both parents in the house; three percent of the children did not live with either parent.
- Of the children who went to work, 12 percent of their fathers were unemployed, 19 percent were laborers, and about 20 percent were skilled or semiskilled mechanics. Approximately 14 percent were factory workers; eight percent teamsters, drivers, and expressmen, and eight percent merchants and peddlers. Only two percent of the children had fathers who were clerical workers.
- Approximately 16 percent of the children came from families in which the mother also worked outside the home.
- Forty percent of the children left school and went to work because their earnings were needed at home.
- The economic need for child labor decreased as the family's length of residency in the United States increased.
- Girls were more likely than boys to take their first positions during a summer vacation.

Today's Housewife Magazine, June 1917, featured a story about the Association for the Study and Prevention of Infant Mortality:

"It has had to deal with the fact that a newborn child has, in this country, less chance of living a week than a man of ninety; less of living a year than a man of eighty. Actually, it had to realize that the mere business of being a baby must be classified as an extra hazardous occupation, and one not nearly as adequately protected as most factory labor."

1918 Profile
World War I: France

Civilian

Livia Sedgwick's lifelong passion for helping the children of her city's poor brought her to war-torn France, where she finds injured people, frightened children and a little orphan named Maria.

Life at Home

- Livia Sedgwick has always loved children.
- Growing up in Springfield, Massachusetts, she often helped her mother with children from the town's largest mill, owned by Livia's father.
- Together, she and her mother would throw parties on special occasions, hold health and hygiene clinics and sponsor tutorials for those who had fallen behind in their schoolwork.
- Livia especially relished teaching English to immigrant children; they were always eager to learn.
- Livia's father did not understand this fascination with helping the less fortunate, but he recognized that it made for a happier and more loyal workforce.
- Even after Livia graduated—with honors—from Smith College and spent a year touring Europe, her interest continued.
- In fact, her desire to help the city's poor children only intensified after her marriage to Edward Sedgwick and their move to Hartford, Connecticut, where he was an insurance company executive.
- Her father and the Sedgwick family both held considerable interests in the company.
- Soon after moving into a large house in one of Hartford's newest and nicest neighborhoods, Livia began focusing on the needs of the city's poorest families.

Livia Sedgwick has joined the fighting to help the children of France.

After marriage, Livia lives in Hartford, Connecticut.

"Thousands of Aeroplanes to Break the Deadlock in Europe," Current Opinion, August 1917:

Why not make it the fixed aim of the United States, says Admiral Peary, to be "the first air-power in the world"? If we will only concentrate upon aircraft, he adds, as von Tirpitz concentrated on submarines, "we will not only have an answer to the submarine menace, but we will have an unequivocal decision of the war, and that within a short time." The suggestion has evidently kindled the American imagination as well as appealed to its common sense. Congress has responded by the passage, in the Lower House, without a dissenting vote, after only four hours of discussion, of a bill appropriating $640 million to build a great air fleet and train an army of aviators. Five universities started courses of instruction several months ago and began graduating students last month, 200 a week being expected to receive their certificates of graduation from now on. . . . In one month's time, 2,000 workmen have erected half a million dollars' worth of buildings at Rantoul, Illinois, for a training field; 3,000 men were at work at the same time near Dayton, Ohio; and 2,000 at work near Mt. Clemens, Michigan. The appropriation bill in Congress does not mention the number of aeroplanes or aviators to be provided. That is to remain a military secret. But the president of the Aereo Club is talking of 100,000 planes and 25,000 men to operate them.

America prepares for war quickly.

Share Your Smoke WITH A Fighting [

When you light your cigar between the acts, think of an American figh[t] [me]n in France who is longing for even a whiff of tobacco. A carton con[taining] 45 cents worth of such favorite brands as Fatima, Lucky Strike, [Du]rham, Chevy Chase, Velvet, Camel, Tuxedo, Stag, Duke's Mixtu[re] [th]em will be sent on receipt of 25 cents from you. A postcard of th[anks] [wil]l come back to you from the soldier who receives the "joy package"

[Soon] as you get back to your desk send 25 cents, $1.00 or $5.00 to "Ou[r] [Tobacco Fund", 25 West 44th Street, New York. (Endors[ed] [b]y of War, Secretary of the Navy, Governor Whitman, Mayor Mitch[el] [Ge]rtrude Atherton, Alton B. Parker, Champ Clark and many others.)

"Jean and Pierre See Sammy," The Independent, August 24, 1918:

(The following extracts from the compositions of French school children are absolutely authentic and were sent to us through the 10th Engineers. While in southwestern France they became acquainted with a village schoolmaster who asked pupils to write, without preparation, compositions on this subject: "American soldiers have been in our village for some time. You have observed them. Describe one of them. What interested you in their work and their habits? Write your personal impressions."

They are all fine men, tall, large shoulders. I know one, a big fellow. He has a scar on his right cheek, which was made by a horse kick. He has a rosy face, long hair, carefully arranged. His feet are small for his size. He has a sweet tooth. He is gay. He is good. He eats chocolates and sweets. There are some going on an errand near their camp. I met him sharing his chocolate with his comrades. Next Sunday I was playing at spinning-top with my comrades. He was looking at us. My small brother had no spinning-top. He gave him two cents to buy one.

The Americans are polite. When they shake hands, they bow down their heads a little. Before entering a house they take off their hats, and wait till they are told, "Sit down."

They have good discipline; no fault is left unpunished. They are more daring than we are; they do not fear expense.

—Jean Laberiote

I know one more particularly. He is of ordinary size. He has a fine face, round cheeks, blue eyes. He likes to laugh at others. He is intelligent. He has got the bad habit of smoking and chewing tobacco. He is fond of sweets. He bathes very often.

The Americans have been very good to France, to come to help her fight the Germans.

—Jean Gaits

I have observed them well. Most of them are close-shaved. They are almost all tall and large fellows. They have quick eyes. They are polite, but some of them are great drinkers. The Americans are very smart. They do almost everything with machines and horses. They are up-to-date in everything.

—André Proustey

The work of the Americans is certainly a curious one. I saw them raise huge logs with large pliers, as easily as they would have moved a straw. Their furnaces for their kitchens are half in the ground, in order not to waste any heat. What struck me especially about the Americans is their cleanliness. All of them are tall, healthy and strong owing to their hygiene. Their teeth are very white; and not to soil their hands, they put on gloves even at work.

—Renée Bourthe

EVERY GIRL PULLING FOR VICTORY

VICTORY

VICTORY GIRLS
UNITED WAR WORK CAMPAIGN

- She organized, lectured and recruited friends into the effort.
- When more than eight years had passed without having a child of her own, Livia increasingly began to see the city's poor as "her" children.
- The arrival of the Great War brought with it a daily barrage of death, starvation and relocation in Europe.
- Livia followed every word, especially as Edward's focus on his work increased and the couple's relationship grew more distant.
- By 1916, before America's entry into World War I, Livia was convinced that her energies were needed in Europe, but was unsure of how to proceed, how it would appear to others, and how she could get across the ocean in wartime.
- Early in 1917, Edward joined the war effort as a "dollar-a-year man" in Washington, where his executive management skills were invaluable.
- His assignment was procurement—locating and purchasing the thousands of items needed for combat from ammunition and airplanes to military clothing.

Selected Prices

Baseball Glove, Horsehide $3.00
Bed, Feather $8.95
Bloomers, Woman's Waist-to-Knee $0.90
Bust, 2.5" Bronze-plated President Wilson . . .$0.10
Card Game, Rook $0.42
Clock, Winding Alarm $2.00
Cup, Collapsible, Aluminum $0.05
Gloves, Woman's Chamois $1.19
Macaroni, Cooks in 12 Minutes $0.25
Magazine, Vanity Fair $0.25
Overcoat, Child's Winter Weight $5.48
Rocking Horse $2.98
Skirt, Girl's Wool $4.38
Steamship Fare, New York to Australia . . .$337.50
Trunk, Wood Veneer $18.75

The children of war-torn France love the escape of reading.

- Proud as Livia was of his contribution, she was also keenly aware that the time between visits and letters grew longer.
- Just before Memorial Day, while having lunch with a Smith alumna, she learned that Harriet Boyd Hawes was leading a recruiting drive for a Smith College Relief Unit.
- Designed to be independent of the much larger Red Cross, the unit's specific goal was to aid French civilians in overcoming the hardships of war.
- Livia was delighted, and wired Hawes of her interest that afternoon.
- Only the next day did she think to call Edward; he was not pleased, but said he would not stand in her way.
- Within days, she was interviewed by a panel; Hawes only wanted serious-minded women of proven ability.
- Livia's fluency in French, her knowledge of Europe and past experience in social work among the poor impressed the committee.
- She was soon notified that she would be accepted for service upon the payment of $300 for uniform,

travel and sundries; she was also required to provide $55 a month for her own support.
- After closing up the houses in Hartford and Old Sagbrook on Long Island Sound, she sailed for France.
- Her parents proudly saw her off, and Edward sent a telegram from Washington.

Life at Work

- Livia and 17 other Smith graduates—ranging in age from 20 to 40—set sail from New York in late 1917, each determined to be of service to her country during the Great War.
- Every member of the Smith College Relief Unit was fluent in French, and many possessed special expertise in health, transportation, agriculture or social work.
- To support the effort, the unit brought two trucks, a car, six portable houses, carpenter's tools, parts for the cars and trucks, cots, blankets, clothing and food for the French.
- Within weeks of arriving, the unit had established itself a few miles from the French front lines in the town of Grecourt.

- Called the "Ladies of Grecourt," their self-appointed task was to assist 16 neighboring villages, with populations totaling 1,650.
- Farms were restocked, war wounds mended, and wood-working classes created to help villagers learn how to rebuild war-torn homes.
- A sewing and knitting shop was set up to provide employment for four women.
- Livia did what she has always done—work with the children.
- She established a library for them, and found that they loved the escape of reading.
- Day after day she worked with government officials to reestablish schools and ensure the fair distribution of food.

Soldiers sometimes pass through the town bringing gifts to the children.

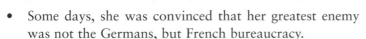

- Some days, she was convinced that her greatest enemy was not the Germans, but French bureaucracy.
- Mostly, she listened to young children, frequently girls, talk about their lives, their families, becoming a woman, and being afraid.
- She spent enormous energy planning Christmas parties for each of the villages.
- Using her own money, she purchased large quantities of food and drink.
- Most important, she made sure each and every child was able to open an individually wrapped Christmas present.
- Many of the children wept with joy—for a moment, the war had gone away.
- Livia's other project is more personal: a girl named Maria.
- Maria, whose parents were killed in an explosion, lost her right leg to an artillery shell.
- Eager, bright and resilient, Maria is devoted to Livia and wants to learn English.
- Livia began exploring the arcane and convoluted regulations of taking Maria to Hartford with her.

- She did not discuss the possibility with the little girl because, if she is unable to cut through the French bureaucracy, it would only bring one more disappointment into Maria's life.
- Occasionally, soldiers would pass through the town and offer gifts.
- Recently, a French officer sent a wagon of pigs, while an English unit provided a load of duckboard to line the muddy village streets.
- Another group of soldiers explained how the ladies could "read" their undergarments on a sunny day to rid them of lice.
- Livia was exhausted, filthy, and happier than she had ever been.
- As spring arrived, signs were everywhere that the war was drawing nearer.
- Some nights, the artillery fire was so loud, she was unable to sleep.
- Then, almost without warning, word came that the village must be abandoned.
- The relief unit was ordered to leave as the Red Cross carried out the evacuation.
- Livia and the other ladies made dozens of trips transporting the sick, the lame, and the children on muddy roads clogged with refugees, livestock and retreating soldiers.
- As each group of children was delivered to safety, Livia returned to the village for more.
- Only the crash of German shells stopped the work.
- Edward, who always wanted children, wrote of his excitement about Livia wanting to bring Maria to America.

Some nights the shooting is so near that Livia cannot sleep.

- He began assisting with the complex paperwork involved in adopting a French orphan.
- A doctor in New York, who also has a house on Long Island Sound, has agreed to fit Maria with a prosthetic leg.
- But first, Livia must complete her work.
- After Maria was entrusted to a group of nuns caring for children, Livia moved to a field hospital to help the many, many wounded.
- A large number of the patients came from units in New England; a few once worked in her father's mills.

- Some soldiers are missing limbs, several are suffering from mustard gas attacks, and others simply have the flu that has killed so many.
- During the day, Livia treats the wounded; at night she listens to their stories.
- Matter-of-factly, they talk of lost friends, cold trenches, and fear so strong it smells, tanks, airplane dogfights, barbed-wire battlefields and dreams of home.
- She helps them write letters and waits for word from Maria and Edward.
- Nine-year-old Maria writes often in her looping cursive handwriting, always working hard to enclose some English words in her messages.
- Edward writes that Maria's passage to America can be secured once the war ends.
- Livia writes about brave men who cry themselves to sleep.

American Involvement in World War I

- To support the war effort, the American government amassed an army eventually totaling four million; the navy numbered 600,000 more, and the Marine Corps, nearly 80,000.
- The United States was involved with the Great War against Germany and Austria for 30 months, but played a significant battlefield role in France, Belgium and Italy for only eight months.
- Commander John "Blackjack" Pershing complained that, because most of the American troops were raised in towns and cities, many had little familiarity with firearms and were poor marksmen.
- U.S. World War I casualties were declared to be 116,516; battle deaths totaled 53,402; other deaths including disease totaled 55,114; total wounded tallied at 204,002; and fatalities worldwide for all nations were placed at 10 million.
- Artillery and machine guns, not rifles, were the biggest killers on the battlefield during World War I.
- The influenza outbreak of 1917-18 killed 52,000 American soldiers, sailors and Marines.
- Thousands of American soldiers were introduced to the concept of regular tooth-brushing by military training during the Great War.

HISTORICAL SNAPSHOT
1918

- Farmers enjoyed a 25 percent jump in real income; many sold their mules to the army and plowed up pastures with their new tractors
- As an energy-saving measure, the nation adopted daylight saving time during the war, 150 years after it was first recommended by Benjamin Franklin
- Girls Scouts collected peach stones, which when heated turned into charcoal for use in gas mask filters
- Women assembled bombs in defense plants, learned to repair cars, carried the mail, directed traffic and worked as trolley car conductors
- The Committee on Public Information turned out patriotic press releases and pamphlets by the millions and drew upon a roster of 75,000 speakers to provide speeches for every occasion
- Civilians abstained from wheat on Mondays and Wednesdays, all meat on Tuesdays, and pork on Thursdays and Saturdays
- Some Americans swore off any beer that had a German name; sauerkraut become "liberty cabbage," hamburger was "Salisbury steak," and dachshunds were called "liberty pups"
- Labor unrest was at its most turbulent since 1890; inflation triggered 2,665 strikes involving over four million workers, more than 500,000 union workers staged a strike in Chicago resulting in riots and the death of 36 people, while New York City saw a strike of 300,000
- The rate of inflation reached 8.9 percent, dramatically increasing prices
- *The Economic Consequences of the Peace* by J. M. Keynes, *Ten Days That Shook the World* by John Reed and *Winesburg, Ohio* by Sherwood Anderson were all published
- Seventy lynchings occurred in the South as membership in the Ku Klux Klan increased to 100,000 across 27 states
- Herbert Hoover was named director of a relief organization for liberated countries, both neutral and enemy
- Peter Paul's Konobar, the Drake Hotel in Chicago and a state gas tax (in Oregon) all made their first appearance
- Hockey's Stanley Cup was cancelled after one player died and many others were stricken with the deadly flu

1919 FAMILY PROFILE

As the heiress to a lumber fortune and wife of a Presbyterian minister, Agnes Forcelle has had the benefit of traveling with her family to Hawaii as missionaries and to Paris as first-class tourists. They have one daughter, Martha, who has announced her engagement.

Life at Home

- The Forcelle family lives in Chevy Chase, Maryland, near Washington, D.C., where Agnes's husband Albert serves as a Presbyterian minister.
- Three years ago, Agnes's mother passed away, leaving an estate of more than $300,000, which has increased the family's economic freedom considerably.
- Agnes's grandfather had made a fortune first in the timber industry, later redoubling his wealth through real estate as the vast land holdings he had acquired for timber became valuable to developers near rapidly growing cities and towns.
- Because her parents had always shared their wealth generously, for most of the past two decades Agnes has traveled to Europe for vacations with her husband and their only daughter.
- Their daughter Martha, now 25, has completed her education at George Washington University and has begun her master's degree.
- Unmarried, she still lives at home, but travels widely with great skill and aplomb—often with her mother.
- Recently, she announced her engagement to a local businessman, but before she is married, she and her mother plan to repeat their 1913 grand tour of Europe with one last trip together, now that the war is over.
- The entire family enjoys traveling when time permits.

Agnes Forcelle is heiress to a lumber fortune.

Martha loves to travel.

- As one of 12 children from a middle-class family in Springfield, Massachusetts, Albert in his younger years did not have the wealth to travel on his own.
- After graduation from Yale in 1878, he spent two years as principal of Connecticut's Rockville High School, then entered Yale Divinity School, graduating in 1885 and spending the next two years touring the world as a guide, tutor and companion to a wealthy young man.
- As the daughter of a wealthy timber magnate, Agnes grew up traveling; she has been to England a dozen times, has visited India, and dreams of Japan.

This couple has traveled extensively throughout their marriage.

- From upstate New York, where her father's timber interests and paper mills were located, she fell in love with New York theater as a child, and often returns to New York City for Broadway plays and opera.
- She is proud to be a member of both the Colonial Daughters and the Society of Mayflower descendants, tracing her lineage through William Bradford, who was the second signer on the Mayflower Compact.
- Their daughter Martha went to Miss Hall's, a private boarding school, and hated the experience.
- During the war, when foreign travel was restricted, they traveled the United States collecting art pottery—a passion that appeals to many well-to-do American women they know.
- The current popularity of these ceramic vessels, which are created for beauty rather than utility, is driven by a rebellion against the machine-made anonymity of mass-produced objects.
- In their quest for pottery, the Forcelles have taken the train to New Orleans, where they bought several pieces of Newcomb pottery depicting a misty moon shining through moss-draped trees; they particularly like the work because it is an outgrowth of the art and design department of Newcomb College, the women's college of Tulane University.
- On another trip, they went to Chicago to buy Roseville pottery, made in Ohio and New York, and found a three-handled vase glazed one color inside and unglazed outside, made by Louis C. Tiffany.

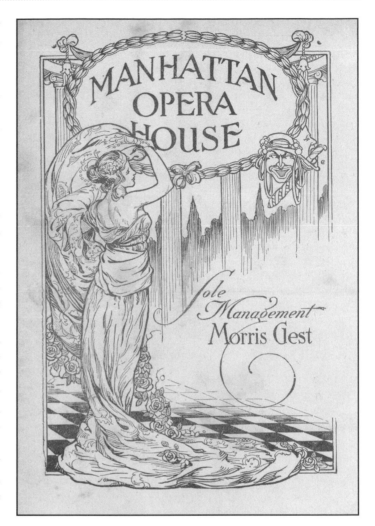

The beauty of Newcomb pottery is a rebellion against machine-made, mass-produced objects.

While in Hawaii the Forcelles learned the language and collected crafts.

- During that trip, they visited the theater and opera, and bought several very subtle Tiffany bowls which had leaves and flowers etched into a monochromatic finish.

Life at Work

- During his many years as a Presbyterian pastor, Albert has served for five years in churches in upstate New York and Allston, Massachusetts, near Boston; four years in Hawaii; then 13 years in Rye, New York, before taking his current pulpit in Chevy Chase, Maryland.
- During World War I, their home had been a center for visiting pastors and soldiers, as well as a refuge for the Korean government in exile, a dangerous political position; the Japanese government currently has a price of $300,000 on the head of dissident Syngman Rhee.
- Albert enjoyed studying at Yale and often returns; from the pulpit, he enjoys telling how in 1638 the Rev. John Davenport and the merchant Theophilus Eaton founded the New Haven Colony to establish a Puritan "Bible State," in which "the word of God shall be the onely rule to be attended into in ordering the affayres of government."
- He particularly feels at home at Connecticut Hall, Yale's first foray into the Gothic Revival architectural style.
- Currently, a building program is under way at his church in Chevy Chase by a builder who is a local man and a friend of Albert known for his ability to construct meaningful worship space using only the finest stone.
- During the flu epidemic of 1918 several children of the parish died within days of each other; their parents and grandparents have all contributed funds for an expanded Sunday School building in their memory.
- Albert is also working on outreach programs with the women of the church who want to help the starving people of Armenia, formerly a part of the extensive Turkish Empire; now that World War I has ended, many countries are calling on the United States to act as their guardians.
- Prior to the war, his church was actively engaged in the Christian Helpers League, designed to help down-and-out men who were often alcoholics.
- Working with other Presbyterian churches in 1915, the League provided meals to 11,352 people, baths to 4,834, clothing to 64, medical care to 102 and jobs to 100; records show that 5,442 of those served also attended religious services.

America Feeding Starving Armenia

Photographs by DONALD C. THOMPSON, LESLIE'S Staff Correspondent

The "Flour Line" in Erivan, with an Armenian representative of the American Relief Administration weighing out flour to the children who come with tickets. The weights on the scales are stones. The A. R. A. makes its investigations in advance and distributes tickets to the needy families in order that each may get its portion and not more than its portion. These photographs are from the land which asks the United States to act as its guardian, a responsibility which our official missions of investigation seem to think unwise. Armenia was formerly an important part of the very extensive Turkish Empire.

Three starving Armenian boys applying for admission to a relief station in Erivan. The boy on the left is in the last stages, as is shown by his emaciated body and the "starvation face" so familiar in the Near-East. The boy in the center has been living on grass and roots, with a distended stomach as the result. Thousands of children are in this distressing condition and other thousands have been brought through the summer by American flour. To continue relief for 150,000 undernourished little bodies the Commonwealth Fund of New York has just given $750,000 to the American Relief Administration.

Armenian children in the public park at Erivan, being entertained by Miss Gertrude Pearson, of Oak Park, Chicago, who is a genius in telling pantomime stories. At this particular moment she is giving the girls a mental picture of the American skyscrapers, in spite of the handicap of not being able to speak the very difficult Armenian language.

"The Street of Little Coffins" is one of the pathetic spectacles seen in Erivan. The death-rate has been so high that it was found necessary to have "dead

Greek refugees making bread at a station in the neutral zone between the new republics of Armenia and Georgia. The woman at the board in the fore-

His church is raising money for the people of Armenia.

- Even earlier, while in Rye, New York, Albert secured contributions from property owners to build sidewalks and improve the looks of the public library.
- Before the turn of the century, the Forcelles lived in the newly acquired U.S. territory of Hawaii, where Albert was serving as a Presbyterian missionary.
- While there they learned some of the language, collected furniture made by local craftsmen and learned to fish from outrigger crafts; they also welcomed the American troops passing through during the Spanish American War.

Washington society is attempting to regain its footing.

Life in the Community: Chevy Chase, Maryland

- With the war over, Washington society is attempting to regain its footing.
- President Woodrow Wilson remains incapacitated following his stroke, and Mrs. Wilson devotes all of her time to his care.
- Belgian and British nobility have dressed up the season recently by visiting Washington.
- A reception for H.R.H. Edward Albert, Prince of Wales, held at the Congressional Library "brought out the gowns and jewels," according to the Washington Post; Cora, Countess of Stafford, the former Mrs. Colgate of New York, arrived in white satin with diamond tiara and corsage ornaments, and Lady Newborough, who has been passing the past few months with American friends, wore "black velvet on modish lines, with diamonds and pearls."
- Albert and Agnes, in recognition for what they had done during the war, were honored by a personal invitation to the White House by Mrs. Wilson, prior to the President's illness.

"Apartment House Sold," Washington Post, November 16, 1919:

"A four-story apartment building at 3516 Connecticut Avenue was sold last week by Harry Wardman to Morris Cafritz for $80,000. The building, which is located just above the Cleveland Park car stop, contains 14 apartments, six of which have four rooms and the remaining eight three rooms. The structure was completed for occupancy October 1. The annual rent is about $9,200."

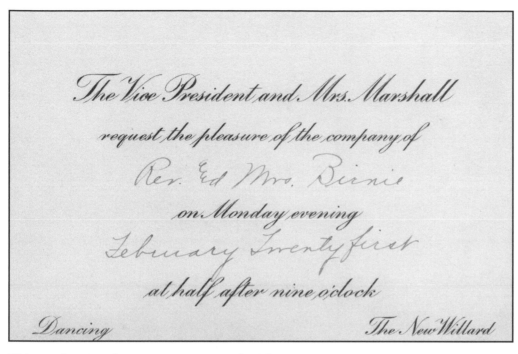

The Vice President and Mrs. Marshall
request the pleasure of the company of
Rev. & Mrs. Birnie
on Monday evening
February Twenty first
at half after nine o'clock

Dancing   The New Willard

This couple enjoys frequent invitations to the White House.

- Women's clubs, created for the purpose of mind improvement, continue to study key issues such as English and French women's war work, prohibition and national efficiency
- General John J. Pershing is still basking in the glow of his victory, even though recently, Ohio Representative Sherwood attracted a firestorm of criticism for suggesting that Pershing was "not on the firing line during the great battles of the western front."

"Society News," Washington Post, November 16, 1919:

"There was an exodus of débutantes and other young people to the White Sulphur for the weekend, parties being made up as soon as it was hinted that the prince was going to be there.

The short and historic visit of the Prince of Wales in Washington has left much-elated the buds of this season and last, who were in the several private parties given for him. Many of the débutantes frankly admit that they hardly know whether they are on their heads or their heels when dancing with a real, delightful prince of the royal blood. This prince left behind a number of personal gifts and souvenirs, which will be cherished probably through many generations. They range all the way from gold purses and silver cigarette cases, to autographed photos of himself, both framed and otherwise. A number of the people with whom he had been thrown together during his visit, and who entertained him, called at the Belmont home just before his departure for the train on Friday night to bid him farewell."

"With the Allies on the Rhine," by Charles Victor, *Leslie's Weekly*, November 15, 1919:

"I wonder how many people thought, when we went into the war, that any part of the American army would be stationed for 10 years on the banks of the Rhine? Very few, I am sure. And not many more, probably, have a very clear idea of the nature of this 'occupation.' Officially, of course, the occupation has one purpose: to enforce the provisions of the treaty of peace. With a hostile army in this country at all times ready for action, it is safely expected that the defeated enemy will be rather particular about 'paying up' promptly. But, as a matter of fact, the army is not, strictly speaking, a hostile one, and its military duties are destined to be perfunctory. Unofficially, however, its presence in the country is bound to have a considerable influence, and incidentally, to bring about consequences that were neither foreseen nor intended by those who decreed the occupation.

These effects, to some extent apparent today, after 12 months, are bound to vary greatly in different zones, according to the temperaments of the nations involved, and according to the policies of their authorities. I have just had an excellent opportunity to observe these differences at close range.

The policy of the British is perfectly clear from the moment you arrive in Cologne. Aside from the primary purpose of the occupation, their objectives are frankly commercial. As soon as the bars of the blockade were let down, the British government considered that it was its particular duty to help British businessmen into Germany as fast as it was physically possible. There is not the slightest attempt to hide this purpose. The corporal in charge of the passport control at the railroad makes you 'show cause' before he allows you to enter the town. If your job is anything but 'business' you are shoved aside, for Cologne is too crowded to accommodate mere pleasure-seekers, journalists, and such-like. . . .

The French are busy at Mayence making the Germans understand that they—the French— are the victors. They have old scores to settle and they propose to settle them here and now. Their policy is not commercial, but political, as their protection of the 'Rhenish Republic' of Dr. Dorten indicates. In the English and American zones harmless army newspapers are published, recording the doings and diversions of the boys; in the French zone there appears a handsomely illustrated weekly, in German and French, recording the latest achievements of the separatists, and 'stimulating French interest in Rhenish affairs.' While the British examine the passports of foreigners, letting the Germans pass without control, a ferocious-looking Algerian in Coblenz scrutinizes every native that attempts to pass the gate. . . .

The American policy is less easy to define. Strictly speaking, we have no policy at all, except to fulfill our engagements with our Allies, irksome as they may be. Our 'Watch on the Rhine' is a purely military action, carried out strictly in conformity with the rules of war, with the minimum amount of discomfort to the natives and no material advantages to ourselves. In the early days of the armistice, when Cologne and Mayence were centers of illicit trading with the enemy, when one truckload of goods after another was smuggled across the 'neutral zone,' and when unscrupulous officers were said to grow rich on bribes, Uncle Sam stood guard over the morals of his men so that not a single case of nefarious dealing could be held against them. The Germans, who abetted this practice for their own benefit, now say that every French officer is a 'schieber' (profiteer), but are obliged to admit the Americans were proof against all temptation."

FIRST IN
THE FIGHT~
ALWAYS
FAITHFUL~
BE A U.S. MARINE!

- General Pershing is also popular with America's mothers; the normally unsentimental general gave the celebration of Mother's Day a boost in 1918 by ordering all his commanding officers to have "every officer and soldier in the American Expeditionary Forces to write home on Mother's Day."

"Same Pay for Loan Flyers," Washington Post, March 25, 1919:

"As a result of the attempt of some flying 'aces' to commercialize their fame by asking fancy prices, the Treasury Department has been flooded with requests from aviators anxious to pilot the captured German planes in the 'victory loan' campaign. A great number have offered their services 'to Uncle Sam, for nothing.' The department, however, ruled yesterday that all will be paid and all the same amount. They will receive the amount paid aviators in the army service, which is, at the maximum, about $250 a month.

'We have a surplus of crackajack aviators now,' said a Treasury official. 'What we are short of is planes. Many of the aviators have exhibited a splendid patriotic spirit by offering to defray their own expenses. One man who tendered his services explained "that in private life [he was] a minister".' "

Women provided America's "manpower" during the war.

- The soldiers were instructed to write "Mother's Letter" on the envelopes so the Army Postal Service could spot them more easily and speed them home.
- According to the Stars and Stripes, one transport alone carried approximately 1.4 million letters from France to the United States that year.
- Pershing also took time to thank the women who worked to aid the war effort.
- During the war, women took a critical role in book drives to create libraries overseas, and even gathered peach stones to combat the effects of poisonous gases; seven pounds of pits were needed to filter a single gas mask, and a million men required masks.
- Many women's groups are now turning their attention to widespread starvation in Europe and the threat of socialism taking hold in America.

HISTORICAL SNAPSHOT
1919

- President Woodrow Wilson went to the Peace Conference at Versailles and proclaimed America's idealism: "Tell me what's right and I'll fight for it"
- While in Colorado promoting the League of Nations, Wilson suffered a paralyzing stroke on his left side
- The inflationary rate was down to 8.9 percent from 13.5 percent; because of the war, unemployment remained at 1.4 percent
- Labor unrest was intense, the worst since the 1890s; an August tally showed 300,000 workers on strike
- After 110 days of striking, steelworkers in Gary, Indiana, returned to work unsuccessful in gaining recognition from U.S. Steel
- The attorney general brought an injunction to halt a United Mine Workers strike
- An actors' strike for recognition of Actors' Equity closed theaters in New York, Philadelphia, Boston and Chicago
- A nationwide plot to mark the Communist May Day with mail bomb assassinations was thwarted when 16 packages were held at the post office for insufficient postage; the intended victims included millionaires John D. Rockefeller and J.P. Morgan
- The American landscape boasted more railroad tracks than any country in the world
- Standard Railway Time became federal law with the Standard Time Act of 1918, establishing five time zones
- The United States first experimented with daylight-savings time
- Created as a war measure, a 10-percent excise tax on a variety of goods, including soft drinks, was still in effect
- When 45,000 strikers threatened to paralyze Seattle, Washington, the mayor set up machine guns and threatened anyone who attempted to take over the city's facilities
- Thirty-one-year-old Conrad Hilton invested his lifetime savings of $5,000 on the Mobley Hotel in Crisco, Texas
- States ratified the Eighteenth Amendment prohibiting the sale of alcohol, starting in 1920
- The dial telephone, the Communist Party of America, a nonstop flight from New York to Chicago and the Drake Hotel in Chicago all made their first appearance
- Henry Ford gained full control of Ford Motor Company by repurchasing the Company for $105 million
- Prices were up 79 percent over 1914; adjusting for inflation, wages had risen only 14 percent in industry and 25 percent in agriculture

1920–1929

In the years following the Great War, women who had worked men's job in the late teens usually remained in the work force, although at lower warges. They were allowed to vote nationally, and society was beginning to encourage women to consider college and options other than marriage. These years were marked by a new nationalism symbolized by frenzied consumerism. By 1920, urban Americans had begun to define themselves—for their neighbors and for the world—in terms of what they owned. The car was becoming universal, at least in its appeal. At the dawn of the century, only 4,192 automobiles were registered nationwide; in 1920, the number of cars had reached 1.9 million. Simultaneously, aggressive new advertising methods began appearing, designed to fuel the new consumer needs of the buying public. And buy it did. From 1921 to 1929, Americans bought and America boomed. With expanded wages and buying power came increased leisure time for recreation, travel, or even self-improvement. Advertising reinforced the idea that the conveniences and status symbols of the wealthy were attainable to everyone. The well-to-do and the wage earner began to look a lot more alike, and many of the most feared diseases of the urban ghetto began to disappear.

Following the Great War, America enjoyed a period of great expansion and expectation. The attitude of many Americans was expressed in President Calvin Coolidge's famous remark, "The chief business of the American people is business." The role of the federal government remained small during the period and federal expenditures actually declined following the war effort. Harry Donaldson's song "How Ya Gonna Keep 'Em Down on the Farm after They've Seen Paree?" described another basic shift in American society. The 1920 census reported that more than 50 percent of the population—54 million people—lived in urban areas. The move to the cities was the result of changed expectations, increased industrialization, and the migration of millions of Southern blacks to the urban North.

The availability of electricity expanded the universe of goods that could be manufactured and sold. The expanded use of radios, electric lights, telephones, and powered vacuum cleaners was possible for the first time, and they quickly became essential household items. Construction boomed as—for the first time—half of all Americans now lived in urban areas. Industry, too, benefited from the wider use of electric power. At the turn of the century, electricity ran only five percent of all machinery, and by 1925, 73 percent. Large-scale electric power also made possible electrolytic processes in the rapidly developing heavy chemical industry. With increasing sophistication came higher costs; wages for skilled workers continued to rise during the 1920s, putting further distance between the blue-collar worker and the emerging middle class.

Following the war years, average family earnings increased slightly during the first half of the period, while prices and hours worked actually declined. Women, now allowed to vote nationally, were also encouraged to consider college and options other than marriage. Average family earnings increased slightly during the first half of the period, while prices and hours worked actually declined. The 48-hour week became standard, providing more leisure time. At least 40 million people went to the movies each week, and college football became a national obsession.

Unlike previous decades, national prosperity was not fueled by the cheap labor of new immigrants, but by increased factory efficiencies, innovation, and more sophisticated methods of managing time and materials. Starting in the 'teens, the flow of new immigrants began to slow, culminating in the restrictive immigration legislation of 1924 when new workers from Europe were reduced to a trickle. The efforts were largely designed to protect the wages of American workers—many of whom were only one generation from their native land. As a result, wages for unskilled labor remained stable; union membership declined and strikes, on average, decreased. American exports more than doubled during the decade and heavy imports of European goods virtually halted, a reversal of the Progressive Movement's flirtation with free trade.

These national shifts were not without powerful resistance. A bill was proposed in Utah to imprison any woman who wore her skirt higher than three inches above the ankle. Cigarette consumption reached 43 billion annually, despite smoking being illegal in 14 states and the threat of expulsion from college if caught with a cigarette. The Hays Commission, limiting sexual material in silent films, was created to prevent "loose" morals, and the membership of the KKK expanded to repress Catholics, Jews, open immigration, makeup on women, and the prospect of unrelenting change.

The decade ushered in Trojan contraceptives, the Pitney Bowes postage meter, the Baby Ruth candy bar, Wise potato chips, Drano, self-winding watches, State Farm Mutual auto insurance, Kleenex, and the Macy's Thanksgiving Day Parade down Central Park West in New York. Despite a growing middle class, the share of disposable income going to the top five percent of the population continued to increase. Fifty percent of the people, by one estimate, still lived in poverty. Coal and textile workers, Southern farmers, unorganized labor, single women, the elderly, and most blacks were excluded from the economic giddiness of the period.

In 1929, America appeared to be in an era of unending prosperity. U.S. goods and services reached all-time highs. Industrial production rose 50 percent during the decade as the concepts of mass production were refined and broadly applied. The sale of electrical appliances from radios to refrigerators skyrocketed. Consumers were able to purchase newly produced goods through the extended use of credit. Debt accumulated. By 1930, personal debt had increased to one-third of personal wealth. The nightmare on Wall Street in October 1929 brought an end to the economic festivities, setting the stage for a more proactive government and an increasingly cautious worker.

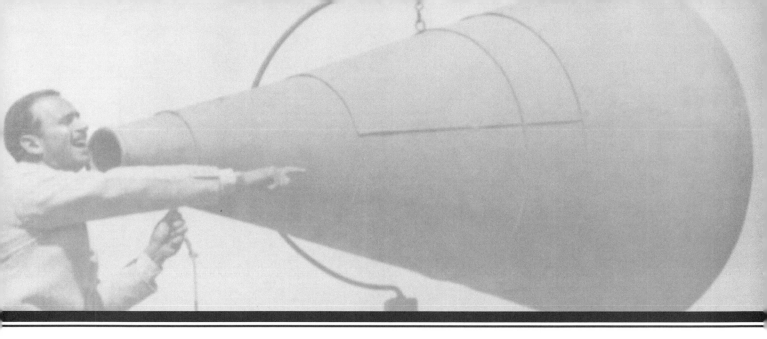

1922 FAMILY PROFILE

Beautiful, tough and driven, Gwendolyn Price is nearing the top of the silent movie star world, due to her mother's ambition, her fabulous good looks and her husband's business savvy. They have no children.

Annual Income: Approximately $650,000; currently, Price commands $50,000 to $100,000 per movie and is able to make four to five movies a year; her husband, Walter Zarnov, will make $350,000 this year through movie productions and the management of several movie stars.

Life at Home

- Gwendolyn and Walter live west of Los Angeles in a sprawling 3,800-square-foot home complete with an Olympic-size pool where Walter exercises; since they both work in the movie industry, they live near the studio, but still enjoy a mountain view.
- Recently, they purchased a Daniels automobile from "back East" that gives them the look they both desire, since the car is not only expensive—something he likes; it is also very sexy—something she likes.
- Gwendolyn began appearing in movies in 1910 when she was only 14 years old, driven by a very determined mother and a desire to be famous.
- One of three daughters, she is now gaining fame, along with her sister, in the movie industry; their mother had taken the three girls to Hollywood with the expressed purpose of their being movie stars.
- The girls knew little of their father, who left them and their mother before the sisters made their first movie.
- Like many of Gwendolyn's contemporaries, "she came from nowhere and nothing," according to the movie magazines.
- For many young actresses, movies are viewed as a way out of poverty.

Gwendolyn Price has gained stardom in silent movies.

The couple's 3,800-square-foot home offers a mountain view.

- When she was featured in the 1911 hit, *An Old Man's Love Story*, her head of thick black hair, full bosom and seductive beauty launched her career, and by 1914, movie scripts were being written around her talent and name.
- That same year, at 18 years old, she married a Russian immigrant who had created a fortune in movies, first as the owner of a chain of movie houses, and later as a movie producer; he is 19 years her senior and she calls him Daddy.
- After their marriage, her husband established a Hollywood-based production company to feature his wife's skills and those of her sister.
- For the past five years, her movies have featured not only her natural beauty, but dozens and dozens of fabulous outfits; women often go to her movies to marvel at the latest fashions she displays on the screen.
- Her roles range from traditional women to exotic, ethnic characters; in recent movies she has played an Asian maiden; the daughter of one of the first families of Virginia fated to marry the wrong man; a Russian in a movie titled *New Moon*, and in *Isle of Conquest*, she is shipwrecked with a man who hates women.
- Her older sister often plays in comedies; they find their parallel careers complementary and rarely compete with one another for attention.
- Her youngest sister, who has only managed to land small parts in a handful of moving pictures, recently married movie star Buster Keaton.

Recently they purchased a Daniels automobile from "back East."

Life at Work

- Gwendolyn belongs to a tiny group of highly celebrated movie actresses who have come to symbolize the romantic ideals of the nation; she is flooded with fan letters, while girls across the nation emulate her clothing, hairstyles and her "way with men."
- Although during the early years she worked an arduous dawn-to-dusk schedule to get parts, her fame is now said to rival that of "America's Sweetheart," Mary Pickford, who is earning more than $100,000 per picture.

- Like many of her fellow movie stars, she is small at only five feet tall, and often plays with leading men who are only six to eight inches taller.
- Her adoring fans see her as a woman with one foot in the 1890s and the other in the 1920s; in a recent movie, she was shown driving her roadster at top speed while planning her "radiophone" dance for the coming evening—a scene displaying both her "new woman" role as the driver of a powerful automobile, and her "old" role of wife, focusing her attention on social events.
- Since her career began, she has appeared in more than 200 movies and can now name her price, often up to $100,000 per picture.
- Silent movies are about emotion and action, and she is talented at displaying both without speaking; title cards displayed throughout the movies provide the viewers with an ongoing conversation, relaying historical information, mood, dialogue and often wit.
- She loves her job, and worships the money she has made as a movie star; having money and power makes her wonder why so many movie directors demand that female actors appear so childlike, helpless and frightened while waiting for heroic men to save them.
- One reason she can command high salaries was the creation of the star system, which began in 1913 when actors began demanding screen credits for their work, allowing them to command higher and higher wages as the public demanded to see their favorite stars.

Life in the Community: Hollywood, California

- In 1910, Hollywood, California, was a quiet, country town near Los Angeles, dominated by lemon groves, churches and a few sprawling estates.
- Four years later, Hollywood claimed 52 moviemaking companies which spent $5.7 million a year to crank out more than a thousand miles of developed film annually.
- The area also offered scenic lands for the shooting of cowboy movies, majestic backdrops such as the Pacific Ocean, and the availability of mountains and deserts only a day away.
- The ability to concentrate production into factory-like studios and integrate virtually all aspects of production allowed Hollywood-produced movies to be shot more quickly, at less cost, with more control.
- The Hollywood system became the model worldwide and its products and stars, such as Charlie Chaplin and Mary Pickford, became cultural icons.

Her roles range from the exotic to the traditional.

Fans across the country emulate Gwendolyn's fashions and "way with men."

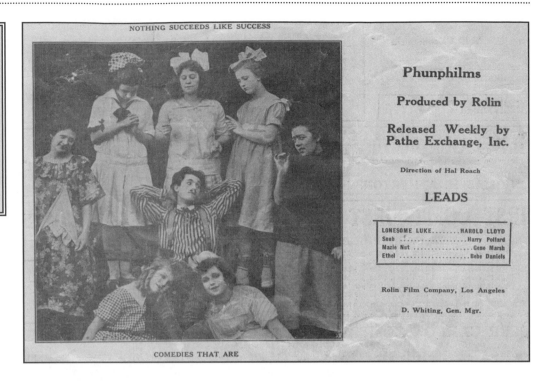

NOTHING SUCCEEDS LIKE SUCCESS

Phunphilms

Produced by Rolin

Released Weekly by Pathe Exchange, Inc.

Direction of Hal Roach

LEADS

LONESOME LUKE	HAROLD LLOYD
Snob	Harry Pollard
Mazie Nut	Gene Marsh
Ethel	Bebe Daniels

Rolin Film Company, Los Angeles

D. Whiting, Gen. Mgr.

COMEDIES THAT ARE

Even Harry Houdini is doing movies to display his greatest stunts.

- Currently, Hollywood-produced movies dominate worldwide; World War I dramatically reduced the ability of many European producers to compete with American films.

- Nationwide, Americans are enjoying all types of entertainment—motion pictures, baseball and boxing are all drawing record crowds.

- Everyone wants to be in the movies and in Hollywood, so the Chamber of Commerce is currently buying newspaper ads to discourage young women from coming to Hollywood—"the land of broken dreams"; the advertisements plead, "Please don't try to break into the movies."

- Even the great escapologist Harry Houdini has made films to display his greatest stunts; unfortunately, his ability to escape from impossible situations is irrelevant on the screen where the stunts can easily be faked.

- Nationwide, more than 20,000 cinemas are now open, 2,000 of which are picture palaces for the showing of exclusive, first-run movies of "feature length," running about 90 minutes.

- Picture palaces are architectural marvels, designed to capture attention, with many featuring colossal electric signs that can be seen for miles, while interior decorations often showcase opulent chandeliers and classical drapery on walls and entrances, plus elegant furniture; many offer free child care.

HISTORICAL SNAPSHOT
1922

- Seventeen-year-old Clara Bow won a fan magazine contest for "The Most Beautiful Girl in the World," while Charles Atlas won the "World's Most Perfectly Developed Man" contest
- During his third trial, movie star Roscoe "Fatty" Arbuckle was exonerated of starlet Virginia Rappe's murder, but not before his name was sullied in a highly publicized sex trial
- The self-winding wristwatch, Checker Cab, Canada Dry ginger ale, and State Farm Mutual auto insurance all made their first appearance
- California became a year-round source of oranges
- Automobile magnate Henry Ford, who earned $264,000 a day, was declared a "billionaire" by the Associated Press
- Radio station WEAF objected to airing a toothpaste commercial, deciding that care of the teeth was too delicate a subject for broadcast
- The first commercially prepared baby food was marketed
- The U.S. Post Office burned 500 copies of James Joyce's Ulysses
- The mah-jongg craze swept the nation, outselling radios
- Protestant Episcopal bishops voted to erase the word obey from the marriage ceremony
- Movie idol Wallace Reid died in a sanitarium of alcohol and morphine addiction
- Thom McAn shoe store introduced mass-produced shoes sold through chain stores for $3.99 a pair
- Hollywood's black list of "unsafe" persons stood at 117
- Radio was a national obsession; people stayed up half the night listening to concerts, sermons and sports
- Syracuse University banned dancing
- A cargo ship was converted into the first U.S. aircraft carrier
- Publications for the year included T.S. Eliot's The Waste Land, F. Scott Fitzgerald's The Beautiful and the Damned and H.G. Wells's The Outline of History; Willa Cather won the Pulitzer Prize for One of Ours
- The tomb of King Tutankhamen, in the Valley of the Kings, Egypt, was discovered
- New York's Delmonico's Restaurant closed
- The first mechanical telephone switchboard was installed in New York
- Broadway producer Florenz Ziegfeld forbade his stars to perform on radio because it "cheapens them"
- In describing the new "flapper," Vanity Fair reported, "She will never . . . knit you a necktie, but she'll go skiing with you. . . . She may quote poetry to you, not Indian love lyrics but something about the peace conference or theology"

1923 Profile

Middle Class

A native of Seaman, Ohio, Jervey Steffens is a dreamer of big dreams, such as becoming a famous jazz saxophone player or writing a controversial book that will rile the censors, although she may settle for secretarial school or a few years in college.

Jervey Steffens loves to discuss her dreams with her best friend.

Life at Home

• Even though her real name is Eleanor, her father has called her by her middle name, Jervey, since she was a little girl; now everyone does.

• She loves having a name different from everyone else's.

• Now that she is 16 and has read about what Napoleon and Mozart did as teens, Jervey believes it is time to have important thoughts and make big discoveries.

• She feels that greatness is her destiny, too, and that she will make her mark on the world through music or literature.

• To play saxophone with Fletcher Henderson's jazz band, or write a great novel that would make the censors cringe—now that would be grand.

• Last year, when she was much younger, she often spent time wondering about her neighbors' real occupations: Was the debonair man who lived down the street really a desperate criminal, the lady next door a world-famous dancer, or a World War I spy, or both, and did the Wilkersons have countless millions buried in their backyard?

• Now that she is a junior in high school, she has put those fantastic notions behind her, although she still wonders about the true nature of the debonair man down the street.

• The family attends the Methodist church, and her mother is a committed Epworth advocate.

Jervey and classmate Dorothy are fashion rivals.

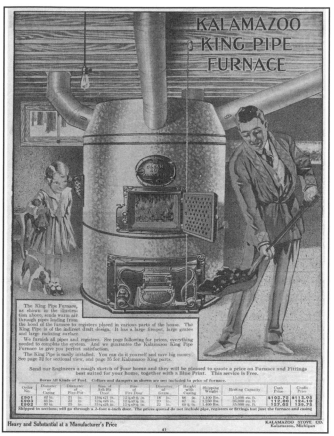

The family recently installed a central heating system.

- Jervey can tell when The Epworth Herald arrives; her mother will either begin to talk about tithing, going to a devotional or helping others—sometimes all at the same time.

- Lately her mother has been devoting her time to the elimination of child labor across America, telling everyone she knows, "Children should have a childhood."

- Jervey and her family live in a turn-of-the-century, Queen Anne-style house that has rooms for dining, living and sitting on the first floor, in addition to a bathroom, pantry and kitchen.

- The front and rear staircases lead to a 790-square-foot second floor with four bedrooms, one of which is Jervey's, and a bath, which she must share with the rest of the family.

- Her father is impossible to figure out; all he ever says to her is, "Turn off the lights when you leave the room; I'm not made of money," yet recently he spent $112 to install a new coal burning central heating system so he won't have to tend to the fire so much.

- For reasons that are beyond her, all of her friends seem to like her mother and come over to the house often, especially now that the Steffens have an electric mixer, which makes cookie and cake baking a breeze.

- The invention of small electric motors has made possible a revolution in household appliances including vacuum cleaners, and reliable refrigerators and washing machines.

Her favorite teacher, Miss Patterson, gave Jervey Tales of the Jazz Age *to read.*

Jervey's home is a magnet for her classmates.

- Many appliances can be bought on the installment plan, which allows payments for a new appliance to be spread over 12 months.
- Jervey's mother says her favorite time of the week is when the two of them sit down in the kitchen together and snap string beans, though Jervey is less enamoured with this ritual.

- Recently the entire family took a trip to the cinema to see Cecil B. DeMille's The Ten Commandments, which was wonderful.
- Seaman's moving picture theater was created when local businessmen banded together and each bought one or two shares in the Star Moving Picture Company so the village could enjoy the movie boom sweeping America.
- Jervey is just dying to go see The Pilgrim, starring Charlie Chaplin, and The Hunchback of Notre Dame when they come to town.
- The only time of the year she hates is the Easter season, when "the butterfly story" gets told and retold.
- When she was six, she overheard her mother say that she didn't know if she would have enough money to buy herself new Easter shoes to match her new Easter outfit, so Jervey secretly created and colored a set of paper butterflies that she could sell to her neighbors for $0.10 each.
- At the first stop, she told her next-door neighbor, Mrs. Middleton, that her mother was too poor to buy shoes and she was working to buy them.

In high school, Jervey is being encouraged to read current literature by F. Scott Fitzgerald.

- At the second stop, Mrs. Holly was told that Jervey's mother was so poor that she was going to be barefooted at Easter, and at the third house, Mrs. Flowers was told even more stories that included Jervey's mother not having anything to wear at all.
- Each woman expressed delight at the prospect of buying a butterfly from the child and each gave her $0.10.
- When Jervey arrived home with three dimes, her mother was on the telephone with Mrs. Middleton, who was relaying the sales pitch and the family's recent descent into abject poverty.
- Jervey wrapped her three dimes in the last butterfly and presented them to her mother to buy shoes, which were bought and proudly displayed at Easter.
- It was the last time she was allowed to sell butterflies, but not the last time the story was told; it has become an Easter ritual to retell it.
- Now that the family has a radio, many evenings are spent listening to the glorious sounds of the Rheingold Quartet or the Lucky Strike Show.
- Jervey loves listening to jazz and pretending that she is sitting in the midst of the orchestra, wailing away.

Life at School
- In class Jervey is known as a reader and a dreamer.
- On more than one occasion she has been caught reading books other than the assigned text; her favorites are adventure stories with girls as the heroines, as in The Radio Girls on Station Island by Margaret Penrose.
- Her favorite teacher, Miss Bertha Patterson, a graduate of Cornell University, understands Jervey's need to read.
- After class, Miss Patterson often challenges her to read current literature, recently giving her F. Scott Fitzgerald's new book, Tales of the Jazz Age.
- Jervey absolutely loves the opening sentence of the story, Jelly-Bean: "Jim Powell is a Jelly-bean. Much as I desire to make him an appealing character, I feel that it would be unscrupulous to deceive you on that point. He was a bred-in-the-bone, dyed-in-the-wool, ninety-nine and three-quarters percent Jelly-bean and he grew lazily all during

Jervey is the only girl in the Saxophone Club.

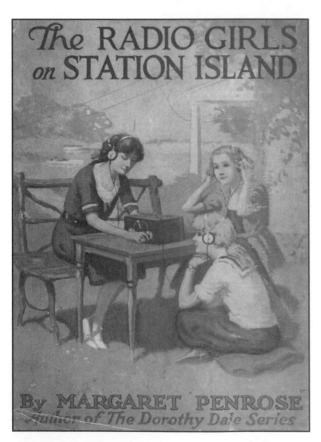

She loves books which feature a resourceful girl.

Jelly-bean season, which is every season, down in the land of the Jelly-beans well below the Mason-Dixon line."

- She wants to write just like that someday—loose, free, strong and sure.
- Jervey is on the girls' basketball team and is the only girl in the school's Saxophone Club.
- The basketball team only played five games during the season, because travelling long distances during Ohio winters can be treacherous.
- They lost four of the five games, defeated in the first game of the season 23 to 6, but they improved.
- After the boys' game against the Columbus Mutes, the Junior Hi-Y staged a "stag" at the YMCA; they played basketball until two in the morning, then went to the game room until 4:30, slept for an hour and held a breakfast on the basketball court at 5:30 a.m.
- The girls' team was not invited.
- She loves being the only girl playing the saxophone with five guys.
- Some of Jervey's neighbors are concerned that a group composed of five boys and one girl does not look proper, so the club holds most of its practices in the front parlor of Jervey's house, where everyone can be properly supervised.
- When she reads the line in the High School Annual that says the Saxophone Club is "the first organization of its

The basketball team has played five games, winning one.

"Just for the Love of Them,"
Mansfield (Ohio) High School Annual, 1923:

Breathes there the girl with creative instinct so dead that never to herself has murmured, "I must do something original"? Probably not. At any rate the senior girls progressed beyond that murmur to the realms of accomplishment. Just in the way of proving their originality they set the pace for future classmen by giving a reception to the faculty, if you please.

Seemingly by magic, the third floor had been transformed into an unusually attractive living room. We were "senior-y" throughout the whole, our old cerise and blue having been carried out to a "T." Here our illustrious guests were welcomed. . . .

Our musical ones performed first. Piano solos were given by Naomi Wigton and Naomi Banks, while Louise Emery gave a violin selection. The senior girls' Sextette also gave a group of selections.

Lest this grow monotonous, however, a one-act play was presented. It was one of Oliphant Down's Pierro and Pierette plays, *The Maker of Dreams*. We never dreamed that Louise Booth could make such a handsome Pierro. (Oh, what a Romeo!) And Marion Bradford as Pierrette had us all at her feet. Mirian Rife, the Maker of Dreams was very good, too.

"Code of Conduct for Teachers," Southern Ohio District, W. W. Fuller, Superintendent, 1923:

Some teachers, 1922–3, have failed for the following reasons: (a) lack of knowledge of subject matter and inability to manage children; (b) attention to card playing, dancing, and other social interests to the neglect of their schoolwork; (c) on account of falling in love with high school pupils; (d) on account of keeping company with sorry men; (e) on account of night riding without a chaperon; (f) on account of attendance at rotten vaudeville and sorry moving picture shows; (g) on account of entertaining company until late hours at night, making good schoolwork the next day impossible; (h) on account of failure to take any vital interest in church and Sunday school work and other community activities.

If you think this applicant will and can avoid all the above sources of failure, I shall appreciate your saying so. If you think there is doubt about her having enough sense to avoid these sources of failure, I shall appreciate your frankness. We are after teachers who are in earnest about doing what they are paid to do. We prefer that other kinds go elsewhere.

type; it is proving to be a popular organization which has been very acceptable to the public and the pupils of the high school," she snickers.

- Everyone knows that if Jimmy Epting's dad hadn't gone to the superintendent's office and threatened to sue if the group wasn't sanctioned, the club would never have been formed.
- She can't wait to be a senior, when she and her friends will be the oldest and in charge.
- Jervey has always thought she would go to secretarial school, but is now thinking about college.
- Last year nearly half of the class went to college, most to Ohio State and Miami University; a few went to Oberlin and Wooster, but she thinks that going to Cornell would be keen.
- She is very pleased that she now has a school dress that includes a clasp-locker, or what some magazines are calling a zipper.

PLAY THE GAME

With Real Equipment for Baseball, Football and Basketball. Camping Supplies of Quality and Worth.

THE SPORTING GOODS STORE

YUNCKER BROS.

MAIN STREET ADAM 1508

The school annual is graced with student art and section headings.

- Since World War I, the device has become more popular, even in clothing for children and young women.
- Jervey was convinced that her rival, Dorothy Lancaster, would have a dress with a zipper first, but is glad it didn't happen.
- She might even wear the dress to the Isaly's Circus, which is making its third trip around the world and plans a stop near her home in Seaman.
- Featured acts advertised in fliers include John Zellnerino Batistichiski, the Italian knife thrower; Clark Brooks Martinique, the cigarette fiend; Helene Foxe, the graceful rope walker, Clara Beard Evans, the bearded lady, Maurice Bair Valintino, the cowpuncher who courts death and laughs at disaster.

Business in Seaman is booming.

Life in the Community: Seaman, Ohio

- The community of Seaman was named for Frank Seaman, a wealthy farmer who bought a 180-acre farm in 1880 at a sheriff's sale on the courthouse steps to settle the Hamilton estate.
- Much of the village is located on that property today.
- Two years later, Frank Seaman donated two acres to the Cincinnati and Eastern Railway on the condition that they name the station Seaman.

> ### "Amusing Incidents," *A Town in the Makin',*
> ### *History of Seaman, Ohio,* by Frank G. Young, 1929:
>
> At the close of the school year in 1920, there was a lot of excitement in "this man's town," due to the activities of the senior class. One night near the close of the term, the freshmen arranged for a party, but the boys were picked up one by one, as they were going to the party, by the seniors and kidnapped. They were taken to an old house west of the village and kept captive until a late hour, when they escaped, after three or four free-for-all fights in which clothes were torn and faces disfigured. The "freshies" finally got to the party. The next morning the seniors were on the streets in full force, and the freshmen, both boys and girls, were out also looking for a chance to even up for the kidnapping of the night previous. They clashed in front of the mayor's office, and engaged in another free-for-all, the girls joining in the mêlée, but the mayor soon put a stop to the scuffle.
>
> Word had gotten out that the freshmen boys intended to kidnap the seniors as they marched from the home of the superintendent to the Presbyterian church for their graduation exercises, so John Hannah, who was the village marshal, was called upon to escort the seniors to the church, and in the name of the law, made this impossible. After the graduation exercises were over, Mr. Hannah escorted them back to the home of Supt. Fred Lott. With the exception of a wire that was stretched across the street at one point, nothing happened. This is the first thing of its kind that ever happened at graduation time, and the last.

- To encourage the construction of a railway to their land, local farmers donated fine oak logs to the railway company and hauled them to a sawmill to be cut into lumber for the station.
- The current high school, constructed of brick and stone, sits on a five-acre tract west of the village, and includes an auditorium-gymnasium.
- Jervey's grandfather operates the town's biggest produce house, dealing in eggs, poultry, cream and veal calves.
- Business is going so well, he now owns two trucks and takes local produce to Cincinnati twice a week.
- Recently, thanks to considerable lobbying, the streets of Seaman were dramatically improved when the State Highway Department scraped the roads and covered them with crushed rock.
- Seaman prides itself on being a well-mannered town, which extends to its dogs; to keep strays under control, "Stringer" Barnes, the freight conductor on the railway, pays small boys to gather up all the unclaimed dogs and haul them to the station, where the dogs are then transported on the train to the neighboring community of Portsmouth and turned loose.
- Recently, after the Nelson brothers escorted a cow into the office of the cinema, the city fathers attempted to establish a 9:00 p.m. curfew for teenagers, though the matter was dropped after Mr. Nelson gave his two boys a sound whipping and paid for the ledger book and tickets eaten by the cow.

HISTORICAL SNAPSHOT
1923

- Even though Prohibition is the law of the land, prescription liquor for those in need remained unrestricted
- Clean Book Leagues formed around the nation to protect America's youth from "smut," while controversy raged about the work of D. H. Lawrence
- Clarence Darrow and William Jennings Bryan debated the issue of evolution versus fundamentalism in the *Chicago Tribune*
- Girls who dressed in the style of flappers in Tennessee were banned from public schools until they rolled their stockings back up over their knees
- The German shepherd Rin Tin Tin captured stardom as a top silent movie star
- Montana and Nevada became the first states to introduce old-age pensions
- The Dow-Jones Average hit a high of 105, a low of 86
- A sign reading HOLLYWOODLAND was erected in Los Angeles; each letter measured 30 by 50 feet
- The rubber diaphragm, Pan American World Airlines, the Milky Way candy bar, Welch's grape jelly, the name Popsicle and the Hertz Drive-Ur-Self all made their first appearance
- President Warren G. Harding died in office and was honored nationwide as his cortège traveled from San Francisco to Washington
- Evangelist Aimee Semple McPherson opened a $1.5 million temple in Los Angeles, which included a "miracle room" where the healed could discard their crutches and wheelchairs
- Music hits included "Yes! We Have No Bananas," "Who's Sorry Now?" and "That Old Gang of Mine"
- Blues singer Bessie Smith's "Downhearted Blues" sold a record two million copies

1928 News Feature

"Troubled Thoughts about Prohibition," by Ida M. Tarbell,
***The Delineator*, June 1928:**

Is prohibition becoming a menace to temperance? A startling question but one which must be considered by the gentlemen who gather in Kansas City, Missouri, and in Houston, Texas, during this month, if they are to frame platforms on which candid Democrats and Republicans can support with some degree of hopefulness and self-respect the candidates for the presidency which they name.

Five years ago I should have laughed at such a question. A menace? Prohibition had established national temperance. I was the more emphatic because a convert. I had not liked a national law dictating what men could or could not drink. Temperance by force seemed to mean an untrustworthy substitute for temperance by choice, which I believed we were slowly achieving. I dreaded, too, the spread through the country of the hateful combination of fanatical dryness and underhanded wetness which I had run upon in more than one so-called "bone-dry" state. However, I was willing to consent to any measure that promised to root out the saloon.

My doubts and fears—wobbling if you wish—were ended by a series of personal experiences in the years immediately following the adoption of the Eighteenth Amendment. At that time I was giving from four to eight consecutive weeks each winter to lyceum work. It took me from coast to coast and from gulf to lakes. It meant night changes in lonesome places, waits in dreary stations, days in questionable hotels. The only real terror that I had ever felt in this hard travel was of the drunken man who, not infrequently, reeled against me, leered at me. Not long after the adoption of the Eighteenth Amendment, I discovered that he was gone. Prohibition had destroyed him.

Another heartening discovery was the new life among working people. Every industrial settlement I visited, or from which I had reports, was taking on order and cleanliness unheard of before the Amendment. The children had more shoes, the women more time at home; there were cars and savings accounts. Prohibition had done this by closing the saloon, forcing the weak and vicious to sobriety. No price, I told myself, was too great to pay for such a shortcut to national temperance.

That was five years ago. Today, I am asking myself whether prohibition is any longer serving as a guarantee of temperance, whether it may not be that, having accomplished its revolutionary purpose—destruction of the saloon—it is not actually becoming a hindrance to further progress and may not in a few years, if things go on as they are now, become a menace to the degree of temperance from choice which the country had achieved before the Eighteenth Amendment was adopted.

These questions had been forced upon me just as my conclusions of five years ago were forced by personal experience in the course of travel necessary to filling lecture engagements in various parts of the country. The comforting security I had come to feel, whatever the loneliness or sordidness, has been disturbed by the reappearance of an occasional drunken man on a railroad platform, or at night on a street.

More disquieting is the evidence that liquor is finding its way into a place which I am obliged to use constantly and in which I had always felt safe—the Pullman car. Liquor on the breath of a Pullman porter was an entirely new experience to me, but in the past few years it has been frequent. Changing cars in the middle of the night three years ago, I was helped to my train by a porter so drunk that I refused to stay in the car unless he was removed, as he was promptly, with profuse apologies by a sleepy conductor. How could this happen under the strict rules of the company in a body of men as self-respecting and altogether admirable as our Pullman porters? Only through passengers, carrying their supply, drinking it on the train, and treating the porter who accepts through weakness, the desire to be obliging, or the fear if he refuses of endangering the fat fee which is almost sure to follow protection of a drinking party.

Drunken men and drinking parties have been frequent on the Pullmans I have used in recent years. I have lain awake and listened to a man babble half the night and nobody protested except myself, and my protest was effective for only brief intervals. I recall at least half a dozen drinking parties going on in state rooms. I do not know that anything could be done about it so long as they remained in their own quarters. They had paid for the room. They carried their own liquor. I have had one convincing proof that they carried an ample supply. It was after a night on a train which a band of revelers had invaded at midnight, keeping the passengers awake for two or three hours by their irrepressible excitement. Everybody changed trains at daybreak. There was confusion about the bags; during the morning I opened the one I had carried off. Lying on top of the other contents were two big bottles of Scotch whiskey—part of the supply of the hilarious party that had caused so much disturbance to the would-be sleepers of the night before.

The hotel, like the railroad, had ceased to be the inviolate place I believed it had become. Even highly respectable hotels sometimes allowed drinking parties to go on until fellow guests protested. In one of the best-managed small hotels I frequent—one to which I always go when I am in that particular city—a large party occupied a room next to mine one night four years ago, and were undisturbed in a noisy drinking bout until around 2 a.m., when I telephoned the office that my patience was exhausted. The men were quickly carried or steered to other quarters. In this case the party was made up of delegates to a convention annually held in the house—a profitable connection not to be disturbed if it was possible to avoid it.

Activist Ida Tarbell questions the effectiveness of prohibition.

Over-Sunday drinking parties in Western and Southern towns—I have never run across them elsewhere—are sometimes of dreadful proportion. Arriving at 8 a.m. one Monday at a trim new hotel in a North Dakota town, I was hardly in my room before a highly exasperated housekeeper appeared to examine what she called the "remains!"

"There have been two bums locked in this room since Saturday—drinking their souls away. Nobody could get in. Look there," she almost sobbed, "so drunk they actually poured their whiskey over my nice new mahogany." True enough, there were long patches of varnish burned down the front of the bureau, and the desk was scarred.

"It was worse than before prohibition in this part of the country," the housekeeper went on. "I thought that the Amendment would end our troubles, but the drinking is more beastly. We have them every week just like this."

"And where do they get it?" I asked.

"They get it here in town. Anybody can that's wise. We are only 60 miles from the border and a whiskey express runs through on schedule time. The drivers stop here at midnight for gas and meals. Anybody can get what he wants from them.

Many of the women I have talked with in Middle West boarding houses and hostelries have been deeply disturbed by what they described as "things that never happened before." Tied up for 24 hours by a storm in a dingy railroad town, I was obliged to stay in a boarding house near the tracks. It was winter and the sitting-room was unheated. My room was cold and inexpressibly dreary. So I took refuge in the big dining-room where a vicious but beautiful parrot, the activities of the incoming and shifting trains seen between the blossoming geraniums and begonias in the big windows, and my landlady kept me entertained.

"See that boy," she said pointing to a little fellow of perhaps 12 years, coming from behind a freight car with a big package in his arms. "That's booze he's got. That happens every day and I don't know how in the world we're going to stop it. This always was a bad town for a drink. We've had a bar in this very house. My husband ran it, but I kept an eye on it. Made him shut down at midnight, throw out drunks. He never drank bad—barkeepers ain't apt to. We women here were all for prohibition and it certainly did clean up the town the first two years. Then the stuff began to be sneaked in. See that garage over there?—nothing but a speakeasy. That's where that boy is going. Men don't dare take it off the train in daylight—use boys—use boys to distribute it, that's what scares me. Bad as the saloons were, boys never went into them. We women would have torn them down first, but how are we going to stop this? They're so cunning about it and sneaky, and with the men back of them like they are. Do you suppose they don't get a drink now and then? Can't make me believe they don't! And how about respect for law—any kind of law? They are growing up without it.

"As for the men—they drink more, at least my husband does. Always was a great hand to visit. The traveling men—railroad hands off work used to come in here nights; now they go over there—so there he goes, and he drinks too much. I ain't got anything like the hold I had on him with the bar in the house. But it's the boys that worry me most—and not knowing what we can do about it."

The here-dry, there-wet practice shows itself frequently in the industrial world. There are no more ardent supporters of prohibition than the heads of great industries. They have profited enormously by it. It has made for the steadiness and efficiency of labor. Because of it, the liberal-minded and progressive employers have seen their safety, stock sharing, educational and housing plans pushed vigorously forward. The men were morally inclined and financially able to cooperate. Prohibition has made, too, for industrial peace. Sober men are reasonable men. Employers of labor are emphatic supporters of prohibition—for their employees; as for themselves, they often "know how to drink" and exercise a privilege which money and power give them.

That is, the employer makes of prohibition an economic class issue. Those who haven't money must not be trusted, those who have may be. The working man does not admit the fairness of the decision. He contends that he is as capable of self-control as his employer and we have organized labor demanding a modification of the Volstead Act which will give back beer to the worker.

The situation we are now in is most difficult and trying for the great body of sincere and consistent prohibitionists who have labored for years for a national amendment, believing that it would put an immediate end to all forms of intemperance. If they are frank and open-eyed, and many of them are, they are suffering the painful disillusionment which inevitably comes to reformers who believe the evil they hate can be cured by law or formulas alone. When they get what they want, they sooner or later are horrified to find law is not enough—that the way out is not so easy—that they still are under the old hard compulsion of persuading men. They have tried to shuffle off responsibility and here it is back on their shoulder, croaking in their ear, that unless they win consent, the law will be nullified—may finally die of disuse.

This is bringing from many a new question: Might not a crusade arouse lawbreakers to the enormity of defying the law of the nation—bring them to what is called by some "willing acceptance" of what has been decided by the majority to be for the good of all? But the old-fashioned appeal was to free manhood. Can you arouse a man willingly to yield to a law which he believes an interference with his right of choice? The strength of the old appeal lay in its power to stir a man to make an effort to control himself. His assent was what was sought. He gave it because he was convinced of its rightness and he was helped toward permanent control largely by his pride in showing that he could, if he would, control himself. Can youth particularly be stirred by appeals to obey laws it did not assist in making? It is doubtful; but it can be stirred mightily by appeals to its ideals of manhood.

May it not be that, in attempting to force total abstinence on all men, we have destroyed the only approach we had to some men—the approach through the intellect, the self-respect, the conscience? If that be true, will much be gained by crusades in favor of "willing acceptance"?

These troublesome questions are not touched by the advice some of our very able citizens are giving: Repeal the Amendment. To be told to do what cannot be done is no help in a bad situation. There is little or no reason to suppose that the country would at this juncture repeal the Eighteenth Amendment. There is too large a part of it that believes firmly that it can be enforced—that enforcement has never had a fair trial. It must not be forgotten that there are hundreds of practically dry communities in the United States. They became dry, many of them, long before national prohibition, through years of continued temperance agitation. Such communities generally admit, when they are cornered or off guard, that there may be some liquor finding its way in, but they consider it the exception that proves the rule. "We enforce prohibition—why can't the nation? It can if it would." They are generally inclined to consider recitals of growing intemperance under prohibition as sensationalism or attempts of the liquor interests to scare the country into repeal.

Should Girls Play Interschool Basketball?

1928 News Feature

"Should Girls Play Interschool Basketball?"
by Henry S. Curtis, Hygenia, November 1928:
There is a great increase in interest in athletics among girls all over the world. In Germany, France, England and America we find the same enthusiasm. Most women physical directors and school authorities believe that contests for girls should be confined to intramural athletics rather than to interschool competition such as men have. But it is by no means certain that women and girls are going to abide by the decision of school authorities. It is a part of their new feeling for liberty and equality of opportunity that they should be allowed to enter interschool competition if they wish.

Such competition of girls in basketball in the past has often been injurious. It has taken place by boys' rules, under men coaches, with long halves and with inadequate training to bear the strain involved.

In Illinois, the rules permit girls to compete only in volleyball and tennis, while in Maryland they may compete in tennis, playground ball, volleyball and dodge ball.

The Women's Athletic Federation has stood firmly against interschool competition for girls, particularly in basketball, and has insisted that when contests did take place the girls should be in the charge of women physical directors, should play quarters rather than halves, and should always play by girls' rules.

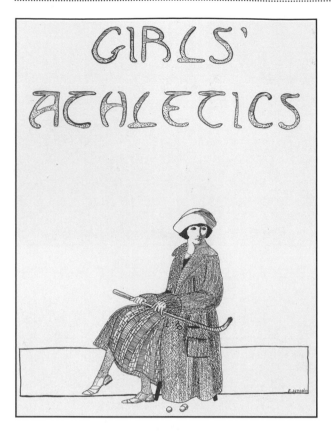

Of the colleges, considerably less than 10 percent allow women to compete in interschool basketball, though such competition is doubtless less objectionable for college women than it is for high school girls. Nearly all women physical directors in colleges are opposed to it.

Some of the reasons given are the following: On the social side it is said that women have not been trained for interschool competition and that they do not thus far have the traditions of sportsmanship that have been impressed upon men's teams for generations; they are poor losers and often lose their tempers along with the game. It is further asserted that girls are nervously more unstable than men and are consequently more affected in the way of distraction from their studies, in the loss of sleep before and after games and in general nervous injuries. It is not good social policy to have girls travel about the country for interschool contests. Oft times there is no suitable place for changing their clothes or for taking showers after the game. Remarks by spectators are often discourteous or even insulting, and the publicity in the papers is usually not the kind that emphasizes feminine ideals.

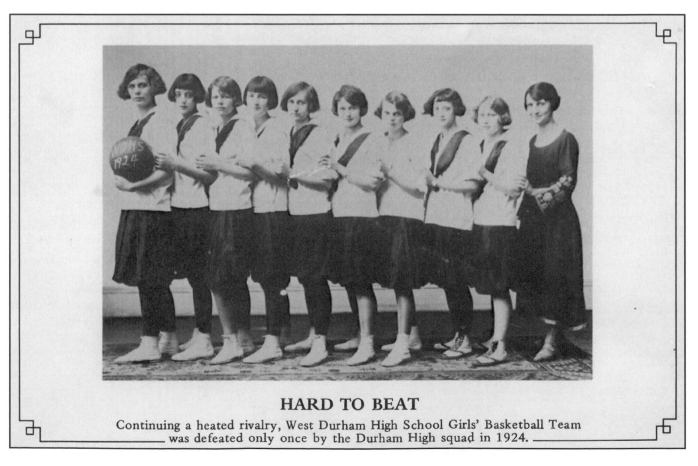

HARD TO BEAT

Continuing a heated rivalry, West Durham High School Girls' Basketball Team
was defeated only once by the Durham High squad in 1924.

On the physical side it is said that a woman has a much smaller heart than a man and that basketball involves a continual strain which a small heart is not well-qualified to stand, even resulting in the girl's fainting or being unable to stand at the end of the half. Strains of the knee and about the body are more injurious to girls than boys. Bruises on the breast and abdomen are likely to be serious. Jumping and falling sometimes result in displacements which may require an operation to prevent sterility.

All these objections are more serious where girls are playing by boys' rules with men coaches. Many former women players believe that these contests are injurious to them.

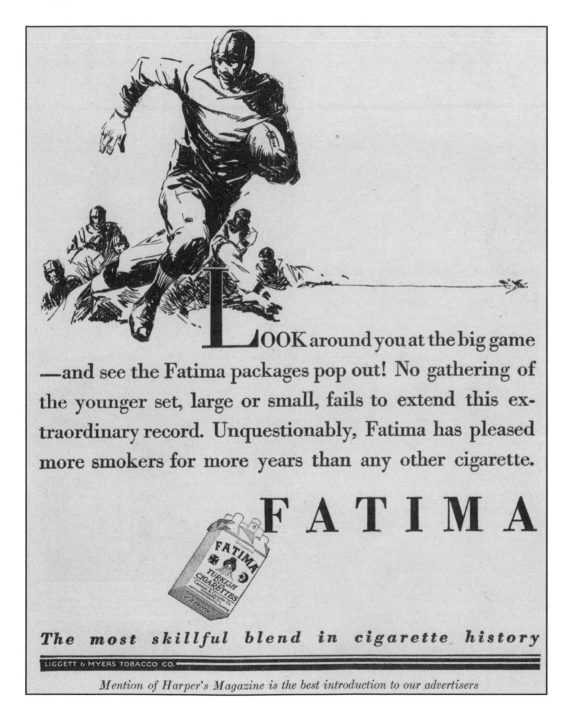

However, this question is far from settled. Basketball by girls' rules, played in quarters, after adequate training and with a competent woman physical director in charge, is quite different from basketball played in halves, by boys' rules and under a man physical director. It may be that when basketball has been led up to by other, less strenuous games, and when adequate preparation has been given in sportsmanship, we should be ready to hold interschool competitions for girls of which the educational authorities can approve.

1930–1939

Few Americans escaped the devastating impact of the most severe depression in the nation's history as banks failed, railroads became insolvent, unemployment rose and factories closed. Women were told they could no longer work because they were occupying a job that could be held by a man. Other workers accepted shorter hours so two or three people could be paid for one 40-hour week. School attendance was cut back to only five months in many states. Fewer couples chose marriage, fewer still had children in this austere environment. By 1932, one in four Americans was jobless. One in every four farms was sold for taxes. Five thousand banks closed their doors, wiping out the lifetime savings of millions of Americans, rich and poor.

The stock market sank into the doldrums. In urban areas, apple sellers appeared on street corners. Bread lines became common sights. The unemployed wandered from city to city seeking work, only to discover the pervasive nature of the economic collapse. In some circles the American Depression was viewed as the fulfillment of Marxist prophecy—the inevitable demise of capitalism. President Franklin D. Roosevelt thought otherwise. Backed by his New Deal promises and a focus on the "forgotten man," the president produced a swirl of government programs designed to lift the country out of its paralytic gloom.

Roosevelt's early social experiments were characterized by relief, recovery, and reform. Believing that the expansion of the United States economy was temporarily over, Roosevelt paid attention to better distribution of resources and planned production. The Civilian Conservation Corps (CCC), for example, put 250,000 jobless young men to work in the forests for $1.00 a day. By 1935, government deficit spending was spurring economic change. By 1937, total manufacturing output exceeded that of 1929; unfortunately, prices and wages rose too quickly and the economy dipped again in 1937, driven by inflation fears and restrictions on bank lending. Nonetheless, many roads, bridges, public buildings, dams, and trees became part of the landscape thanks to federally employed workers. The Federal Theatre Project, for example, employed 1,300 people during the period, reaching 25 million attendees with more than 1,200 productions. Despite progress, 10 million workers were still unemployed in 1938 and farm prices lagged behind manufacturing progress. Full recovery would not occur until the United States mobilized for World War II.

While the nation suffered from economic blows, the West was being whipped by nature. Gigantic billowing clouds of dust up to 10,000 feet high swept across the parched Western Plains throughout the '30s. Sometimes the blows came with lightning and booming thunder, but often they were described as being "eerily slight, blackening everything in their path." All human activity halted. Planes were grounded. Buses and trains stalled, unable to race clouds that could move at speeds of more than 100 miles per hour. On the morning of

May 9, 1934, the wind began to blow up the topsoil of Montana and Wyoming, and soon some 350 million tons were sweeping eastward. By late afternoon, 12 million tons had been deposited in Chicago. By noon the next day, Buffalo, New York, was dark with dust. Even the Atlantic Ocean was no barrier. Ships 300 miles out to sea found dust on their decks. During the remainder of 1935, there were more than 40 dust storms that reduced visibility to less than one mile. There were 68 more storms in 1936, 72 in 1937, and 61 in 1938. On the High Plains, 10,000 houses were simply abandoned, and nine million acres of farm turned back to nature. Banks offered mortgaged properties for as little as $25 for 160 acres and found no takers.

The people of the 1930s excelled in escape. Radio matured as a mass medium, creating stars such as Jack Benny, Bob Hope, and Fibber McGee and Molly. For a time it seemed that every child was copying the catch phrase of radio's Walter Winchell, "Good evening, Mr. and Mrs. America, and all the ships at sea," or pretending to be Jack Benny when shouting, "Now, cut that out!" Soap operas captured large followings and sales of magazines like Screenland and True Story skyrocketed. Each edition of True Confessions sold 7.5 million copies. Nationwide, movie theaters prospered as 90 million Americans attended the "talkies" every week, finding comfort in the uplifting excitement of movies and movie stars. Big bands made swing the king of the decade, while jazz came into its own. And the social experiment known as Prohibition died in December 1933, when the Twenty-first Amendment swept away the restrictions against alcohol ushered in more than a decade earlier.

Attendance at professional athletic events declined during the decade, but softball became more popular than ever and golf began its drive to become a national passion as private courses went public. Millions listened to boxing on radio, especially the exploits of the "Brown Bomber," Joe Louis. As average people coped with the difficult times, they married later, had fewer children, and divorced less. Extended families often lived under one roof; opportunities for women and minorities were particularly limited. Survival, not affluence, was often the practical goal of the family. A disillusioned nation, which had worshipped the power of business, looked instead toward a more caring government.

During the decade, United Airlines hired its first airline stewardess to allay passengers' fears of flying. The circulation of Reader's Digest climbed from 250,000 to eight million before the decade ended and Esquire, the first magazine for men, was launched. The early days of the decade gave birth to Hostess Twinkies, Bird's Eye frozen vegetables, windshield wipers, photoflash bulbs, and pinball machines. By the time the Depression and the 1930s drew to a close, Zippo lighters, Frito's corn chips, talking books for the blind, beer in cans, and the Richter scale for measuring earthquakes had all been introduced. Despite the ever-increasing role of the automobile in the mid-1930s, Americans still spent $1,000 a day on buggy whips.

1931 NEWS PROFILE
BUILDING HOOVER DAM

Massive public works projects like the Hoover Dam were an important part of the New Deal's response to the Great Depression. Hoover Dam was the first of the great multipurpose dams, providing flood control, water for irrigation, and hydroelectric power to the Southwest. The 60-story-high dam across the Colorado River was built by The Six Companies, a consortium mainly of little-known Western construction contractors. This is the story of one family that worked on "one of the monumental engineering achievements of the twentieth century."

Erma Godbey, 1931: "We had heard a lot about the Boulder Canyon Project while we lived in Colorado and took the Denver Post, because the regional offices of the Bureau of Reclamation were in Colorado . . . so we thought what we'd do is come over here. My mother and stepfather came down from Colorado to visit us. They were driving an old seven-passenger Dodge touring car. We had no car, so we had them drive us over here. We put a mattress and two baby cribs and two baby mattresses on the top of the car and tied them on. Then all of us got in the car. We brought a few cooking utensils and very few clothes and some bedding with us—and that's all. We had four children and my baby was only five months old. . . . It was terrifically hot. My God it was terribly hot and dusty. None of the roads were paved in those days. It was just ungodly, it was so hot.

We got into where Boulder City is now, down from where the airport used to be; that's where the Six Company camp was. It was all tents. We stopped there and asked about a job. They said we just have a tent mess hall here, and we have tents for the men that are working, and you'll have to go down into the river bottom. We still had to keep on driving. . . .

It was called Ragtown, but was officially Williamsville, after Claude Williams, who was in charge of it. It looked like anyplace that is just built out of pasteboard cartons or anything else. Everyone had come just in a car, with no furniture or anything. My mother looked around. They got to go back to Colorado. She said, 'Well, I'll never see you again, I'll never see you again.' I said, 'Oh Mom, we're tough. Remember, we're from pioneer stock.' After all, my mother had driven cattle from Texas on horseback to Colorado when she was 14 years old. I said, 'We're pioneer stock; we'll last.' But she cried, and she left us. . . .

We were right in among all these other people that were already camped there. Some had tents, but a lot them just had canvas or blankets or anything they could have for shelter. There was one little fellow that they called 'Johnny behind the Rock.' There was a great big boulder as you came down Hemenway, Washington, to go to into Ragtown. He just kind of moved around where the shade was. He didn't have any tent or anything. He just kept moving wherever the shade was that the rock made.

What I had to do—I had blankets made out of pure wool that I had had made up at Utah Woolen Mills. They had cost me $32.00 a pair, which was a lot of money in those days, when men were only making four bucks a day wage. We got a hold of some clothesline, and we had some safety pins. We put some poles in the ground and pinned those beautiful wool blankets with safety pins to those poles to try to make a little bit of shade from the terrible heat. It would get to be 120 by nine in the morning, and it wouldn't be below 120 before nine at night. It just seemed like the river just drew the heat right down there. You could just see the heat dancing off the mountains, the black cliffs down there. I would wrap my babies in wet sheets so they could sleep. But for my littlest baby, the one that was only five months old, Ila, I would put the wet sheet around her crib so the air would blow through it. But it wasn't enough.

It was about four days that we were like that, just with the blankets for shade. There was a little camp real close to us. The man who lived in that tent worked in drilling the diversion tunnels. He wasn't a miner; he just was somebody who needed to have a job. When they would blast in the tunnels, they would just set the blast off as the men came off the shift. Then the next shift would muck out, but the blast would go off between shifts. This man was so anxious to get in to work to earn his wages that he went in a little ahead of some of the other men, and the blast hadn't finished going off. Just as he put his shovel down to muck out, a delayed blast went off and made the handle of the shovel go like this and it disemboweled him. His wife—the only thing she could do was to have the body sent back home to her relatives or it would be buried in Las Vegas in the old cemetery—that was the Woodlawn Cemetery at the time. Then she'd just have to move on, since she had no way of making a living or anything. So we bought her tent. That way we had a small tent, but it still wasn't big enough for anything but maybe to do a little cooking in it. . . .

We had to haul drinking water from the river. They had dug a couple of holes a little bit in from the river, and when the river would seep through the sand it would be pretty good. But, of course, when people would dip a lot into these wells, it would get riley again, so you'd have to let it settle. My husband didn't want to drink that water, and I didn't either. I had brought over my copper boiler, so I had something to put water in. He would just take the boiler and swipe water from the mess hall when the cooks were busy feeding the men. I didn't give my nursing baby enough water to drink. I gave her about the same amount of water that I had given my other babies that I had raised up in Colorado. She pretty near dehydrated. So one night when all my other children woke up and wanted a drink of water, I picked up the baby to nurse her and she just knocked the cup I was drinking from right out of my hand. It was a 10-ounce white granite cup. It spilled on her. My husband said, 'Mama, I think the baby's thirsty.' We gave her a drink, and she drank 10 ounces of water. She drank it from the cup, and she never did take water out of a bottle after that.

They did have outside toilets that the government furnished. The rangers would put slaked lime in them about twice a week. The only thing you could do with garbage was to burn it. There was no garbage removal or anything. Everybody just had to burn their garbage on their own premises, as best they could.

They would go to work at 7:00 in the morning. It was so terrible hot by noon that men were passing out with the heat. So they decided that they would go to work at 4:00 in the morning and work until noon. Another shift would come on at 4:00 in the afternoon and work until midnight. But nobody would work during the very bad heat of the day between noon and 4:00. So then my husband had to be at work at 4:00 in the morning. That meant I had to get up at 2:30 in the morning and get some breakfast going for him and get his lunch packed. I was still using the campfire. The very first money we got, we got somebody to go into Las Vegas and we got a Coleman camp stove. We had a carbide lamp—that's what miners use, you know. And we had the carbide crystals. So what I would use at night was the carbide lamp.

The reason I left Ragtown was not only the heat. Four people died—four women died in one day. That was the 26th of July, 1931, and it was terribly hot. There was a woman that was 60 years old and a girl 16, and another woman that I don't know how old she was or anything much about her, and then there was a woman that was 28 that was only three tents from me. Her husband was working the swing shift in the diversion tunnels. They had come out from New York State. She was sick. He had done the best he could. He left her with a thermos bottle with ice. We could get ice once a day where they brought the ice in. They had a big dog, a big police dog. She just got to feeling terribly bad, so she tied a note to her dog's collar and told him to get the ranger. He knew what she'd told him, but where was the ranger? Mr. Williams was anywhere. He probably wasn't in his office when the dog went hunting for him. In the note she had asked Mr. Williams to come and get her and take her to the river so she could get in the water to get cooled off. By the time Mr. Williams got to her after the dog got to him, she was just lying across of folding cot and she was dead. They told us women that were close. There were three of us that went over into her tent. We kind of straightened her up on the bed.

They sent for the other ranger or somebody to get her husband out of the tunnels. The woman had been dead for probably an hour by the time he got there. He immediately tried to give her artificial respiration. Then her looked at we three women, and he said, 'Anybody going to Alaska? Anybody want to buy a fur coat?' We all just batted our eyes, hearing this in over 120-degree heat. Who in the heck would want a fur coat? But we got to thinking later that what the poor man was trying to do was get enough money out of the fur coat to bury his wife. They couldn't even move her into Vegas right away, because there wasn't any transportation. They had taken the other three people earlier in the day into Las Vegas. I went back to my tent, and I told my husband, 'We've got to get out of here. We've just absolutely got to get out of here. I've got to get somewhere I can get the babies to a doctor if need be, and also myself.'"

1934 PROFILE

Working Class

Twelve-year-old Martha Hope and her family are preparing to leave their farm and move into town after her father died and the farm had to be sold; the two children were told he died of pneumonia—a story that disregarded the facts.

Life at Home

*   Martha's father's given name was Robert Hope, but everyone called him by his middle name, Meek.
*   A farmer like his father before him, Meek raised cotton, but also kept an orchard of apples, grapes and peaches in York, South Carolina; the rest of the family's food was produced by the cows and chickens they raised.
*   Meek took great pride in his looks and his farm, but his passion was his hunting dogs.
*   Martha loves to tell how her daddy was so smart and his dogs so good, he could tell which dog was closest to catching the quarry based on its howl.
*   He often traveled on weekends to demonstrate their hunting prowess in dog shows around the state.
*   The dogs loved the trips so much they often waited on the running board of the old Ford truck he drove, eager for the next hunt to begin.
*   When he came back from long trips he would bring both children an eight-inch stick of mint candy.
*   Since he died all that has changed.
*   Martha's mother Edna has been offered a job at a dry cleaner's in town, so she is moving her family to live in one part of her great-uncle's house, where she will pay room and board.

Martha Hope is preparing to leave the farm.

After the move into town, Sonny plans to be a super salesman.

- Times are too tough for anyone to take on additional mouths for free, everyone says over and over.
- Even though the house is big, Martha is worried the yard is too small to grow the vegetables the family needs.
- When she found out the farm was going to be sold, she didn't even cry once—until her little brother Sonny started to.
- Sonny says he is excited about the move to town; he won't talk about his father's death, but instead tells everyone he plans to be a salesman for Curtis Publishing Company and win lots of prizes.
- At night he spends hours going through the book of prizes available to top student salesmen; he knows he can sell enough subscriptions to win a Columbia Motobike by gathering 800 brown vouchers.
- He also thinks he may be the "kick-the-can" champion of the world; every day he practices kicking an Esso oil can from the farm to Uncle Ted's store down the road and back to keep in practice.

- Most of their supplies come from the store, where Uncle Ted keeps lots of food in stock, but doesn't allow credit, especially to relatives.
- Sometimes, though, he gives away little treats, and has been generous with Ritz Crackers, which were introduced in the market last year by National Biscuit Company.
- Since the funeral, Martha has had to take on more responsibility for the family.
- Right after her father died, her aunt came to her and said, "You need to make sure your little brother knows that Santa Claus does not exist and won't be coming this year. There is no use pretending now."

Most of the family's supplies come from Uncle Ted's store.

- Martha did as she was told, because an adult said so, even though, until that moment, it had never occurred to her that Santa Claus wasn't real.
- For her entire life, the family cooked and heated their 900-square-foot house with a wood stove, sometimes sleeping in the kitchen for warmth during the coldest days of winter.
- The wood stove also operated around the clock during the summer months, when the temperature outside often hovered near 100 degrees.
- Wood had to be cut weekly to keep it running; pine made a good hot fire, but oak was needed to keep the stove warm.
- On cold mornings, the dogs fought over the chance to lie by the warm oven door.
- The house has no electricity, although the rural electrical cooperative has now extended lines to 10 miles' distance of the farm, with promises to hook up the rest within the year.
- On top of the wood stove rests a skillet of cornbread; even in bad times, cornbread and honey can be filling.
- They say it will be different in town, but she doesn't know if different is good or bad.
- On the farm, everyone has a role; most fieldwork was done by her father and a sharecropper who has a lifetime of experience with a steel plow pulled by a mule.
- Martha is proud that she can butcher her own meat, cut cane and chop cotton.
- Every year after the weather cooled, her family and one neighbor joined together to butcher three or four hogs.

Martha cherishes a picture of herself with her parents.

Until recently, most work was done by Martha's father, a sharecropper, and a mule.

- During that 18-hour stretch, the hogs were killed and bled, sausage was ground, liver pudding made, lard rendered from the fat and hams hung for curing.
- In the garden, her specialty has been growing turnips and string beans that could be sold at the farmer's market.
- Starting when she was nine, she planted her crop early and gambled that frost would not kill her plants so she would be the first to market with produce—earning a better price.
- This year, right after her father died, she convinced her uncle to take her and her turnip crop to market.
- When she arrived there, she found that refrigerator trucks carrying produce from Florida had beaten her there and forced down the prices; on top of everything in her life, it was a huge disappointment.
- She didn't have enough money to buy any extras, particularly bananas, which she loves.
- She is afraid a similar fate awaits this year's cotton crop; last time her father sold cotton it only brought $0.40 per pound, the lowest cotton had fallen since 1894.
- Times are so hard, a neighbor boy got one gift for Christmas—five shotgun shells costing a nickel a piece—and was told, "Make sure those shells bring food to the table."
- To help bring in the best possible crop, Martha has carefully treated the cotton with a mixture of arsenic and molasses, which she mopped on the cottons stalks to kill the boll weevils that seem to be destroying everyone's crop.

Meek's hunting dogs often wait at the car for the next outing.

- When applying the arsenic, Martha is always careful not to get any on her hands or in her mouth; her friend Sarah was poisoned and missed several weeks of school—even missing story day when all the children get to read a tale of their own invention.
- Because she has always been good with numbers, Martha was given the job of helping to keep the purchases straight when the farm was sold.
- For one whole day she watched her father's entire life being auctioned; the day's total came to $841, after everyone paid like they were supposed to.

Partial listing of the estate of Robert Meek Hope, sold at auction, York, South Carolina, December 22, 1934:

Four Mules	561.00	Grindstone	1.45
Three Cows	72.00	Mailbox	0.50
Wagon	15.00	Farm Bell	1.00
Wagon Harness	9.50	Wheelbarrow	1.50
Horse Collars	1.75	Wagon Wheels	0.60
Disc Harrow	8.50	Hack Saw	0.45
Tractor Harrow	26.00	Pipe Wrench	0.75
Four Side Harrows	8.20	Grain Cradle	0.75
Two Drag Harrows	2.25	Mowing Scythe	1.25
Stalk Cutter	0.60	Pitch Fork	0.50
Mower	1.25	Two Shovels	0.55
Seed Fork and Rake	1.00	Gears	3.80
Five Cotton Planters	14.50	Anvil	2.50
Corn Planter	2.60	Hoses	4.40
Guano Plow	1.00	Manure Spreader	1.00
Single Row Oat Drill	3.60	Crosscut Saw	0.45
Three Row Oat Drills	4.70	Dinner Bell	2.00
Four Plow Sacks	0.70	Icebox	2.50
Four Turn Plows	20.00	Cabinet	3.00
Middle Buster	1.75	Wardrobe	2.80
Three Go-Devils	2.50	Table	2.10
Shop Tools	6.50	Baby Bed	0.25
Bellows	1.25	Two Beds and Springs	3.00
Blower	4.50	Bureau	5.75
Corn Sheller	1.20		

- Most of the bidders were from nearby farms, especially aunts and uncles who thought that helping to buy out the farm was a fair thing to do for brother Meek.
- Uncle Neely spent the most, $561, primarily for the mules, but Mr. W. W. Inman only spent $11 because no one wanted him to have anything; Meek's kin folks out-bid him whenever he took a shine to anything.
- She thinks it serves him right for talking bad about her daddy after he died; everyone in the family knows he died of pneumonia, but he kept telling them he died from a knife wound he caught in a bar fight down the road.
- The only things the family kept were two beds, one for Martha and her brother and one for Momma, and the portable Victrola Meek bought for his wife; Momma didn't want to give it up for any amount of money.
- Currently, a big argument has erupted concerning the 13-year-old black girl named Lucinda who lives with the family.
- Two years ago, when Lucinda's father tossed her out of the house for talking back, Edna found her crying on the back steps and took her in.
- Shortly thereafter Lucinda's father moved off the farm and has not been heard from since.

Martha has been pouring over the Montgomery Ward catalog.

- Lucinda has lived with Edna, Meek, Martha and Sonny ever since, sleeping in a cot in the back of the house.
- Martha and Lucinda do everything together—especially if dolls are involved—except go to school.
- Even though Lucinda is a year older, she is still on the third-year reader, and Martha helps her with her schoolwork at night.
- All the relatives are urging Edna to turn Lucinda out when they move into the city, saying, "Let the coloreds take care of their own; you've got troubles enough."
- Martha has begged her mother to take Lucinda when moving day comes, reminding her that when Daddy died, Lucinda acted like family, carefully and quietly stopping all the clocks in the house and draping the mirror with a black cloth.
- Momma says she may have to think about what's best for the entire family.

Life at School and Work

- In preparation for the new school year, Martha has been poring over the Montgomery Ward catalog.
- Some people in the neighborhood are Sears fans, but this family has always found Montgomery Ward to be fair.
- In her heart, Martha knows that no money will be available for new dresses this year, but looking at the wonderful pictures keeps her hopes up.
- In the new school year, Sonny will be in the second grade, and hopes there are pictures on the wall like in his old classroom.
- In the first grade he was able to learn how to tie his shoes by looking at a detailed, step-by-step drawing on the wall; some days they even practiced in class.
- Like most farm boys, before starting school, Sonny rarely wore shoes, except for his Sunday shoes, which fastened with a buckle.
- His first-grade teacher, Miss Gaillard, has attended at least two summer sessions at Newberry College, but was not a high school graduate; her formal education ended in the sixth grade, so she was permitted only to teach through the fourth grade.
- When Miss Gaillard is sick or away, Martha teaches Sonny's class because she is the best reader in the school.
- Martha's sixth-grade class program included a commemoration of George Washington's birthday, featuring a program of readings and songs.
- At Easter a pageant was performed in two acts—"At Calvary on the Green Hill Far Away" and "At the Tomb on Sabbath Dawn," followed by an Easter egg hunt.
- Martha was proud to play the role of Martha at the tomb when the stone was rolled away.
- Her father came to both presentations, but didn't say much afterward—he rarely did.
- For her little brother's birthday, Martha and her mother are making a stuffed character from his favorite storybook, *Where's Angus?*

- It has an embroidered nose, mouth and eyes, and a red ribbon with little silver bells around its neck.
- After the farm was sold, Martha's Aunt Cora gave her a gift—a booklet called "How to Make Draperies" by the Singer Sewing Machine Company.
- Since she was a little girl, Martha has enjoyed helping her mother pump the pedal on the family sewing machine, and has been praying she will learn fast enough so she can sew herself a dress to wear to the new school.
- One of Martha's remaining concerns is the road grader man.
- Ever since she can remember, the man from the county who scrapes the gravel roads three times a year has allowed her to ride in the truck when he cleaned ditches and graded the road.
- At the end of each trip he said, "Thanks for your help; I don't know if I could have done it without you."
- She doesn't even have a way to tell him she can't help him anymore.

Life in the Community: York, South Carolina

- South Carolina's foreign-born population is only one percent, one of the lowest in the nation; of its 1.8 million citizens, the racial mix is 54.3 percent white and 45.7 percent black.
- Agriculture dominates the state's economy, with two-thirds of the state's 166,000 farms operated by tenants who do not own the land they till.
- South Carolina's 110,000 manufacturing jobs rank sixth among the Southern states; the average annual wage is $615.

After her father died, Martha was given a book on how to make draperies.

"Discipline," *The Tompkins School, 1925 to 1953, A Community Institution*, by T. Felder Dorn, 1994:

The switch and the ruler were prominent implements for administering justice and maintaining order. Standing in the corner with our back to the class or standing in the cloak room during recess (which, recalls one culprit, "broke your heart on a nice day") were also used. The types of devilment that merited punishment often were rather banal—sticking out one's feet to trip a classmate en route to the front of the room, fighting or ugly name-calling, backtalk or sass to a teacher, horsing around on the bus or sailing paper airplanes. Other infractions, such as tipping over the girls' toilet, setting the woods on fire, sneaking off to the creek, or playing on April Fools' Day were a bit more daring. Putting a crayon on a hot stove was a stunt that usually permitted the instigator to escape detection, but it made quite a stink.

One or two teachers acknowledged their prowess with the rod, but others spoke of using the switch sparingly, adding that children minded them. Two teachers, whose tenures at the school were separated by a number of years, were recalled by different pupils with identical words: "She was a lovely lady, but she would tear you up." A punishment for younger pupils recalled most vividly by some who received it began with a teacher grasping the offender's hand and giving it some sound whacks with a sturdy 12-inch ruler.

Hop-Along Cassidy is one of Martha's favorites.

- Because the Depression has hit the farm community even worse, the per capita income of South Carolinians has dropped from $261 in 1929 to $150 in five years.
- Only two percent of the state's farms have electricity; with no lights, rural residents of the state tend to go to bed with the chickens.
- To balance the state budget, Gov. Ibra Blackwood reduced state salaries, and employees are paid in state scrip.
- No safety net exists for families.
- The state's constitution permits assistance only for Confederate veterans, their widows and faithful slaves.
- South Carolina is one of six states without old-age pensions, one of 14 without assistance for the blind, and one of two with no aid for dependent children.
- The unemployment rate now exceeds 30 percent, and in some rural parts of the state the elderly are reported to be dying of starvation.
- The Works Progress Administration (WPA), administered by the federal government, is beginning to transform the economic landscape, building roads, schools, bridges and dams.
- Recently, the General Assembly created the Public Service Authority, known as Santee-Cooper, to produce and sell electricity, develop inland navigation along three South Carolina rivers, reclaim swamps and reforest watersheds.

Historical Snapshot
1934

- Leni Riefenstahl directed *Triumph of the Will*, documenting the rise of the Third Reich in Germany
- The Civil Works Administration provided employment for four million people
- Donald Duck, Walgreen's drugstores, Flash Gordon, Seagram's Seven Royal Crown and the term "hi-fi" all made their first appearance
- Ernest and Julio Gallo invested $5,900 in a wine company
- The birth of the Dionne quintuplets in Ontario stirred international interest
- The ongoing drought reduced the national corn crop by nearly one billion bushels
- Edna St. Vincent Millay published *Wine from These Grapes*; F. Scott Fitzgerald completed *Tender Is the Night*
- Dicumarol, an anticoagulant, was developed from clover
- "Tumbling Tumbleweeds," "I Only Have Eyes for You" and "Honeysuckle Rose" were all popular songs
- The Securities and Exchange Commission was created
- The movie *It Happened One Night* won academy awards for Best Picture, Best Director (Frank Capra), Best Actress (Claudette Colbert) and Best Actor (Clark Gable)
- The U.S. Gold Reserve Act authorized the president to devalue the dollar
- Enrico Fermi suggested that neutrons and protons were the same fundamental particles in two different quantum states
- The FBI shot John Dillinger, Public Enemy No. I, generating a hail of publicity
- Greyhound bus lines cut its business fares in half to $8 between New York and Chicago to encourage more traffic

1935 Profile

Julia Stern entered the road less traveled for women—the practice of law. As a judge, she can mete out justice and work for the causes about which she cares the most: the social problems arising from poverty and inequity. Her annual income is $10,000.

Judge Julia Stern is concerned about the welfare of children.

Life at Home

- Julia Stern found her way into law and eventually the role of judge through an unusual route—a textile mill.
- The daughter of a prominent Reform rabbi and an activist mother, Julia was born in 1901 during President William McKinley's administration.
- She grew up in relative economic security in a nation invigorated by the possibilities of commerce and rapidly rising prestige abroad.
- Her mother's work with the poor focused on adopted children, especially the hard-to-place Jews of Oregon whom no one seemed to want.
- Julia often worked alongside her mother on difficult cases and heard as a young girl about the complexities of family relationships.
- Life in the real world harbored more violent beatings, neglect and child abuse than fairy godmothers, she learned.
- The experience would shape her life; as a judge, successful adoptions would bring a special joy.
- Her parents often led by example; her father was an early member of the National Association for the Advancement of Colored People, which was founded nationally in 1909.

- When a local minister told her father he couldn't be expected to sit down to dinner with a black artist also invited to the family's home for a meal, her father said, "Oh, I'm so sorry. May I take you downstairs and help you get your coat?"
- Her grandparents were staunch supporters of the need for a Jewish homeland in Palestine.
- Family lore says they emigrated to America in 1888 from Galicia to promote the Zionist idea in the United States.
- Julia attended Bryn Mawr after she was subjected to an hour-long grilling from the school president, a man determined to keep "undesirables" out of his college.

"Children in Gainful Occupations," *Needlecraft Magazine*, March 1935:

No one who has ever seen a child made prematurely old and careworn by the unrelenting taskmaster, hard work, can fail to sympathize with the efforts which have been put forth from time to time in an attempt to limit the age at which children may be employed in gainful occupations. In his recent message to Congress, President Roosevelt commented upon child labor, stating that it had been "for the moment outlawed" under the various codes of fair competition. For years the question of an amendment to our constitution restricting the labor of children has been agitated. Away back in June 1924, this amendment was first proposed and it has been ratified by 20 states. The resolution reads: "The Congress shall have power to limit, regulate and prohibit the labor of persons under 18 years of age."

Much controversy has been waged over the advisability of ratifying this amendment. Its foes point out that it involves a question which should be determined by each state individually; that climatic conditions have much to do with the age at which young people should be permitted to go to work; and that there is danger in permitting Congress power to absolutely control the life of young people throughout the nation, where conditions vary so decidedly in the various sections of the country. There have always been a considerable number of sincerely-minded individuals who believe the principle of "States' Rights" should not be violated, and that to as great an extent as is practicable, all questions should be decided and adjusted by the individual states; and that the federal government should handle only such as require a central administrative power.

The American Farm Bureau Federation has been, until recently, opposed to the Child Labor Amendment, but of late they have reversed their opinion, and are now lined up with the advocates of the amendment. The American Federation of Labor has always been one of the amendment's warmest friends and defenders, and they are now calling upon the state federations of 28 states to make the passage of the amendment their chief legislative objective this winter.

You and I will probably be called upon later to vote to either ratify or defeat this resolution; so it is not too soon to be thinking the matter over, that we may make up our minds on which side of the controversy we choose to be found. In any event, we can all undoubtedly agree that every child has an inalienable right to leisure, wholesome recreation, opportunity for education, and freedom from adult cares while he is growing, and before he has reached his maturity. It is not only for his welfare but for the future welfare of the nation in which he lives, that this should be possible. That is a consideration we should not overlook.

- After two years, she transferred to Radcliffe, where she thought she might obtain more economics courses.
- During the day she attended classes and taught foreign residents of Boston how to read; nights were spent learning about economic conditions by working in a local factory.
- The experience helped shape her thinking about labor, fairness and the power of capitalism.
- Disillusioned by the bluestocking atmosphere of Radcliffe, Julia finished at Barnard with a degree in economics.
- There, she published an article in the student newspaper calling on young people to "claim responsibility" for solving the social problems of their time.
- In the midst of the roaring twenties, she petitioned the Jazz Age generation to work directly in the industrial communities alongside the poor and the immigrants to gain the firsthand knowledge necessary for developing labor policies.

To learn about mill life, Julia worked in a textile mill.

- In a New Jersey mill, where she took employment under an assumed name, Julia witnessed legions of women arrive for the night shift exhausted and discouraged after a day of caring for children and home.
- She also watched 14-year-old children quit school and then quickly grow old under the strain of trying to make money in the mills night after night.
- In the mill, she came to understand the intimidation tactics of the owners determined to keep out the unions; eventually she was blacklisted from mills in the area and not allowed to work.
- The experience pointed her to law school, an unusual path for a woman.
- Her father encouraged her to pursue the practice of law, especially if her goals included social justice.
- When she was told that only Yale University and the University of Chicago were open to both women and Jews, she chose Yale.
- Five of the 125 students at the law school were women.

- She was well accepted and popular until her second year, when she became heavily involved in the support of a group of striking textile workers.
- While encouraging a mass rally of workers to denounce the employers' "feudal tyranny" and their "octopus-like espionage system," she urged the workers to persist in their strike.
- Prominent members of her father's synagogue resigned the temple, and some Yale law students stopped speaking to her.
- Her visible, activist role did attract the attention of a young law professor, whom she eventually married.
- Currently, Julia is still recovering from the loss of her husband to leukemia three years ago.
- She still wears his small gold Longines wrist watch as a constant reminder of him.
- Julia now has sole responsibility for raising their son, who was four when his father died.
- She has recently met a fellow attorney who shares her passionate devotion to children's causes—and the game of bridge.
- He, too, thinks the courts can be an instrument for good.

"Woman Runs Signal Tower; Handles It 'Like a Man,'" *Grit*, April 18, 1937:

If a woman takes a man's job, she must be able to handle it like a man, contends Mrs. Ella Bower, who, as adeptly as a man, pulls switches and signal levers in the Pennsylvania and Lehigh Valley Railroad's joint signal tower near Stanley, NY.

Nearly three decades of service at a railroad job, held by few women, have made her as efficient as any male tower operator, her fellow workmen say.

Mrs. Bower in her 29 years of service has worked at nearly every tower in the Williamsport (Pa.) Division of the Pennsylvania Railroad.

"I've climbed semaphore poles 35 feet high to display signals," she says. "I have always contended that, if a woman is to take a man's job, she must be ready and capable of doing what is expected of the position when it is filled by the man."

Her hobby is knitting, but there is little time for knitting during working hours, she has discovered.

"You're too busy watching messages and pulling switches and semaphore levers," she explains.

"We Are Much Cleverer. Topic of The Times," *The New York Times*, January 19, 1935:

Easily the best news of the day is the report that we are no longer a people with the average mental age of a 12-year-old child; our mental age is nearly 18 years. That is the finding of an expert who writes in *School Life,* the official publication of the Federal Office of Education in Washington.

This tremendous improvement in American intelligence is not credited to the administration or the New Deal or anything governmental. The Washington specialist simply finds that the celebrated army intelligence tests upon which the 12-year-old mentality of the

American was alleged do not justify such a condition. This point is essentially the same made by critics like Dr. Fabian Franklin at the time. The speed of a person's response to a specific mechanical stimulus does not measure his intelligence, which is his total response in his own way and his own time to the whole world in which he lives. We are now told that the capacity to learn may continue indefinitely. At any rate, it is good to hear that there are no less than 10 million Americans with a mental age of 23 and over, and there are only three million of us with a mental age of 12.

The HOME LOAN BUNK

Lost—Millions of Homes

Foreclosures and tax sales that came in the wake of depression have already swept away two million homes. And with them have vanished the life savings, the sense of security, pride of ownership, courage and hope of more than eight million men and women.

Capitalizing Human Misery for Votes

When home owners read the early and frequent announcements from the White House that President Hoover's Home Loan Bank Act would save their mortgage-menaced homes from the auctioneer's block, they gave thanks that rescue was near. Immediately pathetic appeals for aid flooded the Washington office of the Federal Home Loan Board.

But they soon found out that the Home Loan Banks do **NOT** hold out immediate or substantial help to the small home owners as Hoover publicity deluded them into thinking. The truth is that:

> The Hoover Home Loan Bank Law does not compel banks and loan associations to share the benefits they enjoy at the expense of the taxpayers with the burdened home owner whom the law was supposed to protect. If it is more profitable for them to force payment or foreclose on old mortgages, and with the money make new mortgages on newer homes at higher rates of interest, there is nothing in the Home Loan Bank Law to prevent such action. Furthermore, the home owner as such is definitely barred from membership in the directorate controlling Mr. Hoover's Home Loan Bank. According to the law, only those connected with home financing business can be elected directors.

The Wolf at the Door

Exorbitant interest rates still threaten the home owner. When friends of home owners amended the Home Loan Bank bill to limit service to loaning agencies that charged only *legal* interest, Hoover spokesmen got that amendment twisted to read "legal or *lawful* contract rate"—a loophole through which ruinous rates can continue to menace home owners.

Democrats Pledge Security to Home Owners

The Democratic candidate for President, Franklin D. Roosevelt, said in his acceptance speech:

"Rediscounting of . . . mortgages under statutory restrictions must be expanded and should, in the future, be conditional on the reduction of interest rates. Amortization payments, maturities, should likewise in this crisis be extended before rediscount (*i.e.,* loaning money to banks and loaning agencies on the mortgages they hold) is permitted where the mortgagor is sorely pressed. . . ."

"Take away that spectre of too high interest rates. . . . Save homes; save homes for thousands of self-respecting families and drive out the spectre of insecurity in our midst."

VOTE TO PROTECT YOUR HOME
VOTE FOR ROOSEVELT AND GARNER

Issued by Democratic National Campaign Committee
Hotel Biltmore—New York City 324

Life at Work

- At 34 years old, Julia Stern has recently been appointed to the Domestic Relations Court in Manhattan by Fiorello La Guardia, the first judicial appointment in New York State to elevate a woman above the rank of magistrate.

- For the past year, she has been heading the city's Workman's Compensation Division, where she was able both to implement labor reforms and enrage the business community who have personally attacked her.

- In 1932, she voted for Norman Thomas on the Socialist ticket for president and later toured Russia for three months, fueling the accusation she was a "red," or communist.

- When asked to be a judge, she hesitated; her passion lay in the labor movement.

- Domestic Relations Court judges were reported to have little power but enormous workloads when presiding over what most called "poor people's court."

- A day in Domestic Relations Court watching case after tragic case helped convince her that she could make a difference as a judge.

- According to newspaper reports, a man who had appeared before Julia during one of her first days on the bench said his court appearance went well: "The judge wasn't there," he said, "but his wife treated me just fine."

- Divorce, desertion, adoptions and child abuse flood her court on a daily basis.

- Her current salary is $10,000 a year, a raise of $6,500 over her previous position.
- Currently, she is concerned about the "vast chasm between our rhetoric of freedom, equality and charity, and what we are doing, or not doing, for poor people, especially children."
- Julia does everything possible to avoid identifying herself as a woman judge; merit, not gender, is all that matters in court, she says.

"Ask Birth Control at House Hearing," *The New York Times*, January 19, 1935:

Amendment to the penal laws to permit medically supervised dissemination of birth control information and advice to overburdened parents of "unwarrantably" large families in their own interest and those of taxpayers who are staggering under the "greatest relief load in history" was urged today on moral, economic and scientific grounds at a crowded hearing before the House Judiciary Committee.

Mrs. Thomas N. Hepburn of Hartford remarked in concluding the pleas for birth control that she had six children. One of her children is Katherine Hepburn, the actress.

More than 500 men and women who overflowed the caucus room of the House building applauded the assertion of Dr. Joseph J. Spengler of the University of Arizona that "without birth control the New Deal will be a frizzle."

Margaret Sanger declared "the forgotten women of the nation, including more than 32 million child-bearing mothers, sought not to bring into the world more children than they could care for."

"We are engaged today, publicly, in the greatest relief job in history," Dr. James H. S. Bossard declared. "If it is to mean nothing more than giving out money and more money, then we have learned nothing since the days of the Roman Empire."

Father Charles E. Coughlin of Detroit spoke for half an hour in opposition to the birth control bill pending in Congress, declaring that America's problem was not one of reproduction but of "control of money in the hands of the Reserve Banks."

"We had better turn our minds to the solution of the problem of how to prevent our billions from going into the pockets of a few men and how to get a few more hundred into the pockets of our farmers and workers . . . ."

Representative Pierce, former Governor of Oregon and sponsor in the House of the amendments to the Comstock Law, declared the present law "absolutely unenforceable and in that respect on all fours with the prohibition Amendment."

The three sections of the criminal code from which exemption is sought forbid possession or transmission by mail or express of anything relating to contraception, under penalty of $2,000 fine or five years' imprisonment, or both.

The result, according to Representative Pierce and the medical experts who appeared on behalf of this bill, is the "bootlegging" of contraceptive devices often to the injury of those most in need of help from qualified physicians who are prevented by law from supplying them, or from sending the desired information or advice.

"We want to bring these things out in the open so that legally licensed physicians can give authoritative information to the people who need it," Representative Pierce declared. "No one need worry about race suicide. What we seek is protection of the race from suicidal effects of the present conditions of things."

- Adoptions were among the happiest events in Julia's courtroom, and she champions adoption's civic potential as well as its personal value; providing children with a family to love them would produce more law-abiding citizens.
- Her goal is always the best interest of the child, she likes to say, which means she often is in conflict with the teaching of the Catholic Church, which insists the children must always but awarded to the Catholic member of the couple.
- She likes to make her views known in and out of the courtroom; Julia regularly writes letters to editors to complain about antiquated custody law or the "Oliver Twist treatment" provided by private child care agencies.

Life in the Community: New York City

- Times are hard: one out of four households is on relief; 750,000 farms have experienced foreclosure in the past five years.

- The Civilian Conservation Corps (CCC) employs half a million men, most of them young, in conservation projects; they earn $40 a month.
- Direct relief work through the states, primarily the Works Progress Administration or WPA, employs eight million men and women to build libraries, schools, roads and hospitals.
- Budget-conscious housewives buy day-old bread, warm several dishes in the oven at the same time to save gas, purchase cheaper cuts of meat or cut down adult coats to fit their children.
- First Lady Eleanor Roosevelt has said the Depression means "endless little economies and constant anxiety for fear of some catastrophe such as accident or illness which may completely swamp the family budget."
- Often a woman's role increases as the center of the household in the midst of economic crisis, whether her husband is working or not.
- Many women still refuse to take paid work, believing it would "steal a job from a man."
- Most studies indicate that women's average yearly pay of about $525 is half that of men.

- Divorce rates are falling, along with the number of marriages and births.
- More than a million couples recently told researchers that they postponed marriage for economic reasons.
- A Gallup poll revealed that 63 percent of Americans now favor the teaching and practice of birth control.
- It is a nation in a state of transformation.
- In 1920, a study showed that of the total number of Jewish women at the nation's colleges, 14 percent were studying law, a nearly identical percentage to Jewish male students.
- At the same time, less than two percent of non-Jewish women are striving to be part the masculine world of law, where "doing in your neighbor and doing him in first" discourages women's participation.
- Opportunity is clearly opening to upper-class German and Central European Jews, allowing many for the first time to get an education at some of the nation's most prominent colleges.
- At the same time, second-generation East European Jewish women are well-represented in public colleges and universities, including New York's Hunter College, where many train as teachers.
- According to one study, Jewish women constitute almost half of all New York City's teachers.
- Despite their academic achievements, "foreign students" are considered "raucous, gawky, and afflicted with acne, halitosis and deplorable hair-do's."
- For many, the availability of public libraries is critical to their education; there, many immigrants and children of immigrants, including Jewish women, learn the English language and American ways.
- To receive a New York City teaching license, candidates face both a written exam and a grueling oral interview where candidates are judged on their breeding, energy and alertness.
- A prospective teacher, especially a second-generation immigrant, is required to be audible, articulate, pleasant and well-modulated, without being nasal, high-pitched, monotonous, strident or noisy.
- The prospective teacher must speak without vulgarisms or foreignisms that night be imitated by students.

"4,000 in CWA Put on Short Week; Supply Purchases Hauled by Low Funds," January 19, 1935:

With its $400 million fund of emergency reemployment rapidly nearing exhaustion, [the Civil Works Administration] today placed four million workers now carried on its rolls to a 24-hour week in cities of more than 2,500 population, and 15 hours a week for smaller communities and rural districts. Instructions to this effect were sent to all state directors by Harry L. Hopkins, head of the CWA . . . .

The action of Director Hopkins today thus put squarely before Congress the need for deciding in the near future whether the civil works program is to continue. The $400 million fund originally made available for the work was expected to carry it through February 15 on a full operating schedule. The proposed addition of $350 million is intended to continue the program to May 1.

HISTORICAL SNAPSHOT
1939

- The Supreme Court declared the National Recovery Administration to be unconstitutional
- The word "boondoggling" came to refer to "busy work" created to find activities for the unemployed
- Congress authorized creation of the Works Progress Administration, the National Labor Relations Board and the Rural Electrification Administration
- Group sports in public areas gained in popularity, especially bicycling, skiing, golf and softball
- The average cost of advertising on NBC radio was $360 per minute
- Congress passed the Banking Act of 1935, the Emergency Relief Appropriation Act, the National Labor Relations Act, and the Social Security Act
- Despite the domination of automobiles, Americans still spent $1,000 a day on buggy whips
- Economic recovery had begun as unemployment fell to 20.1 percent
- Popularity of the board game Monopoly exploded, with 20 million sets sold in one week
- Mary McLeod Bethune organized the National Council of Negro Women as a lobbying coalition of black women's groups
- Alcoholics Anonymous was founded
- Average monthly sales of *True Confessions* magazine topped 7.3 million
- New York Attorney General Thomas Dewey gained national attention with the convictions of Lucky Luciano and 70 others for racketeering
- Germany issued the anti-Jewish Nuremberg Laws
- Making their first appearance were: a woman member of the stock exchange, beer in cans, Toyota, Jolly Green Giant, Gallup polls, hot meals served on airplanes and Kodachrome for 16 mm cameras
- Fashion for women featured a severe military look showcasing square, epaulette shoulders, low heels, plumed hats and gauntlet gloves
- Baseball star Babe Ruth was traded by the New York Yankees to the Boston Braves
- *Tortilla Flat* by John Steinbeck, *Taps at Reveille* by F. Scott Fitzgerald and *The Last Puritan* by George Santayana were all published; *Of Time and the River* by Thomas Wolfe was a bestseller
- The Wagner Act (National Labor Relations Act) established the first national labor policy to protect the rights of workers to organize and to elect their own representatives for collective bargaining
- The Guffey Act was passed to stabilize the coal industry and to improve labor conditions
- Andrew Mellon donated $10 million, plus a $25 million art collection, for the construction of the National Art Gallery in Washington, D.C., with the stipulation that no gallery be named for him
- The Massachusetts Department of Mental Health reported that children from small families have a greater tendency to steal; children from large families have a greater tendency to lie
- Popular songs included "You Are My lucky Star"; "I loves You, Porgy"; "I Got Plenty o' Nuthin'"; "Stairway to the Stars" and "I'm in the Mood for Love"
- The Committee for Industrial Organization (CIO) formed within the AFL to foster industrial unionism
- Americans consumed 50 million chickens; the cost of poultry rose above red meat

"Pay-As-You-Listen Is a Riddle of the Age," by Orin E. Dunlap Jr., *The New York Times*, January 14, 1935:

How to levy a fee on millions of unseen listeners is a riddle that has caused more than one economist hours of concentration during the past decade. Recently, several of the calculators have reached what they consider to be practical conclusions, and they presented their suggestions to Uncle Sam for possible use in the "New Deal."

Generally, they open the discussion by calling attention to the fact that automobiles are taxed for their right to use the highways and they display license plates as proof; the driver pays his license fee and pays a tax on gasoline and oil. The railroad is taxed for its right of way across the countryside and ships pay a fee for entering ports. The long distance telephone call is taxed.

So is the radio set in many foreign lands, but not in the United States. That is why twentieth-century physiocrats have caught the idea that broadcasters and listeners should assist in meeting expenses. In the President's budget recommendations, the authorized obligation for the Radio Commission for 1934 was listed at $640,000, and the budget estimate for 1935 at $668,885.

Mindful of the revenue collected on radio receivers in foreign countries—for example, in England, there are approximately eight million outfits, the owners of which pay an annual tax of $2.50—the economists are wondering if radio on this side of the sea has reached an age where it can be called upon to pay its own way. They point to the fact that a property rental is generally paid for billboards erected along the highways or signs painted on barns. Why, then, they ask, should not Uncle Sam collect an annual toll on each wave length? Another argument, frequently expounded, is that circulars going through the mail add to the government's revenue by carrying a postage stamp, but an hour radio program is criss-crossed through space without Uncle Sam deriving any revenue, although he controls the channels. A ship passing through a canal usually pays a toll, but a broadcast flashes across the entire continent without paying "a continental."

All of these factors have caused the economists to scratch their heads and turn toward radio as a source of income.

Selected Prices

Broiler Pan	$0.75
Camera, Kodak Bantam	$22.50
China Cabinet	$32.50
Cocktail Glasses, Set of Seven	$0.79
Flatware, Service for Six	$29.75
Garden Tractor	$242.00
Hamburger, Half-pound	$0.12
Hotel Room, New York Commodore	$4.00
Radio	$49.50
Refrigerator	$169.50
Sofa and Chair	$66.85
Typewriter	$54.50

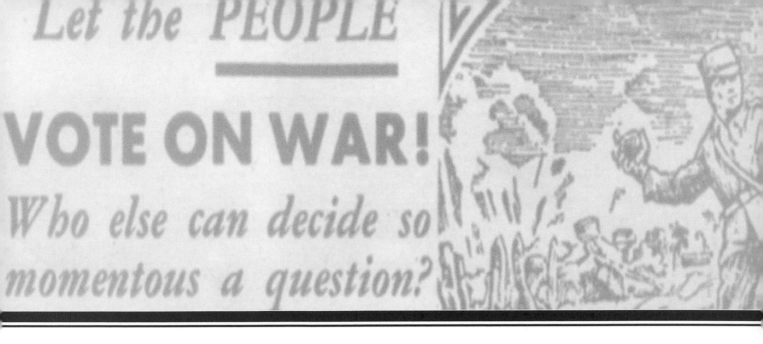

Let the PEOPLE

VOTE ON WAR!

Who else can decide so momentous a question?

1937 PROFILE
FIGHTING FOR PEACE

Civilian

Adele Morrison has found new freedom and excitement by joining with other students at the Colby Junior College for Women in fighting for peace through the Emergency Peace Campaign.

Adele Morrison is an advocate for peace.

Life at Home

- Adele Morrison was crushed when her mother told her—very firmly—that she would be attending Colby Junior College for Women and not the University of New Hampshire as she had planned.
- She knew that her mother's talk about "a more stable environment" was code for little social life and no boys.
- When she appealed to her father, he deferred; he was late for a business meeting.
- Where his children are concerned, he is content with his role as provider, generally agreeing with his wife's decisions.
- Occasionally—but only occasionally—he takes a stand and demonstrates he is the real seat of power in the house.
- This was not to be one of those times.
- Jack Morrison had worked hard to rise from being a car mechanic to owning one of the largest car dealerships in Manchester, New Hampshire.
- He liked to describe himself as the embodiment of the American dream.
- After all, he had achieved his life goals: a brick, two-story home, a new car every three years, and all his children with college degrees—especially the three boys.
- And now that he is able to be active in the Optimist Club and donate regularly to the church, the rumors concerning his involvement with liquor bootlegging from nearby Canada during Prohibition are dying down.

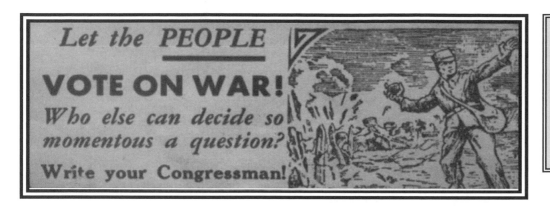

Let the PEOPLE
VOTE ON WAR!
Who else can decide so momentous a question?
Write your Congressman!

Guns will make us powerful; butter will only make us fat.
—Hermann Goering, 1936 radio address

Life at Work

- Adele Morrison dissolved into tears watching her parents drive away from Colby Junior College for Women that first day.
- It was bad enough that her three brothers and all her friends got to attend the University of New Hampshire, but Colby was located in New London, close to nothing but cows.
- Even when classes were under way, Adele felt miserable, spending considerable time composing desperate, tear-stained letters to her friends at the University.
- Her roommate is a quiet, deeply religious girl from near Boston named Evelyn, who frequently asks Adele to participate in activities of the "Commission."
- Adele had heard that the group was involved with the peace movement, but didn't care; she wanted out of Colby, and although war was bad, it wasn't her problem.
- The closest Adele had come to politics was hearing her parents discuss the chances that Franklin Roosevelt will be defeated by a good Republican before he names himself dictator.
- For years, she has heard that the president is a dangerous man, destined to give away America's wealth—and eventually its freedom.
- She also knew from listening to her father that most peace activists were at least leftists, if not outright communists.
- Yet, it was equally obvious that the Commission was one of the most active groups on campus.
- When Adele accompanied Evelyn to her first discussion group gathering of the Commission, she realized it was populated by girls considered to be campus leaders.
- The meeting turned out to be primarily a strategy session for the student mass meeting planned for November 11, Armistice Day.
- The goal was for students to speak about peace to various groups of townspeople.
- The Commission, as it turns out, is one of more than 150 campus units of the Emergency Peace Campaign.
- The campaign got its start in late 1935 after the American Friends Service Committee attracted the involvement of a number of prominent Americans, including First Lady Eleanor Roosevelt and Admiral Byrd, the polar explorer.

WHAT
ARE YOU GOING TO DO ABOUT IT?

THE CASE FOR CONSTRUCTIVE PEACE

BY ALDOUS HUXLEY
PRICE THREEPENCE

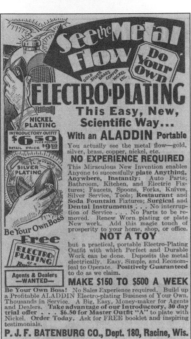

- Conceived as a two-year program, its goal is to assure United States neutrality in the event of another European war.
- The American Service Committee preaches that the use of American armed forces should be restricted to defending U.S. territory.
- Its opposition to war is mixed with a heavy dose of isolationism and a strong anti-communist outlook.
- The Emergency Peace Campaign's primary, short-term goal is educating Americans on the horrors of war; its long-range plan is a grass roots foundation that can impact national policy.
- The passion of the speakers immediately captured Adele's attention.
  - Even her roommate Evelyn seemed to shed her shyness when she spoke to the gathering of her unflinching fervor for peace through the work of the Commission.
  - Back in their dorm room, Evelyn shared with Adele some tracts filled with figures and pictures on the horrors of the Great War and the revolution under way in Spain.
  - Over the next several days, Adele read everything available on war and peace.
  - A couple of student leaders are mentoring Adele, taking her on walks to extol the importance of their work.
  - Adele is now convinced that working with the Commission is the most important thing she can do; if she can help shape a little community's attitude about peace, anything is possible in the wider world.
  - She is so convinced of her mission, Adele is no longer concerned what her parents might think.
  - Besides, once her mother learned that girls from nice families were talking about peace, all would be fine.
  - Adele quickly became active in speaking at local town meetings.
  - Never shy about speaking in public, Adele is on fire now that she has something important to say.
  - Almost the entire student body of 300 girls showed up at the main building on Armistice Day.
  - Adele felt wonderful when her speech received enthusiastic applause.

- Next, the Colby Commission held a joint meeting with the Dartmouth Commission to develop plans to reach much of western New Hampshire.
- Several of the Dartmouth boys, whom Adele had been dying to meet months ago, asked her out.
- Surprising even herself, she decided she did not have time to socialize; boys would have to wait.
- Her room is adorned with pictures of women peace activists such as Eleanor Roosevelt and Jane Addams.
- She is still not exactly sure why she took them down when her father and mother came to visit.
- Maybe it was because she told her mother that day she was not coming home for the summer, but would instead be teaching vacation school through the Commission in a town near the college.
- To further the peace effort, the summer school combines fun and discussions of world affairs.
- Five days a week, the teachers assemble their charges, averaging 75 each day, at the town meeting hall, where they entertain the students with traditional activities such as crafts, games and music.
- Adele is even trying her hand at the piano after years of being out of practice.
- The key element of the program is the importance of world peace, imparted through discussions, plays, dances, movies and study projects, some of which come from the national office, while others are being developed by Adele and her fellow teachers.
- As the summer draws to a close, Adele is delighted by their work.
- During an exhibition for the town, her students showed their handiwork, sang songs and performed skits—many on the subject of peace.
- The reception among students and townspeople alike was overwhelmingly enthusiastic; even members of the local American Legion Post applauded with gusto.

Life in the Community: New London, New Hampshire

- New London, 1,300 feet up in the Sunapee hills of New Hampshire, boasts 1,000 residents, including the 300 women of Colby College.
- The community is 100 miles from Boston, 40 miles from Concord, and eight miles from the railroad.
- New London is clustered along both sides of an elm-shaded main street and includes a white-spire church, a brick town hall, an inn, which once served stagecoach travelers, and a war memorial.
- Except for the growth at the college, New London has changed little in three generations.

The Only Way We Can Save Her

"STAY OUT! STAY OUT FOR MY SAKE, AS WELL AS YOUR OWN!"

WAR MAD EUROPE

DEMOCRACY

AMERICA, THE LAST REFUGE OF DEMOCRACY

Peace advocates believe America will be harmed by war, an angry Europe and leaders like Joseph Stalin.

"Who Wants Peace?" Dorothy Thompson, Survey Graphic, February 1937:

More than any other movement in the United States, that represented by the peace societies is a cross-section of the American mind. At some point it touches all of American liberal opinion, some of the conservative, and much of the radical. For it starts with a premise that few dispute: Peace is the desideratum of all political activity; the condition of freedom, the necessity of sound prosperity, the parent of culture, the demand of orderly social progress.

On the side of peace, therefore, are not only those who hate uniforms and militarism as a primary cause of war, but those who think that peace depends upon international armament against aggressors; for peace, are those who believe that there will be wars until national sovereignties are eliminated in a socialistically organized world, and those who think war will end when every nation has equality. On the side of peace are those who believe wars can be quarantined, and those who think that neutrality is immoral. The result is usually coupled in the mind of its advocate with something else: "Peace and Freedom, against War and Fascism."

- Garages for automobiles exist alongside a large and busy livery stable.
- A chain store is located in New London, but part of it remains dominated by yard goods, house dresses and notions.
- Residents pride themselves on the number of out-of-town papers read in the city and how hard the radio is worked for information.
- The Emergency Peace Campaign became part of the fabric of community discussion in 1936.
  - In late 1935, the American Friends Service Committee and other pacifists such as Devere Allen, Frederick J. Libby, Ray Newton, John Nevin Sayre and E. Raymond Wilson initiated the Emergency Peace Campaign, a nationwide program to keep the United States out of war and to promote world peace.
  - Its focus included a desire to promote world peace through strengthening pacifist alternatives to armed conflict, bringing about political and economic changes as essential to a just and peaceable world order, and recruiting in one dynamic movement all organizations determined not to approve of or participate in war.

Historical Snapshot
1937

- Scottsboro defendant Clarence Norris was sentenced to death for the third time on a charge of rape
- As the depression continued, unemployment reached 14.3 percent
- Howard Hughes flew from Los Angeles to Newark in a record seven hours, 28 minutes and five seconds
- The crash of the dirigible *Hindenburg*, witnessed by hundreds who had come to see its landing at Lakehurst, New Jersey, killed 38 people
- Spam was introduced by George A. Hormel & Company
- President Franklin D. Roosevelt called for an investigation of "immoral" tax evasion by the wealthy
- The principle of a minimum wage for women was upheld by the United States Supreme Court
- General Motors introduced the automatic transmission for automobiles
- Radio quiz shows grew in popularity, including "Melody Puzzles," "Professor Quiz," "Spelling Bee" and "Uncle Jim's Question Bee"
- "Nice Work if You Can Get It," "Whistle While You Work" and "The Lady Is a Tramp" were all popular songs
- Nylon, Santa Claus school, the trampoline, Pepperidge Farm and the Lincoln Tunnel all made their first appearance
- Several thousand Americans, including authors Dorothy Parker, John Dos Passos, Ernest Hemingway, Malcolm Cowley and Upton Sinclair, joined the Abraham Lincoln Brigade to fight with the Loyalists against fascist-supported Franco forces
- Spinach growers erected a statue to Popeye in Wisconsin
- John D. Rockefeller died, leaving an estate of approximately $1 billion
- *Popular Photography* magazine began publication
- After 70 years of failure, the first successful instant coffee was formulated by the Nestlé Company
- A *Harper's Monthly* article concluded that today's young people behaved "without thought of social responsibility"
- Numerous federal parks and fish and game sanctuaries were set up by the National Park Service, which set aside some 600,000 acres
- A revolt against progressive education was under way, led by Robert M. Hutchins, president of the University of Chicago
- Pro-Nazi Bund societies were forming in Germany, ostensibly devoted to social and athletic pursuits
- Studies showed that people were spending 4.5 hours daily listening to the radio
- A *Fortune* magazine story reported, "As for sex...the campus takes it more casually than it did 10 years ago. . . . It is news that it is no longer news"
- *Life* magazine reported that one out of 10 Americans had a tattoo
- Icemen made regular deliveries to more than 50 percent of middle-class households

1938 News Feature

"I was in the Gastonia (N.C.) Strike (of 1929)," by Bertha Hendrix, an excerpt from a *Southern Summer School* autobiography, 1938:

I had been working for the Manville-Jenkes mill in Loray, near Gastonia, for eight years—ever since I was 14. We worked 13 hours a day, and we were so stretched out that lots of times we didn't stop for anything. Sometimes we took sandwiches to work, and ate them as we worked. Sometimes we didn't even get to eat them. If we couldn't keep our work up like they wanted us to, they would curse us and threaten to fire us. Some of us made $12 a week, and some a little more.

One day some textile organizers came to Gastonia. They came to the mill gates at six o'clock, just when the daylight hands were coming out. They began to talk to the workers as they came out of the mill. Everyone stopped to listen. When the night-shift hands came up, they stopped to listen, too. I was on the night shift. None of us went into work that night, for the organizers were telling us that they would help us to get more money and [fewer hours] if we would stick together in a union, and stay out.

National Guardsmen control the strikers.

This was the first time I'd ever thought that things could be better; I thought that I would just keep working all my life for 13 hours a day, like we were. I felt that if we would stick together and strike, we could win something for ourselves. But I guess we didn't have a chance—the way "the law" acted after we struck.

That night we had a meeting, and almost all the workers came. People got up and said unless they got shorter hours and more money, they would never go back to work. We all went home that night feeling that at last we were going to do something that would make things better for us workers. We were going to win an eight-hour day, and get more pay for ourselves.

The next morning, we were at the mill at five o'clock, to picket, but we couldn't get anywhere near the plant, because the police and the National Guard were all around the mill and kept us blocked away. We formed our picket line anyway, and walked up and down a street near the mill.

Every day for a week we picketed. One day my husband, Red, went with me to the picket line. (He worked in another mill on the night shift.) Just as we started on the picket line, two policemen came over and grabbed Red, put him in an automobile, and took him to jail. They beat him with a blackjack, and broke his ring and tore his clothes. They thought he was one of the strikers; they were arresting strikers right and left, hauling lots of them to jail every day.

In the second week of the strike, the bosses went to other towns and out in the country and brought in scabs. The police and the National Guard made us keep away from the mill, so all we could do was to watch the scabs go in and take our jobs.

We kept on with our picket line, though we didn't have much of a chance to persuade the scabs not to go in, because of the police and guards. We were treated like dogs by the law. Strikers were knocked down when they called to the scabs, or got too near the mill. Every day more and more strikers were arrested. They kept the jailhouse full of workers. Strikers were put out of their houses. All over our village you could see whole families with their household belongings in the street—sometimes in the pouring down rain, and lots of them with little children and babies.

We had a relief station where strikers could get food and groceries. Red, my husband, had been fired from his job in the other mill when his boss found out that he was trying to help us strikers, so he opened a drink stand near the relief station. One night about nine o'clock, the police came to the relief station, as they usually went anywhere there were any strikers. I don't know what happened exactly, but there was a gun fight, and the chief of police was killed. Red, who was selling drinks there, was arrested along with a lot of others. Red and six others were accused of killing the policeman.

After Red was put in jail for the murder, my father and I moved to another town. I was expecting a baby soon, but I went to work in another textile plant. Except for what I read in the papers, I didn't know much about what was going on in Gastonia.

Several months after the strike, they tried Red and the six others accused of killing the chief of police. They had been kept in jail all this time. I couldn't attend much of the trial on account of the baby, but Red told me about it.

Almost everybody thinks the workers were innocent, and many people believe that the chief was killed by one of his own policemen. However, Red and the others were convicted of the murder, and given anywhere from five to 20 years in the penitentiary. Red and the others got out on bail, and all of them left the country and stayed away for two years. Then Red came back to get me and the baby and he was caught, and sent to prison. He served three years and four months of his prison term, and got out last year.

After the trial, I moved to High Point, and got a job in a textile mill to support the baby and me. We have had a hard time of it, but I think what we went through in Gastonia was worth it all, because I think people all over the country learned about the conditions of textile workers in the South, and it helped the labor movement in the South.

1940–1949

The dramatic, all-encompassing nature of World War II dominated the lives of all Americans as men went to war, women went to factories and shortages of nearly every consumer commodity became a reality. America's role in the world rapidly shifted from that of passive observer to fierce warrior following the bombing of Pearl Harbor in December 1941. Almost immediately, women were thrust into highly visible leadership roles in their communities, positions that were unthinkable only a few years before. Colleges became more welcoming to women, factories were dominated by trouser-wearing females and society began to open its eyes wider to the full potential of women.

People from every social stratum either signed up for the military or went to work supplying the military machine. Even children, eager to do their share, collected scrap metal and helped plant the victory gardens that symbolized America's willingness to do anything to defeat the "bullies." In addition, large amounts of money and food were sent abroad as Americans observed meatless Tuesdays, gas rationing and other shortages to help the starving children of Europe.

Business worked in partnership with government; strikes were reduced, but key New Deal labor concessions were expanded, including a 40-hour week and time and a half for overtime. As manufacturing demands increased, the labor pool shrank, and wages and union membership rose. Unemployment, which stood as high as 14 percent in 1940, all but disappeared. By 1944, the U.S. was producing twice the total war output of the Axis powers combined. The wartime demand for production workers rose more rapidly than for skilled workers, reducing the wage gap between the two to the lowest level in the twentieth century.

From 1940 to 1945, the gross national product more than doubled, from $100 billion to $211 billion, despite rationing and the unavailability of many consumer goods such as cars, gasoline, and washing machines. Interest rates remained low, and the upward pressure on prices remained high, yet from 1943 to the end of the war, the cost of living rose less than 1.5 percent. Following the war, as controls were removed, inflation peaked in 1948; union demands for high wages accelerated. Between 1945 and 1952, confident Americans—and their growing families—increased consumer credit by 800 percent.

To fight inflation, government agencies regulated wages, prices, and the kind of jobs people could take. The Office of Price Administration was entrusted with the complicated task of setting price ceilings for almost all consumer goods and distributing ration books for items in short supply. The Selective Service and the War Manpower Commission largely determined who would serve in the military, whose work was vital to the war effort, and when a worker could transfer from one job to another. When the war ended and regulations were lifted, workers demanded higher wages; the relations between labor and management became strained. Massive strikes and inflation followed in the closing days of the decade and many consumer goods were easier to find on the black market than on the store shelves until America retooled for a peacetime economy.

The decade of the 1940s made America a world power and Americans more worldly. Millions served overseas; millions more listened to broadcasts concerning the war in London, Rome, and Tokyo. Newsreels brought the war home to moviegoers, who numbered in the millions. The war effort also redistributed the population and the demand for labor; the Pacific Coast gained wealth and power, and the South was able to supply its people with much-needed war jobs and provide blacks with opportunities previously closed to them. Women entered the work force in unprecedented numbers, reaching 18 million. The net cash income of the American farmer soared 400 percent.

But the Second World War extracted a price. Those who experienced combat entered a nightmarish world. Both sides possessed far greater firepower than ever before, and within those units actually fighting the enemy, the incidence of death was high, sometimes one in three. In all, the United States lost 405,000 men and women to combat deaths; many suffered in the war's final year, when the American army spearheaded the assault against Germany and Japan. The cost in dollars was $350 billion. But the cost was not only in American lives. Following Germany's unconditional surrender on May 4, 1945, Japan continued fighting. To prevent the loss of thousands of American lives defeating the Japanese, President Truman dropped atomic bombs on the Japanese cities of Hiroshima and Nagasaki, ending the war and ushering in the threat of "the bomb" as a key element of the Cold War during the 1950s and 1960s.

Throughout the war, soldiers from all corners of the nation fought side by side and refined nationalism and what it meant to America through this government-imposed mixing process. This newfound identity of American GIs was further cemented by the vivid descriptions of war correspondent Ernie Pyle, who spent a considerable time talking and living with the average soldier to present a "worm's eye view" of war. Yet, despite the closeness many men and women developed toward their fellow soldiers, spawning a wider view of the world, discrimination continued. African-American servicemen were excluded from the marines, the Coast Guard, and the Army Corps. The regular army accepted blacks into the military—700,000 in all—only on a segregated basis. Only in the closing years of the decade would President Harry Truman lead the way toward a more integrated America by integrating the military.

Sports attendance in the 1940s soared beyond the record levels of the 1920s; in football the T-formation moved in prominence; Joe DiMaggio, Ted Williams, and Stan Musial dominated baseball before and after the war, and Jackie Robinson became the first black in organized baseball. In 1946, Dr. Benjamin Spock's work, *Common Sense Baby and Child Care*, was published to guide newcomers in the booming business of raising babies. The decade also discovered the joys of fully air-conditioned stores for the first time, cellophane wrap, Morton salt, daylight-saving time, Dannon yogurt, Everglades National Park, the Cannes Film Festival, Michelin radial tires, Dial soap, and Nikon 35mm film.

1942 Profile

Twenty-seven-year-old April Holiday has moved to Huntsville, Alabama, to help the war effort and support herself making ammunition after her husband left their 49-acre Tennessee farm to fight against the Germans and the Japanese. Her annual salary is $792.00.

Life at Home

- Born in Lincoln, Tennessee, April Holiday was named for the month she was conceived by her newly married parents in a honeymoon suite in Memphis.
- Her parents, both 14 at the time, had run away to get married against the advice of nearly everyone.
- Shy and beautiful, April always thought her name was special and grew up believing she was destined to do great things.
- After her father ran off with a neighbor woman, April dropped out of school in the sixth grade, even though she was the best reader in her class.
- April really didn't like the book work of school much, anyway, but she loved being with her friends and talking about who liked whom.
- She also loved listening to country music on the radio, drinking lemonade, but most of all, dancing, which was strictly prohibited in her mother's house unless you were alone.
- When April married at 16, she and Hal Holiday just knew that their love was greater than that of all the couples mentioned in the Bible and even Shakespeare.
- Since then they have struggled for nearly 11 years to make a financial success of their 49-acre farm, struggled to have a baby and struggled to get along.

April Holiday joined the war effort.

> "I am interested in carrying on here while the boys do the fighting over there. It is not a question with me as to what I do, nor how hard I work. The harder I work for them here, the sooner they will come home."
>
> —Marie Owens, a 31-year-old employee of Huntsville Arsenal whose husband was in the army

- Most of their spending money comes from an illegal still Hal and his daddy run; the consumption of the white lightning they make is also the source of many of the couple's arguments.
- Like thousands of men across the South, Hal volunteered for the war immediately after the Japanese attack on Pearl Harbor; he was ready to fight and eager to be out of Tennessee.
- Before he left for training camp 60 days later, Hal spent hours talking about what he planned to do personally to the first Jap or German he met; it helped keep his courage up.
- After Hal's military bus pulled out in February 1942, leaving nothing but dust in its wake, April knew she was really alone and on her own—maybe forever.
- Hal left behind a failed tobacco crop, an aging mule, two plows and lots of farm debts.
- Winter had arrived in Tennessee, and their three-room, shotgun-style house on the edge of the farm needed a new roof.
- April knew one thing: if she was going to survive, she had to work, and working in the dress factory for a dollar a day wasn't going to cut it.
- All she needed was an opportunity that did not resemble the swaying back end of a plowing mule or a noisy spinning machine.
- She read a story in the local newspaper about a new ammunitions plant hiring workers in Huntsville, Alabama.
- At the same time, U.S. Secretary of War Henry L. Stimson announced plans to double the number of women hired in war jobs.
- April packed up and caught a bus to Alabama three days later; the farm could wait—opportunity was knocking.

> I remember when I came to work here last April. I wanted to win the war, naturally. Who didn't? . . . I thought of it in kind of an abstract way. Something that had to be done, but mostly by the boys at the front. You see, I hadn't learned then about the battles of production and assembly lines as I have now. I hadn't learned of the vital necessity of every able-bodied person doing their share no matter how small, and working! working! working! . . .
>
> And when . . . [my husband] and my brother and my cousins and all the other boys come back home, I want to be able to look them in the eye with a clear conscience and say, "I did all I could."
>
> —Eugenia Holman, a Redstone Woman Ordnance Worker (or WOW) published in the *Redstone Eagle Post*, May 1943

- At the last minute, her unmarried younger sister Amanda climbed aboard the bus; she, too, was ready for adventure and a steady paycheck.
- According to the newspaper, the ordnance installation in Alabama was looking for minor engineering aids, positions that involved testing and inspecting various metallic materials, mechanical parts, castings, assemblies and components for ordnance materials.
- On the bus they discussed what an ordnance factory actually makes, then laughed about their big adventure.
- They weren't entirely sure, but the newspaper story clearly said plant workers were to be paid good wages in line with their particular jobs.
- April was pleased that her sister was going to be a part of her life in Alabama.
- April and Amanda filled out the applications, got hired and found an apartment in the upper room of a retired church secretary's home—all within a week.
- Although reluctant to hire women at first, by the time the sisters applied, arsenal officials had discovered that jobs such as tool-crib operators, inspectors, clerks, forklift operators, guards, truck drivers, checkers and press operators could be performed satisfactorily by female employees.

Life at Work

- Before coming to Huntsville Arsenal, April Holiday had only worked at a dress plant in Tennessee, where she earned one dollar for 11 hours' work each day, out of which she paid $0.25 daily for a ride to work.
- The army is paying female production line employees $3.60 a day, though it is lower than the men's pay of $4.40 a day.
- The army pays even higher wages for certain jobs deemed more hazardous, such as the production of deadly mustard gas.
- The men who work in mustard gas production are paid $5.76 a day, while women workers are paid $4.40 a day.
- April had no plans to work there, even at higher pay.
- The eyes and skin of the people employed in that area, April noticed, appeared yellow, and often, the workers looked "just as pitiful as could be."
- Another place to avoid, April learned quickly, was the section that makes colored smoke grenades which are dyed different colors—yellow, purple and green.
- Townspeople in Huntsville not affiliated with the arsenal make fun of the workers and do not understand why they would come to town with such odd shades of hair and skin.
- For security purposes, all workers have to wear different-colored badges to identify the area of the arsenal in which they work.
- Workers are often asked to stay only in their area and not wander through the plant, no matter how curious they might be.
- When April and Amanda began making ammunition, they were put on the production lines with minimal training, since most tasks had to be learned on the job.
- Because of the nation's demand for soldiers, many of the workers on the lines at Huntsville Arsenal are women, most of whom wear trousers to work.
- With her first paycheck, April paid her rent, and with her second, she bought work trousers.
- Even on the farm, April wore dresses most days, since pants seemed so improper.
- She loved the change and felt deliciously naughty, though she did not tell Hal in her weekly letters about her change in dress or about the men she met at the factory.

Across America, women have been hired to meet the production goals demanded by the war.

The few men assigned to the factory attract considerable attention during work breaks.

- The few male workers and assigned military men working in the factory attract considerable attention, especially during work breaks.
- Now that April was part of the Chemical Warfare Service in Huntsville, she understood that her motivation was both economic and patriotic.
- She liked to say publicly, "With all the boys going into the service and fighting for me, surely I can support the war by providing ammunition," but privately she loved making money that was all hers to keep or spend, and thoroughly enjoyed her financial independence.
- She and Amanda were even helping their landlord prepare a victory garden on the vacant lot near their home.
- The plan was to be able to grow enough food to help in the war effort, which was everyone's business.
- Within six weeks of becoming employed at Huntsville Arsenal, both April and Amanda were involved in one of the installation's worst industrial accidents.
- On the day of the accident, the two were assigned to work in Warehouse 642, where Huntsville Arsenal's first production pilot line for the four-pound M-54 thermate incendiary bomb is located.
- The Huntsville Arsenal is well known for its vast production of gel-type incendiaries.
- That day, April was assigned a position on the filling machine in the middle of the long warehouse, temporarily replacing the woman who usually worked there.
- Amanda was working on a mixing machine at one end of the building.
- At 11:50 a.m., April heard a loud explosion.
- She looked up from her work, saw a blaze, and jumped from her stool to run.
- She fell down, but was able to regain her feet and run out of the burning building.
- By the time she reached the exit, she was on fire, but was caught by some men who extinguished the flames.
- About 30 other people also suffered burns from the accident.
- Because of the severity of her injuries, April was taken to Huntsville Hospital, where she remained for seven months.
- The army paid all the expenses associated with her stay.
- Warehouse 642 was completely destroyed by the fire spawned by the explosion.
- Her sister was the only fatality.
- Because of the highly sensitive and secret nature of the work being done at Huntsville Arsenal, no public reports of the explosion and massive fire were made.
- Security awareness is highly emphasized at every turn.

- Signs throughout the arsenal read: "What you see and what you hear, when you leave, leave it here."
- After the explosion, the manufacture of the M-54 bomb at Huntsville Arsenal was halted.
- When April returned to work after her long convalescence, she was no longer assigned to the factory floor, but was asked to work in personnel doing timekeeping.
- Most mornings, April is still very tense about going to work, and sensitive about her burns.
- The scars on her leg and back may always be visible, she fears.
- She is especially nervous on rainy days because the "goop" or gel-type incendiary chemical is more prone to ignite in that kind of weather.
- Even though she writes Hal every week, she has not heard from him in months; she does not even know if he realizes she was injured and that her sister is dead.

A woman was placed on the job here, another there, until it was no unusual thing to see shifts on the fill-and-press lines consisting of about 50 percent women. They did their jobs well, and kept up their end of the work so that the remaining men were often hard put to it in order to keep up with them.

Then, one of the shift supervisors had the idea to form an all-girl line as an experiment. The experiment worked and today, the 10-girl crew in the fill-and-press building . . . is breaking all production records . . .

These girls are all handling a man's job. Every one of them believes she has a personal stake in this war. Their morale is about the highest at the arsenal. They are expert press operators, ball table operators, and they handle these 124-pound to 150-pound pallets with the ease and efficiency of old-timers. . . . Each one of them is capable of substituting for the other in case of need....This spirit of knowing their assigned job well, and the job of the girl working next to them, has made every one of them valuable operators.

—Newspaper reports on the "Modern Amazons," Huntsville Arsenal, August 1945

Life in the Community: Huntsville, Alabama

- When the federal government announced that an ammunitions factory was to be built in Huntsville, Alabama, in 1941, the city's fire trucks raced through the town delivering an "Extra" edition of the local newspaper.
- Everyone knew that the construction of a $40 million war plant would transform life in this quiet town in northern Alabama.
- Within a month, the army's Chemical Warfare Service broke ground on the new chemical munitions manufacturing and storage facility named Huntsville Arsenal.
- In anticipation of war, the arsenal was designed to supplement the production of the army's only other chemical manufacturing plant at Edgewood Arsenal, Maryland.
- Huntsville Arsenal is the sole manufacturer of colored smoke munitions.
- The facility is also noted for its vast production of gel-type incendiaries and toxic agents such as mustard gas, phosgene, lewisite, white phosphorous, and tear gas.

- The army's impact on Huntsville was immediate and profound.
- Hundreds of men poured into Huntsville seeking employment.
- Within a week of the army's site selection announcement, almost 1,200 men stormed the employment office to register.
- The army's initial need for civilian employees was limited to engineers and skilled office personnel.
- But the contractors selected to build the new plant also needed thousands of construction workers.
- At first, the local newspaper reported that, "Few women have registered, but approximately 200 of those placed on file . . . have been negroes."
- The transition has been complex.
- The local labor force available has primarily been trained in agriculture.

"What Women Can Do: Think War, Buy Little, Maintain Our Ideals," *Life*, September 28, 1942:

Up until now the big Jap has pushed everybody around. He has always been at the right spot with the right equipment at the right time, his skin painted the right color. The poor little white men, with wrong plans for using the wrong things in the wrong places (at Singapore even the guns were pointed in the wrong direction) have scurried piteously through the jungles, swatting mosquitoes, leaping hungry crocodiles and ultimately getting shot or captured. But last week from the far Pacific came a different story. Shortly after the U.S. Marines had taken the airfield at Guadalcanal Island in the Solomons, the Japs landed a force of 750 men at the mouth of the Tenaru River. The Marines closed in and there developed a nasty jungle battle, with the Japs lodged among the trees. Suddenly, out of the jungle there appeared the right thing at the right time—a line of American tanks deliberately heading into the coconut grove where the Japs were concentrated. The Marines let out a roar. As the correspondent described it, "The whole American side of the Tenaru front sounded like the bleachers at Ebbets Field when the Dodgers win." The tanks rushed up and down slaughtering Japs, whose rifle bullets pinged harmlessly against the heavy armor. When it was over, not a Jap remained.

What Can We Do?

The American people would like to fight that kind of war, too—a war of getting the right things to the right places on time. But they aren't doing it. The reason is that in order to fight a war like that, you have to think war. And a lot of people responsible for the war effort on the home front—in labor, in agriculture and chiefly in government—are not thinking war.

The problem is this: how can we get this country of 130 million people to act like and think like the Marines on Guadalcanal Island? And when you examine that proposition, you come to what is perhaps an unexpected answer. The ones on whom this chiefly falls are the women. Many women have written in to the news fronts recently asking what they can do to help win the war. This is our reply. If the women of America will take on this war as their own; if they will think war, thoroughly and relentlessly, then this country would begin to look like a real war machine. Then congressmen would not dare to play politics with their country's safety; bureaucrats would not dare to fail; and farm and labor leaders would not dare to advance their selfish interests first. Then we would begin to get the right things to the right places at the right time.

(continued)

(continued)

Women in Action

The simplest way for women, as for men, to think is to get into action. Hundreds of thousands have done so. The WAACs, WAVES and WAFS have accepted without flinching the hard routines of military life. Nurses have worked coolly under fire and in lifeboats on the open sea. Thousands of devoted women are discharging with precision, and without pay, the exacting requirements of the Aircraft Warning Service. There are war workers who, because their husbands have modest incomes, pour all their own earnings into war bonds. The schedules adopted by some women on the home front are almost unbelievable. Mrs. Mildred Feinberg of Portland, Ore., for instance, has three children. Besides looking after them, she helps her husband at his office. And in addition, she supervises the control room of the Aircraft Warning Service four nights a week from midnight to 6 a.m. Even the enemies of Mayor Edward J. Kelly of Chicago acknowledge the tremendous accomplishment of Mrs. Kelly in building up the huge Chicago Service Center canteen, which is entirely manned by volunteers and handles 80,000 servicemen a week. On the job from 8:30 to 6:00 every weekday, and from noon through midnight through the weekends, Mrs. Kelly sees every volunteer, receives about 2,600 separate donations a week, acknowledges every one with a personal letter.

The Frugal Life

Action has glamour, but it is not necessarily the most important contribution that women can make. Besides the visible jobs, there are invisible ones. And the most important of these is conservation. This is not limited to the salvaging of fats, tin cans, and the like, important though these may be. True conservation goes much further. Despite the fact that merchandisers who haven't yet learned to think war are shoving their goods at you, just remember that everything your family consumes retards the war effort. Labor has been required to make it, transport it, retail it. Your money, needed for taxes and war bonds, doesn't fight the Japs when you buy personal comforts. Every luxury you purchase gives Hitler a better chance. Every can you open taxes the war machine just a little more. Try to get the idea—true in wartime—that the resources and products of America are a common trust. This is especially true of your rubber tires, which cannot be replaced but which are essential to victory. But it's true also of anything you consume. The old American idea was abundance, and if we win, that will be our idea again. But the new American idea for winning is frugality. How much, within the limits of good health, can you do without? That's the test.

- The War Manpower Commission estimates that 95 percent of the potential workers are farmers with little factory experience.
- The few workers who have industrial labor experience come from a textile manufacturing background, a process very different from ordnance manufacturing.
- Some of the region's most talented workers migrated months ago to defense plants on the West Coast.
- The area also lacks a sufficient number of local secretarial and clerical personnel. In addition, the army is able to compete in a free market against the higher wages being paid by the contractors for certain types of jobs.
- For workers and employers alike, the transition to boom war economy in Huntsville is hampered by the inadequacy of inexpensive local housing and poor secondary roads.

Black female job applicants have been told to be patient.

- The emphasis at Huntsville Arsenal is for male help of both races to do the heavy work, while white females are employed for production line work.
- The large number of black females in the area have been told to be patient when seeking employment, and that they will be contacted when the market of white females has been exhausted.
- According to government officials, the lack of "toilet facilities to take care of race distinctions peculiar to the South" is the reason given for this decision.
- Approximately 70 percent of all black women are employed as maids, with a high percentage of the rest working on family farms.
- The biggest recruitment problems faced by the Chemical Warfare Service are the scarcity of qualified people with a background in chemistry and the unavailability of competent supervisory personnel.
- To obtain employees with the necessary chemical production background, the Chemical Warfare Service has looked to technical schools and colleges throughout the Southeast.
- The University of Alabama and Auburn University are both offering courses needed by the employees of Huntsville.
- Conducted two nights a week for 12 weeks, these tuition-free "defense training courses" instruct men and women in such fields as basic accounting, structural design, mechanical and electrical maintenance, industrial management, chemistry, and engineering drawing.
- The University of Alabama offers a course in chemical laboratory techniques "for women only, who desire to qualify for jobs in defense laboratories."
- Local women are being urged to take advantage of the available technical training to prepare themselves to replace men who currently hold many of the more technically-oriented and high-skilled jobs.
- Not only would women be helping themselves financially, but also, they are frequently reminded, they would be performing a patriotic service.
- To keep up the morale of all their workers, army officials sponsor special after-hours social events such as picnics, barbecues, dinners and dances.
- Special awards ceremonies are held so that employees can be a part of the recognition given to the production successes, and organized sports teams for men and women have been created.
- They include activities such as softball, basketball, tennis and bowling, each designed "to promote physical fitness and [provide a] diversion from strenuous duties."
- Even so, female absenteeism is high.
- Official reports disclose that the pressures of work, the strain of trying to keep up with family obligations, the stress of worrying about loved ones fighting in the war or being held prisoner behind enemy lines, the lack of adequate rest and nutrition, and ill health have all contributed to higher levels of absenteeism among women workers.
- But that does not prevent them from being chastised for failing to display an adequate amount of patriotic fervor.
- Huntsville Arsenal has also hired a registered nurse to deal with problems hampering the productivity of individual employees.
- She even travels to the homes of absent workers to determine if the illness keeping employees off the job is being treated properly.

HISTORICAL SNAPSHOT
1942

- The Nobel Prize celebrations, discontinued in Stockholm since 1939 because of the war, resumed in New York City
- A Japanese submarine fired 25 shells at an oil refinery near Santa Barbara, California, the first attack on the American mainland
- The U.S. Post Office in New York hired more than 900 translators to censor mail going to foreign countries
- The lights in New York's Times Square and several leading hotels were blacked out so ships at sea could not be seen by German U-boats
- Daylight Saving Time, nylon parachutes, blackout drills, zinc-coated pennies, Paine Webber, Dannon yogurt and Kellogg's Raisin Bran all made their first appearance
- Forty percent of all vegetables consumed in the United States were grown in small, local victory gardens
- The movie *Mrs. Miniver* won Academy Awards for best picture, best director for William Wyler, and best actress for Greer Garson
- Victory Book rallies were held nationwide; 600,000 books were donated to the armed services through a two-week-long New York City Public Library book drive
- RCA Victor sprayed gold on a recording of Glenn Miller's song "Chattanooga Choo Choo" after it sold one million copies, creating the first gold record
- The sales of women's trousers increased by 10 times after millions of women took their places in factories
- One billion pounds of plastic were produced for use in everything from airplanes to hose nozzles so that scarce metals could be spared for the war effort
- African-American leadership quickly and loudly protested ongoing racial discrimination in the military, especially the navy
- Popular songs included, "Praise the Lord and Pass the Ammunition," "Rosie, the Riveter," "A String of Pearls," and "This Is the Army, Mr. Jones"
- Los Angeles, California, alone contributed six tons of tires to the nationwide rubber drive
- Tubeless tires were successfully tested
- Hollywood produced 80 war movies
- Carole Lombard and 20 others died in a TWA transport crash while on a tour selling war bonds
- *Go Down, Moses* by William Faulkner, *The Just and the Unjust* by James Gould Cozzens, *The Moon Is Down* by John Steinbeck and *Storm over the Land* by Carl Sandburg were all published
- The first safe, self-sustaining nuclear reaction was achieved at the University of Chicago by Enrico Fermi, Edward Teller, and Leo Szilard
- Bell Aircraft tested a jet-propelled airplane

"Against that Day!" *The American Home,* January 1943:

Your government has created a War Damage Corporation and now, through the facilities of the fire insurance companies in the country and their representatives, you can obtain war damage insurance on your home and property for as little as $0.10 per $100 per year. This insurance is not obligatory, but your government wants you to know that it is available for you to purchase and urges you to do so for your own protection . . . .

Our entire country is vulnerable to enemy attack. It is entirely conceivable that, instead of, or in addition to, sending bombers to the coastal areas, the enemy might send planes into the Hudson Bay area by boat and from there fly them into the various industrial centers of the Middle West. The tactics of the enemy are not only to destroy defense plants, air fields and army concentrations, but to terrify the citizens and break down the morale of a country. Moreover, bombs do not always reach their objectives, but sometimes hit defenseless residential areas. Consequently, there is no part of the country that would be absolutely safe from enemy attack—not even the deep interior.

Selected Prices

Automobile, Pontiac Wagon	$1,340.00
Brassiere	$1.50
Coca-Cola	$0.25
Coffee Table	$75.00
Fur Coat, Beaver	$595.00
Haircut, Woman's	$2.00
Iron	$12.95
Mixer, Sunbeam	$23.75
Movie Ticket	$0.40
Seagram's Whiskey, Fifth	$2.70
Shotgun, Remington	$39.30
Tea Kettle, Copper	$3.49

"I always add an extra pinch of nitroglycerin."

MAEDCHEN IN OVERALLS

WORKING WOMEN OF WORLD WAR II

- America's war effort began in earnest in late 1939 as factories began tooling up to support its allies in Europe against German aggression.
- Prior to the Japanese attack on Pearl Harbor and America's declaration of war, women were rarely hired at defense plants.
- More than five million men, many unemployed for years during the Depression, were readily available.
- Many industrial executives believed and publicly said that women lacked the needed mechanical skills to work in factories.
- During the months just before the war, female employment actually fell because of the scarcity of materials.
- In Pennsylvania alone, 11,000 women in the silk mills and 16,000 in the hosiery mills lost employment as silk was diverted into war production.
- More than 30,000 workers in radio production and 41,000 workers in auto manufacturing lost their jobs for the same reason.
- After the thousands of men left their jobs to be in Uncle Sam's army, the Office of War Information declared, "Working is a woman's way in war time; America at war needs women at work."
- Prior to that time, nearly every major publication emphasized the necessity of women staying home and away from factory work, where they might deny a man the opportunity to support his family.
- After World War II began, women were told they had a special stake in victory.
- If the Nazis or the Japanese were successful in world conquest, American women would be enslaved.

- The government published stories saying that if the enemy conquered America, a woman's place in society would be restricted to "kinder, kuche, kirche, and knipe" (children, kitchen, church and the brothel).
- Women were urged to work if they wanted to "earn the feeling they were doing their full part to help speed the day of victory."
- In July 1941, the American Red Cross called upon "every woman and girl in Huntsville and Madison County who knits, crochets or sews..." to cooperate in meeting the deadline for completing the area's assigned quota of sewing.

You Can Help the War Effort

We are all in this together. We don't want anyone to feel the shortage of medical and nursing care unduly. When sickness strikes let's pool our skill and strength and good humor to minimize its effects

BY CONSERVING MEDICAL AND NURSING CARE!

- As a result, women across America sewed for the Red Cross and helped to wind the thousands of bandages desperately needed in the battle zones of Europe and the Pacific.
- They were also active participants in the civilian defense effort, forming "bicycle brigades" to conserve gasoline and rubber tires; volunteering to work at the local USO; buying and selling war bonds; leading drives to salvage scrap metal and rubber for armaments, and silk and nylon stockings for use in making powder bags; and conserving cooking grease for producing glycerin.
- Nationally, women promoted the Women's Victory Food Units, which was on the forefront of promoting such activities as victory gardening, nutrition and conservation.
- While some leaders urged women only to continue such traditional roles as knitting, buying bonds, stretching rationed foodstuffs, and keeping up the nation's morale, others on the home front challenged women to join the ever-growing ranks of America's "production soldiers."
- Uncertainty about the willingness and ability of American housewives to assume a larger defense role was being expressed nationally as well as locally.
- One labor analyst warned that, "The employment of millions of untrained workers, including old men, youths, and housewives, . . . [would] inevitably result in a material and gradual dilution of labor skills, which . . . [means] a decline in manpower output."
- The previously successful employment of women defense workers, according to this same analyst, was ". . . attributable to the fact that the more experienced and best adapted have naturally been the first employed. As . . . [the nation drew] more and more upon inexperienced and untrained homemakers, the average efficiency of women . . . [would] decline."
- Before the start of war, 85 percent of women who worked were employed in the nondurable goods industries such as textiles, apparel, leather, food and paper.
- After the war began, increasing numbers found higher wages and greater prestige making communications equipment, small arms ammunition, electrical equipment, iron and steel, automobiles, and scientific equipment.
- Women gained few opportunities in governmental policy making and were rarely offered positions in the war agencies.

1947 PROFILE
OCCUPIED JAPAN

Civilian

When Nora Steiner decided to put away her travel magazines and start visiting some of the places she'd read about, her life was opened to possibilities she had never even considered.

Life at Home

- Nora Steiner was at work in the spring of 1945 when she received the news that her brother Tom had been shot during a minor battle near the Elbe River.
- Her mother had called to tell her that he was taken to a field hospital with a chest wound, but did not make it.
- Two years later, Nora decided it was time to pursue her lifelong interest in travel—with or without her father's permission.
- Since she was a small girl growing up in Wildrose, North Dakota, she had dreamed of traveling the world.
- The money she earned from the eggs laid by her chickens paid for a subscription to *National Geographic Magazine* and travelogues by female writers.
- Upon taking a job as a clerk for the federal government in Bismark, she embarked on a saving campaign that would allow her to travel.
- Ready to make those countries on the map come alive, her first step was to investigate the availability of jobs overseas.
- Nora first considered positions associated with the occupation in Germany, but when word arrived of clerical jobs with the occupation forces in Japan, she couldn't contain her excitement.
- In an uncharacteristic display of emotion, she squealed out loud with delight when the letter arrived offering her a position.
- For her grand adventure, she packed carefully—including all of her travel books.
- For weeks she carefully constructed list after list of places she wanted to visit.
- And the trip—when it became reality—was better than the dream; her first train ride across the country was a thrill.
- The Rocky Mountains were taller than she had expected, San Francisco more charming and exciting, the ocean vastly larger than the books had said.

Nora Steiner is headed to occupied Japan.

Selected Prices

Baseball Glove, Horsehide	$3.00
Adding Machine	$120.00
Aftershave, Mennen Skin Bracer	$0.98
Board Game, Ouija	$1.59
Cereal, Nabisco Honey Grahams	$0.27
Chemise, Frederick's Gay Paree	$5.98
Chicks, Box of 100	$4.95
China, Wedgwood Woodstock, 20-Piece Starter Set	$75.60
Cycle Goggles	$3.49
Hairstyling	$6.50
Hatchet, Craftsman	$1.69
Lotion, Jergens	$1.00
Mirror, Full-length	$14.90
Television, Emerson, 10-Inch	$295.00
Vacuum Cleaner, General Electric	$39.95
Washer, Kenmore	$119.95

"The Reconversion of Douglas MacArthur," Martin Summers, Saturday Evening Post, May 25, 1946:

The Douglas MacArthur you are thinking about when you arrive here, the one you expect to find, is the relentless warrior who fought the Southwest Pacific war. You recall an unforgettable picture, MacArthur, on the shell-torn sands of bloody Los Negros, in the Admiralties, standing over the naked body of a Jap—one looking thoroughly dead, as only a Jap can look dead—and saying with satisfaction, "This is the way I like to see them."

But that is not the MacArthur you find here, not at all. You find a Douglas MacArthur who is, mirabile dictum, one of the most popular men in Japan, whose fan mail includes letters from intelligent (by Jap standards) Japanese women who want to have a son sired by him because they believe in some fashion this will fuse superior virtue into the Japanese people. You find a MacArthur who is working so hard at the systematic pacification of the Japanese people through constitutional government that his thoughts have turned away not only from killing and the art of war, but also from any presidential ambitions he may have had. You find a Douglas MacArthur who has come to take his job as overseer of 60 million obedient and peaceful people so seriously that he believes he may, through leading them in the creation of a sort of model democratic state without an army or navy, eventually point the way to world peace.

- After days of haunting the library and bookstores of San Francisco for literature on Japan, she felt prepared.
- On the date her ship arrived in Tokyo harbor, she stayed up all night, too excited to sleep.
- But even with all the reading, she was unprepared for postwar Tokyo, once the world's third-largest city.
- Nearly all of the wooden buildings in the city had been destroyed during the wartime bombing.
  - For miles in every direction, she found only a desert landscape, where once seven million people had lived.
  - Three million people were crammed into the buildings that survived the bombing and subsequent flames.

Life at Work
- Downtown Tokyo is filled with people from the Allied nations, especially Americans, and is the headquarters of the occupation forces, including 20,000 civilian War Department employees like Nora, one of 4,000 American women in clerical jobs.
- Japan has established a national government, but Gen. Douglas MacArthur, whose authority is absolute, exercises the real power.
- He is assisted by a large civilian staff.
- Since arriving, Nora has been assigned to the Surugadai Hotel, one of 10 downtown hotels where single women are housed.

BUY WAR BONDS

General Information for DEPENDENTS Coming to the TOKYO AREA

- The Surugadai is considered particularly desirable.
- Because of her newcomer status, she shares a large room with two other women of similar age—Midge Arndt, whose father manages a small fertilizer plant outside Spokane, Washington, and Celeste Amato, whose father is a stevedore in Bagonne, New Jersey.
- In addition, they have the services of room girls—young Japanese women who work as personal servants.
- Nora quickly learned that their room girl would wake her in the morning, tend to her clothes, clean the room, help her dress and even give massages.
- Nora's job requires that she work from 9 a.m. to 5 p.m. five days a week, similar to her stateside government job.
- All three roommates work in offices close to the hotel.
- Celeste is a typist/stenographer for the medical supply division in the Public Health and Welfare Section.
- A small, almost silent girl whose olive skin, large brown eyes and devout Catholicism advertise her Sicilian origins, she felt called by God to work in Japan.
- Even though her assigned job is largely clerical, Celeste envisions her efforts bringing healing drugs and supplies to the most destitute people of Japan.
- At 5 p.m., when others are heading home, Celeste catches a bus to the Our Lady of Lourdes Home in Yokohama, a Catholic orphanage specializing in occupation babies—children with Japanese mothers and occupation-force fathers, including Americans.
- These mixed-race children are often deserted by the fathers and rejected by the family and community of the mothers.
- Many of the babies are abandoned on the steps of the orphanage.
- The hardest lot, Celeste believes, falls to children with black fathers, since most Japanese consider blacks to be an inferior race.
- For several hours each evening and all day on Saturday, Celeste helps the nuns with the 130 babies in their care, taking time to feed them, change their diapers, play games and teach them to walk and talk.

- The half-black children are her special focus; she thinks they need her help most.
- Nora wonders whether Celeste secretly yearns to be a nun.
- Their other roommate, Midge, works for the government section responsible for transforming Japan into a self-governing democracy, including universal suffrage.
- Her actual goal is to meet men; work is simply a way to pass time between dates.

Nora has two roommates in Tokyo, a city heavily damaged by war bombing.

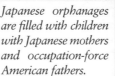

Japanese orphanages are filled with children with Japanese mothers and occupation-force American fathers.

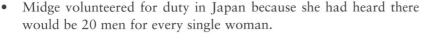

- Midge volunteered for duty in Japan because she had heard there would be 20 men for every single woman.
- A tall blonde with a full figure and vivacious personality, Midge does not need 20-to-1 odds to be popular; nearly every night is spent out partying at bars, restaurants and private homes.
- A current focus of her attention is a divorced, balding major with a pot belly and vast tracts of land in his native Virginia.
- She often remarks that she would have no contact with the Japanese people were it not for the servants who wait on her.
- The best thing about Midge, in Nora's opinion, is that she isn't in the room often.
- Nora's job is with the information division of the Civil Information and Education Section, the function of which is to improve the status of women in Japan.
- In America, Nora had never considered the status of women.
- The rigidity of Japan's patriarchal society is not only shocking, but is a mirror of her own life.
- Since she was five years old, she has known that—merely because of his gender—her older brother was her father's favorite.
- College was affordable for her brother, but not for her, and good grades were discouraged because "boys don't like girls that are too smart for their own good," her mother had whispered like a close friend.
- For the first time, she is angry that she accepted this underclass status without a fight.
- In Japan, many of the women around her are professionals—graduates of prestigious colleges—who are in charge and making decisions without having to ask for permission every time something needs to be done.

NAME

DATE | EARNINGS | DEDUCTIONS
$ | O. A. B. | FED. INC.

NO. OF HOURS | CLOCK NUMBER | NET AMOUNT $

EMPLOYER

Small
LOANS
◦ ◦ ◦

When you need money
ask about our

EASY-PAYMENT PERSONAL LOAN PLAN

No red tape. Small monthly pay-
ments adjusted to your income.

MEMBER FEDERAL DEPOSIT INSURANCE CORPORATION

The Wilber National Bank
245 Main Street
Oneonta, N. Y.

FORM 944—COPYRIGHTED 1939—CURTIS 1000 INC.

On weekends, Nora travels to Japanese landmarks and museums to understand the culture. She is also saving for college—a new dream.

- Nora finds herself eavesdropping on the conversations of these intelligent women, and has even asked their advice on reading lists and colleges to attend.
- Several times a week, mostly in the evenings, she attends Japanese-language colleges or lectures on Japanese art and culture.
- On weekends, she journeys to museums or nearby historical sites that have survived the war.
- She is growing to love the quiet beauty of Japan, and has invested in a Leica camera so she can capture the incredible world around her.
- During these trips, she takes every opportunity to practice her Japanese on natives, who are almost universally friendly and pleased that one of the "conquerors" is willing to learn their language—even while giggling politely behind their hands.
- Clearly, she has come to understand that the rural areas suffered less destruction than the cities did, but that economic hardship is everywhere.

- Her letters home, which include pictures she has taken, describe a nation struggling to rise from the ashes of absolute defeat.
- She does not mention her growing savings account, or her plans to attend college when she returns.

Life in the Community: Japan
- During the Second World War, over a third of Tokyo was devastated.

Under American occupation, Japan's caste system is being transformed.

- In Hiroshima and Nagasaki, almost a quarter of a million people lost their lives under the atom bombs; millions more were killed, maimed, or made homeless in the ruins.
- The bombing of the steel mills of Yawata, the shipyard of Kobe, and the aircraft factories of Yokohama resulted in the destruction of most of the country's major industries.
- In the "new" Japan, many small manufacturing plants—which were not targeted—are now up, running and competitive in the national economy.
- Like Americans, many Japanese citizens want to buy the goods that were unavailable during the war, allowing factories to switch smoothly from manufacturing planes to making aluminum kitchenware.
- With the dismantling of the social caste system, American officials believe a great leveling is under way which will completely destroy the power of the upper class who controlled Japan—and with that, the country's power to wage war.
- As part of this process, the lowly are being raised; the farmer, once a poor peasant, is discovering that his needs and welfare are of interest to his government.
- In addition, young men both rich and poor have lost their lives in the fighting.
- One wealthy Japanese businessman says, "The past year has dealt no more lightly with me than it has my gardener. Truly, the war has made him my equal."
- Another blow to the roots of the social system is the passage of the Election Bill, which lowered the voting age from 25 to 20 and gave women the right to vote for the first time.
- In the first election after the voting reforms, 66 percent of the eligible women voters cast their ballots.

- To provide economic equality, no person is allowed to draw out more than 1,800 yen per month—no matter their wage.
- Anything workers make over that sum is deposited to their accounts and frozen, to become available at some time in the future.
- American soldiers are contributing to this equality; observers say, "You Americans don't seem to care about a man's social position at all. You would just as soon joke with a common laborer as with the chief of police."

HISTORICAL SNAPSHOT
1947

- A Gallup poll reported that 94 percent of Americans believed in God
- Gerber Products Company sold two million jars of baby food weekly
- *A Streetcar Named Desire* by Tennessee Williams opened on Broadway
- The Freedom Train, carrying 100 of America's greatest documents, toured the United States
- The American Meat Institute reported that Americans abandoned wartime casseroles for meat five nights a week
- Seventy-five percent of all corn production was now hybrid
- *Esquire magazine* promoted the "bold look" for the man of "self-confidence and good taste," featuring wide tie clasps, heavy gold key chains, bold striped ties, big buttons and the coordination of hair color and clothing
- Bikini bathing suits arrived on American beaches to great excitement
- The American Friends Service Committee won the Nobel Peace Prize
- One million homes now had television sets
- Gillette and Ford paid $65,000 to sponsor the first televised World Series, during which an estimated 3.7 million people watched the Brooklyn Dodgers fall to the New York Yankees
- Returning GI veterans took advantage of the GI Bill, sending college enrollment to an all-time high
- New York began a fluoridation program for 50,000 children
- The new innovation of drive-in facilities at banks was spreading rapidly
- A house costing $4,440 in 1939 retailed for $9,060; the price of clothing was up 93 percent over the same period
- Minute Maid Corp., Ajax, Everglades National Park, the Cannes Film Festival and the Tony Awards all made their first appearance
- The United States was urged by the American Association of Scientific Workers to study bacteriological warfare

1947 NEWS PROFILE

In 1945, this 17-year-old woman became a switchboard operator in Dublin, Georgia, where she joined the Communications Workers of America (CWA). Here she describes her life and first labor strike in 1947 as post-war America began to turn its attention to working conditions and workers at home. In the 1950s and 1960s, Selina Burch became a top official of the CWA, an administrative assistant to one of the union's 12 district vice-presidents.

"I grew up in Dublin, Georgia. My father was a farmer and my mother was a homemaker. My mother died when I was 13 and I moved in with my grandmother and four old-maid aunts—three of them were schoolteachers. There was no labor background in my family at all.

I began work for Southern Bell on August 7, 1945, as an operator. I had graduated from Dublin High School and had worked in a coffee shop for about a year—there's no labor market in Dublin, Georgia. After a year, I applied for a job with the telephone company. The chief operator had gone to school with my father, so I was put ahead of all the other applicants.

At that time, remember, there was a manual board where you said, "Number, please." There was no automatic dialing in Dublin. If you've ever walked into a telephone company, you've seen all these cords being put up. It became a fascinating thing to me to see if I could put up all the cords and then move over to another position, because I was very adept at handling telephone calls. There was one other girl from Dublin who could keep up with me, but only one. This was a challenge to me, to see how fast I could work the switchboard.

In 1946, some people from Macon came to Dublin and signed us up to a union. If you were a female, you paid $0.75 a month to belong to a union, and if you were a male, you paid $1.00. I was an operator and was working eight to five every day, the best shift because of my family's relationship with the chief operator. Suddenly, I was assigned to that horrible tour of one to ten. Someone had come along and taken my privileges away. I was young and carefree, though, 17, 18, and it really didn't make any difference to me, that part of it.

Also, right away in 1946, we obtained our first wage increase. At that time, I was making $15.00 a week as an operator and I got a $10.00 increase. It had a real impact on me that somebody had almost doubled my salary, but I did not understand at that

time what it was all about. I had no idea what unionization meant. Pay, it meant more pay. But as for any other privileges, all it meant was that I went to the bottom of the list, because I was the junior person there.

I remember the first union meeting I ever went to—over in Macon. It was during a strike, and we wanted to see what we were striking for, but we didn't find out. I'm not sure that anyone in Macon knew.

The strike didn't bother me because even though my family were schoolteachers, we had a car. There was only one movie in Dublin, so driving to Macon was something for us to do. I could borrow a quarter to buy a little gas. The Western Electric guys were out on strike also. Everybody would get together at meetings and we'd laugh and talk about the strike, whatever it was about.

Dublin was a pretty small place. We were a close-knit group. I guess that we were friends more because we worked together all day than because we were members of the union. When we returned to work in '47, I remember that we gave the two who had not come out on strike a pretty hard way to travel. I resented them.

It was like being out of school on vacation. In fact, the day we were supposed to return to work, I had a big date that night, what I considered at that time a big date. I called the chief operator and said that I couldn't possibly come to work because I had such a sore throat.

We were so young and naïve that we did not even think of picking up the phone and making calls. You see, with only a manual board there, if we had been militant and known what we were doing, we could have driven Mother Bell nuts. But we did not want to inconvenience in any way. We thought we were a big inconvenience just being out on the street. It was part of this Southern upbringing: we respect authority at all costs. And with Dublin so small, I didn't think of "the company" as huge, nationwide Bell Telephone Company. I thought of the company only as the people I worked with. My grandmother broke her hip during this time, and the chief operator called me at home—my grandmother's home where I was still living—to assure me that she would make sure that any calls from our number went through, even though they were having trouble keeping up on the switchboard because of the strike . . ."

1950–1959

As the 1950s began, the average American enjoyed an income 15 times greater than the average foreigner, optimism was rampant, and much of the nation's energy was focused on family and making up for lost time. Women tended to marry at an earlier age and bear children in their twenties. Many were able to maintain the independence obtained during the 1940s and continued to work after "the boys" returned from the war. Many more found a new lifestyle in suburbia, where they could take advantage of a prosperous America. Surveys showed that the vast majority of Americans considered themselves middle class, many enjoyed the benefits of health insurance for the first time, and everyone knew someone who owned a television set. On the world stage, the United States manufactured half of the world's products, 57 percent of the steel, 43 percent of the electricity, and 62 percent of the oil. The economies of Europe and Asia lay in ruins, while America's industrial and agricultural structure was untouched and well-oiled to supply the consumer and industrial needs of a war-weary world.

In addition, the war years' high employment and optimism spurred the longest sustained period of peacetime prosperity in the nation's history. A decade of full employment and pent-up desire produced demands for all types of consumer goods. Businesses of all sizes prospered. Rapidly swelling families, new suburban homes, televisions, and most of all, big, powerful, shiny automobiles symbolized the hopes of the era. During the 1950s, an average of seven million cars and trucks were sold annually. By 1952, two thirds of all families owned a television set; home freezers and high-fidelity stereo phonographs were considered necessities. Specialized markets developed to meet the demand of consumers such as amateur photographers, pet lovers, and backpackers. At the same time, shopping malls, supermarkets, and credit cards emerged as important economic forces.

This economic prosperity also ushered in conservative politics and social conformity. Tidy lawns, bedrooms that were "neat and trim," and suburban homes that were "proper" were certainly "in" throughout the decade as Americans adjusted to the post-war years. Properly buttoned-down attitudes concerning sexual mores brought stern undergarments for women like bonded girdles and stiff, pointed, or padded bras to confine the body. The planned community of Levittown, New York, mandated that grass be cut at least once a week and laundry washed on specific days. A virtual revival of Victorian respectability and domesticity reigned; divorce rates and female college attendance fell while birth rates and the sale of Bibles rose. Corporate America promoted the benefits of respectable men in gray flannel suits whose wives remained at home to tend house and raise children. Suburban life included ladies' club memberships, chauffeuring children to piano and ballet classes, and lots of a newly marketed product known as tranquilizers, the sales of which were astounding.

The average wage earner benefited more from the booming industrial system than at any time in American history. The 40-hour work week became standard in manufacturing. In offices many workers were becoming accustomed to a 35-hour week. Health benefits for workers became more common and paid vacations were standard in most industries. In 1950, 25 percent of American wives worked outside the home; by the end of the decade the number had risen to 40 percent. Communications technology, expanding roads, inexpensive airline tickets, and a spirit of unboundedness meant that people and commerce were no longer prisoners of distance. Unfortunately, up to one-third of the population lived below the government's poverty level, largely overlooked in the midst of prosperity.

The Civil Rights Movement was propelled by two momentous events in the 1950s. The first was a decree on May 17, 1954, by the U.S. Supreme Court which ruled "that in the field of public education the doctrine of 'separate but equal' has no place. Separate educational facilities are inherently unequal." The message was electric but the pace was slow. Few schools would be integrated for another decade. The second event established the place of the Civil Rights Movement. On December 1, 1955, African-American activist Rosa Parks declined to vacate the white-only front section of the Montgomery, Alabama, bus, leading to her arrest and a citywide bus boycott by blacks. Their spokesman became Martin Luther King, Jr., the 26-year-old pastor of the Dexter Avenue Baptist Church. The year-long boycott was the first step toward the passage of the Civil Rights Act of 1964.

America's youths were enchanted by the TV adventures of *Leave It to Beaver*, westerns, and *Father Knows Best*, allowing them to accumulate more time watching television during the week (at least 27 hours) than attending school. TV dinners were invented; pink ties and felt skirts with sequined poodle appliqués were worn; Elvis Presley was worshipped and the new phenomena of *Playboy* and Mickey Spillane fiction were created only to be read behind closed doors. The ever-glowing eye of television killed the "March of Time" newsreels after 16 years at the movies. Sexual jargon such as "first base" and "home run" entered the language. Learned-When-Sleeping machines appeared, along with Smokey the Bear, Sony tape recorders, adjustable shower heads, *Mad Comics*, newspaper vending machines, Levi's faded blue denims, pocket-size transistor radios, and transparent plastic bags for clothing. Ultimately, the real stars of the era were the Salk and Sabin vaccines, which vanquished the siege of polio.

1951 PROFILE

Born as a slave on a plantation in South Carolina, Ida Davis is the proud matriarch of four generations. For over 70 years, she has lived in the same cabin she and her husband built after they were married.

Life at Home

- Ida Davis is a very old woman, and though she tells friends she is 88, she is not sure of her exact age.
- Born as a slave on the Davis Plantation in Pine Tree Bluff, South Carolina, Ida has lived on the same property, occupying only two houses in her entire life.
- The first was the wood cabin in which she was born.
- She lived there until she was 16, when she married Columbus Davis, known to all as Boy-Boy.
- They built a cabin together on the Davis Plantation, where she has lived ever since.
- Neither house boasts running water or an indoor bathroom.
- Electricity arrived 11 years ago, thanks to the rural electrical cooperatives that brought service to the farm regions of the state.
- Together Ida and Boy-Boy had 14 children, 10 of whom lived to adulthood.
- Over time, eight moved away: one to New York, three to Baltimore, two to Columbia, SC and two to Sumter, SC.
- One child moved to the nearby town of Summerton, while the oldest child, known as Junior, sharecropped with his daddy in Pine Tree Bluff.
- Today, Ida has 56 grandchildren and more great- and great-great-grand children than nearly anyone can count, except for Ida.
- She has meticulously created a set of scrapbooks, dedicating a page or two for each child, using pictures, locks of hair and other memorabilia to honor every birth.

Ida Davis meticulously creates scrap books to honor her grandchildren, her great grandchildren and her great-great grandchildren.

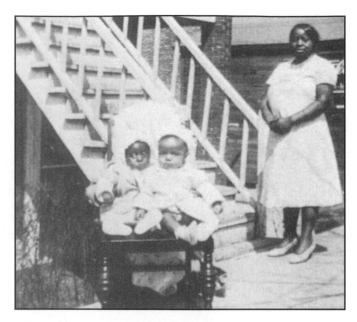

Ida's children and grand-children visit often.

Ida married Columbus Davis when she was 16 years old.

- Only Ida remembers the name and birthday of each and every child.
- Her favorite leisure activity, after churchgoing, is to look at the pictures and drawings in the "sweet memory" books, or listen while her children read her letters or the newspaper clippings stored in the books.
- Born during the Civil War, Ida never had an opportunity to learn how to read or write; times were hard and schools few for the former slave children of the Reconstruction South, when Ida was a girl.
- Following a lifelong habit, Ida listens hard and remembers well when the Bible, letters and articles are read aloud.
- Ida places great stock in the belief that education is the key to lifting the Negro out of poverty.
- She is proud that all of her children managed to stay in school until at least the eighth grade; two even graduated high school, as have many of the grand-children.
- Her children come to visit regularly; they all know that Ida lives for news of the children.
- Many of the grandchildren, who were raised in the North, have returned to Summerton to raise their children and live near the family matriarch.
- Currently, Ida is particularly focused on the progress of the great-grandchildren who have been drafted into the newly racially integrated army to fight in Korea.
- Ida is almost beside herself with joy that one of the great-grands has just been accepted at the new law school for Negroes in nearby Orangeburg, SC.
- Having one of the family on the verge of becoming a lawyer ranks alongside the moment her grandson Zebulon became a minister, or when the first of several granddaughters became teachers.
- Most of the family up North have jobs in industry, a couple still work as domestics, two sons in Baltimore own a grocery together, and one son is a porter on the railroad.
- Though she has never considered herself an activist, Ida has always been keenly interested in seeing that the members of her community had opportunity and education.

Memories of Sharecropper Fannie Lou Hamer, Montgomery County, Mississippi, 1937:

One day when I was about six, I was playing beside a gravel road and the landowner came and asked me could I pick cotton. I told him I didn't know.

He told me if I picked 39 pounds of cotton that week that they would carry me to the commissary store on the plantation that Saturday, and I could get Cracker Jacks and Daddy-Wide Legs and cherries. And this was things I had never had. I picked 30 pounds that week. Then the next week I was tasked to 60 because what he was doing was trapping me into work. I had to pick more and more. By the time I was 13 years old, I was picking 300 and 400 pounds.

Letter to the Reverend J. A. DeLaine, Lake City, SC, October 7, 1955:

"We have been notified by the best of authority that you are the one that started school segregation mess at Manning, S.C. and that you was run out of manning four dirty filthy work. Maybe you don't know Lake City but you are going to find out real soon. Several hundred of us had a meeting and pledged ourselves to put you where you belong, if there is such a place. I wonder if you ever heard about the Negrow (cq) Postmaster that was sent to Lake City and notified to Leve. (cq) He refused. However he left, but in a coffin. So we have decided to give you 10 days to leave Lake City and if you are not away by then rather than let you spread your dirty filthy poison here any longer. We have made plans to move you if it takes dynamite to do so. This is final."

"There are not enough troops in the army to force the South to give up on segregation and admit the Negro race into our schools, our theaters, our swimming pools, and our houses."

—South Carolina Governor J. Strom Thurmond, 1948

Life at Work

- Ida Davis was trained by her aunt as a midwife, and for more than 60 years she cared for most of the black babies and many of the white ones born in her part of the county.
- Her family insisted she "retire" on her eightieth birthday.
- The family offered to build her a nice brick home with electricity, running water and a septic system, but she figures that the little unpainted frame house where she has spent the last 72 years has too many memories, most of them happy.
- The house started out with a large main room and a small bedroom.
- Two other bedrooms were added over time, one for the boys and one for the girls.
- The living room is neatly wallpapered with the covers of *Life* magazine, a project of many years for which Boy-Boy took great pride.
- One of the bedrooms is where she now makes quilts.
- It is filled with cloth scraps that family members bring whenever they come to visit.
- All the descendants have come to expect a Mama Ida quilt on their sixteenth birthday.
- She says often that she's getting too old to sew anymore and will have to stop soon.
- Her family knows that when she stops, her last breath will be near.
- She goes to the Mt. Hebron Methodist Church where her grandboy Zeb now preaches.
- He often complains, only half in jest, that she knows the Bible better than he does, even though she can't read.
- Years of careful listening have made an impression.
- When Ida was in her forties, she was so active in the church, the congregation asked her to represent them at a church convention in Little Rock, Arkansas.
- She traveled by train and was quite proud of going, but never accepted another call by the church to travel that far again.
- The unfamiliar places and names were just too hard to comprehend without knowing how to read.

"We are all children of one God, and all members of one race, the Human Race."

—The Reverend J. A. Delaine, 1950

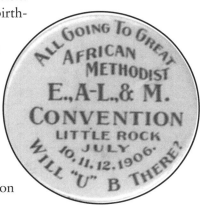

- Her illiteracy has also prevented her from voting, although she knows of many of her neighbors who can read, but who have been prevented from voting by draconian "literacy" and poll taxes.
  - In her part of the state, it cost $2.00 if you wish to vote in a local or national election.
  - Just a couple of years before, South Carolina's governor, Strom Thurmond, ran for president on the States' Rights ticket, promising to preserve segregation.
  - Still, things are better now than they were earlier in the century when the Klan ran rampant.
    - During those days, one of her sons-in-law was lynched.
- The newspaper ran a picture of the lynch mob with his body; later, the photographer ran an advertisement to sell postcard-sized prints of the lynching to anyone with $2.00 plus postage.
- No one was ever punished, and no trial ever held.
- Over the years, many of her family members have been threatened and harassed by the Klan and less formal groups.
- By and large, however, white people have treated Ida well over the years, especially the women whose babies she has delivered.
- It still galls Ida that even when delivering babies in the middle of the night, she was often asked to enter the house through the back door.
- Five years ago, after her husband Boy-Boy died, the Davises, the white family still in possession of the plantation, told her doctor to send all his bills to them.

"Summer Crisis Arrives in Race Relations," *The Christian Century*, July 13, 1949:

Nearly every summer, race disorders threaten to engulf some American cities. This year is unfortunately no exception. Brawls and tension are again making headlines in many places. Most notable among the trouble spots is Washington. The nation's capital ought to set for the country an example of racial justice and concord. It should stand before the world as a demonstration of democratic fair play and equality. It does neither. Instead it handles race relations in a way that shames other Americans, brings the nation into international disrepute and makes inevitable the dangerous hostility now manifest. Why? Behind the current swimming pool brawls is a contest for control of recreational facilities. The Department of the Interior is opposed to segregation, and it seeks to make public pools on all the same terms. The District of Columbia Recreation Board is attempting to capture all recreation facilities and to enforce a segregation policy. The latter is dominated by the real estate interests in the capital. Its chairman is a leader in the movement for restrictive covenants. All this and much more was set forth last November by the National Committee on Segregation in the nation's capital in its booklet *Segregation in Washington*. It revealed that a battle between human and property rights runs all through the life of the capital city, which is controlled by a "benevolent dictatorship" organized by the 8,000 members of the Board of Trade. This regime, which is opposed to democratic home rule, tries to keep children segregated in the schools, parks and playgrounds, and adults separated in housing and business. Surprisingly, this disgraceful state of affairs is of recent origin, going back only to the administration of Woodrow Wilson.

- Her biological Davis family protested that they could take care of their own, but the white Davises finally prevailed, saying that in many ways Ida was their family, too.
- She still keeps a garden beside her house, although the grandchildren and great-grandchildren do most of the work now.
- Depending on the season, she grows corn, okra, tomatoes, cucumbers, collards, mustard and turnip greens, lima beans, field peas and peanuts.
- When peanuts are in season, Ida will have a kettle of them boiling in the yard whenever large numbers of young guests are expected.
- Ida is known countywide for her boiled peanuts.
- Until electricity came to the area, vegetables had to be used up quickly, but now they can be stored almost indefinitely in the refrigerators and freezers of several relatives in the area.
- That takes much of the worry out of winter, when food of all kinds, especially vegetables, used to be scarce.
- Fall is Ida's favorite time of year.
- During September, October and often November, she can sit in a chair Boy-Boy made for her, located just outside the door of her home, and smoke her hand-carved pipe.
- It makes her feel close to Boy-Boy and the life they had together.
- This is where she likes to sit and look at pictures.
- One of her favorites is of her and Boy-Boy pretending to drive Mr. Davis's car many years ago.

Ida loves this picture of her and Boy-Boy in their younger days.

- Her porch chair is also a great place to watch for the elderly Ford truck belonging to her grandgirl Lucsata's husband Tom.
- These days, they regularly bring a meal that includes steaming greens and cornbread, as well as a mess of children that demand Ida's loving attention.

Life in the Community: Summerton, South Carolina

- Currently, the Summerton community is in an uproar since the school district refused to buy a school bus to transport black kids to their school a number of miles away.
- Every school morning, the whites' school bus rolls past black children walking several miles to the colored, segregated school.
- Nationally, a movement has started to integrate the schools, Ida's children tell her.
- The NAACP is determined to fight the issue in the courts.
- Ida is not sure how she feels about this.
- She knows she wants her family to receive the best education.
- She also believes that the Lord made the races different for a reason.
- Since the school integration talk started, one local gas station and store has posted signs reading, "No Nigger or Negro allowed inside building."
- Another sign, which has been professionally painted, reads, "Negros not wanted in the North or South. Send them back to Africa where God Almighty put them to begin with. That is their home."
- With the backing of the NAACP, 20 parents of the black schoolchildren filed a lawsuit on May 16, 1950, a case known as *Briggs v. Elliott,* challenging the unequal treatment of their children.
- Many of the people employed in the white community were immediately dismissed from their jobs.

"New Rebel Yell in Dixie," by Hodding Carter, *Collier's*, July 9, 1949:

A strong flame, brighter and infinitely more cleansing than the fiery cross of the Klan, is burning throughout the South today. Increasingly, there are hands to feed it and voices to proclaim its meaning. The hands are not clenched in hate as are the demagogue's, nor are the voices as shrill and blatant, but the flame of purposeful liberalism is lighting up dark and tragic corners of a harried region.

Liberalism, progressiveness, vision. These are abused words, loosely used, often narrowly defined. The Southern liberal fits into no mold. He is rarely a theorist. He is not bound to an ideology, nor does he recite a manifesto as if it were a prayer. He is as often condemned by the left as by the right. He has a deeply rooted, provincial love for his homeland. His objectives are usually what are termed limited ones, and he may differ even from his fellows in his proposals for attaining them. But he shares a common determination to make democracy work and thrive through individual and concerted effort on the battle line itself and not from a distant ivory tower.

You don't hear too much about him. He is an educator, an editor, a churchman, a representative of organized labor, a writer, a political leader, a business or professional man, a farmer. Usually he would be embarrassed if you praised him for his courage, or labeled him a liberal. Even when he organizes, his organization is loosely knit, and he may be unaware that his neighbor shares his own convictions.

As Harry Ashmore, the brilliant young editor of the *Arkansas Gazette,* puts it: "I figure there are thousands in the region, men of goodwill who are getting the job done where it counts, and the hell if it is that us so-called experts on the South don't even know who they are." But there are multiple thousands who know who Harry Ashmore is, and of the conscientious, day-in-day-out job he and many others do on the editorial page and from the platform to put the South's problems, achievements and unreachable goals in perspective.

And certainly this much is true. No other region in the nation is producing today so many and such effective spokesmen for social and economic progress and for a new evaluation of human relationships as is the South. And nowhere else do such men of goodwill work against as difficult and complex a background. . . .

The Southern liberal is aware of his past. He works within its receding restrictions, if for no other reason than there is yet no other way for him to work effectively. A suspect among the defiant reactionaries at home, who brand him a Communist, a "Nigger lover" and a Yankee tool, he is no less a target for the militant, all-or-nothing crusaders who wage their war at a distance.

If I may be personal about so personal a matter as mail, I can be sure that if I advocate or praise the local attainment of such objectives as equal hospital facilities, equal pay and facilities in the separate school systems or the inclusion of a Negro juror on a trial jury, I will get equally condemnatory letters from opposed correspondents whose only common ground is a dislike for what I have said. The proponent of ending segregation—a favorite phrase is "at the point of the bayonet"—will denounce me for endorsing the status quo. The yearner for the good old days will whiplash me for endangering it.

This continuous experience is shared by the scores of fellow Southern Rebels with whom I have swapped stories. Yet the concrete objectives we espouse are those which are most despised—according to so eminent a student as Gunnar Myrdal—by the Southern Negro, and the least objected to by the resisting white and therefore the most readily attainable.

Putting first things first, we work for equality in the courts, school facilities, job opportunities and the right to vote. Northern critics of both races attack us for leaving the issue of mass segregation alone, for being unconcerned about that nebulous thing called social equality, for questioning the overall wisdom of the present civil rights program, or for discouraging the idea that assimilation is the only way out.

"Methodist Women Seek End to Segregation," *The Christian Century,* **October 8, 1947:**

Women of the Methodist Church may force their denomination to deal with a racial issue which that large communion would like to soft-pedal. At the annual meeting of the Methodist Board of Missions, held this month in Buck Hill Falls, Pennsylvania, the Women's Division of Christian Service adopted a resolution demanding that the Methodist General Conference, which is to meet in Boston next May, "take such steps as may be necessary to abolish the pattern of racial segregation in the Methodist Church." Behind this resolution lies the fact that the Methodist Church, as now organized, is on a racially segregated basis. The union brought about a few years ago was consummated by adoption of a division into six American jurisdictions. Five of the jurisdictions are geographical, but the sixth is entirely racial. It places the Negro churches in the denomination in a unit by themselves. Such sporadic and half-hearted attempts as have hitherto been made to do away with this segregated pattern have been resisted mainly on two grounds: first, to change the jurisdictional setup would be to go back on an understanding by which the former Methodist Episcopal Church, South, was persuaded to vote for the union; and second, that the Negroes in the Methodist Church are satisfied with their separate jurisdiction and want to keep things that way. However, Southern women were conspicuous at Buck Hill Falls in passing the anti-segregation resolution. It is not likely that the women's demands will produce action at the Boston General Conference. But when the women's societies of Protestant denominations once start agitating for definite changes in their communions, it is generally not long before something happens.

HISTORICAL SNAPSHOT
1951

- World War II inflation continued to drive up prices
- The Korean conflict was underway
- After 16 years, *Time* discontinued the "March of Time" newsreels shown in movie theaters
- Metropolitan Life Insurance Company reported obesity as a cause of early death
- Television advertising companies discovered that dressing actors as doctors to peddle health products dramatically improved sales volumes
- The top television shows included *Arthur Godfrey's Talent Scouts, I Love Lucy, The Red Skelton Show, The Roy Rogers Show* and *Superman*
- Sugarless chewing gum, Dacron suits, the telephone company answering service, and power steering in cars all made their first appearance
- Monogram Pictures cancelled a movie about Henry Wadsworth Longfellow because of their concern that Hiawatha, an Indian peacemaker, might be viewed as a communist sympathizer
- *An American in Paris* received the Academy Award for Best Picture, beating out *The African Queen, Detective Story* and *A Streetcar Named Desire*
- An estimated three million people turned out for a New York City parade honoring General Douglas MacArthur
- African American baseball star Willie Mays was the National League Rookie of the Year
- Avis Rent-a-Car charged $6 a day and eight cents a mile
- Scientists led by Edward Teller set off the first thermonuclear reaction
- *The Grass Harp* by Truman Capote, *Requiem for a Nun* by William Faulkner, *The Ballad of the Sad Café* by Carson McCullers, *The Strange Children* by Caroline Gordon and *Betty Crocker's Picture Cook Book* were all published
- The U.S. Census Bureau purchased Remington Rand's UNIVAC, the first commercially produced, large-scale computer
- Hit songs for the year included "Cold, Cold Heart," "Mockin' Bird Hill," "Tell Me Why," "In the Cool, Cool of the Evening" and "Unforgettable"
- Glenn T. Seaborg won the Nobel Prize in chemistry for the discovery of plutonium
- The five-cent phone call rose to 10 cents in New York and other large cities
- Hiroshima A-bomb survivor Shigeki Tanaha, 19, won the Patriots Day Marathon in Boston

Selected Prices

Dress, Linen, Sleeveless	$30.00
Girdle	$6.95
Refrigerator, Frigidaire	$199.75
Record Album	$4.85
Cake Mix, Betty Crocker	$0.35
Blanket, Fieldcrest	$9.95
Blender, Waring	$44.50
Vaporizer	$5.95
Lip Balm, Chapstick	$0.25
Automobile, 1951 Buick Riviera	$1,995.00
Wallet, Leather	$3.50
Set of Old Spice After-Shave and Cream	$1.65

"Daddy Doesn't Live Here Anymore," *McCall's Magazine*, April 1950:

"There are in this country today hundreds of thousands of young women who are war widows in the most explicit sense, even though their husbands did not meet death in combat. They are widows by decree. Their marriages did not survive the grotesque distortions of wartime living and so ended in divorce.

A husband who has died honorably in the service of his country is not a morbid presence in the thoughts of the woman who loved him. His widow turns herself once more to the realities of living. But the husband who was observed a little furtively last night with a pretty girl on his arm, the husband who comes to see his children and expects all the privileges of their companionship with none of the duties—that man is a more haunting ghost than a man recently dead can ever be.

It is a proud and simple duty to tell the children their father died in the service of his country. It is a difficult moment when the children first ask, 'Mother, what does divorce mean?'

The war widow whose husband died in uniform is cushioned economically, at least to some extent, by the pensions and allowances the government provides and by such life insurance as her husband might have carried. The widow by decree receives none of these benefits. Her only outside source of funds is the alimony granted by the courts. For the rest she is on her own.

Of course, this is not a war problem. We still live in the aftermath of those years of incredible excitements and bewilderments. The notion of divorce, of getting out of a situation that seems hopeless, comes to the heads of half the wives of the land at some time or other . . .

Pauline Long was born on her father's small farm near Huntington, Ohio, and was graduated from the country high school when she was 18. As in most of the rural districts of the land, teachers were scarce, the formal education required of them was not too elaborate, and so Pauline got a job for the very next school year teaching in the primary grades.

Pauline lived at home and was quite happy with her work for five years. Then, when she was 23, she married Clarence Schroeder, who was 26. He was a machinist, an extremely capable and conscientious workman, who earned good wages. He insisted that Pauline stop working at once. He said that he was able to earn quite enough money for the two of them and that he wanted her to make a nice home and enjoy life.

Even before they were married they decided not to think about children for a while. Both of them were young. It seemed best to have a few carefree years before they took on the responsibilities of a family.

As a matter of fact, six years went by before Judith was born, in 1942. By this time, of course, we were at war. Clarence Schroeder was working at one of the great munition plants in the Cleveland area and had found a home for himself and Pauline and the new baby at Elyria, a pleasant town of about 25,000 some 30 miles from the metropolis. He was engaged in high-precision work, and though he made no effort to avoid the draft he was classified as essential on the home front.

Pauline says, 'He worked terribly hard for long hours every day. Looking back on it, I think he may have worked too hard. But he has always been like that. Ever since I have known him he has worked 12 and 14 hours a day, and even now when he has his own business he does the same thing. The one thing he hates in anybody is laziness . . . '

Toward the end of the war, in fact, they had almost enough money to do something Clarence Schroeder always had wanted to do—get out of the shop and start a small business of his own. The little town of Wakeman, Ohio, was the crossroads for a whole region of Ohio farm country, and a hardware store there came up for sale. Pauline's mother agreed to lend them enough money, at trifling interest, to stretch out their savings, and they not only bought the business but also a small house to live in.

(continued)

(continued)

'That was a happy time for all of us,' Pauline says. 'I wanted to work at the store, but he wouldn't let me. He just could not stand the idea of a woman working outside of her home. So I joined the church clubs and made as many friends as I could.'

In 1945 Pauline found herself pregnant again. Very shortly after V-E Day her son Dennis was born. The baby was exactly three months old when Clarence Schroeder made his announcement to Pauline. He was fed up with bills and responsibilities. Being the head of a family was too much for him. He was through.

There were, of course, other things involved in his decision to call it quits. They have to do with complex human emotions, with the immemorial urge of the male to cast off his encumbrances and look for new adventures, and so they lie with the causes of the divorce, which is not our subject here.

In retrospect, Pauline is of the opinion nowadays that she could have conquered her hot resentments and saved the situation. But the fact is she did not. She was shocked and angered by Schroeder's announcement. And so she went to see a lawyer. She wanted a legal separation rather than a divorce, and she is still a little bitter because the lawyer talked her out of that idea. He told her that such separations never worked, that a clean break was the only thing.

The upshot of it was a divorce granted to Pauline on the grounds of mental cruelty. The court gave her full and unconditional custody of the two children. It also gave her half the proceeds of the sale of the business and house in Wakeman. And in addition the court ordered Schroeder to pay her $60.00 a month toward the upkeep of his children.

So it was that after nine years of marriage, which seemed as happy and satisfying as most marriages, Pauline found herself on her own once more. She was 32 years old. She had $5,000 in the bank and the court order demanding that her former husband pay her $60.00 a month. She realized at once that her new responsibilities lay beyond the mere feeding and sheltering of her two infants. She had to give them a chance in life . . .

She found a job almost at once in the small town of Columbia, about 10 miles from Elyria, but she couldn't find a place to live there. Pauline's father had died some years before, and her mother had married an elderly farmer. Now her mother bought a pleasant little house on a quiet street in Elyria and rented it to Pauline. Normally the property would bring about $60.00 a month. She gave it to Pauline for $35.00. In the division of the property at Wakeman, Pauline had been awarded the family car, and so her transportation was taken care of.

'I figured it all out as carefully as I could,' Pauline said. 'My teaching job that first year would pay me about $2,100 and my alimony would come to $720.00—a total of a little more than $2,800. I thought that the only way to get a woman to take care of the house and the children while I was away would be to find someone who needed a home.'

She advertised in the newspapers. It was almost inevitable that the woman who finally came to work for her was herself divorced . . . The woman brought a teenaged daughter to live in the house on Marseilles Avenue. Her own divorce had been an affair of extreme unpleasantness. Her hatred for men—all men—had become ingrained, deep, and relentless. Presently Pauline began to realize that it was her chief subject of conversation . . .

Pauline has another housekeeper now. Perhaps it should be said again that she could not work to earn her living if she did not have a housekeeper. She pays the woman $72.00 a month, plus board and room. In the last four years she has taught her third-grade class of about 30 pupils in Columbia. Pauline's salary has

(continued)

DADDY DOESN'T LIVE

A divorced mother says:

"Don't quit your marriage if you can possibly help it. If you do, brace yourself for tough times"

BY MORRIS MARKEY

THERE are in this country today hundreds of thousands of young women who are war widows in the most explicit sense, even though their husbands did not meet death in combat. They are widows by decree. Their marriages did not survive the grotesque distortions of wartime living and so ended in divorce.

A husband who has died honorably in the service of his country is not a morbid presence in the thoughts of the woman who loved him. His widow turns herself once more to the realities of living. But the husband who was observed a little furtively last night with a pretty girl on his arm, the husband who comes to see his children and expects all the privileges of their companionship with none of the duties — that man is a more haunting ghost than a man decently dead can ever be.

It is a proud and simple duty to tell the children their father died in the service of his country. It is a difficult moment when the children first ask: "Mother, what does divorce mean?"

The war widow whose husband died in uniform is cushioned economically, at least to some extent, by the pensions and allowances the government provides and by such life insurance as her husband might have carried. The widow by decree receives none of these benefits. Her only outside source of funds is the alimony granted by the courts. For the rest she is on her own.

Of course, this is not simply a war problem. We still live in the aftermath of those years of incredible excitements and bewilderments. The notion of divorce, of getting out of a situation that seems hopeless, comes into the heads of half the wives of the land at some time or other.

The dream of starting all over again is as old as time — not only with marriage but with life itself — of writing off the losses, wiping out the mistakes, beginning with a clean slate. We know that we cannot climb back into the cradle and look at the world once again with eyes which are innocent and hopeful and expectant. But almost anybody can go into a court of law and wipe out a marriage. Sometimes that [Turn to page 108]

The court gave Pauline Schroeder unconditional custody of the children. She says, "I want to keep them as normal as I can. I've seen in other children's faces the marks of the hatred and the quarrels they've listened to. I don't want my children to look like that"

Getting the screens up in the spring is a job for the man of the house—when there is one. Now all the odd jobs are up to Pauline

Teachers who have a college degree can command more money than those who do not. So while she taught she worked for her degree

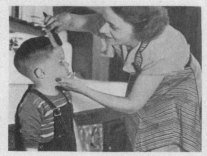

During the school term she leaves her home each morning at seven-thirty and rarely makes it home again before five in the afternoon

(continued)

increased twice, and she now earns $2,450 a year. When her alimony is added this gives her a gross income of $3,170.

Against this income her fixed, overhead expenses for a year amount to $2,388 in a budget that is capitulated like this:

Groceries and Milk $740
Heat $120
Light and Water $94
Rent $420
Servant $864
Upkeep of Car $150

This gives her an apparent surplus of $782.00 over her major costs of living, which would seem to be a fairly comfortable margin, particularly in view of the fact that Schroeder's parents supply the larger part of the clothing for the children.

But every woman knows that the major costs of living are not the whole story by any means. There are doctors and dentists. Even in a small town the schoolteacher must be careful of her dress. And the unexpected extras make a ceaseless assault upon the pocketbook."

"Marriage Is a Way of Life," by Amy A. McGregor, *Nautilus Magazine*, March 1951:

" 'I wish I weren't married; then I'd be able to afford a car.'

The young man who made this statement is not at all dissatisfied with his wife; he is more than ordinarily proud of his little girl. But the fetters of married life chafe him. So does the constant sacrifice—the doing without something he would like to have, and could afford if he were single. In truth, he is dissatisfied with marriage itself.

The squabble over sex education has distorted and overemphasized the physical side of marriage. Some preparation for the responsibilities of marriage is given to our young girls, but that also is physical. It is important to learn to budget one's earnings, to learn to care for a house, to look after the welfare of a small baby, to sew, to cook and to do the various things which promote physical well-being. But of what use is a spic-and-span house, a healthy, happy baby, a well-balanced budget, or a well-cooked meal, if the husband always refers to things he would like to have but cannot because he is married? Would anyone in his right mind call that a happy marriage?

If it is important that a girl be taught such details appertaining to the physical side of marriage, how much more important is it that both boys and girls should be taught the one most obvious lesson they will need for marriage: the art of living together?

The family group, on which our present civilization is based, is supposed to teach this lesson. But our modern news items, particularly those concerned with juvenile delinquency and divorce, testify that it does not. From the other members of his family, the child is supposed to receive his first true impressions of the world, and his first contacts with it. From that group, he should learn the fine art of living with others, and be made aware that the universe does not center directly about him.

Instead, what happens? The child is born, and immediately becomes the pivot around which the household revolves. The parents can deny him nothing, and the whole routine of the household is disrupted to fit his pleasure, instead of gradually fitting the child into the already established routine.

As he grows older, there is an eager rush to keep him from realizing the world of reality. He is fed with fairy stories and tales of the world as his parents imagine it should be. Each idle wish is fulfilled as if by magic, even though the parents have to go without necessary comforts for themselves.

When he enters adolescence, he is thoroughly self-centered. He really knows nothing of the world. His ideas of his playmates are based on the world of make-believe in which he has lived all these years. Physically, he is becoming aware of himself as never before, and this tends to make him even more self-centered. At the same time, he feels the need of companionship from those of his own age, and is unable to meet them on an equal footing. Is it any wonder that the process of growing up is so difficult? Is it any wonder that the divorce rate soars to even higher levels each year?"

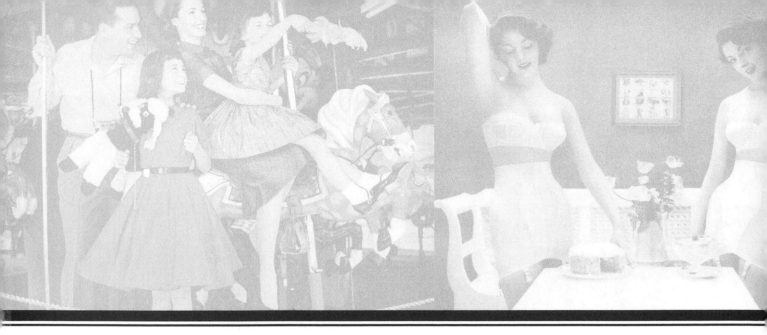

1956 PROFILE

A native of Queens, New York, Mary Cronin has found an opportunity in Miami, Florida, where she can fulfill her dream of being a teacher.

Mary found the fulfillment teaching in Miami, Florida that she never could in Queens, New York.

Life at Home

- Thirty-one-year-old Mary Cronin grew up convinced that she was an ugly duckling with no chance of ever becoming a swan.
- Fairy tales, she frequently reminded herself, did not happen in Queens, New York.
- The product of a college-educated father and a bright mother—who dropped out of school to be married—Mary loves the process of learning.
- Being smart is the next best thing to being pretty, she tells herself.
- Science, medieval wars, modern literature, even homemaking—it all fascinates her facile mind.
- While still in high school, Mary decided that teaching could be a satisfying career.
- Her first serious opportunity to teach came when she was a junior in high school in New York City.
- One afternoon her chemistry teacher called her aside to explain that his 15-year-old son who had cerebral palsy couldn't attend school.
- He offered her an after-school job of teaching his son to read.
- Mary had no idea how to teach reading, but accepted the challenge anyway, especially since the pay of $2.50 per week seemed an enormous sum.
- For their first, very awkward meeting, she brought books ranging from her sister's fourth-grade reader to her high school texts, along with a copy of *The Collected Poetry of W. H. Auden*.
- Her new pupil rejected the textbooks and asked for a poem.

- Quickly, it became clear that he fully understood many words, but because of his limited experience, he was unable to visualize the meanings of certain words like "dive" for a tavern, or to imagine New York's Fifty-second Street.
- Mary then had an opportunity to open this young man's eyes to the wonder of new places, people and experiences.
- More than simply the appearance of New York's Fifty-second Street, she also described the smells and tastes of the place.
- She felt for the first time in her life that she had done something truly powerful and positive for another person.
- Wanting to teach, she concluded, was like wanting to have children or write a novel or think through a math problem that others couldn't solve.
- Her dream of being an elementary school teacher maintained its strength throughout college, despite the tumult of war and the persistent admonition that people didn't attend Radcliffe to become schoolteachers.
- While in college, Mary watched with fascination and confusion the debate raging about women and college.
- The year she graduated, 1943, was the first year that Radcliffe students could attend classes at Harvard.
- At the same time, Harvard Medical School was engaged in an internal struggle over the role of women in medicine.
- One side argued that the ravages of the Second World War demanded that America produce a steady flow of physicians, thus necessitating the admission of women.
- Traditionalists said that despite the war, the economy or the interests of women, society should protect the role of women as child bearers and keepers of the home.
- Following the debate closely, Mary felt torn by the arguments, especially since she was engaged to a man who proudly stated that his wife would "never work if I can help it, by God."
- She struggled with what was to be her role in a country at war, and the fact that she was about to become a Mrs.
- It was a question quickly answered when she became pregnant on her honeymoon, then saw her new husband shipped off to fight the Japanese in the Pacific theater.
- Her role as mother was all-consuming.
- Two years later, when her husband returned, the love of her life didn't recognize his two-year-old son or his new, independent wife, but was interested in moving forward with a career interrupted by war.
- A wife and child, remnants of his life before the war, seemed to be a greater burden than he could handle, and the couple divorced in 1948.

"The worst way to torture the average woman is to lock her in a room with a hundred hats and no mirror."

—John P. Medbury

"While I am willing to agree that there are some very able women in medicine, the pro-feminists are apt to overlook the fundamental biological law that the primary function of woman is to bear and raise children, and the first social duty of woman is to develop and perpetuate the home."

—John T. Williams, Assistant Professor of Gynecology, Harvard Medical School, during Harvard Medical School's debate concerning the admission of women in 1943

A Foreign Language for First Graders, *Life*, May 28, 1956:

Though they are only first graders, the students are doing their French lesson—with the help of TV. In their classroom at Paige Elementary School in Schenectady, N.Y., they follow Anne Slack on Station WRGB as she acts out the phrases she sings. On the screen she sings a French song, "Picota," about a hen pecking bread who lifts its tail ("leve la queue") and then goes away ("et puis s'en va").

Mrs. Slack's Monday program, *Fun with French*, is aimed at first- to sixth-graders, teaching by songs and conversation about everyday subjects. This new hearing-speaking method—"aural-oral" teachers call it—is coming into wide use in public schools. Though few use TV, over 270,000 elementary pupils are learning languages from Italian to Japanese.

Life at Work

- The first time Mary attempted to find a teaching job was a disaster.
- Despite a degree from one of the finest schools in America, she had failed to obtain any education courses, and therefore was not qualified for a teaching job in the New York system.
- To teach, she needed a teaching certificate, which required that she go back to school.
- Then she discovered that private schools were not as strict about teaching certificates.
- That sounded fine to a recent divorcée in a world wary of unattached women, so she took a job at a private school.
- However, the challenges of raising a son alone and teaching school were immense, even when she was able to arrange for her son to attend the same school with her.
- Fellow teachers scolded her for not finding a way to keep the marriage together; others were scandalized by her decision to take back her maiden name when the divorce was final.
- After five years of struggle and tears, she awoke one day ready for a change.
- Teaching wasn't the problem—it was New York.

- Within days she made the decision to move to Miami, Florida, where the climate would be good for her son's asthma; surely there, a job would be available.
- At the same time, the Cold War was creating opportunity.
- To stop the spread of communism, America was willing to spend billions on defense, including the reopening of Homestead Air Force Base just south of Miami.
- Thousands of airmen and their families assigned to the base needed everything: housing, runways, restaurants, laundromats, new schools and, most of all, new teachers.
- Mary found her place immediately, teaching fifth grade at Tangerine Elementary School, a collection of 14 detached, surplus Quonset huts donated by the military.

Growing Minds, On Becoming a Teacher, by Herbert Kohl, 1990:

James T. turned out to be a very skilled artist. He told me that when he saw colors he could taste them in his mouth, and I once caught him dipping fingers in our tempera paints and licking them. I surprised him one day by giving him a box of pastels. I made up some story that the school was providing special art material to students of talent to help decorate the halls. James T. made several pastel drawings. A particular favorite of mine (which I still have) is a drawing of Moby Dick on black construction paper. The black underlies the pastel white whale, deep blue water, and pale blue sky, giving the whole an appropriately ominous feeling.

I mounted a number of James T.'s pastels on poster board and hung them in the hall. This got me in trouble several weeks later when the district art supervisor came into my class and in front of the students told me to take down James T.'s posters. I remembered what had happened to me (before) and decided to stall. I muttered something that could have been taken for assent, but explained that we were about to take an important phonics test. By this time I'd learned that phonics always takes preference over any other matter.

The supervisor didn't give up easily on the pastels and was waiting in my classroom when I returned from dismissing the class. The assistant principal accompanied her. Lois was a very sympathetic woman who protected her teachers. I could see James T. and Felipe hiding behind the swinging doors down the hall. The supervisor advised me that pastels were a sixth grade medium, and since I was teaching fifth grade, my students couldn't use pastels. She showed me a passage in the school district's art curriculum manual that confirmed her contention and insisted again that the offending art be removed. She also wanted to confiscate the pastels in my room. I politely objected, pointing out that the 5-1 class, of so-called gifted students (my class was 5-7, the bottom of our grade), used pastels. My motivation was to show my students and particularly James T. that he could do work that was as good or better than that of some of the students in 5-1. She said the only reason 5-1 was allowed to use pastels was that they all read and did math on a sixth grade level. By now I was getting angry and was about to argue that art and reading skills had no direct relationship, that the development of any skill could lead to confidence in other areas, that there was no set sequence of the use of art materials, that. . . . Lois put her hand on my shoulder and shrugged. Her eyes told me what I quickly realized. We were in an educational madhouse and my students and I would be losers if I protested further. James T.'s work came down. The supervisor even demanded that I turn over the pastels, but since they were not the brand bought by the school, I was able to keep them.

- The huts were located in neat rows in a flat, treeless field; pour a few sidewalks and a school was born.
- Most of the long, rounded, metal Quonset hut classrooms had windows down both sides to bring in light, all had fans to push the Florida air around, and a few had air conditioning.

- Because of the Cold War, the new military base and the resulting influx of workers, everything was happening so quickly there literally was no rule book for the school.
- In this atmosphere, Mary began to blossom.
- Her first quest was to get to know her students, many of whom are children of construction workers imported to Southeast Florida to build this overnight air base, or military kids who are so used to moving they rarely remember each other's last name.
- In New York and across the nation, teachers are taught that chatting with students or meeting with them during breaks instead of taking coffee in the teacher's lounge would contribute to the breakdown of discipline in the classroom.
- On at least two occasions in New York, Mary was called to the principal's office for talking to her students outside of class.
- In Florida, she is ignoring that tradition of teaching.

A 24-year-old housewife from Trenton, New Jersey, describes her day, *Workingman's Wife* by Lee Rainwater, Richard Coleman and Gerald Handel, 1959:

"Well, naturally, I get up first, make breakfast for my husband and put a load of clothes in my washer while breakfast cooks. Then I wake him up, give him his breakfast and he's off to work. Then I make breakfast for the children. After the children eat I dress them and they go out to play. Then I hang the clothes up and clean lightly through the house. In between times I do the dishes—that's understood, of course. Then I make lunch for the children and myself and bring them in, clean them up, and they eat. I send them out to play when they're done and I do the dishes, bring the clothes in and iron them. When I'm ironing it's usually time to make supper, or at least start preparing for it. Sometimes I have time to watch a TV story for half an hour or so. Then my husband comes home and we have our meals. Then I do the dishes again. Then he goes out to work again; he has a part-time job at his uncle's beverage company. Well, he does that two or three nights a week. If he stays home he watches TV and in the meantime I get the kids ready for bed. He and I have a light snack, watch TV awhile and then go to bed."

- One of her first challenges was to assist a young girl who needed help in reading.
- A product of the deep South, the child had been in seven different schools because her migrant family moved so often.
- Because of Mary's heavy New York accent, using phonics to teach reading was difficult; she and the young Southerner simply did not pronounce their vowels the same way.
- Yet, the meaning of sentences and the content of stories made communication possible.
- So everyday she talks about books and discusses the stories that have been read; then she listens.
- The more Mary and the students talk about books, the more they read.
- One night she realized that the children could teach themselves if given the right opportunity to learn; every child should be both student and teacher if the process is to work.
- Mary has also found that the more she immerses herself in the life of her students, the more ready they are to learn—and the more she loves being a teacher.
- From her Cuban students she is learning to properly cook rice and beans; from the military kids, she has gotten a picture of life in Germany, England and the Philippines; and from the Floridian children she learned how to throw a cast net and spot motionless black crown night herons in the Everglades.
- She has met Florida's environment at its best and worst.
- Recently, thousands of migrating fiddler crabs invaded the base and the land around the school, covering every inch of space and causing dozens of automobile accidents when car tires slid on thousands of slick, crushed crab bodies.
- She has also experienced the informality of south Florida, where wearing shorts after school is accepted and no one seems to care about one's past.
- It is the perfect place for a divorced woman who loves her son, her students and the uniqueness of Florida in the midst of change.
- The standard dress for her students is still dresses every day for girls, blue jeans and collared shirts for boys.
- Because the school is so new, it has no cafeteria, so the children ride their bikes home at lunch and often return with locally grown oranges for an afternoon snack.

Lady sings the blues
Lady sings the blues
She's got 'em bad
She feels so sad
Wants the world to know
Just what the blues is all about
Lady sings the blues
She tells her side
nothing to hide
Now the world will know
Just what the blues is all about
The blues ain't nothing but a pain in your heart
when you get a bad start
When you and your man have to part
I ain't gonna just sit around and cry
And now I won't die
Because I love him
Lady sings the blues
she's got 'em bad
She feels so sad
The world will know
She's never gonna sing them no more
No more
—"Lady Sings the Blues"
Billie Holiday, 1956

- Often in the afternoons, Mary takes the children outside to play music, which gives everyone a break from the Florida heat that builds in the classrooms.
- After work she goes home, changes clothes and goes touring in her blue 1947 Plymouth through the Everglades, where alligators and herons await.
- Twice she has even gotten to the nearly deserted place called Key West.

Short Shorts Become Permanent in U.S. Scene, *Life*, September 10, 1956:

On a Detroit street corner a willowy young woman, hurrying along in high-heel shoes, paused to tug her tourniquet-tight and abbreviated britches ever so slightly down her trim, summer-tanned legs. It might seem an incongruous spectacle but her wriggling adjustment drew not so much as a glance from the young man who was peddling past on a bicycle.

It was no wonder, because the wearing of shorts in public, not only by teenagers but also by many thousands of older females, had become a permanent accepted—and generally welcome—part of the American scene as the summer season drew to a close.

The phenomenon seemed to be part of the growing informality of suburban living in an age that has placed ever greater emphasis on leisure and play. As more and more skin came into view, manufacturers were finding a still-growing market for shorts of all types, from the relatively Bermuda garment to the briefest of shorts. In short, it had been as scenic a summer as a man could want. While this caused dismay in some places and peevish countermeasures by police in just a few others, nowhere did the phenomenon produce much astonishment. . . .

Nearly all U.S. cities have ordinances governing the clothes that girls and women may wear in such public places as downtown streets and stores. . . . The ordinance for Southampton, Long Island, reads, "No person shall walk or ride in any vehicle upon or along the public streets of the Village in any bathing suit, shorts, trunks or other apparel which does not cover properly the body and limbs from midway between the knees and hips to and including the shoulders. Any person who violates this ordinance shall be liable to a penalty of not more than TEN ($10) DOLLARS for each offense. . . ."

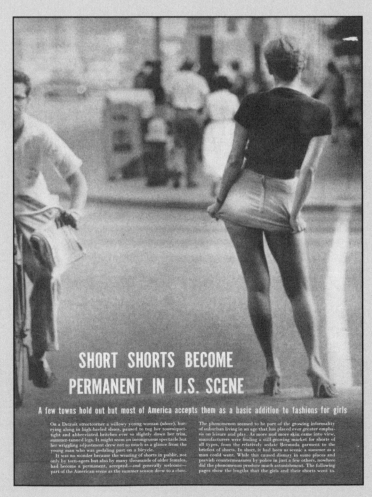

Life in the Community: Homestead Air Force Base, Florida

- Mary lives with the Cold War every day because of the school's location near Homestead Air Force Base, which is located in southern Dade County, Florida, approximately 25 miles southwest of Miami.

- The base is seven miles northeast of the town of Homestead and five miles east of the Everglades.

- Because of the military, Mary sees the composition of her class change often as children transfer to other bases with their families.

- Since arriving in Florida, she has attended the funerals of three men whose planes crashed on take-off or failed to come back from a mission.

- Most parent-teacher conferences only involve mothers; the fathers rarely are seen at school except at the annual Christmas pageant.

- Last year, one fifth-grade boy was in tears before the Christmas play; his father had sent word from Morocco that he would not be home for Christmas.

- It was the fourth straight Christmas he had missed because of an overseas assignment.

- The international flavor of the base also creates interesting classroom assignments.

- When Mary assigned a scrapbook on an African country, three children brought in pictures their Air Force pilot fathers had taken on recent trips to Egypt, the Gold Coast and South Africa.

- One set of boy-girl twins even showed up at school in authentic Moroccan costumes complete with a tall fez for the boy and lacy veils for the girl.

- The community is sensitive to the needs of the base; Spanish-language classes are taught beginning in the first grade on new television sets placed in every classroom.

- The School Board has proudly said that the worker of tomorrow must be bilingual, and that teaching could be delivered in different ways, like a television instructor.

- Mary has two children in her class for whom English is a second language; their fathers both came to Homestead to do construction on the rapidly expanding military base.

- Homestead Air Force Base covers an area of 2,940 acres and houses the Strategic Air Command 19th and 379th Bomb Wings.

- The base traces its beginnings to the early days of WWII.

- Shortly after the Japanese attack on Pearl Harbor, Army Air Corps officials began using an existing runway as a maintenance stopover point for aircraft being ferried to the Caribbean and North Africa.

- In September 1942, officers with the Caribbean Wing of the Air Transport Command began constructing a fully operational military base.

- As the need for trained transport pilots grew during 1943, officials in Washington decided to beef up the training program at Homestead.

- As a result, the entire base was transferred to Air Transport Command's Ferrying Division, and by the end of the year, the 2nd Operational Training Unit's sole mission was to prepare C-54 air crews to fly the famed "Hump" from Burma to China.

- By 1945, Homestead AAF represented the largest four-engine transport training operation in the entire Air Transfer Command: the 2nd Operational Training Unit had graduated 2,250 C-54 pilots, 14,505 copilots; 224 navigators; 85 radio operators; and 1,375 flight engineers.

HISTORICAL SNAPSHOT
1956

- Elizabeth Bishop received a Pulitzer Prize for *Poems, North and South*
- Josephine Bay was named president and Chair of the brokerage house A.M. Kidder and Company to become the first woman to head a New York Stock Exchange member company
- Popular songs included "Blue Suede Shoes," "Love Me Tender," "Too Close for Comfort" and "Mr. Wonderful"
- Approximately 26 percent of all adult women smoked cigarettes; 56 percent of men were smokers
- Acclaimed jazz singer Billie Holiday published "*Lady Sings the Blues*"
- French actress Brigitte Bardot became an international sex symbol after starring in *And God Created Woman*
- The DNA molecule was photographed for the first time
- Former first lady Eleanor Roosevelt received the first Woman of Valor award
- M. E. Tower was the first woman ordained in the Presbyterian church in Syracuse, New York
- Former Milwaukee schoolteacher Golda Myerson became the Israeli prime minister and accepted Premier Ben-Gurion's suggestion that she Hebraize her name to Meir
- Maria Callas's debut in *Norma* at the Metropolitan in New York City grossed $75,500
- Movie premieres included *The King and I* featuring Deborah Kerr and Yul Brynner, *The Ten Commandments* directed by Cecil B. De Mille, and *The Invasion of the Body Snatchers*
- Comet, Raid, Midas Muffler shops, Salem cigarettes, and the adoption of the motto "In God We Trust" all made their first appearance
- Boston religious leaders urged the banning of rock 'n' roll
- In men's fashion, crew cut or flattop haircuts were in; for women the play *My Fair lady* ushered in both flowing and clinging fabrics, and large hats with ribbons and feathers
- The first American test rocket for sending a manmade satellite into orbit ascended 125 miles at 4,000 mph
- Ford Motor Company went public and sold more than 10 million shares to raise $650 million
- The Academy Award for best picture was presented to *Around the World in Eighty Days*, starring David Niven
- Broadway openings included *My Fair Lady, The Diary of Anne Frank, Damn Yankees*, Samuel Beckett's *Waiting for Godot* and Eugene O'Neill's *Long Day's Journey into Night*
- The last Union veteran, a former drummer boy who fought in the Civil War at age 17, died
- Eleven percent of all cars sold were station wagons

- But it all came to a rather abrupt end.
- On September 15, 1945—three years to the day of the base's founding—a massive hurricane barreled through, sending winds of up to 145 mph howling through the cinderblock buildings.
- Enlisted housing facilities, the nurses' dormitory and the base exchange were all destroyed; the base laundry and fire station were both declared total losses, and the few remaining aircraft were tossed about like leaves.
- Following an evaluation of the damage, the decision was made that Homestead AAF would shut down, with a target date for complete closure of December 1, 1945.
- By the time a separate Air Force was created on September 18, 1947, the old Homestead Field lay in ruins.
- When the Soviets began the total land blockade of Berlin in June 1948, the Air Force responded with an unprecedented airlift effort known as Operation Vittles.
- Twenty-four hours a day, seven days a week, for 16 months, Air Force "Skymasters," many of them piloted by Homestead graduates, were winging into and out of Berlin, keeping one of the world's great cities alive.
- In the early 1950s, as the Korean conflict was winding down, defense officials once again looked toward Homestead with an eye to making the site a key player in the continental defense of the U.S.
- In mid-1954, an advance party arrived at the old base to begin cleaning it up, and on February 8, 1955, the installation was reactivated as Homestead Air Force Base.
- The base quickly became home for the 823d Air Division, an umbrella organization encompassing the 379th and 19th Bomber Wings.
- Within a year, Homestead housed more than 4,000 permanently assigned members and a fleet of B-47 "Stratojet" bombers.

Selected Prices

Baby Food, Gerber's, Four Jars	$0.87
Ballet Ticket	$9.50
Boy Scout Uniform	$8.97
Coffee Percolator	$16.88
Girl's Raincoat	$5.74
Ironing Board	$13.95
Lawn Sprinkler	$9.95
Man's Florsheim Shoes	$19.95
Nylons, Kotex	$1.00
Radio, Transistor	$44.00
Stereo	$129.95
Television, Zenith, with Remote	$550.00

1959 PROFILE

Seattle, Washington, native Ronnie Pettigrew, a 26-year-old hairdresser who loves being paid to help people look and feel beautiful, frets so often about being unmarried, she has begun secretly smoking cigarettes after work. Her annual income is $2,855.

Ronnie Pettigrew is paid to make women look and feel beautiful.

Life at Home

- Ronnie Pettigrew has been a hairdresser since she graduated from high school.
- While still in school, Ronnie was worried sick about what she was going to do for a living.
- The high point of her high school career was her time as a majorette, a role she wanted desperately.
- The rest was an endless succession of lectures about her potential, obvious IQ and apparent lack of ambition.
- She couldn't continue living at home, that was for sure; she could not even suggest it to her father.
- With no steady boyfriend, marriage was an unlikely possibility; she was painfully aware that half of all American women were married by age 20.
- As for going to college, that was something others did, or at least talked about.
- Besides, most of the kids who went off to the state university returned after one year with tales of wild parties, little money and less chance of returning to school.
- Then they looked for jobs at Boeing.
- Lots of Ronnie's friends have a love-hate relationship with the city's largest employer, including her Boeing mechanic father.
- "Boeing's like the benevolent kings of Europe," he would repeatedly orate after his second drink of the evening. "They have the power to make or break you based on their whim. The workers are simply well-paid serfs."

- At first, Ronnie did temporary work at the hospital, where she discovered she hated blood, sick people, bossy doctors and trauma.
- She also found that she loved helping the ladies prepare their hair when it was time to return home.
- Washing and styling the hair of new mothers was particularly satisfying; for days the baby had gotten all the attention and finally, for one deliciously guilty moment, it was the mother's turn.

"She Got Her Boots for a Song," by Carlene Grivois, *Reminisce*, September/October 2001:

In the spring of 1952, I was about to graduate from sixth grade in Van Buren, Maine, a tiny town along the St. John Valley, on the Canadian border. More than anything, I wanted to join the town's most prestigious girls' group, the Van Buren Majorettes.

My older sister was already a member. She got to wear the smart-looking uniform royal blue jacket with golf braid and shiny buttons; a short, pleated white skirt; and an elegant, tall, white fur hat with puffy blue plumes. The finishing touch was high white boots with royal blue tassels.

Because I was willing to practice in the town gym every Saturday, I was approved for membership. Now all I needed was a baton and the white boots. The uniform was provided free.

I'd saved enough for the baton but needed $7.98 for the boots. The group's director said that if I started coming to practice, and had my boots, I could debut in the Memorial Day parade—just four weeks away.

Each weekend, I earned $1.25 babysitting. That was $5. But I still needed $2.98, so I scrubbed the porches of two neighbors' homes. One gave me a quarter, the other 20 cents. Then I searched the ditches for empty soda bottles. That got me another 15 cents.

A couple of afternoons, I entertained a toddler for 50 cents while his mother worked. And I helped a younger brother on his paper route for 50 cents more. Then I lucked out babysitting on a school night for 50 cents.

The Friday before Memorial Day, I was still almost $1 short. That night, my father brought his boss home. Dad liked to entertain his guests, and as I was the only one home that night, I sang "On Top of Old Smokey."

The boss applauded, in appreciation or relief, and handed me a dollar!

The next morning I was waiting at the door of Mrs. Belzile's shoe store when she opened for business, and on Memorial Day, I was one of the proud majorettes in the parade.

- Her mother encouraged Ronnie's decision to attend cosmetology school, and even secretly supplied most of the tuition.
- Her father was happy to have his daughter out of the house; after all, doing other ladies' hair wasn't really a career, simply a stopover on the road to marriage.
- When Ronnie got her first paycheck, her dad even suggested that part of it be set aside for her wedding.
- Ronnie bought clothes instead.

"Bell System Rings Up a Fancy New Line," *Business Week*, October 8, 1960:

This year Mother Bell has really lived up to her name; she's given birth to a whole new brood of telephonic devices for the home. Since January, the Bell Telephone System has announced:

The Princess, a demure, newly styled telephone that comes in several colors.

The Farm Interphone, a network of telephones, microphones, and loudspeakers that link a farmhouse, its barns and yards, along with providing standard outside calls.

The Home Interphone, similar in concept to the farm hook-up, but permitting room-to-room communications and even letting you answer the doorbell by telephone.

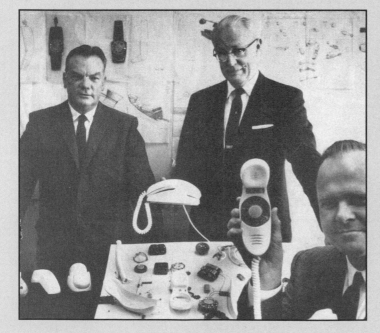

The Bell Chime, which can be set up away from the phone, but will still announce calls by chimes, soft bells, or loud ones.

All this is quite a switch from Bell's traditional approach toward its home customers: All it used to give them was the conventional phone, with no frills at all. Toward its office customers, Bell has long been more liberal, offering them a broad line of communications equipment. But even here the newest policy is a marked stepping up in the tempo of new products. Among the office developments are:

Data-Phone Equipment, which enables computers to chat with one another over telephone lines.

The Call Director, a telephone set that is almost a desk-sized switchboard.

The Bellboy, a little pocket gadget by which your office can signal you to call in or your wife can bid for your attention.

This spate of new product development has sprung from interplay between two company units: (1) a special marketing group for new product planning at the parent American Telephone & Telegraph Co. headquarters in New York, and (2) the company's famous research branch on the other side of the Hudson River, Bell Telephone Laboratories in Murray Hill, N.J.

Life at Work

- Every morning, Ronnie Pettigrew wakes up knowing she's going to make someone's day.
- Simply put, she gets paid to make people look and feel beautiful.
- Working her magic with scissors and gel, Ronnie shapes limp strands of hair into well-styled coifs.
- And when that is not enough, she sharpens her creativity through formal up-dos and inspired color treatments, making clients feel like the most important person on the planet.
- "I love to see them leave smiling," she says when people ask how she is faring in the competitive world of hairdressing.
- The work hours are long, normally eight to 10 hours on her feet, six days a week.
- Saturdays, when all her friends are at the lake having a good time, Ronnie is helping to beautify the good, the potential, and the ugly.
- She especially enjoys doing weddings; on more than one occasion the bride and bridesmaids agreed to let Ronnie work her magic on them.
- Ronnie works with clients of all ages, providing coloring, styling, washing and cutting hair.
- The work is fun and demanding: Mrs. Mildred Johnson is always so picky, as though Ronnie caused the bald patch on the top of her head; Mrs. J. P. Holland is indifferent one week, then a tiger the next—what a witch!
- Mrs. A. G. Wahl talks endlessly about how she is spending her husband's newfound fortune in the real estate business, thanks to the booming economy of Seattle.
- Most of all, the ladies like to talk about when Ronnie is going to get married.
- They have tried repeatedly to arrange blind dates for her with their sons, nephews or friends, all of which have been disasters.
- It's bad enough to hate your date, but its simply awful to have to explain yourself to his mother while she is sitting in the beauty parlor chair.
- The pressure to find a mate and get married has upset Ronnie so much, she now secretly smokes cigarettes to calm herself down.

Ronnie especially enjoys doing weddings.

- The other hard part of working in a beauty parlor is being on her feet all day.
- Standing for long periods can make Ronnie's back ache, but the ladies never want to hear about her woes, Ronnie has found.
- Day after day, she keeps her young mouth shut about her troubles while she learns about life from a steady stream of talking heads.
- She has learned to ignore hunger and hurt hands, too.
- When Ronnie looks in the mirror at night, she is concerned that she is becoming round-shouldered from the work, and thus, will never get a man.

"Speed-Up on Atomic Plane, Air Force and Navy Submit Competing Proposals for Nuclear-powered Craft," *Life*, January 20, 1958:

Last week, spurred by news that the Russians were hard at work on a nuclear aircraft program, the U.S. took steps to speed its own building of an atomic plane—a plane whose all-but-inexhaustible fuel supply would give it almost unlimited range. The new sense of urgency made it certain that someone would soon get the money and authority for high-priority action. The Navy favors developing an atomic seaplane which, it claims, could be safely flown and tested far from populated areas. But the Air Force will probably get the job, on which it has already spent over $200 million.

The Air Force began planning a nuclear plane 10 years ago. But aside from research on the ground and a few test flights in which a B-36 carried a reactor aloft to study radiation effects, not much was done. The Department of Defense and the AEC saw so little military justification of pushing the program, in fact, that at one point it was in danger of being killed.

The first nuclear plane decision facing the Defense Department is this: whether to put nuclear power into an existing plane or whether to build a new plane around a nuclear system. If an existing plane were used, it could be flown in two to four years with consequent help in U.S. prestige. If a new plane were built, it would take longer but would produce a more operational craft.

- Thursdays are particularly hard, since the shop stays open from 8 a.m. to 8 p.m.
- The money is good, particularly the tips from after-hours customers, but it hardly enriches her social life.
- For Ronnie, who is slow and methodical by nature, hairdressing can be a physical and mental strain.
- With a client coming in every half hour, extra care for one lady means being late to tend to another.
- And even when she thinks the clients' comments are stupid, she has to pay attention and remember *everything* in case the customer wants to pick up that old conversational string weeks later when she comes for another appointment.
- After eight years, Ronnie can predict the conversational flow of many of the ladies; some talk about children, others focus on recent country club parties, while several simply love to exchange gossip.
- Nothing and no one is sacred, she has learned.
- Since becoming a hairdresser, Ronnie has begun reading the local newspaper to keep up with the people under discussion in her chair.
- Most Thursdays, Ronnie does the hair of Mrs. Karen Martin at 10 a.m., and then of Mr. Martin's mistress at 1:30 p.m.; each describes the activities of the past week with the same man from a different perspective.
- Much of the talk is about Boeing and its future, and what it will mean for Seattle.
- Everyone has an opinion about Boeing, and not everyone is for the growth predicted for it.
- At work, Ronnie feels confident and in control because she knows how to make her clients happy.

Advertisements often feature the science of homemaking.

- When she leaves the shop, she becomes shy, often deferential and sometimes awkward.
- Always good with her hands, she finds she is more creative than her high school teachers had believed, and despite her normal shyness, she communicates well with her customers once they have seated themselves.
- Ronnie sees herself as a professional with a real career.
- When traveling around the city, she is always looking at people's hair.
- Television has been a particular inspiration; often the New York fashions take a while to reach Seattle, and Ronnie loves to talk about the latest looks, even if she will never go to New York or Paris.
- Currently, the top style-setters are Jacqueline Kennedy, Marilyn Monroe, Audrey Hepburn and Sophia Loren.
- Their looks reflect total glamour, made possible only because they are close friends with their professional hairstylists.

Life in the Community: Seattle, Washington

- After some post-World War II readjustments, the United States hit its economic stride in the 1950s, rolling up a 50 percent increase in the gross national product.
- Seattle, Washington, in particular has benefited from both the postwar prosperity and the looming spectre of war with Communism, popularly known as the Cold War.
- Nationwide, real wages and employment have risen.
- Consumers are on a spending spree, eager to buy television sets, power mowers, decorator telephones, poodle skirts, flashy cars and the ubiquitous barbecue grill.
- On New Year's Day, 1956, a *Seattle Times* front-page story detailed the state's economic good news: The 1955 demand for lumber had been solid; plywood and paper manufacture was thriving; hydroelectric and natural gas construction projects rushed ahead to meet demand; the aluminum industry was expanding its capacity; and the Port of Seattle raced to accommodate increasing cargo tonnage, up nearly 40 percent above the previous year.

JET AHEAD WITH TORRINGTON BEARINGS—

Extra heavy outer race for heavy rolling loads. Also available in double row type.

ON **ALL** THE GREAT NEW JETS

Heavy outer race, integral stud permit cantilever mounting for use as track roller.

specially designed to withstand heaviest rolling and shock   and the utmost in dependable commercial jet service

- For Seattle, Boeing is *the* real success story.
- Boeing's payroll pumps $8.5 million into the local economy every two weeks.
- About 35,000 men and women work for The Big B, slightly more than half of all manufacturing employees in the metropolitan area.
- Some fret about Seattle being a one-company city, but generally it is proud of its role in growing the industry giant from its modest beginnings in 1916.
- As a result, the newspaper is always eager to provide coverage of Boeing's resurgence as a Cold War military contractor for the B-47 Stratojet and the B-52 Stratofortress jet bombers, and as a developer of jetliners for the commercial airlines.
- President Dwight Eisenhower's proposed defense budget is also getting big headlines.
- Military projects for Boeing total more than $1 billion and include 72 LC-135 jet tanker transports, 40 B-52H Stratofortress bombers, a secret number of Superbomarc missiles, and nearly $500,000 for the DynaSoar, Boeing's candidate for the manned space program.
- For the past several years, the news media has also featured the race between Boeing 707 Stratoliners and competitor Douglas Aircraft Company DC-8s to win the commercial jet transport market.

HISTORICAL SNAPSHOT
1959

- Eighty-six percent of the population owned a television set; the average person watched TV 42 hours each week
- Reports of contaminated cranberries at Thanksgiving frightened millions
- Lorraine Hansberry won the New York Drama Critics Circle Award for *A Raisin in the Sun,* the first play to appear on Broadway that was written by a black woman
- Weather stations, a nuclear merchant ship, the Lark automobile, movies with a scent (*Behind the Great Wall*), and transparent plastic bags for clothing all made their first appearance
- Television premieres included *Peter Gunn, The Donna Reed Show, The Rifleman, The Lawman* and *Concentration*
- The U.S. restored citizenship to Japanese Americans who were disenfranchised during the war
- Kraft Foods signed a $25 million contract with singer Perry Como
- Russian Premier Khrushchev was denied entrance to Disneyland because his safety could not be guaranteed
- Lee Krasner painted her *Earth Green* series, while Mark Rothko created *Four Darks in Red, Red, Brown and Black* and Jasper Johns produced *Three Flags*
- Radio and television star Gertrude Berg received a Tony Award for her role in the Broadway play *Dear Me, the Sky Is Falling*
- The average car cost $1,180
- Rock and roll stars Buddy Holly, Richie Valens and the Big Bopper were killed in a plane crash
- Movie premieres included *Gigi, Cat on a Hot Tin Roof, South Pacific, Touch of Evil* and Alfred Hitchcock's *Vertigo*
- Fads included Go-karts, black leotards and parachute jumping as a sport
- The American Football League was organized by Lamar Hunt with eight teams
- Paleontologist Mary Leakey discovered the fossilized molars of a humanlike creature in Tanzania, believed to be 1.75 million years old
- Stereo records were introduced by EMI and Decca Records
- Bestsellers included *Kids Say the Darndest Things!* by Art Linkletter, *Please Don't Eat the Daisies* by Jean Kerr, *The Better Homes and Gardens Salad Book, Dear Abby* by Abigail Van Buren and *Inside Russia Today* by John Gunther

The Twentieth Century History of Seattle, Washington

1901–1910

- Seattle's first Sephardic Jews arrive in 1902
- Seattle Symphony Orchestra performs for the first time in 1903
- Olmsted arrives in Seattle to design city parks in April 1903
- The Alaska Building, Seattle's first steel-framed skyscraper, is completed in 1904
- Cedar River Power Plant, the first municipally owned power plant in the United States, starts on January 10, 1905
- The Carnegie-funded Public Library opens in downtown Seattle in 1906
- American Messenger Service, forerunner of UPS, begins in Seattle's Pioneer Square on August 28, 1907
- Pike Place Market in Seattle opens on August 17, 1907
- Seattle's first "World's Fair," the Alaska-Yukon-Pacific Exposition, was held in 1909
- A transcontinental auto race ends in Seattle on June 23, 1909
- Women in Washington state win the vote on November 8, 1910
- An airplane flies in Seattle for the first time in 1910
- The population of King County reached 284,000 in 1910

1911–1920

- King County voters create Port of Seattle in 1911
- Smith Tower, the tallest building west of the Mississippi, opens in 1914
- William E. Boeing builds his first airplane in 1916
- Washington voters prohibit the sale and possession of alcohol in 1916
- Lake Washington Ship Canal is completed on May 8, 1917
- The Stanley Cup is won by the Seattle Metropolitan hockey team on March 26, 1917

- Seattle takes over ownership and operation of the streetcar system on April 1, 1919
- A general strike paralyzes Seattle for a week in February 1919
- Western Washington's first radio station begins broadcasting in 1920
- According to the 1920 Census, the population of Seattle tops 315,000, and that of King County nears 390,000 in 1920

1921–1930

- Community bonds fund construction of the Olympic Hotel in 1924
- Seattle elects Bertha K. Landes as first woman mayor of a major U.S. city in 1926
- Boeing begins forming United Airlines in 1927
- Boeing Field, Seattle's first municipal airport, opens on July 26, 1928
- The stock market crash halts the downtown building boom in 1929
- The final phase of the Denny Regrade section of Seattle is completed in 1930
- The population of Seattle tops 365,000, and that of King County tops 460,000 in 1930

1931–1940

- Aurora Bridge is completed in 1932
- "Hooverville" shantytown forms south of Pioneer Square in early 1932
- The Seattle Art Museum opens in Volunteer Park on June 23, 1933
- The West Coast waterfront strike spreads to Seattle Harbor in 1934
- The Boeing 247, first modern airliner, debuts in 1933
- A prototype of the Boeing B-17 makes its maiden flight in 1935
- A strike shuts down the *Seattle Post-Intelligencer* in 1936
- According to the 1940 Census, the population of Seattle stagnates at 368,000, and that of King County tops 500,000 in 1940

(continued)

(continued)

1941–1950

- Trackless trolleys and buses replace streetcars in the Seattle Transit System on April 13, 1941
- Japanese Americans are ordered to evacuate Seattle on April 21, 1942
- Boeing intensifies production of bombers at Boeing and Renton factories in 1940s, and for the first time hires large numbers of women and African American workers
- Boeing B-29s drop atomic bombs on Japan on August 6 and 9, 1945, ending World War II
- The University of Washington opens a medical school on October 2, 1946
- The Canwell Commission begins investigating "Un-American Activities" in 1947
- The First wide-audience TV broadcast is seen around Puget Sound on November 25, 1948
- The Port of Seattle dedicates Seattle-Tacoma International Airport in 1949

- According to the 1950 Census, the population of Seattle tops 465,000, and that of King County tops 730,000 in 1950

1951–1960

- The first summer "Seafair" is held in 1951
- The Alaskan Way Viaduct, first downtown "freeway," opens in 1952
- Bellevue incorporates in 1953
- Seattle expands its boundaries in 1954
- Boeing 707 prototype makes its maiden flight on July 15, 1954
- King County voters approve "Metro" plan to clean up Lake Washington in 1958
- Dr. Arno Motulsky, a medical geneticist at the University of Washington, collects a blood sample in Africa of the first documented case of HIV in 1959
- The Port of Seattle expansion is approved by King County voters on November 8, 1960
- The population of Seattle tops 550,000, and that of King County tops 925,000 in 1960

AN UP-TO-DA
FROM B

- As recently as 1956, Boeing depended on federal money for 98 percent of its business; this year, 50 percent of the company's revenues come from America's growing love of flying.
- Currently, 1.5 million air travelers pass through Seattle-Tacoma Airport, another good signal to dispel fears that air travel would remain a luxury and the airport would be an empty failure.
- Instead, commercial jet flight is a raging success.
- In 1959, Boeing booked orders for nearly 200 707 airplanes.
- In Seattle, local retail sales nearly doubled, and the average family income increased from $5,255 to $7,042, a 34 percent jump during the boom between 1951 and 1960.
- By all indications, Seattle has arrived: its streets and shops are bustling, while its theaters, restaurants and cultural institutions are more sophisticated and cosmopolitan than ever before.
- The Alaskan Way viaduct was completed along the waterfront, and the Washington, Logan and Norton buildings are changing the city's skyline.

Selected Prices

Airfare, TWA, Chicago to Los Angeles $76.00
Automobile, Cadillac Eldorado $13,075
Brassiere, Playtex $3.95
Guitar, Acoustic $35.00
Hotel Room, Ritz-Carlton, Boston, per Night $9.00
House, Chicago Area, Four Bedrooms $34,000
Iron $9.88
Lighter, Zippo, Chrome Finish $4.75
Makeup, Revlon $1.35
Mattress, Simmons Beautyrest $79.50
Milk, Quart $0.60
Paneling, 12' x 8' Wall $47.00

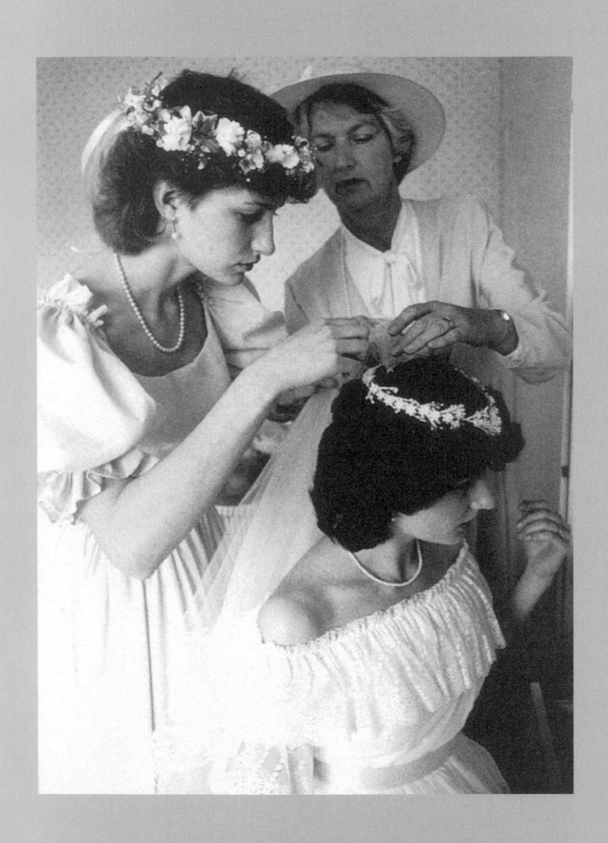

1960–1969

No aspect of American society escaped the tumult of the 1960s. Morality, education, the role of the family, the purpose of college and even the need for parents came into question. Following the placid era of the 1950s, the seventh decade of the twentieth century contained tragic assassinations, momentous social movements, remarkable space achievements, and the longest war in American history. Civil Rights leader Martin Luther King, Jr., would deliver his "I have a dream" speech in 1963, the same year President John F. Kennedy was killed. Five years later in 1968, King, along with John Kennedy's influential brother Bobby, would be killed. Violent protests against American involvement in Vietnam would be led and heavily supported by the educated middle class, which had grown and prospered enormously in the American economy.

From 1960 to 1964, the economy expanded; unemployment was low and disposable income for music, vacations, art or simply having fun grew rapidly. Internationally, the power of the United States was immense. Congress gave the young President John F. Kennedy the defense and space-related programs Americans wanted, but few of the welfare programs he proposed. Then, inflation arrived, along with the Vietnam War. Between 1950 and 1965, inflation soared from an annual average of less than two percent (ranging from six percent to 14 percent a year) to a budget-popping average of 9.5 percent. Upper class investors, once content with the consistency and stability of banks, sought better returns in the stock market and real estate.

The Cold War became hotter during conflicts over Cuba and Berlin in the early 1960s. Fears over the international spread of communism led to America's intervention in a foreign conflict that would become a defining event of the decade: Vietnam. Military involvement in this small Asian country grew from advisory status to full-scale war. By 1968, Vietnam had become a national obsession leading to President Lyndon Johnson's decision not to run for another term and fueling not only debate over our role in Vietnam, but more inflation and division nationally. The antiwar movement grew rapidly. Antiwar marches, which had drawn but a few thousand in 1965, grew in size until millions of marchers filled the streets of New York, San Francisco, and Washington, DC, only a few years later. By spring 1970, students on 448 college campuses made ROTC voluntary or abolished it.

The struggle to bring economic equality to blacks during the period produced massive spending for school integration. By 1963, the peaceful phase of the Civil Rights movement was ending; street violence, assassinations, and bombings defined the period. In 1967, 41 cities experienced major disturbances. At the same time, charismatic labor organizer Cesar Chavez's United Farm Workers led a Civil Rights-style movement for Mexican-Americans, gaining national support which challenged the growers of the West with a five-year agricultural strike.

As a sign of increasing affluence and changing times, American consumers bought 73 percent fewer potatoes and 25 percent more fish, poultry, and meat and 50 percent more citrus products and tomatoes than in 1940. California passed New York as the most populous state. Factory workers earned more than $100 a week, their highest wages in history. From 1960 to 1965, the amount of money spent for prescription drugs to lose weight doubled, while the per capita consumption of processed potato chips rose from 6.3 pounds in 1958 to 14.2 pounds eight years later. In 1960, approximately 40 percent of American adult women had paying jobs; 30 years later, the number would grow to 57.5 percent. Their emergence into the work force would transform marriage, child rearing, and the economy. In 1960, women were also liberated by the FDA's approval of the birth-control pill, giving both women and men a degree of control over their bodies that had never existed before.

During the decade, anti-establishment sentiments grew: men's hair was longer and wilder, beards and mustaches became popular, women's skirts rose to mid-thigh, and bras were discarded. Hippies advocated alternative lifestyles, drug use increased, especially marijuana and LSD; the Beatles, the Rolling Stones, Jimi Hendrix, and Janis Joplin became popular music figures; college campuses became major sites for demonstrations against the war and for Civil Rights. The Supreme Court prohibited school prayer, assured legal counsel to the poor, limited censorship of sexual material, and increased the rights of the accused.

Extraordinary space achievements also marked the decade. Ten years after President Kennedy announced he would place a man on the moon, 600 million people around the world watched as Neil Armstrong gingerly lowered his left foot into the soft dust of the moon's surface. In a tumultuous time of division and conflict, the landing was one of America's greatest triumphs and an exhilarating demonstration of American genius. Its cost was $25 billion and set the stage for 10 other men to walk on the surface of the moon during the next three years.

The 1960s saw the birth of Enovid 10, the first oral contraceptive (cost $0.55 each), the start of Berry Gordy's Motown Records, felt-tip pens, Diet-Rite cola, Polaroid color film, Weight Watchers, and Automated Teller Machines. It's the decade when lyrics began appearing on record albums, Jackie and Aristotle Onassis reportedly spent $20 million during their first year together, and the Gay Liberation Front participated in the Hiroshima Day March—the first homosexual participation as a separate constituency in a peace march.

1963 PROFILE

Betty Jean Cargill, who grew up in a small, isolated community in West Virginia, wants her photographs to impact a much wider world. Her annual income is $3,886.

Life at Home

- Betty Jean Cargill grew up in a mountain community so small even the locals considered it "the backside of beyond."
- Spencer, West Virginia, is situated in the center of the state, approximately 90 minutes from Parkersburg and three hours from Huntington.
- Or, like Betty Jean's daddy might have said, "Slap dab in the middle of nowhere."
- The roads are so circuitous that distances are always explained in minutes, not miles, such as, "The grocery store is 20 minutes from here, about three miles the way the crow flies."
- The town does boast the Robey movie theater, opened in 1907, which the historical society believes to be the longest continuously operating movie house in the U.S.
- Betty Jean can't verify its age, only that it is old—real old.
- But that movie theater may have been where Betty Jean fell in love with pictures and images of all kinds.
- She likes to tell those who ask, "As a mountain girl, the whole idea of being able to create pictures that others would see around the world simply feels magical."
- That's why she became a photographer.
- Besides, during WWII the military was looking for women recruits to fill in on non-combat jobs, a perfect place for a smart woman eager to learn.
- At first she was assigned principally to developing film in a darkroom the size of a deluxe closet.

Betty Jean Cargill got her photography training in the military.

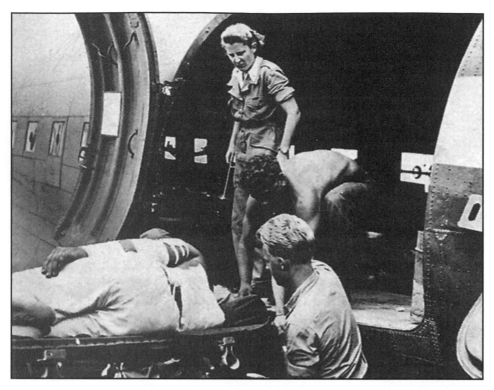

Betty Jean proved herself after a train derailment.

- Then the military allowed her to shoot photographs of promotions, parades and medal awarding ceremonies on base.
- Then came the train wreck.
- Betty Jean was off duty, but still carrying her Rolleiflex twin lens camera, when she heard about the troop train derailment and its resulting injuries.
- In the midst of chaos, Betty Jean worked methodically to record everything that night—the train, workers, the injured, the dead.
- Then, going without sleep, she spent the night developing pictures and making prints that would be available immediately.
- The praise was thunderous.
- After that, Betty Jean's assignments included field maneuvers and combat deployments.
- Betty Jean thinks that women have an advantage over men in many situations because they might be less confrontational or aggressive when pursuing stories.
- This does not mean she is any less prepared than men to be as forceful as necessary in order to get the photo.
- Betty Jean rarely has trouble with troops; they respect her and allow her to do her job because she makes it clear she will not take any of their guff.
- Although all of her assignments during the war were stateside, she was ready and willing to be deployed to the European or Asian theaters of war.

"The ideal newspaper woman has the keen zest for life of a child, the cool courage of a man and the subtlety of a woman."

—Annie Laurie

"Feb. 18, 1952, Rome, Italy. The Realta Hotel in a white room with watermelon curtains. I think that the wonderful thing that is happening or has happened to me is that I am growing up; or I am grown up and enjoying it. I have found the human race. It is like finding one's family at last. I have no more silly questions about what is art or why is art. Seeing the great works of the Italian Renescance [sic] has answered them. It is a personal thing. These people are my ancestors in spirit if not in fact. I think feeling like this must be akin to feeling religion although it is different. No questions are answered but they need not be."

—Diary of photojournalist Esther Bubley

Life at Work

- After her military experience, Betty Jean Cargill returned to Spencer, West Virginia, eager to show the world what she had learned.
- Spencer, she quickly learned, was not ready or very interested in the adventures of a woman photographer, especially since the town boasted half a dozen male war veterans, complete with purple heart-winning injuries.
- She tried shooting pictures of farm activities for a fee, but few in this impoverished industry wanted to pay.
- Many thought that Betty Jean was simply working on a newfound hobby.
- Most were as taciturn as her father.
- So in 1953, she set up a photo studio and occasionally shot pictures for the local weekly newspaper.
- That first year, she gained considerable recognition for using a box kite to shoot aerial photographs of the Christmas parade.
- Within months she was inundated with work, all from brides eager to escape the glare of local male photographers who loved to imply that there was more than one way to pay for pictures of beautiful girls.
- The young women of West Virginia felt safe with Betty Jean, and she made enough money to buy some great photography equipment before becoming completely bored.
- Nearly every shoot shared several elements: a nervous bride-to-be, a bossy mother, disagreements about hairstyle, a panic over the way the dress fit, at least one shouting match between mother and daughter about "whose wedding this was" and, of course, lots of white fabric.
- Betty Jean became an expert at lighting wedding dresses to capture subtle shadows in their folds, while highlighting the best facial features of the bride.
- She considered herself a good photographer who performed magic in the darkroom.
- In her hands, with the proper lighting, pounds melted away, ruddy farm faces glowed and neglected teeth sparkled.
- The other mainstay in Spencer was pictures of children.
- Kids, Betty Jean quickly learned, were never as cute or as well-behaved as their parents believed; she hated photographing babies, in particular, except when she could capture the perfect tear streaking down the cheek of a howling youngster.

"Party Line," by Marcy Shwam, *Teen Magazine*, November 1964:

Flash! Biggest Fad with teens at Jefferson High, Pittsburgh, Pa., is pulling the hooks off blouses or shirts, and the practice is becoming fanciful. For example, the person claiming the hook is known as fairy godmother to the person who forfeits the hook. Your fairy godmother is supposed to grant you three wishes. If she does, she is a real princess. Got it?

The scoop from Wollaston, Massachusetts, right outside Boston, is that Beatle fashions are in everything from sweatshirts to hats. "Bye Bye Birdie" blouses are the cutest and everyone digs them. They're worn mostly with dungaree Bermudas, and denim skirts worn with checkered blouses are still going strong.

"Low-Altitude Aerial Photos Taken from Box Kite," by C.L. Meehanm, Lakeview, Ontario, Canada, *Photokinks*, 1951:

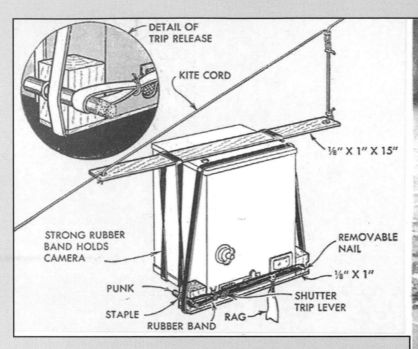

Here's a novel way to take clear aerial photos of homes in your neighborhood with the lowest possible investment in practical aerial photo equipment. Any kite capable of lifting an ordinary box camera in light to moderate winds will do. An automatic shutter-release mechanism consisting of two wooden blocks, two rubber bands and a punk of the kind used to ignite fireworks is attached to the camera. Then the assembly is fastened to the kite cord as indicated. Note that a cord is knotted around the rubber band just under the shutter trip lever and also that a small piece of white rag is attached to this band. In taking the picture, you ignite the punk and send up the kite with camera attached. As soon as the punk has burned sufficiently, it releases the rubber band, which trips the shutter and falls clear, the telltale cloth indicating when the shutter has been released. Remember, there is some danger of fire when shrubs and grass are dry.

- In 1956, after eight years in business, Betty Jean walked out of her studio in the midst of a particularly vicious mother/daughter fight and never went back.
- A month later she was working as a news photographer in Youngstown, Ohio, where they didn't mind having a female photographer as long as she knew her place.
- That was seven years ago.
- Now, at 43, Betty Jean is accustomed to making her own way in a man's world, especially one as brimming with testosterone as a newsroom.
- In the beginning, she knew that she would have to earn every assignment and every picture placement; she also knew that in the newspaper business, reporting and after-hours drinking were part of the same world.
- After almost a decade of politely sipping her father's high proof moonshine whiskey, she was ready for a bunch of beer-and-a-shot-glass guys who needed to prove something night after night.
- Besides, she knew from the beginning she could let her photos speak for themselves.
- Her break came when she was assigned to do a series of pictures in the steel mill.

Betty Jean turned a routine industrial assignment into a much-beloved photographic feature story.

"Can She Boil a Pot of Water, Billy Boy?" by Jeanne Lamb O'Neill, *American Home*, October 1966:

I hope that with all the whoop-de-do about science in the schools today we're not forgetting about dowdy old domestic science. I hope that we're not too busy making our daughters physically fit to make them femininely fit. I'd hate to think we're raising a brand-new breed of egg-headed, ham-legged super girls who can't boil water.

Not that I think the schools are to blame. Most schools make some attempt to expose our children to the homely arts. Sean made cranberry relish in school one year. Cindy once "cooked" some sugar-coated dates. I hear that in our local junior high, girls get three hours of home economics a week (four, I believe, if they're not "gifted or superior" students selected for higher things). That may not be much, but I think we can be grateful Susie's getting any domestic education at all in school. Because I'm not sure Susie's even learning which end of the mop is up at home.

So far as I can see, some of today's young things may never be able to leave their mothers. Never mind if they can make a cherry pie. I know teenager girls who can't make a bed properly, professionally, with snappy hospital corners. I know teenage girls who can't peel a potato or iron a hanky. We've had babysitters who couldn't get the children's dinner if you put a can of spaghetti in their hands and opened it for them. Maybe I shouldn't talk about babysitters; it's possible they're perfect whizzes in their own homes but purposely helpless in mine. But I can't help wondering about the ever-so-willing dumb Doras who load the dirty dishes on top of my clean ones and scrub my antique Italian marble with scouring powder. Obviously, Dora missed a lesson somewhere. And think of all the

Doras in our college dorms who blithely boil their cashmeres and wash their red things with white things—unless they ship the dirty laundry home to mom each week.

I don't mean to pick on teenagers. I've read that teenagers are generically good-for-nothing. (Okay, I remember that teenagers are good-for-nothing.) Teenagers are supposed to rebel against responsibility and suddenly switch from mother's little helpers to Satan's little lounge-lizards. So let's grant that this, too, shall pass and half of today's helpless Hannahs will be tomorrow's crackerjack housekeepers—and let's pick on even littler kids. You just have to observe the young friends your children bring home for dinner or to spend the night. You can tell right away who's being brought up by mother and who's bringing mother up. Some children automatically swoop up their dishes when they leave the table and automatically tuck their pj's and trading cards back in the suitcase, and automatically make their bed. Other children wouldn't pick up a plate if they dropped it right in the middle of the kitchen floor. They're the ones, I'm sure, who couldn't cook a piece of toast or run water in the bathtub without screaming for mom. Interestingly enough, some of the best little table-cleaners who visit our house are boys. It's not surprising at all these days to hear of strapping young he-men who can cook and sew and iron as well as they can throw a pass or make a basket. In fact, a third of the junior contestants in the Pillsbury Bake-Off this year were boys. Ditto for the Delmarva Chicken Festival. Now wouldn't it be a pretty pickle if our girls start asking Billy Boy if he can bake a cherry pie?

- The other photographers thought it was a puff piece until they saw what Betty Jean produced using natural light techniques that dramatically captured the heroics of working in the mill.
- After that, and a perfectly lit photograph of a young couple's car that lost a late-night race with a speeding train, Betty Jean became "one of the guys."
- She did not consider it the compliment they meant it to be, but knew that the assignments and pay would get better.
- The pay was good enough that the bank agreed to lend her $2,000—without a man's signature—to buy a car.
- Before agreeing to the loan for an unmarried woman, however, the bank president called Betty Jean's managing editor to check on her employment status and quietly make it clear to the newspaper that they now owed him a favor.
- Because of its roominess and German engineering, Betty Jean purchased an Opel Caravan wagon, advertised as the "big small car built in Germany by General Motors."
- It boasts 30 miles per gallon, 56 horsepower and lots of space for camera equipment.
- Despite better equipment and the resources to buy it, her favorite camera remains the Rolleiflex 6X6.
- First introduced in 1929, the Rolleiflex quickly became famous worldwide because of its versatility, sharpness of focus and flexibility.
- The film and negative are large, giving a darkroom professional lots of room to correct lighting mistakes made in the field.
- It is perfect for unexpected news jobs such as fires, accidents, murders, or anything that happens suddenly or in which the lighting conditions are uncontrollable.
- Recently, a rural farmhouse fire required that she walk half a mile through a muddy field to get the right view, while a male reporter, refusing to get his trousers dirty, hung back to talk with the fire chief along the main road.
- Betty Jean didn't have to say a word when the two arrived back at the newsroom; anyone who looked at them knew who was the real journalist.
- Her true victory was when she was able to take her pictures back to the family whose farmhouse had caught fire; they invited her to dinner and said a blessing in her honor, despite all they had lost.
- Photography is how Betty Jean connects to the community.
- Even though it is bigger, Youngstown is like her hometown in West Virginia; the subjects of her photographs are neighbors, friends or people she sees in the grocery store.
- It doesn't pay to have a falling out in a small community; word gets around quickly.
- Betty Jean is thinking about an assignment for the Chamber of Commerce; they want a pretty picture piece of a town that has more than a few blemishes.
- The pay is excellent—almost a month's wages for a weekend's work, but Betty Jean is unsure about taking the money of the most powerful men in the community.
- She thinks she would rather be broke than bought.

Betty Jean's car is an Opel Caravan wagon built in Germany.

Life in the Community: Youngstown, Ohio

- The cityscape of Youngstown, Ohio, features few new tall buildings.
- With a population of approximately 165,000, the city, Betty Jean thinks, looks frozen in time at about 1940.
- The day President John F. Kennedy was shot, she learned to see the town in a whole new way.
- Sent out by the newspaper to shoot pictures of the public's reaction, she found that Youngstown was united in grief, disbelief and tears.
- Some people were angry, others sad, but most were stunned as they absorbed the impact of the news.
- Betty Jean shot pictures until her arms were weary; long after she had completed the assignment she continued to point her camera into the face of grief and expose herself to the national tragedy.
- On Sunday, when Kennedy's accused assassin was shot and killed, that death, too, was a moment for Youngstown to gather again to watch over and over on television the shooting of Lee Harvey Oswald.
- In that moment, Betty Jean was proud of the unity she discovered in her community, and confused that this type of violence was possible in the country she loved.
- Her pictures of that day, many of which captured national honors after being transmitted by the Associated Press, are framed in her tiny apartment duplex rented from an 86-year-old woman.

Betty Jean's pictures captured high emotion the day President Kennedy was assassinated.

"JFK IS ASSASSINATED," by Frank Cormier, *Associated Press*, November 23, 1963:

A hidden gunman assassinated President Kennedy with a high-powered rifle Friday.

Three shots reverberated and blood sprang from the president's face. He fell face downward. His wife clutched his head crying, "Oh, no."

Within half an hour, John F. Kennedy was dead and the United States had a new president, Lyndon B. Johnson.

Within the hour, police arrested a 24-year-old man following the fatal shooting of a Dallas policeman. Homicide Capt. Will Fritz said Friday night witnesses had identified the man as the slayer of the policeman and he had been charged with murder.

Fritz said it had not been established that the man killed the president—but it had been established that he was in the building from which the shots were fired at the time of the assassination.

He is Harvey Lee Oswald [sic] of Fort Worth, who four years ago said he was applying for Soviet citizenship. He has a Russian wife.

Oswald denied that he had shot anybody.

HISTORICAL SNAPSHOT
1963

- President John F. Kennedy was shot and killed in Dallas, Texas
- Betty Friedan published *The Feminine Mystique,* challenging the image of the happy housewife
- Television premieres included *The Fugitive, The Patty Duke Show, My Favorite Martian, Petticoat Junction* and *Let's Make A Deal*
- Katherine Graham became president of The Washington Post Company, and the only female head of a Fortune 500 company
- The Beatles crashed the American music scene with their first big hit, "I Want to Hold Your Hand"
- U.S. factory workers earned more than $100 a week, a new record
- The March on Washington for Jobs and Freedom attracted thousands to hear Martin Luther King deliver his "I Have a Dream" speech
- Julia Child prepared boeuf bourguignon on television to launch her popular French cooking program
- Fifty women each week applied to *Playboy* to become "Playmate of the Month"
- American poet and novelist Sylvia Plath published her autobiographical novel *The Bell Jar*
- Sidney Poitier won the Academy Award for best actor in *Lilies of the Field,* while *Tom Jones* won best picture
- Broadway openings included *Barefoot in the Park, Enter Laughing, One Flew over the Cuckoo's Nest* and the musical *Oliver!*
- Fourteen thousand people were arrested in 75 southern cities during civil rights demonstrations
- Mary Petermann discovered Petermann's particles, or ribosomes, the sites of protein synthesis
- Hit songs included "Wipeout," "Call Me Irresponsible," "If I Had a Hammer," "Puff (the Magic Dragon)," "Da Doo Ron Ron" and "The Times They Are a-Changin'"
- The Kodak Instamatic camera, the New York Hilton, Weight Watchers, the Trimline phone and Spiderman all made their first appearance
- Illegitimate births among teenage mothers were up 150 percent over 1940
- California passed New York as the most populous state
- Police Chief Bull Connors of Birmingham, Alabama, used police dogs, fire hoses and cattle prods on civil rights marchers to break up a demonstration
- New Hampshire authorized government-sponsored lotteries designed to raise money for education
- Congress approved legislation guaranteeing equal pay for equal work

- Youngstown was named for John Young, who settled here in 1797 after purchasing the entire township from the federal government via the Western Reserve Land Company.
- The area was part of the Connecticut Western Reserve, to which most early European-American settlers came.
- Within a year "Youngstown" was settled by 10 families near where Mill Creek meets the Mahoning River, and the town was incorporated in 1802.
- Because the area was endowed with coal and iron, the first blast furnace was built east of the city in 1803, and the town soon developed a thriving steel industry.
- Youngstown was on the Pennsylvania-Ohio Canal, completed in 1839, and the railroad came to the town in 1853.
- In 1867, Youngstown was incorporated as a city, and the county seat was moved there from Canfield in 1876.
- From the 1920s through the 1960s, the city became an important industrial hub with large furnaces and foundries of such companies as Republic Steel and U.S. Steel.
- It is headquarters for the huge Youngstown Sheet and Tube Company, one of the most important industrial metal producers in the country.

Selected Prices

Air Conditioner, 5,800 BTU $158.00
Board Game, Monopoly $3.33
Camera, Bell and Howell Canon $149.50
Drive-in Movie, per Car $1.50
Man's Shirt, Hathaway $8.95
Mixer, Sunbeam $49.95
Movie Ticket $2.25
Purse, Leather $5.00
Socks, Woman's Knee-High $2.00
Stereo Phonograph, Magnavox $650.00
Swimsuit, Woman's $24.00
Whiskey, Canadian Club, Quart $7.85

"A Word to Wives, by JFK's Doc," *San Francisco Examiner*, June 16, 1961. "Dr. Janet Travell, President Kennedy's physician, today offered some rules for housewives":

"Scramble your work. Don't spend all of one day cleaning, another day doing laundry, and a third ironing. That way you use some muscles too much, others not enough.

Cultivate a rhythmic pattern. Don't hurry; don't jerk the movements. Just do your housework as if you doing a modern dance.

Take short rests at frequent intervals.

Don't tolerate bad physical and mechanical arrangements in your home. Don't tolerate uncomfortable chairs or too-low sinks.

Counteract housework with an entirely different kind of muscle movement, a variety of exercises."

"Working Girls Beat Living Cost," *San Francisco Examiner*, March 2, 1961:

"The working girl kept a skip and a jump ahead of the rise in the cost of living last year. In fact, she received the equivalent of an extra week's pay—enough to buy one good suit.

John Dana of the Department of Labor disclosed yesterday that the average office girl received a 4.3 percent raise in salary while the cost of living was going up 1.6 percent. This gave her a 1.9 percent increase in real earnings after allowing for high prices and taxes.

Her boyfriend received a somewhat smaller percentage increase, but about the same amount of cash if he worked the year 'round. One analyst remarked that the lower increase for the boyfriend was the more important statistic. The analyst, a woman, explained: 'After all, how is the poor working girl going to get married if her boyfriend can't earn more money?'

Dana, the department's assistant to the Regional Director of Labor Statistics, said local stenographers, with an average weekly salary of $84.00, have received a 47.3 percent boost in wages since January, 1952. In the same period, the cost of living has risen 18.5 percent, giving her a net increase in real spendable earnings of 21.5 percent.

The weekly salaries of women office workers ranged from an average $60.50 for file clerks to $96.50 for secretaries. The report showed that the average woman elevator operator receives $2.05 an hour, $0.22 more than the average male elevator operator, while the average woman janitor or cleaner receives $2.08, $0.07 less than the male janitor. In most skilled occupations studied, men averaged more than $3.10 an hour, with tool and dye makers drawing $3.53, carpenters $3.22, and painters $3.15."

1968 Family Profile

The Whitley family lives in Memphis, Tennessee, where she now works at a leading manufacturing plant in the city, one of the first to allow Black workers. They own a single-wide mobile home on property she inherited from her father. He works on farms in the area; they have one child, who is in the third grade.

Annual Income: $9,375

She makes $3.09 per hour or $124.84 a week creating an annual income of $6,375; he makes approximately $3,000 yearly working on farms, fixing tractors, hauling feed, selling fertilizer, and odd jobs. The fruits and vegetables he grows on their own farm and the game animals he hunts supplement their income.

Annual Budget

The study does not provide family expenditures; nationally the per capita expenditures in 1968 are:

Auto Parts	$22.92
Auto Usage	$338.80
Clothing	$178.87
Dentists	$19.93
Food	$605.86
Furniture	$39.36
Gas and Oil	$92.67
Health Insurance	$15.60
Housing	$397.09
Intercity Transport	$15.45
Local Transport	$11.96
New Auto Purchase	$122.07
Personal Business	$141.00
Personal Care	$52.81

Physicians $54.31
Public Education and
    Research $49.33
Recreation...$182.85
Religion/Welfare Activities $51.32
Telephone and Telegraph $41.35
Tobacco $46.83
Utilities $100.15
Per Capita Consumption...........................$2,785.67

Life at Home

- The Whitleys live in a single-wide mobile home located on the family farm.
- The man farms the family land and hires out to neighbors, many of them White, in the spring and fall; he also sells fertilizer to earn extra income.
- In addition to growing vegetables for sale and use at home, he prides himself on his hunting skills; deer, squirrel, and turtle are part of the family diet.
- The woman experiences a long drive to work; 40,000 people drive into Memphis to work each morning.
- Developers are buying nearby farms for the expanding suburbs of rapidly growing Memphis; land speculation is rampant. The family is uncertain whether to sell the family farm if asked.
- If they agree to sell the farm, they are uncertain where they will live; most African-Americans in Memphis—even those with money—live in homes in the older section of town that are often substandard, because Memphis has few integrated neighborhoods.
- The approach of suburbs also brings libraries; Memphis now offers nearly 20 library branches. This family's third-grader considers herself a good reader.
- Both parents believe that their third-grade daughter will have a better life with more opportunities than they did, especially if she does well in school.

Life at Work: The Manufacturing Plant

- This nationally-known electronics company began manufacturing operations in Memphis in 1947 with 100 employees producing electronic components such as headphones and condensers.
- Currently the plant employs 1,200 workers, spread evenly over three shifts.
- The bulk of the work force are middle-aged White women who work at machines producing small, delicate components.
- The first Black employee is hired in 1961 during a period of expansion.
- African-American workers are added at the Memphis facility because of corporate pressure and a gradual change in the racial climate in Memphis of such desegregated facilities as cafeterias, drinking fountains, and toilets.

The first Black employee of the company, Katie Fuller, described the early days of her employment in 1961:

"I didn't know I was the only colored person. I thought they had hired a bunch of them, you know. And when I got out there—nobody but me and the good Lord knows what I went through. But I just pray. I asked God to help me. I said: 'Help me Jesus, I got to work somewhere . . .'

And they would have to come down this certain aisle going out. See, they would be getting off, while we would still be working. They'd get off at 3:10, and we'd be working almost to 4:20. And they come through there hollering 'Nigger,' and talking all kind of ugly talk. Cursing. And I would look over to the side, to the space next to me. And I thought these people are crazy. And I'd look at 'em and I would laugh. I'd kinda smile. It took a whole lot out of me, you know. And I never worked with anybody like this before. A whole plant of people in here were—I don't know how to describe it. Devil Action."

- At the plant racial relationships are considered good by both Black and White workers; in the cafeteria Black workers normally sit together separate from the White workers out of tradition and choice.
- Black leaders believe that changes in hiring practices take place not because of marches or demonstrations, but on the requirements for a non-discriminatory workplace that are placed on government contracts.
- Most African-Americans hired by the company have a high school diploma and one-third have college experience; approximately one-fourth of the White workers do not have a high school diploma and only seven percent attended college.
- By 1968, 50 percent of the new hires are Black women; only 16 Black men are employed among 1,200 workers.
- Typically the jobs require little training; the plant has experienced little unionization.
- The electrical manufacturing industry, dominated by companies such as Westinghouse and General Electric, is growing rapidly.
- From 1923 to 1958 total employment in the electrical manufacturing industry grew by three times; electric power consumption, measured in kilowatt hours, grew by 16 times.
- In 1968 sales for appliances and electronic products increases nine percent and profits, 18.2 percent.

Life in the Community: Memphis, Tennessee

- Memphis, sitting in the extreme southwest corner of Tennessee, sits high on a bluff overlooking the Mississippi River.
- Memphis and the river have long been tied; the city grew as a center where cotton bales were sold, loaded onto river-boats, and shipped down the waterway.
- Firestone, RCA, International Harvester, General Electric, and other well-known industries have settled in the city once known best for the blues, gambling, and catfish.
- Following a national pattern, more neighborhoods near downtown Memphis are becoming Black, while new all-White suburbs have sprung up around the city.
- With a population of nearly 550,000, Memphis is the largest city in not only Tennessee, but the border states of Mississippi and Arkansas.
- About 40 percent, or 200,000 people, are Black.
- Many migrants from the cotton and soybean farms of the Mississippi delta have settled in the city; only 56 percent of the population was born in Tennessee, and more than 25 percent have lived in Memphis less than five years.
- Approximately 57 percent of the African-American families have incomes below the poverty level of $3,000 a year; only 13.8 percent of White families live below the poverty level.
- The median educational level of Memphis Blacks over 25 years old in the 1960 census is 6.7 years; the median White has completed 11.1 years of school.

- Achievement tests show that Black eighth-graders test two grades behind White eighth-graders.
- The Shelby County school system is not desegregated until 1963; by 1968 the vast majority of the public schools are de facto segregated.
- Three of 13 city councilmen are Black in 1968; five percent of all the school boards are African-American.
- Earlier in 1968, Civil Rights activists encourage the Black garbage workers strike, supported by the American Federation of State, County, and Municipal employees Union and Black ministers in the area; Martin Luther King is to take a leadership role.
- Pay for garbage workers is $70.00 a week; supervisors are all White, while workers are typically African-Americans recruited from farms.
- The mayor feels the strike is unwarranted, declaring "I don't make deals"; King is branded an irresponsible rabble-rouser.
- Memphis' Black ministers use their pulpits to compare the strikers with the Old Testament prophets who crusaded against injustice, take up special collections for the workers, and ask their congregations to join them in daily marches to downtown Memphis.
- In less than a week $15,000 is raised to support the strikers; downtown sales drop by 35 percent.
- On March 14, NAACP Executive Secretary Roy Wilkes speaks to a rally of 9,000; four days later Martin Luther King, Jr., speaks to an even larger audience and calls for a one-day general strike of all workers.
- Riots break out during a downtown march on March 28; one person is killed, 60 injured, 300 arrested.
- The president of the Local Chamber of Commerce blames the violence on activist preachers, saying, "If the Negro ministers would tend to their ministering instead of trying to stir things up, we wouldn't have had this trouble."

WILL NEGRO BLOC VOTE CONTROL SOUTH CAROLINA?

CORE worker carries Communist placard in voter registration march. CORE leader James Farmer said in Columbia that the defeat of Senator Strom Thurmond was one of CORE's main goals.

Martin Luther King shakes hands in Florence, S. C. after a voter registration rally. King said: "We must be an independent force in the Democratic Party in years to come." King predicted this would give Negroes control.

"I believe the Negro vote will have a greater impact this year than any since Reconstruction." said by Rev. I. deQuincy Newman of South Carolina NAACP, March 13, 1966

This year, over 200,000 Negroes are registered to vote in South Carolina. The Negro leaders have made it clear that they will vote as a solid bloc for their Democratic friends who support L. B. J. This means that if the white people remain divided, the Negro vote will decide the election.

It is the oldest story in politics: an elected official must be faithful to those who put him in office. A politician who is elected by the Negro bloc vote will have to answer to the NAACP everytime he casts a vote or makes an appointment. If the bloc vote gains control of OUR STATE GOVERNMENT, OUR SENATORS, AND OUR REPRESENTATIVES, then as surely as night follows day, the Black Revolution which struck Los Angeles, Chicago, Cleveland, and Atlanta will strike South Carolina. THAT MUST NOT HAPPEN!

Stand Up For The Men Who Will Stand Up For You! Support . .
Strom Thurmond — Marshall Parker — Joe Rogers

They Will Represent The People—Not The NAACP Or The Democratic Bosses in Washington.

Lucius Burch, White leader on the Memphis Committee on Community Relations in 1963 to the (MCCR):

"It is now clear beyond argument that no public institution has the right to deny equal facility of use to any citizen because of color. The Negro citizens are naturally restive at being thwarted and delayed in the exercise of their clearly declared rights. Having been successful in establishing their rights through litigation, they now seek to obtain them by 'demonstrations.' These so-called demonstrations are ancient and constitutionally authorized remedies in that all citizens have the right to assemble peaceably, to petition for the redress of their grievances, and to publicize by picketing and other legal means their contentions. There is no legal, moral, or historical basis for condemning the assertion of rights by these methods. Indeed a nation looking with pride at such vigorous precedents as Runnymede, the Boston Tea Party, and Concord Bridge must praise rather than condemn any citizen or group of citizens vigilant and active in the establishment and protection of their liberties. This is straight talk and not calculated to please or flatter or to do other than speak the truth to tough-minded men and women sufficiently concerned to band together to achieve a solution. The trust is that if the White leadership of this community does not actively concern itself with the obtaining of legally declared rights and by its prestige and influence further rather than restrain the exercise of these rights, we must expect the Negroes to exert themselves vigorously to gain these ends which have been judicially declared their legislative due. The Negro leadership in this community is effective and responsible. It is composed of men who have a personal stake in the continued tranquility and future growth of the community. The Negro leaders are ministers, merchants, teachers, bankers, lawyers, etc., and they will suffer even more than their White counterparts from disorder and they have done a magnificent job in preaching responsibility and restrain to those who look to them for leadership. But they first and foremost are members of their race and have a keen sense of injustice. Moreover, they will not remain as leaders of their people without tangible exertion and perceptible progress toward the attainment of their rights. If there is a failure of their leadership, it will be replaced by more radical groups not concerned with long-term and overall community consequences."

- Martin Luther King, Jr., is shot and killed on April 4, 1968, at the Memphis Lorraine Motel while organizing a nonviolent march in support of the garbage workers' strike; Memphis, along with cities across the nation, experiences rioting that night.
- The city eventually agrees to pay the garbage workers an extra $0.10 per hour and to permit union dues check-off if handled through a credit union and then paid to the Union.

HISTORICAL SNAPSHOT
1968–1969

- The U.S. gross national product reached $861 billion
- The Vietnam War and student protests intensified across the nation
- Richard Nixon was elected president
- 4,462 corporate mergers took place
- BankAmericard holders numbered 14 million, up 12 million in two years
- Civil Rights leader Rev. Martin Luther King, Jr., was assassinated at a Memphis, Tennessee, motel; riots occurred in over 199 cities nationwide
- Senator Robert F. Kennedy was assassinated in Los Angeles shortly after winning the California Democratic primary
- In response to the King and Kennedy assassinations, Sears & Roebuck removed toy guns from its Christmas catalog
- Automobile production reached 8.8 million
- Volkswagen captured 57 percent of the U.S. automobile import market
- Television advertising revenues hit $2 billion, twice that of radio
- First-class postage climbed to $0.06
- Inflation was now a worldwide issue
- Yale College admitted women
- The Uniform Monday Holiday Law was enacted by Congress, creating three-day holiday weekends
- Crimes of violence reportedly had increased 57 percent since 1960
- Nationwide 78 million television sets existed
- The average farm subsidy from the government was $1,000
- Neil Armstrong walked on the moon
- The average U.S. automobile wholesaled for $2,280
- Pantyhose production reached 624 million pairs in 1969, up from 200 million in 1968
- The average U.S. farm produced enough food for 47 people
- Blue Cross health insurance covered 68 million Americans
- Penthouse magazine began publication; Saturday Evening Post folded
- The National Association of Broadcasters began a cigarette advertising phase-out
- The U.S. began the first troop withdrawals from Vietnam; Vietnam casualties now exceeded the total for the Korean War
- Richard Nixon's 43.3 percent victory was the lowest presidential margin since 1912
- Pope Paul VI's ban on contraception was challenged by 800 U.S. theologians
- 20,000 people were added monthly to New York's welfare rolls; one-fourth of the city's budget went to welfare
- The Vietnam War became the longest war in U.S. history

1968 Economic Profile

Income, Standard Jobs

Bituminous Coal Mining	$8,169.00
Building Trades	$8,332.00
Domestic Industries	$6,759.00
Domestics	$3,254.00
Farm Labor	$3,327.00
Federal Civilian	$9,002.00
Federal Military	$5,148.00
Finance, Insurance, Real Estate	$6,994.00
Gas, Electricity, and Sanitation Workers	$8,666.00
Manufacturing, Durable Goods	$8,002.00
Manufacturing, Nondurable Goods	$6,849.00
Medical/Health Services Workers	$5,292.00
Miscellaneous Manufacturing	$6,252.00
Motion Picture Services	$7,946.00
Nonprofit Organization Workers	$4,655.00
Passenger Transportation Workers, Local and Highway	$6,279.00
Personal Services	$4,960.00
Private Industries, Including Farm Labor	$6,772.00
Public School Teachers	$7,129.00
Radio Broadcasting and Television Workers	$9,563.00
Railroads	$8,663.00
State and Local Government Workers	$7,255.00
Telephone and Telegraph Workers	$7,506.00
Wholesale and Retail Trade Workers	$8,142.00

Selected Prices

Argus 35-mm Cartridge Camera, with Flash	$69.95
Black and Decker Drill, Electric	$10.99
Child's Fruit of the Loom Briefs, Package of Three	$2.65
Colgate Toothpaste, 6.75 Ounce Tube	$0.55
Custom 7 Transistor Radio	$12.95
Cut-Glass Glasses, Includes Six Tumblers	$2.49
Daisy Golden 750 Rifle	$7.50

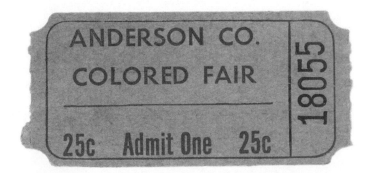

Davis Super Highway Tire, Six-Ply Rating $26.95
DeLong Red Worm Fishing Lure, Package of Three $0.49
Delta Airline Fare, Chicago to Miami $74.70
Dual-Exhaust Kit for Corvair $18.45
Goldblatt's Air Conditioner, Whole House $498.88
Hunts Catsup, 14-Ounce Bottle $0.22
Jarman Man's Dress Shoes $22.00
Lady Kenmore Electric Shaver $13.97
Mattel Teenage Barbie $2.29
Pepsi Cola, 10-Ounce Bottles, Six Pack $0.59
Seagram's VO Whiskey, 86.8 Proof, Fifth $5.79
Solid-Oak Nightstand $25.95
Truetone Riviera Television, 16" B&W $149.95
Western Auto Sunburst Wall Clock $16.25
Wizard Long Life Light Bulbs, Four Pack $1.29
Wizard Washer, 10-Pound Capacity $99.88

Civil Rights in Memphis

- On December 1, 1955, 42-year-old Rosa Parks helped launch a movement by refusing to surrender her bus seat to a White passenger; the federal courts ruled segregation of the Montgomery, Alabama, buses unconstitutional in 1956.
- In response Memphis post office employee O.Z. Evers filed a suit against the Memphis bus company in 1956 to desegregate that city's buses.
- Black banker and NAACP board member Jessie Turner filed a desegregation suit against the Memphis Public Library in 1958.
- John F. Kennedy promised during his 1960 presidential campaign to exercise "moral and persuasive leadership" to enforce the 1954 Supreme Court decision calling for desegregated schools.
- By 1960 a generation of high school Black students had grown up knowing that the Supreme Court had ruled the educational apartheid they were experiencing was against the law of the land.
- Resentment and frustration burst to the surface in the 1960s across the nation.
- Challenges to the official barriers to Blacks seeking public accommodations included sit-in demonstrations at drug stores, freedom rides on public buses across the South, and marches in hundreds of cities across the nation, although principally in the South.
- Student sit-ins began nationwide in 1960; 41 Memphis College students were arrested for entering two segregated libraries.
- The racially mixed Memphis Committee on Community Relations urged voluntary desegregation; the buses were desegrated in the fall of 1960, libraries in October, and the Overton Park Zoo in December of that year.
- To avoid a Black boycott, the Memphis downtown merchants agreed to volunteer desegregation in January 1962—provided that no changes were required during the 1961 Christmas season.

> **Reverend Jimmy Grant, who led a voter registration drive in 1961, recalls adjacent Fayette County, Tennessee, in 1940:**
>
> "I can remember the lynching of '40. I remember my father saying, 'We don't go out of the house for the next day or two. We don't go downtown. If anyone knocks on the door, let me answer.' And we had his gun behind the door, and he would always peep out before. Because everyone was frightened and leaflets had been circulated saying, 'We got Elbert Williams. Who will be next?' (Williams had organized an NAACP meeting.) And when they found him it was a hideous thing. I didn't know what lynching was, and when I questioned my daddy, he said, 'A man was killed. And you just don't bother, if you don't understand it. I'll tell you later.'"

- Thirteen Black students integrated four Memphis schools in the fall of 1961 without incident; officials were so fearful of riots that even the teachers were not informed of the planned integration of their classrooms until the night before.
- In 1962 the movie theaters of the city were integrated secretly. With the cooperation of the theater managers, a Black couple was selected to integrate the Malco Theatre. When nothing happened to the couple, the following week two Black couples were sent to integrate another theater; by April, 1963, 14 theaters had been integrated in this way.
- When publicity about the progressive work of the Memphis Committee on Community Relations appeared in the Memphis newspaper, the White chairman, a respected former Memphis banker, received anonymous letters addressed to the "nigger lover" and stating, "race mixing is communism."
- As part of an agreement to voluntarily integrate the 20 largest restaurants in the city, and thus avoid picketing, the restaurant owners insisted that the Memphis Appeal not report that integration of the eating establishments was taking place.
- Until 1965 the Tennessee Department of Employment Security maintained segregated offices; employers who wanted White workers called one office, for Black workers, another separate facility.
- Many Black workers who applied for jobs through the Tennessee Department of Employment Security were told they were too short, too tall, or too young for the jobs; their applications were not taken or processed.
- Reacting to change, the Memphis American Legion raised $10,000 to finance a sustained showing of J. Edgar Hoover's film Masters of Deceit in every public school.
- But the South was not singled out for change: race riots in the Watts section of Los Angeles in 1965 resulted in 34 deaths and $40 million in property damage. In 1967 in Newark, New Jersey, 26 people died and 1,500 were injured; in Detroit that same year 40 people died and more than 1,000 were injured in an eruption that required 4,700 U.S. paratroopers and 8,000 National Guardsmen to quell.

"A New Cash Crop for Rural America," advertisement by National Association of Real Estate Board, Life Magazine, November 15, 1968:

"The biggest migration of this century has been from America's small towns to the big cities in search of jobs. The Make America Better program of the Realtors salutes Mountain Home, Arkansas, a small community that is successfully reversing this trend. Like most farming communities, Mountain Home was steadily losing its people to the cities. The economy slumped steadily until the town grabbed itself by the bootstraps and began to pull. Though handicapped by limited assets, it succeeded in attracting two industries to locate in the county. As a result, while most rural areas continue to lose population, Mountain Home is gaining steadily. Now that good jobs are available at home, a surprising number of former residents are coming back. And families who otherwise would have emigrated to overpopulated cities are staying at home...Help make America better. Join with the 85,000 Realtors in their Make America Better Program."

1969 PROFILE
PROTESTING VIETNAM

Civilians

Greg and Ellen Watson of Charleston, West Virginia, have found that the decision to voice their opposition to the Vietnam War, even at the risk of social, financial and professional consequences, has yielded some unexpected results.

Greg and Ellen Watson were concerned about the direction of war in Vietnam.

Life at Home

- Ellen Watson was never considered a radical, not even a quality rabble-rouser on a cranky day.
- She rarely attended public meetings, except for the PTA and Women's Club at the church, and never, ever spoke up, unless it was to volunteer for the food committee.
- Her husband, Greg, was even less flamboyant.
- Greg always preached to Ellen and the three girls that he was performing his civic duty when he got up every day and worked hard to support those who didn't.
- So, the Watsons speaking at an antiwar rally was a strange sight indeed.
- After all, Greg had served in World War II, and Ellen's father had been decorated for his service in France during World War I.
- Ellen would claim that their daughter Carol led them to this decision, but Greg insisted the momentum had been building for a while.
- A sophomore at Marshall College in Huntington, West Virginia, Carol had been talking about the nationwide moratorium planned for October 15.
- The youngest of three girls, Carol was polite, adventurous, challenging—and always Carol.
- Moratorium participants were asked to stay home from school, and for businesses to close on October 15 to send a message to President Nixon that the war should end now.

- After first broaching the subject to her parents of cutting class in protest, Carol asked how they would feel if she attended a rally and maybe was arrested.
- Clearly, this was not the type of thing children from Charleston, West Virginia, had been raised to do.
- Greg had been willing to support the war for President Johnson, believing the president knew things he couldn't reveal, but when the death toll continued to mount, Greg grew silent.
- He recalled that Eisenhower had misled America on the U2 incident, Kennedy on the Bay of Pigs, Johnson on the Gulf of Tonkin, and now Nixon was talking peace and acting war.
- It did not help that America was spending $2 billion a month to help a South Vietnamese government that appeared authoritarian and corrupt; at this pace, inflation would definitely be right around the corner.
- Besides, during the 1968 election, Nixon announced he had a plan to end the war.
- Greg was a man who took politicians at their word, and wanted to see the plan.
- For the first time, the Watsons talked about the war and the nearly 1,000 soldiers who had died in combat during the past two months.
- They began reading the Washington Post to see what the big city papers had to say about it.
- None of it was good.
- The peace talks were in disarray, drug use among soldiers was rising, the politicians and generals were fighting each other, and the Negro civil rights leaders said that too many black men were dying in southeast Asia.
- The Hiltons down the road still were unable to believe they had lost to the war their oldest son, who was supposed to take over the hardware store.
- Big Bob had trained Little Bob in everything from fertilizer to plumbing supplies.
- Everyone in town, it seemed, was at the funeral.

B52s Hammer Suspected Viet Jungle Base

U.S Pushes Buildup; 4th Division Men Fly to Highlands

SAIGON, South Viet Nam (AP) — High-altitude B52s from Guam poured 750-pound bombs today into a suspected Viet Cong jungle base south of Da Nang where the Communists are believed massing for operations.

A military spokesman said the eight-engine jets hit almost the same region plastered by a B52 strike yesterday. The target today was a suspected Viet Cong concentration and base camp area.

Da Nang, site of a big U.S. air base, is about 380 miles north of Saigon.

Although the air war continued unabated, no significant ground action was reported either early today or late yesterday, a U.S. spokesman said.

Infantry Sweep Ends

One military operation, named Kolo, ended Saturday night, U.S. military headquarters said. The two-week sweep by the U.S. 25th Infantry Division about 25 miles northwest of capital accounted for 40 Viet Cong dead and 25 captured.

In the central highlands, a 3,-man U.S. infantry brigade flash from the United States flew in yesterday to beef up American forces blocking a Communist attempt to slice South Viet Nam in two. The new troops raised U.S. manpower in

- Since the Hiltons were just simple folks who worked hard and minded their own business, they didn't know how to protest.
- When Ellen decided that Carol was leading them in the right direction, she finally found the courage to tell Mary Sue Hilton that she was planning to attend the moratorium and read out the name of William Edward Hilton, among others.
- Ellen held her breath waiting for a reaction.
  - Mary Sue simply said that would be fine.
    - Greg was experiencing similar struggles: How do you tell your coworkers at a car dealership you think America should tuck tail and run from a fight?
      - As parts manager, he was well-respected for his work, knowledge and cooperative spirit, but he was hardly an opinion leader.
      - What would people say when he didn't show up for work? Or should he just take the day off? Or be really bold and tell the boss to shut down that day?
  - He was afraid they would think he'd turned hippie.
- The moratorium began as a campus-based program, with college-town canvassing, leaflet distribution, class-cutting, seminars, candlelight processions and readings of the names of the war dead at colleges and universities.
  - The aim of the activities was to pressure President Nixon into altering his course and bring the troops home faster than he intended.
    - Carol was pleased with her parents' decision, but her oldest sister Helen was furious.
    - Helen vented over the phone to her father: This type of thing could harm her husband's law practice; the Watson name would be mud; her children—their grandchildren—would be shunned; could her parents even be trusted to keep the kids anymore? Wasn't he aware that bank loans could disappear because of his weirdo ideas?
- Greg finally told his daughter to grow up, and hung up the phone on her ranting.
- Neither Ellen nor Greg expected Helen and the kids to appear for customary Sunday supper after church.

Life at Work

- The night before the moratorium, Ellen created black crepe paper armbands as a sign of solidarity, and though Greg said it was silly, he wore one anyway.
- Shortly after Ellen and Greg Watson arrived at the gathering site near the town's war memorial, several people tried to start an antiwar chant, "Out Now, Out Now," but it died at birth.
- A few moments later, efforts to sing "Blowin' in the Wind" fared little better.
- Ellen knew she needed all her energy just to read the alphabetized E through J names of the war dead.
- When the moratorium organizers learned that Ellen was willing to participate, they offered to let her go first with the A through D names, but she knew that would be too hard.
- Being second would suit her just fine, if she could get through the Hs without tearing up at the name William Edward Hilton.

"I've never marched, rallied, picketed, demonstrated or otherwise created a public fuss in my life— but this war has gone on too long."
—Lifelong Republican Alan Coburn of Washington, DC

- Clearly, this group was not gathering for fun; most attendees had never opposed anything before, especially nothing as significant as the U.S. president and his policy in Vietnam.
- For about 10 minutes, they simply stood awkwardly.
- Then, as the first candle was lit, Greg knew there was no turning back.
- For a moment, he wished he could have mustered the courage to read the names himself, but then he looked at Ellen and realized how nervous she was.
- Unsure of what was proper etiquette at an antiwar rally, it had been decided in advance that church candles would be lit first, then an Episcopal priest would lead the Lord's Prayer, followed by the reading of names.
- The first name read was one Ellen did not know, but the second, Alfred Allen Anderson, was the son of a high school classmate.
- She hadn't even known of her friend's loss, but realized she had no time to mourn now.

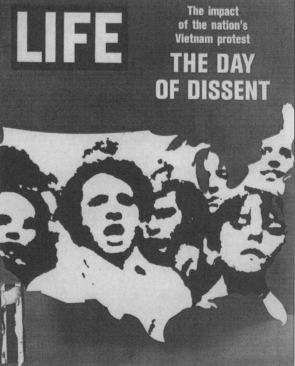

LIFE
The impact of the nation's Vietnam protest
THE DAY OF DISSENT

On October 15, spectators came to support the President and the war; others, like Eugene McCarthy, came to condemn the fighting.

- The first reader was nearly through the D names; Edmund Perry Dallas . . . David Templeton Dukes. . .
- For Ellen, these moments were terrifying and exhilarating.
- She wanted to throw up, but couldn't possibly consider such an act in public.
- When she started reading the names out, she was startled by the flash of a photographer's camera, and realized that tomorrow, all of Charleston would know what she had done.
- "Ellen the activist and the quiet Greg are now a hippie couple. . . . What do you think of that?"
- Well, let them talk, she thought; Greg and Ellen Watson want the war to end.
- Then, she saw Mary Sue Hilton, still wearing black and carrying the American flag that had been draped on Little Bob's casket.
- Big Bob wasn't there and Mary Sue seemed unsteady in her mission.
- She had come to hear the name of her son read out in public as one of America's war dead, while she clutched the flag.
- Old Mrs. Rice, dressed in her Sunday best, stood defiantly with a sign taped to her pocketbook reading, "God Bless our President."
- Two teenagers drove by, yelling, "Dirty commies!" but did not stop.
- The next morning, the *Washington Post* reported that "uncounted and uncountable thousands of Americans demonstrated their opposition to the Vietnam War yesterday in one fashion or another all across the nation."
  - According to the story, crowds ranged from 100,000 on Boston Common to a rain-drenched 1,500 in San Francisco, 30,000 on the New Haven Green to 10,000 at Rutgers University, about 5,000 in the center of Minneapolis to 50,000 on the grounds of the Washington Monument.
  - The reporters said: "3,500 braved a six-inch snowfall in front of the state Capitol in Denver to hear speeches and the reading of names of the state's 567 war dead."
  - Despite snow and 15-degree temperatures, 20 stood through the night in front of a war memorial on the Wyoming University campus at Laramie.

Some students protested by ringing a bell for each life lost in Vietnam.

- Sixty-five people in small, conservative Charleston, West Virginia, felt about right, Greg told Carol, as she relayed her own protest activities.
- Carol had helped ring an old church bell for three days, striking the bell once every four seconds in memory of each U.S. soldier killed in Vietnam.
- There were only minor incidents of violence nationwide, and few arrests.
- In Phoenix, Texas, a mother of a sailor killed in the war demanded that his name be excluded from a list being read at a moratorium rally.
- The crowds were overwhelmingly white, generally but not always predominantly young, and included a number of middle-class, middle-aged "respectables" who now believed direct action was necessary to end the war.
- After the rally at the Monument grounds in Washington, DC, 30,000 marched past the White House carrying candles.
- According to aides, President Nixon kept a business-as-usual schedule, having stated that he does not propose to be the first American president to lose a war.
- He has begun a unilateral withdrawal of the bulk of American forces in Vietnam, and some military commanders have been reined in so tightly, a unilateral cease-fire prevails.
- Life magazine is calling the one-day moratorium "a display without historical parallel, the largest expression of public dissent ever seen in the country."

The October 15 Vietnam Moratorium

- The nationwide protest was initiated by three activists: David Hawk, Sam Brown and David Mixner.
- They raised $75,000 and enlisted the pledged support of more than 100 student-body presidents.
- Brown is 25 years old and the main fundraiser, beginning as a National Student Association activist during the "Dump President Johnson" movement that lead to Sen. Eugene McCarthy's presidential challenge.

- He has won a reputation as a first-rate choreographer of mass movements.
- Twenty-four-year-old Hawk, whose primary focus is opposing the draft, has a background in civil rights work in Georgia and staff work for Allard Lowenstein, the student protest leader.
- Currently, he faces imprisonment as a draft-resister; last spring, he directed a we-won't-go letter to President Nixon from 250 student presidents and editors.
- Mixner, also 24 years old, is a union organizer with a specialization in farm laborers—his father being one.
- Mixner is also a member of the McGovern Commission for Reform of the Democratic Party.
- In addition, the moratorium gained support from nationally recognized individuals such as baby doctor Benjamin Spock and Coretta King, wife of the civil rights leader, Martin Luther King, Jr.
- In Washington, thousands gathered to participate in a candlelight parade led by Mrs. King.
- In her remarks, she said, "Forty thousand Americans have been given as sacrificial lambs to a godless cause. When will it cease? While we spend billions of dollars in Vietnam, we have ignored our problems at home."
- Sam Brown is planning another massive demonstration for November 14 and 15 if Nixon refuses to change the present policy and accelerate withdrawal.

HISTORICAL SNAPSHOT
1969

- To protest the Miss America Pageant, feminists dropped girdles and bras in the trash
- Approximately 484,000 U.S. soldiers were fighting in Vietnam
- After weeks of debate, the delegates from the United States and Vietnam were only able to agree on the shape of the table to be used when South Vietnam and the National Liberation Front joined the talks
- Black militant defendant Bobby Seale was ordered bound and gagged by Judge Julius Hoffmann when Seale repeatedly disrupted the Chicago Seven Conspiracy Trial
- Rock concerts drew millions as groups such as the Rolling Stones, the Who, Joan Baez, Jimi Hendrix and the Jefferson Airplane launched tours
- A copy of the first printing of the Declaration of Independence sold for $404,000
- One study of deferment policies showed that a high-school dropout from a low-income family had a 70 percent chance of serving in Vietnam, 64 percent for a high school graduate, and 42 percent for a college graduate
- The Johnny Cash Show, Hee Haw with Buck Owens and Roy Clark, and The Bill Cosby Show premiered on television
- U.S. universities made ROTC voluntary or abolished the program altogether following student protests
- Neil Armstrong, Buzz Aldrin and Michael Collins landed on the moon; Armstrong and Aldrin collected nine pounds, 12 ounces of rock and soil, and remained on the moon 21 hours, 31 minutes
- Richard Schechner's Dionysus in 69 emphasized group participation in the theater: Each night a woman from the audience was selected to have sex on stage
- John Lennon and Yoko Ono married
- Nationwide, 448 universities experienced strikes or were forced to close; student demands included revision of admissions policies and the reorganization of academic programs
- Penthouse magazine, vasectomy outpatient service and automated teller machines made their first appearance
- The 17-point underdog New York Jets, led by quarterback Joe Namath, upset the Baltimore Colts to become the first AFL Super Bowl winner
- Robert Lehman bequeathed 3,000 works valued at more than $100 million to the Metropolitan Museum of Art
- Bestsellers for the year included Portnoy's Complaint by Philip Roth, The Love Machine by Jacqueline Susann, The Godfather by Mario Puzo and Naked Came the Stranger by Penelope Ashe
- Hippie cult leader Charles Manson and followers were charged with the Hollywood murders of pregnant Sharon Tate Polanski and six others
- The first draft lottery was held

Selected Prices

Acne Solution	$2.98
Airline Fare, Delta	$74.70
Camera, Polaroid	$50.00
Dinette Set, Five Pieces	$119.88
Flag Set	$44.88
Food Processor	$39.95
Guitar	$97.95
Locomotive, Tyco	$16.77
Pepsi, Six Bottles	$0.59
Sewing Machine, Kenmore	$149.95
Shoes, Women's Flats	$6.97
Spray Paint	$1.49
Television, Magnavox	$650.00
Tile, Vinyl Asbestos Floor	$12.50
Vitamins, 100 Tablets	$1.49

"In Duluth, a Mother of Five Joins the Campaign against War," Nan Robertson, The New York Times, October 16, 1969:

Mary Carolyn Lennon Fleege shivered in the frigid wind off Lake Superior at her first peace rally today, whispered a few "Hail Marys" to herself and tied a bit of white rag to her sleeve in public mourning for the men who died in Vietnam.

She sang antiwar songs and "America the Beautiful" in a light soprano in front of the county courthouse and confessed that never in her life had she done anything nearly so daring.

Mrs. Fleege is a 34-year-old housewife with a broad, open Irish face, the mother of five small children and the wife of an engineer for the Minnesota Highway Department. She describes herself as a "ghetto Catholic" who has just begun to move out into a world of new and sometimes painful ideas.

Today, she took her children out of classes for 90 minutes to go to a memorial service at the Duluth campus of the University of Minnesota and later joined several thousand persons, mostly high school and college students, at the downtown demonstration. Her actions climaxed a year of private worry about the war.

For 30 minutes, Mrs. Fleege and the others sat mutely on the cold ground before the courthouse. When the rally dispersed, after the Mayor of Duluth had complimented those present on their good behavior, Mrs. Fleege went home to tend her children, put another load of washing through the machine and bake the supper casserole.

"Antiwar for Everyman," The New Republic, September 6, 1969:

On the nation's campuses, when young men still face the draft, the antiwar clock has begun to tick again. Beginning October 15 with a one-day "moratorium" (to sidestep the more inflammatory word "strike"), the Vietnam Moratorium Committee plans to retool the dormant campus antiwar machine and launch it on a campaign to pressure the Nixon administration to do either of two things: Negotiate a Vietnam settlement or get out fast. The emphasis in both cases is speed.

Moving from the teach-in of 1967-68 to the teach-out, college students this year will be asked to forsake the homogeneous campus and go out into the community, where the door-to-door canvassing techniques that worked so well for Sen. Eugene McCarthy in New Hampshire will be used. The committee hopes to involve labor, business, professional and academic groups in a revived antiwar effort which would escalate to a two-day moratorium in November, a three-day affair in December and so on. The goal is a national moratorium to protest the war—a day when normal activity ceases and everyone's business is some sort of antiwar activity.

The purpose of the October 15 Moratorium is that of "putting an end to the most tragic mistake in our national history—the cruel and futile war in Vietnam. We meet today to call our government away from folly into the paths that lead to peace."

"The Search for a Nexus—Vietnam and the Negroes," William F. Buckley, Jr., *National Review*, August 22, 1967:

There is a shift in the making—a shift in public opinion on the question of the Vietnam War, and in the strange way it relates to the Negro problem, or rather is being made to relate to the Negro problem. There are signs everywhere, and from very important people. The most significant, in my judgment, is the recent declaration of Bishop Fulton Sheen that we should unilaterally pull out of Vietnam. Bishop Sheen is neither senile nor loose-minded. His anti-Communism is unalloyed, and his knowledge of the strategic realities is unsentimental. I put off for another day an analysis of the bishop's reasoning—for the present purposes it is significant to note merely that he has taken that position, and that he is an enormously influential priest.

Moreover, a priest who is grimly engaged at the moment, as Bishop of Rochester, in attempting a substantive reconciliation between the Negro and white people in that tense city. Notwithstanding his great urbanity and learning, he is at heart an evangelist—and he is asking for nothing less than reconciliation, between white and Negro, but also between white and yellow.

At this point, the mind sets out doggedly in search of a nexus. Is there one between the Negro problem and the Vietnam War? The effort is being made to find one, and we can trust to the ingenuity of the politician to discover one. During the weekend, Senator Robert Kennedy went on a paralogistic spree. The occasion was a Democratic fundraising dinner in San Francisco, the immediate purpose of which was to show the great big biceps of Speaker Jesse Unruh, who was recently worsted at the O.K. Corral by the deft gunmanship of Ronald Reagan. Senator Kennedy got his usual running ovation. But it was interrupted by a special ovation when he called on the American people to note the "monstrous disproportion of anyone willing to spend billions for the freedom of others while denying it to our own people." That is one of the political effusions which are the highest testimony to the moral and intellectual emptiness of the political idiom.

The costliest riot in United States history took place a few weeks ago in Detroit, whose Democratic mayor, a long-time hero of the National Association for the Advancement of Colored People, can hardly be said to have conspired against the freedom of the Negro people. But the senator was just warming up. "We cannot allow involvement in the name of independence and democracy in Vietnam to interfere with democracy for our own people." Another burst of applause, more testimony to non-thought. Who is asking that democracy for the Negroes be put off until the end of the Vietnam War? Lyndon Johnson? Ronald Reagan? Abigail Van Buren?

And then the old blackmail: "We must reject the counsel of those willing to pass laws against violence while refusing to eliminate rats." It's sentences like that one that discredit the democratic process. Sentences like that one plus the applause they receive.

But the outline emerges. Somehow, our commitment in Vietnam is one cause of the riots in the United States. Get it? Remember it: The one-two will be very prominent in the rhetoric to come. This is to begin with the sick-at-heartness over the Vietnam war of which Bishop Sheen's manifesto is the expression. Then there is the dazed American attitude towards the riots. . . . why? why? why? There are politicians around who think they can supply a viable answer.

"From GIs in Vietnam, Unexpected Cheer," *Life*, October 24, 1969:

To find out how American troops fighting in Vietnam regard the moratorium, *Life* correspondent Hal Wingo interviewed about 100 men in eight different units scattered from I Corps in the north to III Corps in the provinces around Saigon. He concentrated on young draftees and enlisted men who had been in combat recently. Here is his report:

My conversations led me to four main conclusions:

- Many soldiers regard the organized anti-war campaign in the U.S. with open and outspoken sympathy.
- The protests in the U.S. are not demoralizing troops in the field.
- Nearly all feel the Paris peace talks are a fraud.
- The troops believe President Nixon has done a good job so far in pulling Americans out of Vietnam.

The biggest frustration comes from the feeling that nothing has been accomplished in Vietnam, and that nothing is likely to be. To some men, the moratorium makes particular sense because they feel forgotten. "Outside our families," says Army Pfc. Chris Yapp, a 4th Division civil affairs team member in a Montagnard village, "I think the protesters may be the only ones who really give a damn about what's happening."

Repeatedly, even those opposed to the idea of peace demonstrations at home admit to uncertainty about what the United States has bought with its investment of 39,000 lives. "I don't even know what I'm fighting for," says Marine Pfc. Sam Benson. "I'm just out in the bushes getting shot at." Few men argue that we are here to stop communism and give the Vietnamese a chance for a better life. Most feel the Vietnamese themselves couldn't care less what kind of government they have. "I don't see the threat to these people if they do have a communist government," says SP4 Richard Beshi, 25th Division infantryman at Cuchi. "They're going to be rice farmers regardless of who is running Saigon. . . ."

For some of these young men, the disillusionment has been far more painful than for others. Pvt. Jim Beck, 19, from Philadelphia, had high personal motives for coming to Vietnam. His brother was killed at Khesan on July 4 last year. The brothers were Italian immigrants who hoped to gain American citizenship more quickly by volunteering for military service. "I came partly for revenge," says Beck, a 101st Division medic. "but now I have lost all faith. The demonstrators are right to speak up because this war is wrong and it must be stopped."

By no means are all the troops opposed to the war. Some would like to get on with it in a bigger way, and one repeated complaint heard against the demonstrators was that voiced by Marine Sgt. Howard Clarke, who is on his second tour in Vietnam. "People who haven't been here and suffered," Clarke argues, "have no right to bitch and moan about what is going on." First Division Infantryman Hascal Dennison, 21, sees the protests only slightly differently. "They have the right," he says, "but they are wrong."

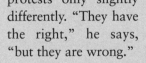

"Vietnam Debate, Will it Help or Hinder Peace?" *U.S. News & World Report*, October 20, 1969:

"NEVER MIND HOW FAST TH' WAR IS WINDING DOWN !!"

Fighting dropped off in Vietnam—but there was no breathing spell in Washington. Pressures, protests and discussion swirled around the White House. Critics—of all stripes—demanded the president "do something to end the war."

There was argument, too, whether the protesters were doing more harm than good in the hazardous search for peace.

Almost before many realized what was happening, Richard Nixon found himself in the vortex of a Vietnam "Great Debate" not unlike the one that dogged Lyndon Johnson's last year in the White House.

President Nixon wanted a "60-day moratorium" on national discussion of Vietnam in hope that he could use the time to break the deadlock with the communists.

What Mr. Nixon got, instead, was a torrent of public reaction from prominent men in both of the major political parties, from the military, from campuses and elsewhere.

The president was confronted with a variety of demands.

Some insisted the war be stopped immediately, at whatever cost. Others wanted the president to set a rigid deadline for troop withdrawal—or risk having Congress set one for him.

At the other extreme, there were demands that the president reverse course, step up the war and strike a decisive blow against North Vietnam.

Through the swelling debate and argument ran only one common thread: "Do something."

Accompanying all this was a parallel and important issue: Will the mounting debate over Vietnam help or hinder the search for peace?

On October 7, the view of the Nixon administration was presented by Defense Secretary Melvin R. Laird, who charged that antiwar forces were trying to pressure the White House "into capitulation on Hanoi's terms."

Said the defense chief in a speech to the AFL-CIO in Atlantic City:

"Hanoi's strategy is clear: Expect to achieve victory by waiting for us to abandon the conflict as a result of the antiwar protest in this country."

Other administration sources, speaking privately, were deeply embittered by the outburst of dissent in Congress and on the campuses. One official emphasized: "There is no doubt that each and every speech, and each and every demonstration helps the communist cause."

The president's critics gave no sign of letting up. A massive nationwide "Vietnam Moratorium" on October 15 won the open support of a group of senators and congressmen who urged that the demonstrations continue until all troops are brought home.

On October 8, Senator Frank Church (Dem.), of Idaho, and Senator Mark Hatfield (Rep.) of Oregon, teamed up to introduce in the Senate a resolution demanding complete disengagement from Vietnam.

The Church-Hatfield move, one of several of a similar nature, was regarded as a key proposal because of its bipartisan basis. At the heart of the resolution was a complaint that President Nixon was moving too slowly in bringing home the troops-a total of 60,000 during all of 1969.

"At the present rate of withdrawal," the resolution said, "American troops will be engaged in Vietnam for the next eight to 10 years."

The essential argument of "doves" is this: It has been decided to get out of the war, so let's get out right now.

1970–1979

The turbulent legacy of the 1960s spilled into the 1970s, igniting racial unrest in the schools, rapidly shifting musical tastes and a plethora of women who declined to use their husband's name after marriage or insisted on being addressed as "Ms." Female enrollment in professional schools such as medicine or law grew rapidly, as did programs focused on the special problems of women such as job discrimination or the crime of sexual abuse. Social change was only one reminder of the 1960s and the Vietnam War; another was the spiraling cost of living set off by several waves of inflation. The result was a nation stripped of its ability to dominate the world economy, and a country on the defensive. In 1971, President Richard Nixon was forced to devalue the U.S. dollar against foreign currencies and allow its previously fixed value to float according to changing economic conditions. By year's end, the money paid for foreign goods exceeded that spent on U.S. exports for the first time in the century. Two years later, Arab oil producers declared an oil embargo on oil shipments to the United States, setting off gas shortages, a dramatic rise in the price of oil, and rationing for the first time in 30 years. The sale of automobiles plummeted, unemployment and inflation nearly doubled, and the buying power of Americans fell dramatically.

The economy, handicapped by the devaluation of the dollar and inflation, did not fully recover for more than a decade, while the fast-growing economies of Japan and western Europe, especially West Germany, mounted direct competitive challenges to American manufacturers. The value of imported manufactured goods skyrocketed from 14 percent of U.S. domestic production in 1970 to 40 percent in 1979. The inflationary cycle and recession returned in 1979 to disrupt markets, throw thousands out of work, and prompt massive downsizing of companies—awakening many once-secure workers to the reality of the changing economic market. A symbol of the era was the pending bankruptcy of Chrysler Corporation, whose cars were so outmoded and plants so inefficient they could not compete against Japanese imports. The federal government was forced to extend loan guarantees to the company to prevent bankruptcy and the loss of thousands of jobs.

The appointment of Paul Volcker as the chairman of the Federal Reserve Board late in the decade gave the economy the distasteful medicine it needed. To cope with inflation, Volcker slammed on the economic brakes, restricted the growth of the money supply, and curbed inflation. As a result, he pushed interest rates to nearly 20 percent—their highest level since the Civil War. Almost immediately the sale of automobiles and expensive items stopped.

The decade also was marred by the deep divisions caused by the Vietnam War. For more than 10 years the war had been fought on two fronts: at home and abroad. As a result, U.S. policy makers conducted the war with one eye always focused on national opinion. When it ended, the Vietnam War had been the longest war in American history, having cost $118 billion and resulted in

56,000 dead, 300,000 wounded, and the loss of American prestige abroad.

The decade was a time not only of movements, but of moving. In the 1970s, the shift of manufacturing facilities to the South from New England and the Midwest accelerated. The Sunbelt became the new darling of corporate America. By the late 1970s, the South, including Texas, had gained more than a million manufacturing jobs, while the Northeast and the Midwest lost nearly two million. Rural North Carolina had the highest percentage of manufacturing of any state in the nation, along with the lowest blue-collar wages and the lowest unionization rate in the country. The Northeast lost more than traditional manufacturing jobs.

The largest and most striking of all the social actions of the early 1970s was the Women's Liberation Movement; it fundamentally reshaped American society. Since the late 1950s, a small group of well-placed American women had attempted to convince Congress and the courts to bring about equality between the sexes. By the 1970s, the National Organization for Women (NOW) multiplied in size, the first issue of Ms. magazine sold out in a week, and women began demanding economic equality, the legalization of abortion, and the improvement of women's role in society. "All authority in our society is being challenged," said a Department of Health, Education, and Welfare report. "Professional athletes challenge owners, journalists challenge editors, consumers challenge manufacturers . . . and young blue-collar workers, who have grown up in an environment in which equality is called for in all institutions, are demanding the same rights and expressing the same values as university graduates."

The decade also included the flowering of the National Welfare Rights Organization (NWRO), founded in 1966, which resulted in millions of urban poor demanding additional rights. The environmental movement gained recognition and momentum during the decade starting with the first Earth Day celebration in 1970 and the subsequent passage of the federal Clean Air and Clean Water acts. And the growing opposition to the use of nuclear power peaked after the near calamity at Three Mile Island in Pennsylvania in 1979. As the formal barriers to racial equality came down, racist attitudes became unacceptable and the black middle class began to grow. By 1972, half of all Southern black children sat in integrated classrooms, and about one-third of all black families had risen economically into the ranks of the middle class.

The changes recorded for the decade included a doubling in the amount of garbage created per capita from 2.5 pounds in 1920 to five pounds. California created a no-fault divorce law, Massachusetts introduced no-fault insurance, and health food sales reached $3 billion. By mid-decade, the so-called typical nuclear family, with working father, housewife, and two children, represented only seven percent of the population and the family size was falling. The average family size was 3.4 persons compared with 4.3 in 1920.

1972 Profile

Elizabeth Clayton may have been educated back East, but her roots are Western, firmly planted in New Mexico. She is a surgeon who has had to prove her expertise time and again to patients, other doctors, and even her grandfather, but has finally won the respect she deserves.

Life at Home

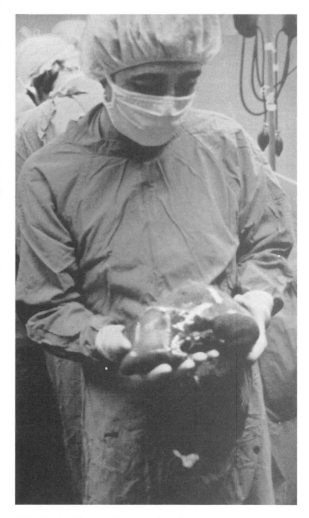

- Thirty-seven-year-old Elizabeth Clayton traces her Western roots to a decision her mother's side of the family made in 1838 to move to New Mexico when it was still part of Mexico.
- There, Elizabeth's grandmother met an American man named Clayton and they started a life, ranch and legacy together.
- Today, her grandfather Bill Clayton is one of the largest landowners in the state of New Mexico and a political power throughout a four-state area.
- The long family history in New Mexico includes the founding of what became one of the largest banks in town, a pharmacy, a railroad depot and a cattle empire.
- Elizabeth's father is a senior officer at the bank where he still lives in the shadow of his larger-than-life father.
- Elizabeth went to exclusive private schools back East for both her secondary and higher education.
- After a year in Washington, DC, working for a lobbyist friend of her grandfather, she entered the University of Pennsylvania School of Medicine.
- Her grandfather was opposed to the idea of women doctors, but Elizabeth proved once again that she was the one person who could stand him down.

Elizabeth Clayton is proud to be a surgeon.

- Ultimately, he not only agreed to the idea but decided to pay for it, as well.
- Eventually, medical school was all his idea.
- Today, he loves to tell friends that he has long felt Albuquerque needed a surgeon of Elizabeth's brains and talent.
- She feels that her one great error in life was falling for Dudley Bannon when she was in college.
- He was a scholarship student at the men's college near her school.
- Dudley had charm, the looks of an Adonis, and was captain of the golf team.
- In many ways he was the antithesis of Elizabeth, who is a sometimes blunt, plain-spoken intellectual who is most kindly described as "looking like she came from a good family."
- Elizabeth stands six feet tall, and is rail-thin with a prominent hook nose and piercing dark eyes; she was known in school behind her back as "the Raptor."
- She married when she was in medical school and Dudley was working on the Philadelphia Stock Exchange.
- After her medical residency, she joined a practice in her home town where they moved, with Dudley joining the local office of a national brokerage firm.
- Many people were delighted to give their business to the charming young man with the excellent family connections.
- The couple built a Spanish adobe-style house in a developing subdivision, despite her grandfather's repeated offers of a house and land on his ranch.
- They had a full-time maid/cook who watched their two young daughters, Alexandra and Caroline.
- The girls, like their mother, were raised to be bilingual in English and Spanish, a fact which infuriated Dudley when the entire household, including the maid Esmeralda, would converse in Spanish, which he still struggled to understand.
- The high life soon got to Dudley; he was drinking heavily, and there were rumors of drug abuse.
- When the private detective hired by Elizabeth's grandfather caught him with a pretty, young cocktail waitress, his time in the sun ended abruptly.
- Those people who had used his services because of the family connections began to avoid him.
- He now lives in a small apartment and sees his daughters every Thursday night and every other weekend.
- Elizabeth has retaken her maiden name, a rather daring step.
- She would like to start dating again, but many men in New Mexico are intimidated by her success, her straightforward demeanor and her grandfather's towering reputation.
- Only when she is alone with her girls does she allow herself to relax and be a little silly.
- The oldest girl, Caroline, who prefers to be called Caro, is fascinated by the space program; she and her mother have put together scrap books on every U.S. mission including the first time a human walked on the moon.
- At the time of the walk in 1969, Caro was seven and Alex five; they sat together as one and watched the first steps with amazement and unbridled excitement.
- Caro was quick to say, "I'm going to do that one day."
- Being smart has value in the Clayton home.

Caro is fascinated by the space program.

- It's always a big day when the *National Geographic* arrives in the mail.
- After dinner, the family reads through the issue together, finds the places it talks about on the globe, examines the enclosed map and talks about trips they would like to take.
- Elizabeth thinks Caro and Alex are getting a good education in the public schools, although late at night she worries whether her girls are being challenged enough.
- She cannot imagine her children going East as she had for prep school; losing the company of her precious girls would be too much.
- The center of the children's social life is the country club.
- Esmeralda takes the girls there to go swimming on many afternoons.
- Caro swims like a fish; Alex spends all her time scrambling from the pool to the diving board and back again; no dive or dare is too much for her.

Elizabeth enjoys the unique style of Western art.

- Some weekends, they drive out to her grandfather's ranch, across broad stretches of New Mexico that are rapidly being converted into the housing developments around Albuquerque.
- The girls love horseback riding with their great-grandfather, who tells them wonderful stories of New Mexico's past in the last century and beyond.
- It is hard for the girls to imagine that New Mexico was once part of other countries—Spain, then Mexico—but most of all they fret that the interests of the original settlers, the Indians, were swept away by settlers, ranchers or cattlemen.
- On several occasions, their great-grandfather has taken them to ancient Indian dwellings, where they could explore natural caves containing dozens of rooms.

- When the girls return, they are full of stories and questions, reminding Elizabeth of her growing-up experiences of discovering those mysterious markings created by the Anasazi.

Life at Work

- When Elizabeth Clayton first moved back to New Mexico after years of medical training in the East, considerable adjustment was required.
- The West is much more informal, and even in a town as rapidly growing as Albuquerque, everyone, it seems, knows everyone worth knowing.
- At first, Elizabeth felt she was under a microscope.
- And, as a female surgeon, returning home after a dozen years away, she was certainly the focus of immense curiosity and some hostility.

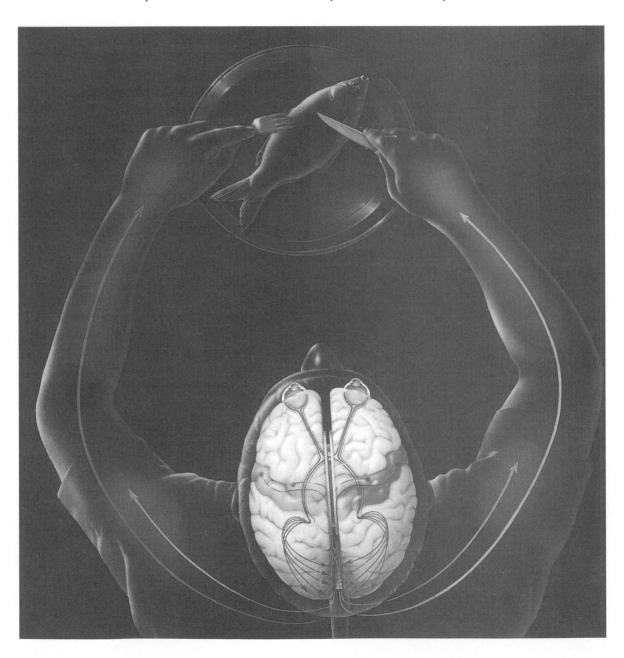

- Men and women expressed anger at her position.
- Men were concerned that she would soon "waste society's investment" in her; women talked endlessly about the "motherless children" who would surely be neglected in the hectic life of a surgeon.
- But eventually, coming home felt good.
- One of her early surgical procedures involved a Navajo man who insisted that a sing ceremony, called a chant way, be performed before the operation.
- Elizabeth's extensive Eastern education had neglected this form of healing, but intuitively she knew that it was critical to the health of her patient.
- During the sing, his blood pressure stabilized and a new red flush of circulation flowed into his cheeks.
- The operation, as well as the chant way, proved a grand success.
- Elizabeth knows she was invited to join the city's most prestigious medical practice because of her grandfather; several of the older doctors, who harbor a clear prejudice for women in their profession, went out of their way to tell her so.
- However, through sheer determination and competence, she has made believers of her fellow physicians.
- The first time she was lead surgeon and the patient began to hemorrhage, the senior surgeon assisting was greatly impressed by the calm way in which she evaluated the situation.
- Elizabeth's even-voiced, precise instructions brought the emergency under control, earning her a measure of early respect.
- At the same time, Elizabeth is often frustrated, even appalled by the actions of fellow doctors who are ignorant of Western ways.
- Many came to New Mexico to take advantage of the growth of Albuquerque without taking time to learn about the local culture.
- Recently, Elizabeth heard a Chicago-bred doctor ask an Indian nurse to help him communicate with a patient who spoke no English.
- "Sorry. I can't help you," she relied. "That man is a Navajo, and I am a Pueblo."
- Elizabeth was embarrassed when this educated man replied, "But you both speak 'Indian,' don't you?"

Life in the Community: Albuquerque, New Mexico
- Sparsely populated New Mexico is the nation's fifth-largest state, but boasts a population of only 1.04 million people, or approximately eight people per square mile.
- Seventy percent of the population lives in urban areas, one-third in and around Albuquerque.
- Currently, Albuquerque's population of 330,000 is similar to the state's total size when New Mexico was admitted to the union in 1912 as the forty-seventh state.
- The Old Town of Albuquerque dates back 250 years.
- Proud of its title, Land of Enchantment, New Mexico has one of the largest populations of Indians in the nation, most of whom have preserved their traditional way of life.
- Three major groups settled New Mexico: first Indians, then the Spaniards, and finally English-speaking Americans.
- Because the Spaniards intermarried with the Indians, their descendants are called Spanish-Americans or Hispanos.

The beauty of New Mexico is a constant delight.

The family often travels to the site of ancient Indian dwellings.

- Hispanos comprised the largest portion of the New Mexico population until the 1940s, but today represent only 25 percent of the census as a result of the rapid growth of the Anglo population in recent decades.
- At the same time, the number of Indians has also increased, growing from just under 35,000 in 1940 to 73,000 today.
- The largest tribe is the Navajo, whose reservation is in the northwest corner of the state.
- More than 20,000 Pueblo Indians are scattered around the state on 19 different land grant areas.
- New Mexico's Indian heritage extends back 20,000 years, according to fossil and stone tool remains.
- Starting around 1500 AD, the Navajo and Apache tribes moved into the region from the north, followed some years later by the Utes and Comanches.
- European civilization got its first toehold in 1598 when Juan de Onate established a colony near the Chama River.
- Pedro de Peralta moved the capital of the colony to Santa Fe in 1610; today it is still the capital of New Mexico, making it the oldest seat of government in the United States.
- Despite Indian revolts, hard living and unpredictable rainfall, the colonists maintained control of this lonely outpost

of the Spanish empire until 1821, when Mexico won independence from Spain and made New Mexico part of its territory.

- That same year, William Becknell opened the Santa Fe Trail to bring goods there from Missouri, cementing the region's role as a frontier trading and travel center.
- The Mexicans controlled the region for 25 years until the outbreak of war between the United States and Mexico in 1846.
- Two years later, the Treaty of Guadalupe Hidalgo ended the war and gave the United States possession of New Mexico.
- In 1850, when Congress officially organized New Mexico as a territory, it included what is now Arizona and parts of present-day Colorado, Nevada and Utah.
- New Mexico obtained its present boundaries in 1863 when Colorado and Arizona were organized as territories.
- At the outset of the Civil War, Confederate troops captured much of New Mexico, including Albuquerque and Santa Fe, but the area was recaptured by Union soldiers in 1862.
- These battles were followed by the bloody Indian wars with the Mescalero Apache and the Navajo tribes, forcing them to live on reservations.
- More fighting followed in the 1870s when cattlemen and other groups fought for control of the state.
- The Indian wars continued; one of the last native Americans to surrender was Geronimo in 1886.
- After railroads linked the territory to the rest of the nation in the late 1800s, cattle and mining fed the prosperity of the state.
- Albuquerque was incorporated as a town in 1885; six years later, it was incorporated as a city.
- The University of New Mexico, the state's largest university, was founded in 1889.
- In 1926, Route 66 gained its designation when the federal government first implemented its highway numbering system; the "Mother Road" supports a host of tourist and travel business.
- Two years later, Albuquerque entered the age of air travel with the opening of its International Sunport facility.
- During World War II, the federal government secretly built the town of Los Alamos in New Mexico's mountains, and in 1945 tested the atomic bomb built there in the White Sands proving grounds in southern New Mexico.
- Albuquerque's high-tech era also began with World War II, which saw the founding of Kirtland Air Force Base in 1940 and Sandia National Laboratories in 1949.
- Atomic power development, including the mining of uranium and the space program, have been part of the state's economy ever since.

HISTORICAL SNAPSHOT
1972

- In a 5-4 decision, the Supreme Court ruled that capital punishment was "cruel and unusual," pending further legislation from the states
- High-rated TV program *Bridget Loves Bernie* was canceled after religious groups objected to its Catholic and Jewish intermarriage scenario
- Porno films such as *Deep Throat* found a wide audience; the X-rated cartoon movie *Fritz the Cat* premiered
- Hit songs included "Let's Stay Together," "Lean on Me," "I'd Like to Teach the World to Sing," "Anticipation," "Rocket Man" and "You Turn Me On I'm A Radio"
- After 3,242 performances, *Fiddler on the Roof,* the longest-running show on Broadway, closed
- The reported annual salary of news anchorman Walter Cronkite was $250,000; a New York Yankees pitcher's annual income was $120,000
- President Richard Nixon won re-election over Democrat peace candidate George McGovern by a landslide
- Movie openings included *The Godfather, Cabaret, Deliverance, The Poseidon Adventure, Play It Again, Sam, Lady Sings the Blues* and *Last Tango in Paris*
- The American Heritage Dictionary for children became the first to recognize "Ms." as a title
- Albert Einstein's prediction of a time difference in a moving clock was validated
- Disposable diapers were introduced
- Time/Life HBO subscription cable television began with a National Hockey League contest and the film, *Sometimes a Great Notion*
- Emmy Awards for the year were awarded to *The Waltons* for drama, *All in the Family* for comedy and *The Julie Andrews Hour* for variety
- Feminist leaders Gloria Steinem and Patricia Carbine founded *Ms.* magazine
- Following President Richard Nixon's visit to China, lacquer-red colors, silk pajamas and lotus-patterned gowns became part of women's fashion
- The First International Festival of Women's Films was held in New York City
- During the Summer Olympics in Munich, 11 died when Arab terrorists seized Israeli athletes as hostages
- Hawaii became the first state to ratify the Equal Rights Amendment
- Black militant Angela Davis, who was once on the FBI's most wanted list, was acquitted of murder conspiracy charges
- The Players Association strike delayed the start of the professional baseball season by 13 days in the first major sports strike
- Congress passed Title IX prohibiting sex discrimination in federally funded education programs to include sports
- Bestsellers included *Jonathan Livingston Seagull* by Richard Bach, *August 1914* by Alexander Solzhenitsyn, *The Winds of War* by Herman Wouk, *Dr. Atkins' Diet Revolution* by Robert A. Atkins and *I'm O.K., You're O.K.* by Thomas Harris

Selected Prices

Automobile, Volkswagen Sedan	$2,999.99
Biofeedback Monitor Kit	$125.50
Bundt Pan	$2.99
Calgon Bath Oil Beads	$0.98
Camera, Kodak Pocket	$28.00
Cassette Tapes, Package of Three	$1.99
Flashcubes	$36.00
Hair Spray, Adorn	$1.09
Microwave Oven, Radarange	$450.00
Pasta Machine	$30.00
Staple Gun	$4.95
Tires, Radial, Each	$16.95

"If You Help Babies, They'll Do Well," *Life*, August 4, 1972:

(Baby) Michele is at the other extreme of pediatric surgery from (seven year old) Lisa. She is only six weeks old, weighs 6.5 pounds and was born with a tumor in her chest. At first her pediatrician thought she had pneumonia, but at Johns Hopkins, Dr. (Alex) Hollar and Dr. Patricia Moynihan, who was completing the final year of her two-year residency in pediatric surgery, made the diagnosis: a massive and malignant tumor was growing in the baby's chest. Already she was having severe problems breathing, and without emergency surgery she would surely die. Dr. Moynihan's team faced enormous problems. Not only do infants present special surgical difficulties because of their size, but on the operating table and afterward, their bodies are subject to mercurial and dangerous shifts in heart, lung and kidney function. Special precautions are necessary. Against sudden loss of body heat, Michele was warmed by a heating pad and an overhead sunlamp, and her arms and legs were wrapped in cotton padding. Her temperature, as well as her other vital signs, was constantly monitored. Anesthesia was given in carefully regulated doses. And as Dr. Moynihan operated on Michele's tiny chest with miniaturized instruments, the fluids leaving the body were measured and replaced drop by drop. Since not all of the tumor could be cut out, silver clips were used to mark its perimeters and trace the effectiveness of the cobalt treatments that would follow. In all, surgery lasted an hour and a half. Then later, in intensive care, Dr. Moynihan listened intently as the baby's compressed lung began to inflate and work again. (See graphic)

There are about 200 surgeons in the U.S. today qualified to operate on and care for a baby like Michele. In a year, less than 20 are trained, under the guidance of experts like Dr. Hollar, at the dozen or so institutions that offer pediatric surgery as a specialty. More are needed, but the training is long—seven years in all

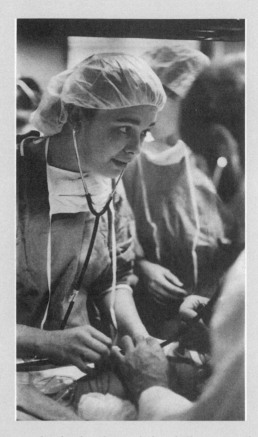

after medical school—and the skills required to suture blood vessels no thicker than a kitchen match are as demanding as any in the surgical field. If and when surgery to correct defects is attempted on living fetuses, it will be done by just these surgeons. Right now, the most important and difficult parts of a pediatric surgeon's practice involve malignancies, as in Michele's case, or congenital—imperfectly formed or connected parts of the body—that instantly threaten the life of an otherwise healthy newborn. "For too long," Dr. Hollar says, "we have said if a baby dies because it was born with a faulty trachea, for instance, that it's an act of God, or 'I did my best but he wasn't strong enough to survive.' Well, I don't accept that. Babies are designed to live, and they're pretty hardy creatures when they are born. If you can help them, they'll do well."

"Quotas: The Sleeper Issue of '72?," *Newsweek*, September 18, 1972:

The way to end discrimination against some is not to begin discrimination against others." Richard Nixon, Miami Beach, August 23

Every presidential campaign, no matter how predictably it may begin, seems inevitably to produce its surprise issue. This year, amid all the expected talk about the war in Indochina and the economy at home, the sleeper has turned out to be quotas—the real or imagined presence of statistical targets for the inclusion of women, blacks or some other minority groups in American industry, colleges and professions. Richard Nixon took aim at the issue in his acceptance speech, has kept up a steady fire ever since and pounded away at it with special vigor in his Labor Day oratory. And despite George McGovern's nimblest efforts to dissociate himself from the quota cause, the president seemed to be scoring political points.

For the issue appears to have touched raw nerves and prompted what might be called the first respectable backlash since the civil rights movement began. The impetus toward quotas springs from a decade of effort, both governmental and private, to open up avenues of American society long closed to minorities. And it illuminates the obstacles that still exist—particularly for women in professions such as college teaching and for blacks in such traditionally white-only trades as the construction industry, where apprentice programs are just beginning to break the color bar.

At the root of the controversy is the concept of "quota" itself a code word with enormously different meanings for different groups. For many women, blacks, Latinos and other minorities, it means simply a guaranteed floor under efforts to achieve reasonable representation in fields previously inhospitable to them. But for many people, the word is a curse. To American Jews, a quota has been historically not a floor but a ceiling—or a lock on the door. Only in the last generation have quotas restricting Jews all but disappeared from American life. To ethnic blue-collar workers, "quota" has come to mean the force-feeding of blacks at their expense. What's more, many fear that the philosophy of quotas may ultimately be taken to its logical extreme, a system of ethnically proportional representation in the U.S. that is finally unfair to individuals and stultifying to society as a whole.

"A Renewal of Broken Treaties," *Interfaith Reporter*, **published by the San Fernando Valley Interfaith Council, May 21, 1971:**

On Sunday, May 23, the Valley Interfaith Council, in cooperation with churches and temples throughout the area, will be sponsoring a forum with representatives of Indians of All Tribes.... The purpose of this forum is to call on Christians and Jews to listen and respond to the crisis facing the Indian community of California. It is as religious people that we have been asked to respect and preserve the sacred heritage of our Indian brothers. It is as American citizens that we are summoned to cherish and protect the right to religious freedom guaranteed to us in the First Amendment.

On April 22, 1971, twelve Indians were sentenced for trespassing and disturbing the peace at the Southwest Museum in Los Angeles. They had protested, in a very orderly manner, the public display of several religious articles. The facts of this issue have not been presented adequately by the news media for fear of political repercussions. Therefore, the Indians have had to come directly to you and me, the people.

Financial assistance is urgently needed by the victims of this unjust action. Yet, more important is the support of the religious community to call into question the legality and morality of this profoundly religious issue.

"The Moon, 'A Giant Leap for Mankind,' " *Time*, July 25, 1969:

The ghostly, white-clad figure slowly descended the ladder. Having reached the bottom rung, he lowered himself into the bowl-shaped footpad of Eagle, the spindly lunar module of Apollo 11. Then he extended his left foot, cautiously, tentatively, as if testing water in a pool—and, in fact, testing a wholly new environment for man. That groping foot, encased in a heavy multi-layered boot (size 9_ B), would remain indelible in the minds of millions who watched it on TV, and a symbol of man's determination to step—and forever keep stepping—toward the unknown.

After a few short but interminable seconds, Neil Armstrong placed his foot firmly on the fine-grained surface of the moon. The time was 10:26 p.m. (EDT), July 20, 1969. Pausing briefly, the first man on the moon spoke the first words on lunar soil:

"That's one small step for man, one giant leap for mankind."

With a cautious, almost shuffling gait, the astronaut began moving about in the harsh light of the lunar morning. "The surface is fine and powdery, it adheres in fine layers, like powdered charcoal, to the soles and sides of my foot," he said. "I can see the footprints of my boots and the treads in the fine, sandy particles." Minutes later, Armstrong was joined by Edwin Aldrin. Then, gaining confidence with every step, the two jumped and loped across the barren landscape for two hours and 14 minutes, while the TV camera they had set up some 50 feet from Eagle transmitted their movements with remarkable clarity to enthralled audiences on Earth, a quarter of a million miles away. Sometimes moving in surrealistic slow motion, sometimes bounding around in the weak lunar gravity like exuberant kangaroos, they set up experiments and scooped up rocks, snapped pictures and probed the soil, apparently enjoying every moment of their stay in the moon's alien environment.

After centuries of dreams and prophecies, the moment had come. Man had broken his terrestrial shackles for the first time and set foot on another world. Standing on the lifeless, rock-studded surface, he could see the Earth, a lovely blue and white hemisphere suspended in the velvety black sky. The spectacular view might well help him place his problems, as well as his world, in a new perspective.

"Angela Davis Legal Defense Fund Furor Described," *Interfaith Reporter*, published by the San Fernando Valley Interfaith Council, June 17, 1971:

Presbyterian churches across the Valley and nation are reverberating in response to the allocation of $10,000 by the Council on Race to the Angela Davis Defense Fund. VIC member Dick Bunce gives this background information: "At last year's General Assembly, the Council on Race was instructed to establish the Emergency Fund for Legal Aid, a fund budgeted for the amount of $100,000 per year. The purpose of the fund is to provide financial help for people of color who are incarcerated and cannot afford the cost of bail or the cost of hiring defense counsel adequate for a fair trial. The Session of the Presbyterian Church in Marin County and the Ethnic Church Affairs Office of the Synod of Golden Gate became convinced that Angela Davis was in particular need of an adequately financed defense in light of the negative publicity that surrounds her case. COCAR responded with the disbursement of $10,000 for the Angela Davis Defense Fund.

The Reverend Elder Hawkins, a former moderator of the General Assembly, Co-Chairman of COCAR, and a black person himself, explained the action...saying that equal justice is an inalienable right of all Americans, which means being assumed innocent until proven guilty. Mr. Hawkins and other Council spokesmen reminded the Assembly that in our society, even a person who is a black militant and a member of the Communist Party has a right to a fair trial when charged with a crime. Mr. Hawkins stated that his strong hope is that her political affiliation would not be used to confuse the issue, and that it would be understood that COCAR was acting in support of a fair trial and not of Miss Davis's personal views . . .

Many churches in the Valley have protested the allocation. The session of Dick Bunce's church defeated a resolution to censure the COCAR action, and supported a resolution affirming the Presbyterian connectional system. (This system allows for disagreement between decision-making bodies.)

Meanwhile, six prominent black clergymen have promised to repay the Church the $10,000 "as an affirmation that the cause of justice and liberation will triumph," Mrs. Ralph M. Stair, new moderator of the United Presbyterian Church, U.S.A., has said.

1972 NEWS FEATURE

"Woman Lawmakers on the Move," by Louie Robinson, *Ebony*, October 1972:
When black members of Congress take their seats for the 93rd annual session beginning in January, they will find their numbers bolstered to record proportions—some 17 or so, depending upon the outcome of several November elections—three of them certain to be black women. The Congress of the United States may never be the same.

Already stunned by the dazzling emergence of N.Y. Congresswoman Shirley Chisholm as the first major woman candidate for president, the staid old legislative body will now have to deal with California's pretty Yvonne Braithwaite Burke and Texas' no-nonsense Barbara Jordan, both such tough political entities back in their own home districts that they wiped out their opponents in Democratic primaries. The Republicans will be able to mount only token challenges this fall.

Identical in sex, race and the ability to get things done, the three women are, however, almost totally different in styles, making their presence in Congress all the more exciting. Mrs. Chisholm, of course, has made her mark, but the House will now have to recognize the congresswomen from California and Texas. It will have little trouble in doing so.

Yvonne Braithwaite—as she is best known, the Burke having been added only last June by her marriage to businessman William Burke—is a 39-year-old Los Angeles attorney whose six years in the California assembly have been highlighted by her work in changing garnishment and housing development laws, and in bringing about equal minority opportunities in housing and jobs, and creating better consumer

California Assemblywoman Yvonne Braithwaite Burke.

protection. Last year alone she introduced 72 bills (almost twice the normal number sponsored by a lawmaker), winning legislative passage of 31. Of these, 25 were signed into law. California Gov. Ronald Reagan vetoed the other six.

But to win the Democratic congressional nomination this summer, Assemblywoman Braithwaite had to defeat colorful Los Angeles City Councilman Billy Mills. Both had large, loyal followings in the district. The fight could have been bitter and divisive, but the two candidates recognized, as Assemblywoman Braithwaite puts it: "We could destroy the community in the campaign, or we could carry on at a level that would not destroy the community."

The resulting contest was lively but friendly. Mills went for the kind of local issues he knew best: better-lighted communities at night, cleaner streets. Assemblywoman Braithwaite talked about education, child care, the policies of lending institutions, the

Senator Barbara Jordan of Texas.

changing priorities in terms of the war and defense spending. "I believe the black electorate is very sophisticated," she declares. "Black people felt my experience on the state level was more comparable to what would have to be done on a national level." She took 54 percent of the vote and Mills announced he would support her in the general election.

In Texas, Barbara Jordan has been chalking up a string of "firsts" to go with her legislative record. She is the first black woman state senator, the first black woman ever to preside over a state senate (she was elected senate president pro tempore for a special session of the Texas senate this summer), and, as governor for a day on June 10 during the absence from the state of both the governor and lieutenant governor, the first black person to ever serve as her state's chief executive officer.

Like Assemblywoman Braithwaite, Sen. Jordan has seen about half of her bills passed in six years. Her legislative work has included preventing a highly restrictive voter registration act, giving Texas its first minimum wage bill ($1.25 an hour), bringing the first raise in workmen's compensation in 12 years, and setting up the state's Department of Community Affairs "in an attempt to bring identifiable state focus on urban areas, housing and transportation."

Sen. Jordan won her Democratic congressional nomination by forging a coalition of black, Mexican-American and labor votes in Houston's 11th district. But the Texas campaign differed in tone from the California one. "I ran my campaign on effectiveness—who got what done while he ran his campaign on me," Miss Jordan says of State Rep. Curtis Graves, the principal of her three opponents for the congressional seat, who described her as "the best congresswoman that money can buy," in an obvious reference to her well-financed, Lyndon Johnson-endorsed campaign. She responded by pointing out that, as a lawmaker, her opponent had managed to get only one bill through the legislature in six years. Sen. Jordan was also accused of trading her Texas senate seat for a slot in Congress, since recent redistricting in her home territory now

New York Congresswoman Shirley Chisholm.

That's about what four years of college costs these days. More than a lot of families can handle. The Army is awarding over 1,000 four-year ROTC Scholarships this year. If you're accepted, we'll pay for your tuition, your books and your lab fees, plus $100.00 a month. For up to 10 months each school year. And ROTC only takes up about three to five hours a week of your time.

You choose your own academic major. And you can select from over 290 colleges and universities. No matter where they are. No matter how much they cost.

If you like the idea of going to college with a big part of the costs taken care of, see your high school Guidance Counselor about Army ROTC Scholarships. You owe it to yourself. And your family.

Army ROTC. The more you look at it, the better it looks.

makes it improbable that another black can be elected to the state senate in the near future. The senator declared that the special board drew up the new senate districts last year and she had no part in it.

When the dust had settled over all the controversy, Barbara Jordan had smashed her opponents by rolling up an overwhelming 80.6 percent of the vote.

Going into the November elections, Sen. Jordan will be facing an undistinguished Republican opponent in an area that is 42 percent black, nearly 15 percent Mexican-American and 70 percent Democratic.

1979 PROFILE

Anna Martignetti is an art student who has struggled all her life against her family's and community's view of a woman's place; finally, as a senior in college, she is finding an environment in which she can flourish.

Life at Home

Anna Martignetti is finding herself as a woman and an artist.

- Anna Martignetti is in her senior year at Massachusetts College of Art in Boston, only a short distance from the home she had lived nearly all her life.
- She grew up in a poor area of the city, in a small three-decker apartment with her parents, and her older brother and sister.
- Her parents were first-generation Americans; both sets of grandparents had come to the United States from Sicily early in the twentieth century.
- Between 1880 and 1924 more than four million Italians arrived in America, many settling in major eastern cities such as Boston.
- The National Origins Act of 1924 was passed to halt the massive immigration of Italians, Poles, Slavs, and Eastern European Jews.
- The family follows the "old school" Sicilian rules of family structure—sons are treasured and privileged, while daughters are considered to be of far lesser value.
- Even as a very young child, Anna questioned this thinking, inciting animosity in her father.
- He often told Anna that he would have preferred that she had been born a boy.

Anna feels that boys are granted more privileges.

- She keenly felt the inequality at home, where she had to clean her brother's room and iron his clothes.
- Every Saturday, Anna and her sister did all the major house-cleaning before preparing Sunday dinner—alongside their mother, who worked full-time at a bank in downtown Boston.
- As a child, Anna was often angry that her older brother had no household responsibilities, angry that she and her sister were not allowed to go out with friends as her brother did.
- When her father assigned Anna a task, he would sit glaring at her while she worked.
- Anna felt as though he was daring her to make a wrong move; frequently, he would scream at her in a rage she couldn't understand.
- The children were all sent to Catholic school.
- There, when students lined up for class, girls had to walk behind the boys, and were secondary in every aspect of education; even in the roll call, all the boys' names were called out first.
- Girls were not even allowed to take physical education, as the boys were.
- Anna's escape was music; she loved the Beatles, the Rolling Stones, Carole King, Carly Simon, Steely Dan and David Bowie, among many others.
- When *Goodbye Yellow Brick Road* by Elton John was released, she had to have a pair of platform shoes and a jacket as much like the ones depicted in the drawing of him on the album cover as she could get.
- She always carried a picture of Mick Jagger and a photo of the Beatles in her purse, for the rough times.
- In her senior year of the girls' Catholic high school Anna attended, each student had to meet with the guidance counselor before graduating.

Listening to music, especially the Beatles, is Anna's escape.

- When Anna, who was an honor student, told the counselor she wanted to go to college, the nun asked why she would want to do that when she could get a job as a secretary.
- This made Anna more determined to get an education.
- To study for the college entrance exams, Anna had to take time from her housework, angering her father.
- Once, he bellowed at her, "I hope you don't make it into college!"
- She did not say a word to her father the day her acceptance letter arrived from Massachusetts College of Art.

Life at School

- Founded in 1873, Massachusetts College of Art was the first public art college in the United States.
- The college is considered one of the three top art schools in the country.
- Anna loves the stimulating atmosphere at college—the exchange of ideas, the enthusiasm of the teachers, and especially the opportunity to be creative.
- This is a completely different world from anything she's ever known before; from the moment she arrived, she felt she belonged.
- Finally, her gender was not an issue.
- She marvels at the attitude of the male students and teachers, who are sincere in their praise of her artwork and do not expect special treatment for themselves.
- As a freshman, Anna became involved with the Drop-in Center, where students come to talk to other students about personal and school problems.
- It provided her with a new perspective about herself and the larger world.
- As a prospective staff member, Anna was required to attend thorough training with the school nurse to learn first aid and various methods of dealing with the problems students might want to discuss.

Anna attends the Massachusetts College of Art in Boston.

Virginia Slims looks back upon the afternoon soap opera of 1901.

VIRGINIA SLIMS

Slimmer than the fat cigarettes men smoke.

You've come a long way, baby.

15 mg "tar," 0.9 mg nicotine av. per cigarette by FTC Method.

Warning: The Surgeon General Has Determined That Cigarette Smoking Is Dangerous to Your Health.

- The candidates for staff positions stayed for a weekend at the nurse's house in Cape Cod for the intensive training.
- Anna's jaw almost dropped when she saw her male counterparts automatically picking up their own dishes after meals and doing their share of the cleaning up.
- This was truly an enlightened crowd, she decided.
- Upon returning home, she took a part-time job selling shoes on commission in a department store and soon moved into an apartment in Boston's South End with two other art students.
- Her mother said she would never forgive Anna for moving out.
- Work permitting, Anna goes to every women's rights or pro-choice rally she can; the women's movement is alive and kicking at school and in the country.
- It is invigorating, but confusing.
- Not all women agree with many of the tenets of the emerging philosophy; some are content with the status quo and have little interest in changing the status of women in the country.
- Anna can't understand why some women say they don't think they should be entirely equal with men; how can they insult themselves in that way?

College is opening Anna's vision of what art can be.

- How could women object to the statement in the Equal Rights Amendment proposal: "Equality of rights under the law shall not be denied or abridged by the United States or by any state on account of sex"?
- Anna and other supporters of the Equal Rights Amendment lobby, march, rally, petition, picket, and commit acts of civil disobedience, but it will be a long road toward real equality.
- She is convinced that women's equality won't happen in her lifetime.
- Anna gets by on very little money.
- The bus ride to and from school costs $0.25 each way.
- On days she doesn't bring her lunch, she buys a Greek salad, which normally costs $1.25, in the school cafeteria.
- Most of her earnings go toward art supplies and the tuition of $450 per semester for in-state students.
- Anna loves watching her own views mirrored in films such as *An Unmarried Woman* with Jill Clayburgh.
- Colleges are also adjusting to the women's movement.
- MassArt recently added a course called "Women Artists" to supplement the handful of female artists included in the large art history textbooks each course is assigned.
- Powerful female authors like Germaine Greer are also tackling issues such as the role of women artists in history.
- Anna is inspired by what seems to be going on in many places in the country.
- Women are demanding that barriers to their gender be broken.
- Just recently, Boston women marched on several restaurants and bars that prohibit women from being served in certain sections of these establishments.
- They are also demanding equal pay for equal work; right now, a woman earns $0.59 for every dollar a man makes for the same job.
- Anna says wryly, that's fine, as long as women receive corresponding discounts on rent, utilities, and groceries, since these things cost the same for both men and women.
- Recently, Anna's work has begun to garner attention from several teachers.
- She has been influenced by a teacher who is an abstract painter, and her work is coming alive.
- Her painting, she and her teachers feel, is entering a bold, new, confident level.
- She has begun to add mixed media to the oil paint to create rich textures and shapes based on trees and bark.
- Anna is finding her style—at least for now.
- Her work had been chosen for a show at the college gallery, and although the painting was not for sale, someone told the gallery director he wanted to get in touch with the artist so he could buy it.
- They settled on a price—$60.00—and Anna made her first sale!
- When one of her painting teachers found out about the sale, he offered her a job to help design a brochure for a local radio station, and Anna jumped at the chance.
- Susan Tighe, a friend of Anna's on the Cambridge Arts Council, had shown Anna's work to some gallery owners.
- They came to visit Anna in her small workspace at school, and though she had been nervous at first, they all got along famously, drinking coffee and talking about art for two hours.
- That's how Anna got her first gallery show.
- She would be showing work with two other artists in a group show.

- It was announced in several local newspapers, along with a picture of one of her paintings.
- When it came time for the opening, Anna was excited, and looked her best.
- Many of her friends came, along with people from the Arts Council, her mother and sister, and guests of the two other artists.
- She bemoaned the fact that she didn't have a business card.
- Some of the people who attended were extremely pretentious, but Anna knew they would be good people to know after college ended.
- She was exhilarated, selling three paintings out of six, and enjoyed the opening and the attention immensely.
- It was hard to let the sold paintings go, but she knew she would have to get used to it—she was now an exhibited artist, with more shows on the way.

Life in the Community: Boston, Massachusetts

- Boston is a small city compared with other major cities in the country.
- It is a historic place, with its Beacon Hill district boasting nineteenth-century brick buildings with exquisite stone carvings and wrought iron fences.
- Its fashionable thoroughfare is Newbury Street, where galleries and boutiques are clustered within eight blocks.
- The Boston Common was the first public park in America, and was first used for grazing cattle.
- Now, along with the Boston Public Gardens, it is a picturesque setting with statues, flowers, a frog pond, and lovely weeping willow trees gracing the perimeter of the pond.
- In addition to the galleries, Boston is home to the Museum of Fine Arts, the Institute of Contemporary Art, and the large Boston Center for the Arts, where *The Dinner Party*, an installation by artist Judy Chicago, is coming next year.
- Premiering in San Francisco this year, it comprises a triangular table set for 39 eminent women from history; the table rests on a porcelain floor inscribed with the names of 999 other historical or famous women.
- The women represented are chronologically named, from "Primordial Goddess" and Hiawatha to Mary Wollstonecraft and Georgia O'Keefe.
- The installation is yet more evidence of the exciting liberation art and artists are experiencing.
- Many artists are redefining what is art, while casting aside formal traditions and techniques.
- Anna has arranged with some contacts at the Center to be involved in setting up the installation when it comes to town.
- She hopes to be exposed to new artists and gallery directors so she can continue the momentum in her work.

HISTORICAL SNAPSHOT
1979

- Jane Fonda and Tom Hayden spoke out against the use of nuclear power during a 50-city tour
- The U.S. Treasury issued the Susan B. Anthony dollar coin
- The U.S. National Weather Service began naming hurricanes for both men and women
- More than 315,000 microcomputers were purchased
- The United States Supreme Court ruled that husbands-only alimony laws were unconstitutional
- More than 290 women held seats on Boards of major corporations, double the total in 1975
- A *New York Times* poll reported that 55 percent of Americans saw nothing wrong with premarital sex, double the response a decade earlier
- Video digital sound discs, electronic blackboards, throwaway toothbrushes, *Drabble* cartoon in *Seventeen* magazine, and railroad trains operated exclusively by women all made their first appearance
- Jane Margaret Byrne became Chicago's first female mayor, defeating the man who had fired her as consumer affairs commissioner
- The divorce rate increased 69 percent over 1968; the median marriage lasted 6.6 years
- The National Coalition Against Sexual Assault formed rape crisis centers in 20 American cities
- The U.S. Air Force and Navy introduced maternity uniforms for pregnant military women
- Mother Teresa of India was awarded the Nobel Prize for Peace
- Important paintings of the year included Susan Rothenberg's *Pontiac*, Ida Applebroog's *Sure, I'm Sure* and Alice Adams' *Three Arches*
- Controversy erupted in Boston when Gilbert Stuart's portraits of Martha and George Washington were moved from the Boston Atheneum to the National Gallery
- *Viking I* discovered a thin, flat ring of particles around Jupiter
- Control of mild hypertension was found to greatly reduce the incidence of heart attack
- Movie openings included *Kramer vs. Kramer*, *All That Jazz*, *Apocalypse Now*, *Star Trek—The Motion Picture* and *The China Syndrome*
- The high for the Dow-Jones Industrial Average was 907
- Franchise rights for a Dunkin' Donuts store cost $45,000
- TV premieres included *Archie Bunker's Place*, *The Dukes of Hazzard* and *Knots Landing*
- Marcia Carsey was named senior vice president of all prime-time series on the ABC network
- Massachusetts joined several other states in raising the legal drinking age from 18 to 20
- The John F. Kennedy Library, designed by I. M. Pei, opened in Boston
- U.S. Trust reported that 520,000 Americans were millionaires, one in every 424
- Judie Brown founded the American Life League whose goal was to prohibit abortion by constitutional amendment
- Judith Krantz received a record $3.2 million advance for the paperback rights to *Princess Daisy*
- An amendment to the 1964 Civil Rights law said employers with disability plans must provide disability for pregnancy

Selected Prices

Coffee Maker, Norelco..$23.88
Microwave Oven...$168.00
Calculator, Pocket, Texas Instruments.......................................$74.95
CB Radio, Basic 40-Channel $39.88
Turntable, Automatic $199.95
Trash Bags, Box of 500 ....$19.95
Bathroom Scale $17.99
Pressure Cooker $10.88
Vacuum Cleaner, Eureka $49.88
Automobile, Toyota Corolla..$2,788.00
Sunglasses..$7.99
Perfume, Chanel No. 19...$9.50

Gas: A Long, Dry Summer, *Time*, May 21, 1979:

By tradition, Memorial Day starts the American summer. Beaches, amusement parks, resorts welcome their biggest crowds since the previous Labor Day. The roads are jammed with city families streaming out to picnic areas or campgrounds. Next weekend, however, the stream may be more of a trickle, and some who venture forth may even be stranded, unable to find a gas station that will fill their tanks for the haul back home. Memorial Day could mark the point when the gasoline shortage of 1979 starts to hurt nationwide—and when American families finally realize that the nation's growing addiction to undependable supplies of foreign oil can really jeopardize its prodigal way of life. And although President Carter asked for standby authority to impose gas rationing, Congress last week rejected his proposal. The vote, a stunning defeat for Carter, reflected all too accurately a national unwillingness to face the facts about energy if doing so would mean any change in cherished habits. It left drivers vulnerable to what Press Secretary Jody Powell called "allocation by chaos."

A so-far irresistible force is about to collide with an immovable object. The force is the average American's desire to climb into his auto and take off, regardless of revolutions in Iran, soaring gasoline prices or presidential appeals to drive less. Gasoline demand has increased three percent since last year. No decrease at all has been noticeable since President Carter in April called on every motorist to reduce driving by 15 miles a week.

The immovable object is the empty service station. Why it may be empty is a complicated question, but the fact is inescapable: Gas stations just do not have as much fuel to sell as they did a year ago. Each month, oil companies are allotting their station chains anywhere from five percent to 20 percent less gas than in the same month of 1978. Every month, many stations are drained early, and in the last week of the month they start closing early in the evening, or on weekends, or until they get the next shipment. Come Memorial Day and the start of the great summer driving orgy, most experts predict serious trouble.

"Hell, No, We Won't Glow," *Time*, May 21, 1979:

With varying degrees of apathy, Washington has witnessed a demonstration by coal miners, farmers, chiropractors and bird watchers, by mimes protesting the imprisonment of six mimes in Spain, Tibetan-Americans complaining about their passports, and Strippers for Christ. But last week, in the wake of one of the largest marches since the Viet Nam era, in which more than 70,000 people assembled to protest the proliferation of nuclear-power plants, the capital began wondering whether an important movement may be in the process of being born.

The most concrete evidence of such a process was the unexpected approval by the House Interior Committee of a six-month moratorium on all new nuclear plant construction or licensing. Chairman Morris Udall had urged postponement of the vote until after a full investigation of the accident at Three Mile Island, Pa. But he found conservative Republicans joining liberal Democrats to pass the measure, and the full House is expected to pass it, as well. Said Udall afterward: "The potential is there for making nuclear power the centerpiece of politics in 1980. It has an intensity of its own." Representative Edward Markey, 32, a Democrat from Malden, Mass., who proposed the moratorium, was in his district last month talking to a man in his 70s. "You know," the old man told him, "I think those kids may be right again."

"Remembering the 1970s," *The Boston Globe*, December 16, 1979:

The 1970s will be remembered as the dance boom decade in the United States when, in one year, more people attended ballet performances than NFL football games; when Russian defectors put dance into the political arena and onto the front page; when movies such as *Saturday Night Fever* and *A Turning Point* and musicals like *A Chorus Line* and *Dancin'* glorified and glamorized dancing; when millions of amateurs took the plunge and enrolled in ballet and modern dance classes.

It was the decade when New York's position as undisputed dance capital of the world was solidified and when every dance company—ballet, modern, or ethnic—gained credibility with New York reviews. It was the tapering off of an era of dominance by several of the greatest choreographers in the history of dance, now in their 70s and 80s: Balanchine, Ashton, and Graham have no obvious successors.

Was the dance boom a craze or an indication that dance no longer occupies its traditional position as the stepchild of the arts, always underfunded and overlooked? Whatever the answer, there is a consensus that, coinciding tidily with the closing of the decade, the boom has peaked. There is less general, but growing, agreement that we are on the edge of an abyss full of economic woe and lacking in the strong artistic purpose which can make economic struggle worthwhile.

Why did dance boom? Americans in the 1970s had more time and more money. Two of the most popular ways to spend these resources are in the arts and in physical fitness, and in dance, Americans got both for the price of one. We are fitness mad, as witness all the bestsellers on diet, running, sports and exercise. It has been convincingly documented that ballet is more physically strenuous than virtually all sports, and the large number of adults flocking to beginner ballet and other dance classes testifies to a growing awareness of dance—but as exercise rather than as art. Part of our adulation for male Russian dance defectors is akin to our adulation for sports heroes. Their bodies are like ours, only better. They do the same things, only in extremes. Part of the current ascendancy of the male dancer is because he is more obviously an athlete than is the female dancer, who more often masks the difficulty of what she is doing to seem traditionally delicate. One sideline of the association of dance with fitness and the desire to look like a dancer is that in the 1970s the dancer's uniform, the leotard, became high fashion.

"Greer's Incisive Look at Female Creativity," by Robert Taylor, *The Boston Globe*, November 7, 1979:

The Obstacle Race, The Fortunes of Women Painters and Their Work, by Germaine Greer. Farrar, Straus & Giroux, 373 pp., $25

The literature of the women's movement has produced few volumes more incisive than this. Germaine Greer (*The Female Eunuch*) is a writer of skill who marshals her arguments on the kinship of female creativity to male-dominated culture with a refreshing lack of the tendentious. Unfortunately, she sometimes contradicts herself, the book is uneven, and, as an art historian she casts too wide a net. "Why have there been no great women artists?" is the question she sets forth to answer. Though one may quibble over her terms (doesn't Berthe Morisot qualify, or Sonia Dclaunay?), her intention is plain, and through the sheer volume of her examples she demonstrates convincingly it was no accident nearly all women painters before the ninteenth century were either daughters or mates or relatives of men. Of course, she is speaking about a modern activity practiced in a limited area of the planet, since it would be peculiar to speak of a great woman artist of the High Gothic period or from a culture that values arts other than the portable easel picture.

The author has patently done a tremendous amount of research. The names flow past in a cascade of surprises—Mary Beale, Lady Butler, Marie-Guilhelmine Leroulx de la Ville, a host of the unacknowledged and forgotten. The first section of the study, arguing that family, romantic love and the masculine art establishment crippled women's efforts, is by far the best. Here she is able to consolidate historical data with feminist issues; later, scholarship takes over, and with the exception of a couple of lively chapters devoted to single artists such as Artemisia Gentileschi and Angelica Kauffman, the book devolves into a dry-as-dust compilation of lists.

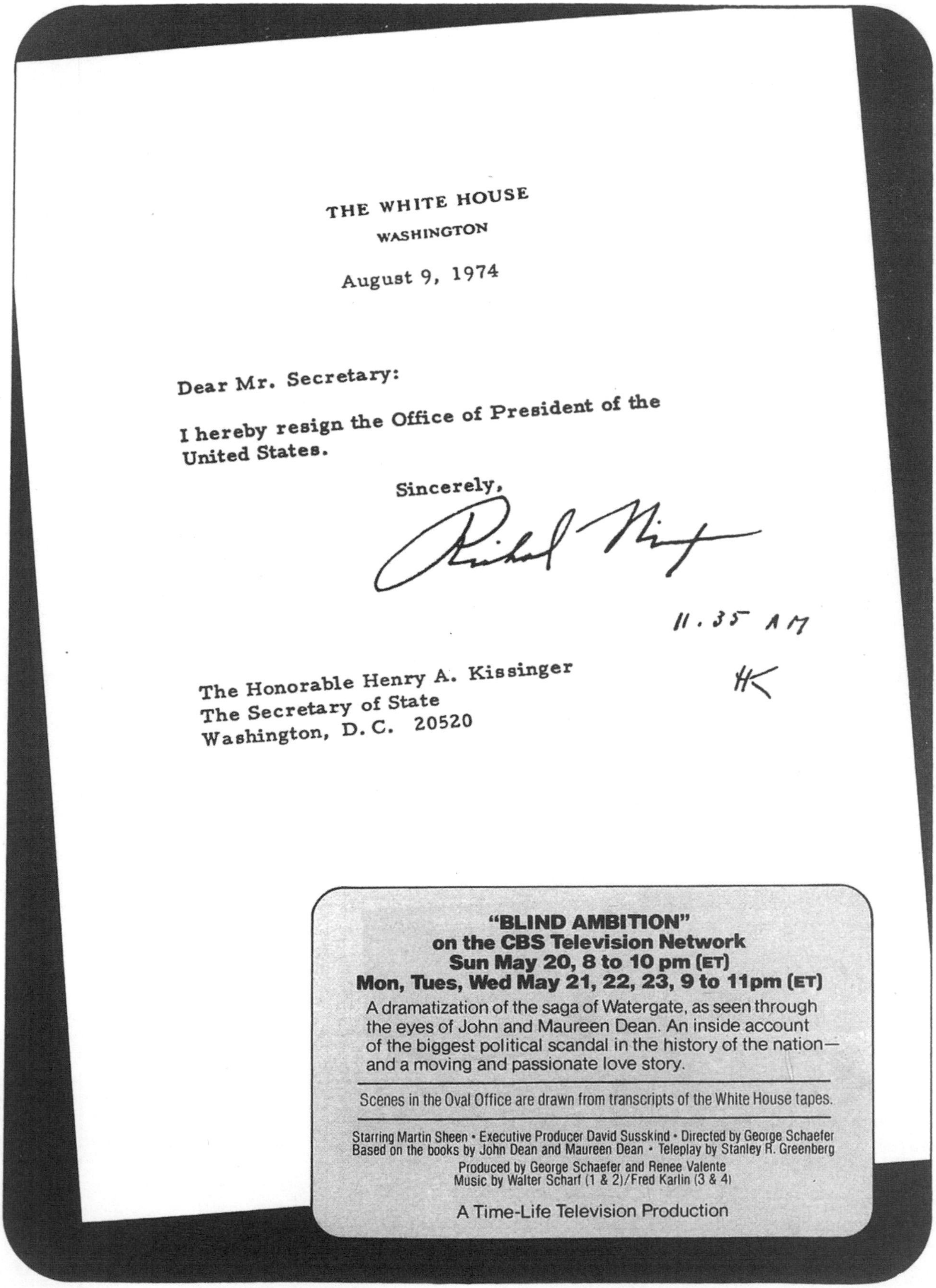

THE WHITE HOUSE

WASHINGTON

August 9, 1974

Dear Mr. Secretary:

I hereby resign the Office of President of the
United States.

Sincerely,

Richard Nixon

11.35 AM

HK

The Honorable Henry A. Kissinger
The Secretary of State
Washington, D.C. 20520

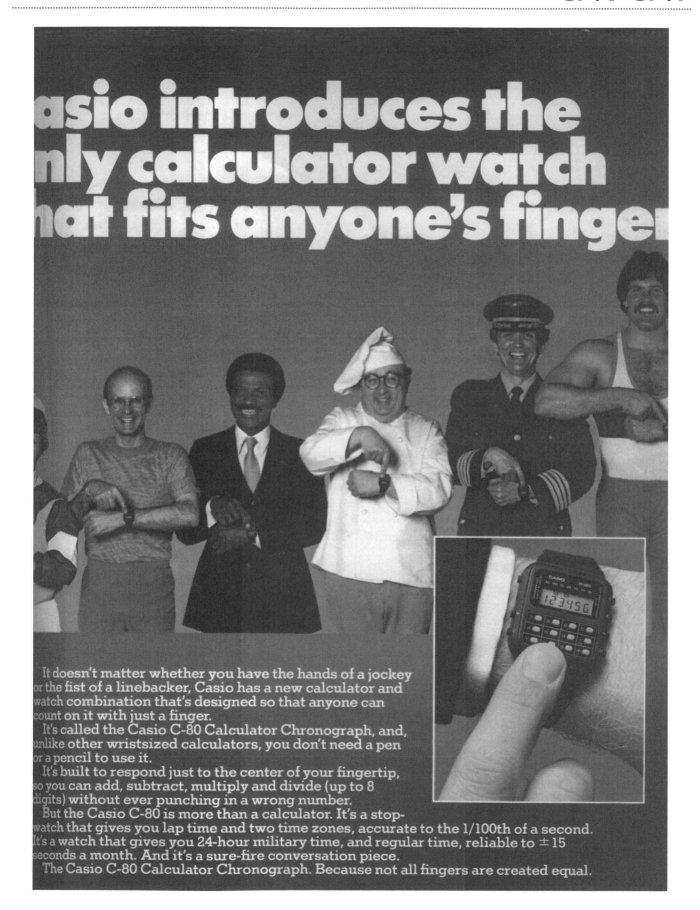

asio introduces the nly calculator watch hat fits anyone's finger

It doesn't matter whether you have the hands of a jockey or the fist of a linebacker, Casio has a new calculator and watch combination that's designed so that anyone can count on it with just a finger.

It's called the Casio C-80 Calculator Chronograph, and, unlike other wristsized calculators, you don't need a pen or a pencil to use it.

It's built to respond just to the center of your fingertip, so you can add, subtract, multiply and divide (up to 8 digits) without ever punching in a wrong number.

But the Casio C-80 is more than a calculator. It's a stopwatch that gives you lap time and two time zones, accurate to the 1/100th of a second. It's a watch that gives you 24-hour military time, and regular time, reliable to ±15 seconds a month. And it's a sure-fire conversation piece.

The Casio C-80 Calculator Chronograph. Because not all fingers are created equal.

"A Decade of Change: From Supermom to Superwoman," by Ellen Goodman, *The Boston Globe*, December 20, 1979:

In one moment, she wrapped it all up, the whole decade of change, the remaining problems, the new anxieties. Betty Friedan, the founding mother, the astute and caring observer of the women's movement, stood in front of a New York audience last month and said: "We told our daughters you can have it all. Well, can they have it all? Only by being Superwoman. Well, I say NO to Superwoman!"

By any media calculation, the audience was a collection of superwomen. They wore their raised consciousness layered with dress-for-success suits. Yet they broke into spontaneous applause. They, too, were saying no to the Superwoman myth.

That moment is as good a place as any to stop and assess, to review and preview.

For all the social change in the past decade, all the rhetoric and action, we have moved from one national ideal of True Womanhood to another—from Supermom to Superwoman. The girl who was told that when she grew up she should get married and have children and keep house is now a grown-up woman being told that she should be married, have children, keep house and a job, or better yet, a career.

While mothers at home have felt increasingly pressured for "not working," mothers in the work force feel increasingly pressured by the double burden. They have been "liberated" to the Russian model—have a new role on top of an old one. Every study shows the same things. The overwhelming number of working mothers do the overwhelming amount of housework and child care. They may not have it all, but they seem to do it all.

Why has the change been so lopsided? I have asked that question a hundred times and heard a dozen different answers, ranging from the psychological to the economic. One feminist psychiatrist says that women spent the decade proving themselves. A sociologist believes that the person who initiates the change—the person who goes to work even out of necessity—accepts the personal responsibility for it.

A woman from a working-class neighborhood in Baltimore tells me that women are stretching their own energy to cover both their traditional and non- traditional values: the desire or demand to make Christmas pudding and a salary. An economist offers a different theory: "The average woman earns $0.59 to her husband's dollar. She sees her time as worth less and overworks herself. She gets it twice."

And last week a union leader said: "Remember three things. One: A lot of women with lousy jobs hope they'll be able to quit. By doing everything, they think they're keeping their options open. Two: The home is the only place some women have any power. They sure don't want to let go of that. Three: Never underestimate the power of the men in their lives to resist."

Perhaps single mothers were the first to wipe off the upbeat Superwoman makeup that covered the lines of fatigue. But now it seems to many women that the Superwoman model who looked so chic at the beginning of the decade looks worn at the end.

In 1970, women had just begun to agitate collectively for new choices. But in 1980, the "daughters" who were to "have it all" face new choices that are still limited, frightening as well as attractive.

Many women, especially those "up against the clock" of their thirties, approach motherhood with fear and trembling. Those for whom homemaking, even temporary, is not a psychological or economic possibility see only two choices: superdrudge or childlessness.

In Washington, a 45-year-old woman says ironically, "I saw my mother frustrated at

(continued)

(continued)

home. My daughter sees me overworked. I'm not such a great role model myself."

Superwoman was in part a creation of the self-help, self-reliant, self-improvement Seventies. This was the flip side of the so-called Me Decade. It was not new narcissism, but new isolation masked as independence.

"I used to take pride in being a Superwoman," said a Manhattan woman listening to Friedan that afternoon. "Now I see it, not as a personal victory but as a failure. A failure of my relationship with my husband, a failure of the work world, maybe even a failure of the society that just isn't adjusting to the way we live."

The Superwoman myth is exploding like an overstuffed sofa. Women are no longer willing to look inside themselves for all the answers and all the energy. At the turn of the decade, they don't want a Superwoman pep talk any more. They long for something more precious and more realistic: a support system—of families, the workplace and the community—to fend off this cultural kryptonite.

1972–1979 NEWS FEATURE

Letters to *Ms.*, 1972-1987, edited by Mary Thom, 1987:

Dear Ms.

Recently I was "called in" by a secondary-school district where I substitute-teach. I was told I would be dropped from their list of substitute teachers unless I stopped using "Ms." writing my name on the board at the beginning of a new assignment—"because "Ms." makes students think of "sexuality and liberation."

When I asked if there weren't other women on the faculty using "Ms." with their names, I was told, "No, we don't have very many young, unmarried women working for us." Click . . . crash!

—Patricia R. Bristowe, La Honda, California, October 1973 Issue

Dear Ms.

I thought you might enjoy hearing a discussion I heard between my son and his neighbor friend. They were playing together and the little boy got the giggles. "Hee-hee-hee-hee," he giggled, whereupon my son replied in a very condescending tone, "What are you, Danny, some kind of chauvinist? In this house we say, "Her-her-her-her!"

Her who laughs last,

—Name Withheld, August 7, 1975

Dear Ms.

I finally got up the courage to challenge an old established male tradition in my office. I do telephone sales. Our working area in the office has always been covered with "girlie" pictures and photographs of devastating (and devastated) maidens. This made us few women in the office feel terribly uncomfortable.

When the majority of the male staff was out to lunch, we proceeded to rape the latest issue of *Playgirl* of its best. Over my desk now hangs one gorgeous specimen of the male species, the centerfold. Everywhere there was a girlie picture there are now beautiful stud photographs.

I think the reactions of the men in the office could best be summarized in terms of shock. Although everyone tried to be good-humored about it, joking or otherwise, they all compared themselves in some way to the models. It was a marvelous experience to

see super-duper macho stud types go all to pieces with the same thing we had to face for years—images of ourselves as seen only in the minds of men.

—Name Withheld, October 13, 1975

Dear Ms.

You have given me the supreme insult of my life by offering to let me subscribe to *Ms*. I hate the sound of it. It sounds like the hiss of a snake.

Are you proud of what you have helped do to our world? The family is almost destroyed; children by the millions have no parents or homes; divorces, crimes, dehumanization are the norm now. Has it been worth all this just to get some women in the military academies?

—Mrs. H. Sims, Mount Olivet, Kentucky, January 1977 Issue

Dear Ms.

I have been working for six years in a suburban law office in New Jersey, where the staff consists of seven secretaries (female) and four lawyers (male). It has always been the custom in this office for each "girl" to have her turn at "kitchen duty." She is expected to set the table in the library with dainty place mats, napkins, spoons, and eatables (such as crackers, which the firm finances) and to make coffee. At twelve o'clock everyone in the office, including the lawyers (if they are so inclined), comes into the library, and we all have lunch. Afterward, the woman who has kitchen duty for the day wipes up the table and washes the dishes, including the lunch containers that each person brings in.

I have participated unwillingly in this program for six years. Three weeks ago I decided that I had had it and announced that I was no longer to be given kitchen duty, that I would go out some of the time and when I had lunch in, I'd do my own dishes.

To say that my announcement caused a sensation is to put it mildly. At present none of the women is speaking to me except when absolutely necessary in the course of work. I have been told by one of the lawyers that no one can understand my attitude and that the women (and, I assume he) have completely lost respect for me.

I have taken a stand. How it will turn out, I have no idea.

—Name Withheld, March 1978 Issue

Dear Ms.

Recently, I was visiting my eighty-two- and eighty-six-year-old parents. My father was in the process of sorting through an old box of letters. My father's aunt Emma received a letter from an individual named Eunice on September 2, 1883. We were unable to come up with a last name; however, I do know that Eunice was a Baptist and she was much into saving "souls." We were able to surmise that Eunice was not married and approximately in her early thirties:

"I don't know as they would hire a woman teacher in the winter, yet I think if one would teach cheaper, she would stand a chance of getting the school. I won't teach cheaper just because I'm a woman, so I should probably be considered as very wicked and mercenary if I wanted $1.25 a day and board, the same as they pay some inferior sort of creature, who has the good fortune to be of the masculine gender, and just educated enough to know that there is such a gender."

It is so unfortunate that we will never be able to talk to this woman nor her friend my great-aunt Emma.

—Marjorie Wagner Chodack, Ravena, New York, November 28, 1979

NATIONAL ACADEMY OF SCIENCES

1980–1989

By the 1980s, the two-career family became the norm. Forty-two percent of all American workers were female, and more than half of all married women and 90 percent of female college graduates worked outside the home. Yet, their median wage was 60 percent of that of men. The rapid rise of women in the labor force, which had been accelerating since the 1960s, brought great social change, affecting married life, child rearing, family income, office culture, and the growth of the national economy.

Convinced that inflation was the primary enemy of long-term economic growth, the Federal Reserve Board brought the economy to a standstill in the early days of the decade. It was a shock treatment that worked. By 1984, the tight money policies of the government, stabilizing world oil prices, and labor's declining bargaining power brought inflation to four percent, the lowest level since 1967. Despite the pain it caused, the plan to strangle inflation succeeded; Americans not only prospered, but many believed it was their right to be successful. The decade came to be symbolized by self-indulgence.

At the same time, defense and deficit spending roared into high gear, the economy continued to grow, and the stock market rocketed to record levels (the Dow Jones Industrial Average tripled from 1,000 in 1980 to nearly 3,000 a decade later). In the center of recovery was Mr. Optimism, President Ronald Reagan. During his presidential campaign he promised a "morning in America" and during eight years, his good nature helped transform the national mood. The Reagan era, which spanned most of the 1980s, fostered a new conservative agenda of good feeling. During the presidential election against incumbent President Jimmy Carter, Reagan joked, "A recession is when your neighbor loses his job. A depression is when you lose yours. And recovery is when Jimmy Carter loses his."

The economic wave of the 1980s was also driven by globalization, improvements in technology, and willingness of consumers to assume higher and higher levels of personal debt.

The rising economy brought greater control of personal lives; homeownership accelerated, choices seemed limitless, debt grew, and divorce became commonplace. The collapse of communism at the end of the 1980s brought an end to the old world order and set the stage for a realignment of power. America was regarded as the strongest nation in the world and the only real superpower, thanks to its economic strength. As democracy swept across eastern Europe, the U.S. economy began to feel the impact of a "peace dividend" generated by a reduced military budget and a desire by corporations to participate in global markets—including Russia and China. Globalization was having another impact. At the end of World War II, the U.S. economy accounted for almost 50 percent of the global economic product; by 1987, the U.S. share was less than 25 percent as American companies moved plants offshore and countries such as

Japan emerged as major competitors. This need for a global reach inspired several rounds of corporate mergers as companies searched for efficiency, market share, new products, or emerging technology to survive in the rapidly shifting business environment.

The 1980s were the age of the conservative Yuppie. Business schools, investment banks, and Wall Street firms overflowed with eager baby boomers who placed gourmet cuisine, health clubs, supersneakers, suspenders, wine spritzers, high-performance autos, and sushi high on their agendas. Low-fat and fiber cereals and Jane Fonda workout books symbolized much of the decade. As self-indulgence rose, concerns about the environment, including nuclear waste, acid rain, and the greenhouse effect declined. Homelessness increased and racial tensions fostered a renewed call for a more caring government. During the decade, genetic engineering came of age, including early attempts at transplantation and gene mapping. Personal computers, which were transforming America, were still in their infancy.

The sexual revolution, undaunted by a conservative prescription of chastity, ran head-on into a powerful adversary during the 1980s with the discovery and spread of AIDS, a frequently fatal, sexually transmitted disease. The right of women to have an abortion, confirmed by the Supreme Court in 1973, was hotly contested during the decade as politicians fought over both the actual moment of conception and the right of a woman to control her body. Cocaine also made its reappearance, bringing drug addiction and a rapid increase in violent crime. The Center on Addiction and Substance Abuse at Columbia University found alcohol and drug abuse implicated in three-fourths of all murders, rapes, child molestations, and deaths of babies suffering from parental neglect.

For the first time in history, the Naval Academy's graduating class included women, digital clocks and cordless telephones appeared, and 24-hour-a-day news coverage captivated television viewers. Compact disks began replacing records, and Smurf and E.T. paraphernalia were everywhere, New York became the first state to require seat belts, Pillsbury introduced microwave pizza, and Playtex used live lingerie models in its ads for the "Cross Your Heart" bra. The Supreme Court ruled that states may require all-male private clubs to admit women, and 50,000 people gathered at Graceland in Memphis, Tennessee, on the tenth anniversary of Elvis Presley's death.

1986 PROFILE

German-born Maria Knapp holds the patents for more than a dozen scientific developments derived from a lifetime of molecular research, though the millions she has earned interest her little. At 66, her focus remains her first and only love—science.

Annual Income: More than $150,000, including salary and interest on investments managed by Bank of America.

Life at Home

* At 66, Maria Knapp displays the Old World manners she learned growing up in Germany; unfailingly gracious, she enjoys entertaining guests—as long as the topic is science.
* To stay in shape, she runs every day and continues to do push-ups and calisthenics in the privacy of her bedroom, since she finds public gymnasiums distracting, disorienting and frivolous.
* Although she bought a car last year—an Oldsmobile that is "all American"—she is often driven to work by an associate from the lab.
* Lab assistants also help with her paperwork and chores such as changing the batteries in her hearing aid.
* Her first research paper—published when she was only a 14-year-old child living in Germany—described a series of fruit fly mutations that cast whisker-thin rays of light on the knowledge of embryo development.
* Her parents' home was often populated with eminent scientists from around the world who came to Berlin, the epicenter of brain research in the 1930s.
* She even traveled with her parents to Moscow, where her father was invited to study Lenin's brain, which had been preserved after his death.

Maria Knapp is unfailingly gracious—as long as the topic is science.

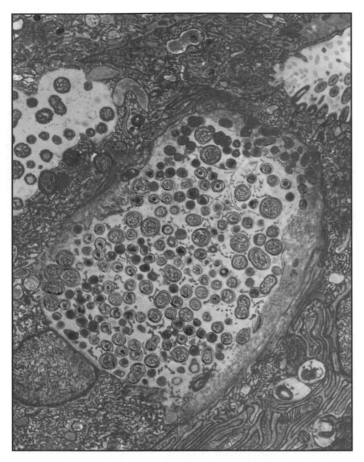

Maria has spent her life studying viruses and telomeres.

- As a university and medical student in Germany, she often skipped classes to putter around the lab, making up the missed lectures by memorizing the textbooks.
- Her work continued throughout the Nazi era, even after her parents were thrown out of a leading institute in Berlin, where her father was director.
- His previous trips to communist Russia, along with the couple's close association with many fellow scientists who were Jewish, made the family untrustworthy; thus, they were banished.
- Thanks to the intervention of a prominent German family who had been her father's patients, Maria's family was not imprisoned.
- Using money provided by their wealthy benefactors, her father established a private institute in the backwoods of Neustadt where their work could continue; there, they were able to offer refuge to many Jewish scientists and their families.
- During this time, Maria avoided every man, refusing to date; "I did not want to end up dating a Nazi, and in Germany at that time, you could never be sure of someone's politics."
- Devoting herself to science, she never married or had children; "Science was my milk," she likes to say.
- Her older sister, a scientist studying the biochemistry of the brain, has also opted against marriage and children.
- Maria wishes to die as her father did—in the laboratory, his last glimpse of life being the view through a microscope.
- She emigrated to Great Britain before the war broke out, becoming prominent in neuroscience, which has earned her election to the Royal Society of London.
- Repelled by her wartime experiences, she jumped at the opportunity to leave Germany in 1950 and come to the United States, even though it meant abandoning fruit fly genetics; "There was no interest in Drosophila research, so I had to take up something new," she recalls.
- She then emigrated to the United States when she was 30 years old, going first to the California Institute of Technology, and afterwards accepting a job at the Salk Institute.
- There, she participated in groundbreaking studies of how the polio virus forms distinctive plaques in tissue culture—an essential discovery in the development of the polio vaccine.
- Her intensity for her work has often superseded her own safety; while studying the polio virus, she did much of the work while laboring alongside a pathogen that other biochemists would not touch.
- Her parents were very angry when they learned that she was working with the polio virus.
- When she emigrated to the U.S., the only possession she brought with her was a grand piano, which she still plays regularly, often on Sundays when fellow musician-scientists hold recitals.
- Otherwise, she left Germany behind; when young German scientists come to the lab to meet the famous researcher and chat with her in their native tongue, she replies, often sternly, in English.

- By contrast, when a visiting Sorbonne student recently met with her and spoke in French, Maria's responses were also in French.
- She is known as a soft touch, often lending money from her own pocket to students in need.

Life at Work
- She has spent a lifetime in her own personal toy store—a scientific laboratory.
- Even at 66, she works 10 hours a day, seven days a week; "If I were to stay at home, I'd be bored," she says.

Her fellow scientists have lobbied her to donate her money to the education of women scientists.

She has worked with Dr. Barbara McClintock, who won a Nobel Prize in 1983.

- Her credits include groundbreaking studies on the polio virus and how a type of mammalioma virus called the polyoma virus transforms ordinary cells into cancer cells.
- This type of early research has helped lift the study of cancer biology from simply cataloging the gross anatomy of a tumor cell to an exploration of the genetic mutations underlying the disease.
- Two of her colleagues have been awarded the Nobel Prize for research, but she does not like or seek awards, saying, "When you get too famous, you stop being able to work."
- Fellow scientists say she deserves more recognition.
- She has been awarded patents for 16 of her scientific breakthroughs, earning her millions of dollars, most of which are invested in a trust managed by Bank of America.
- Her Last Will and Testament states that her wealth is to be used to promote science.

- Although some of her fellow female scientists have lobbied her to donate her money exclusively to the education of women scientists, she has not responded; money, grants, wills and recipients are not subjects she likes to think about or discuss.
- Her research through the years has ranged from oncogenes, the genes that when mutated result in cancer; immunology; and the behavior of telomeres—the distinctive chromosome tips that serve as molecular timepieces in healthy cells, but play a nefarious role in cancer when they fail to shorten as anticipated.
- She has worked with some of the finest talent in the world, including Dr. Barbara McClintock, the corn geneticist who won a Nobel Prize for her research.

"0.5 Percent of Families Found to Hold 35 Percent of Wealth," Michael Wines, *Los Angeles Times*, July 26, 1986:

"More than a third of the nation's net worth is held by 0.5 percent of America's households, a concentration of economic clout that has snowballed to levels not seen since the Great Depression, Democrats on Congress' Joint Economic Committee concluded in a study released Friday.

Their report, using 1983 figures compiled for the Federal Reserve Board, stated that the 420,000 richest U.S. families controlled $3.7 trillion in assets after debts. That is 35.1 percent of total wealth.

An earlier Fed study using 1962 data concluded that the same 0.5 percent of the population then controlled 25.4 percent of the national wealth. By comparison, the report stated the share of assets held by the poorest 90 percent of Americans dropped during those 21 years from 34.9 percent to 28 percent.

The committee Democrats' report provided the first public comparison of the two studies, both of which were conducted for the Fed by the University of Michigan's prestigious Survey Research Center. The 1983 study was based on projections from a survey of about 4,000 Americans. The sample included 432 members of the country's wealthiest families. . . .

In the report the 1983 data is divided into four classes of households:

- 420,000 'super rich' families with more than a third of the wealth and comprising 0.5 percent of families. None of these families were worth less than $2.5 million; their average wealth after debts was $8.85 million.
- 420,000 'very rich' with 6.7 percent of all net assets and an average wealth of $1.7 million.
- 7.6 million 'rich' with net wealth ranging from $206,000 to $1.4 million and an average net worth of $419,616. The rich, nine percent of all households, owned 29.9 percent of the wealth.
- 'Everyone else,' the 75.5 million households that make up the remaining 90 percent of the population. Their net worth ranged no higher than $206,000 and averaged $39,584.

The wealthy excelled in another crucial statistical measure as well. The net worth of the super rich rose during the 21-year period by 147 percent, adjusted for inflation. The very rich managed only a 64 percent increase and the rich, a 66 percent gain. Everyone else posted a more modest 45 percent increase. . . .

Nearly half the net assets of the bottom 90 percent were tied up in real estate, most of it in homes. Real estate was among the fastest appreciating assets, more than doubling in value from 1962 to 1983.

The super rich, meanwhile, had less than a fifth of their money in real estate in 1983. But the worth of their property holdings grew sevenfold during the 21 years between surveys."

Hotel del Coronado, Coronado, Cal.

She loves collecting old postcards featuring her adopted city of San Diego.

Life in the Community: San Diego, California

- Maria loves her adopted city of San Diego; now the second-largest city in California, it is not only picturesque, but has learned how to manage its growth well.
- The seventh-largest city in the United States, San Diego boasts a wonderful climate and a wide range of recreational activities.
- Several years ago, Maria began charting the number of times an executive in the building across the way—who often works the same long hours she does—slips out early in the afternoons for a spin in his sailboat; her chart shows he plays hooky 6.4 times a month.
- On a lark, a dozen years ago, she began collecting postcards of her beloved San Diego; today, she has hundreds.

Broadway looking East.

- She has especially enjoyed watching downtown transform itself from a seedy city center into a vibrant downtown, housing 120 shops, 30 eating establishments, seven movie screens and two performing arts theaters.
- The showcase is Horton Plaza, painted 49 different pastel colors, bordering the historic Gaslamp Quarter, which is now undergoing renovation.
- Today, seven Amtrak connections run from Los Angeles to San Diego daily, taking about two and a half hours, including a stop at Del Mar.
- When scientists come to visit, she always puts them up at the Horton Grand, a 110-room restored Victorian hotel in the downtown section.
- On Sundays, she will sometimes take brunch at the hotel and then rent a horse-drawn carriage for a gentle ride through the city.

HISTORICAL SNAPSHOT
1986

- Harvard University celebrated its 350th birthday
- Consumers who sought professional assistance with home decorating spent an average of $15,584 on the living room
- A New York Stock Exchange seat sold for $1.5 million
- The Dow Jones Industrial Average hit 1,955; the prime rate dropped to seven percent
- The U.S. Supreme Court upheld Affirmative Action hiring quotas
- Federal workers in sensitive jobs were randomly drug-tested after a presidential commission estimated that each month, 20 million Americans smoked marijuana, five million did cocaine and 500,000 used heroin
- Eight airlines controlled 90 percent of the domestic market
- Approximately 35 percent of high school graduates entered college
- The first bio-insecticides, designed to eliminate insects without harming the environment, were introduced
- A supercomputer capable of 1.720 billion computations per second went online
- The average salary of elementary and secondary schoolteachers was $26,700
- Office Depot, one of the first office supply warehouse-type stores, opened in Lauderdale Lakes, Florida
- The national debt passed $2 trillion—twice the level in 1981
- The Supreme Court held that the military may enforce a uniform dress code in a case involving three men who were prohibited from wearing yarmulkes indoors
- The official observance of Martin Luther King, Jr.'s Birthday, the Honda Acura, the one-stick Popsicle and the outdoor testing of genetically engineered plants all made their first appearance
- Estimates of America's homeless included 40,000 in New York City, 38,000 in Los Angeles and 25,000 in Chicago
- Drexel, Burnham, Lambert executive Dennis Levine pled guilty to insider trading, by which he had earned $12.6 million
- The Hands Across America chain, stretching from New York City to Long Beach, California, raised $100 million for the poor and homeless
- Fitness foods high in fiber and low in sodium, fat, cholesterol, calories and caffeine accounted for 10 percent of the $300 billion retail food market

Proof at last that money can buy happiness.

Spend a happy moment with Chateau Ste. Michelle's Cabernet Sauvignon.

Chateau Ste. Michelle

CABERNET SAUVIGNON

Of 59 gold medal cabernets, it was named American Champion by *Wine & Spirits*.

1986 ECONOMIC PROFILE

The national consumer expenditures (per capita income) in 1986 were:

Auto Parts	$76.46
Auto Usage	$1,411.96
Clothing	$576.75
Dentists	$97.65
Food	$1,981.67
Furniture	$130.16
Gas and Oil	$331.18
Health Insurance	$91.83
Housing	$1,752.69
Intercity Transport	$94.32
Local Transport	$32.83
New Auto Purchase	$416.77
Personal Business	$891.31
Personal Care	$180.22
Physicians	$349.46
Private Education and Research	$245.16
Recreation	$846.84
Religion/Welfare Activities	$292.12
Telephone and Telegraph	$187.40
Tobacco	$137.54

"Shopping by TV Becomes New Mania,"
Los Angeles Times, July 21, 1986:

"Jane McElveen had seen bargains on TV before, but this one lit up her life like flares in the night.

Budget Bob from the Home Shopping Network was selling miniature figures by Limoges. Heavens, some of them were only $8.75.

And it was new stuff, too—tiny porcelain shoes and a sewing machine and a grand piano. A feeling came over her a little like madness and a lot like rapture.

She looked over at Duncan, her cockateel. His cage hangs near the display cases where Jane keeps her figurines. 'That's dirt cheap for Limoges,' Jane said out loud.

Then she began dialing Home Shopping's toll-free number, ordering 10, 15, 20 items. Who can remember? It was mania.

To this day, Jane—single and 56—cherishes that one special night. 'It was the best $300 I ever spent.'

Such is the grip of home shopping fever. And what Jane McElveen of Clearwater, Florida, has long known, much of America is finding out. Discount shopping shows—hypnotic as a price tag 50 percent off list—are spreading wholesale across cable TV.

Most often, the shows are run by perky hosts who breathlessly present marked-down goods as if each item had just been excavated from a pharaoh's tomb. First, they give a retail price, then they slash it down to tempting size. Anyone with a credit card or a checkbook can order.

By September, these shows are expected to reach 20 million cable-equipped homes. Some already are broadcast daily, non-stop. The never-ending sales may be the biggest advance in shopping since the mall."

Utilities $487.41
Per Capita Consumption $11,845.00

Annual Income, Standard Jobs
Bituminous Coal Mining $34,837.00
Building Trades $23,590.00
Domestics $10,061.00
Farm Labor $10,216.00
Federal Civilian $27,833.00
Federal Employees, Executive
    Departments $24,273.00
Finance, Insurance and
    Real Estate $25,778.00
Gas, Electricity, and Sanitary
    Workers $33,222.00

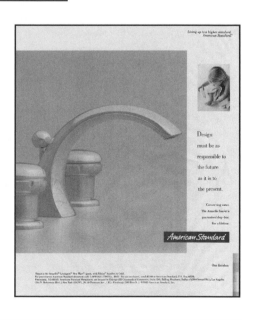

Manufacturing, Durable Goods . .$27,147.00

Manufacturing, Nondurable
Goods $23,313.00

Medical/Health Services
Workers $21,652.00

Miscellaneous Manufacturing . . .$20,145.00

Motion Picture Services $28,363.00

Nonprofit Organization
Workers $14,350.00

Passenger Transportation
Workers, Local and Highway . .$16,239.00

Personal Services $13,403.00

Postal Employees $26,362.00

Private Industry, Including
Farm Labor $21,699.00

Public School Teachers $21,920.00

Radio Broadcasting and
Television Workers $28,721.00

Railroad Workers $37,673.00

State and Local Government
Workers $21,949.00

Telephone and Telegraph
Workers $33,705.00

Wholesale and Retail
Trade Workers $26,119.00

Selected Prices

Ballet Ticket, *The Nutcracker* $18.00

Bracelet, Sapphire and Diamond $129.00

Bronze Shoes, Baby's First Shoes $5.99

Car Phone $995.00

Compact Disc Player $229.95

Computer, Apple $795.00

Computer Game, Chess $149.00

Easter Lily $4.99

Glue Gun $24.99

Hose, Women's, Three Pairs $8.07

Ice Cream, Dove Bar $1.45

Pen Set, Cross $30.00

Potato Chips, Ruffles 6.5 Ounces $1.19

Radar Detector, FuzzBuster $69.00

Sofa, 82" Leather $599.00

Sweater, Man's Bulk Knit $29.25

Synthesizer, Yamaha $188.88

Television Satellite Dish $1,995.00

Wine, Liebfraumilch $3.99

"High Blood Pressure? It May Be in Your Genes,"
Business Week, April 3, 1985:

"Hypertension has long been the scourge of many active, hard-driving people, and no amount of research has been able to pin down its cause or find a cure for the condition once it has developed.

Now, after 15 years of work in this field, Dr. Lewis K. Dahl, of Brookhaven National Laboratory's medical department, has found a cure that may ultimately reduce the incidence of the disease. Dahl, the man who established a correlation between salt and high blood pressure, has laboratory evidence that heredity plays a role in essential hypertension, the most common form of high blood pressure. Estimates vary, but it's believed that hypertension affects more than 10 percent of the U.S. adult population.

People don't inherit hypertension, Dahl thinks, but may inherit a susceptibility that somehow can be triggered by other factors: kidney infection, emotional stress or, more commonly, too much intake of table salt in the diet.

In his lab, Dahl has bred two strains of rats. Under certain conditions, one strain quickly develops hypertension; under identical conditions, the other strain doesn't.

Dr. Dahl, a senior scientist in Brookhaven's medical research center and chief of medical services for its 48-bed hospital, is among the first to admit this genetic research on rats can't be applied directly to human patients. But it sheds new light on possible predisposition of people to hypertension, and perhaps on how people can avoid triggering the disease."

"One need not go so far as to accept the dictum that money is crystallized freedom. But it is hard to argue that money and freedom have nothing to do with each other. . . . Men will die for freedom but they will not necessarily starve for it. A society that wants to be free must not expose its members to this alternative."
—Economist Henry Wallich

"First Human Vaccine Produced by Genetic Engineering OK'd by FDA," by Marlene Cimons, *Los Angeles Times*, July 24, 1986:

"The Food and Drug Administration on Wednesday announced its approval of the first human vaccine produced by genetic engineering, which will be used to protect against Hepatitis B.

'This vaccine opens up a whole new era of vaccine production,' FDA Commissioner Frank E. Young said in a press conference. 'These techniques should be able to be extended to any virus or parasite to produce other vaccines that normally cannot be propagated in the laboratory.'

Until now vaccines have been made from viruses that have either been killed or weakened.

Young said the recombinant DNA, or gene-splicing, technology could be applied to many diseases for which there are now no preventive vaccines, such as AIDS or malaria. 'The same principles could be tried with an AIDS-related virus, or with the parasite that causes malaria.'

Federal health officials said they expect the new vaccine to be more widely accepted than the existing Hepatitis B vaccine, which uses plasma obtained from infected members of the group also at high risk for AIDS.

Fewer than 30 percent of those at risk for Hepatitis B—including male homosexuals, intravenous drug users, dental and medical workers, immigrants from countries where Hepatitis B is prevalent, and pregnant women in high-risk groups—have been vaccinated using the older vaccine, Young said. . . .

The vaccine, developed by scientists at the University of California, San Francisco, the University of Washington, and Chiron Corporation of Emeryville, California, results from combining brewers' yeast cells with the gene from the outer coat of the Hepatitis B virus.

The yeast cells become 'factories' producing large quantities of the antigen portion of the virus—the part that triggers the human body to manufacture the protective antibodies against future assault by the disease. While the antigen stimulates immunity, it is not itself infectious.

The vaccine, called Recombivax HB, will be manufactured by Merck Sharp & Dohme, which also produces the plasma-derived vaccines.

The vaccine is the fifth major genetically engineered product to be approved for human use, and the third this year."

1987 NEWS FEATURE

These two workers work for Ford Motor Company, one of the leading automobile manufacturers in the country. In their own words, they present two views of the company.

This Cuban worker was born in 1934, and began working for Ford Motor Company in 1965. He is a check and adjustment person.

"I don't let people at the plant harass me. If they have prejudice, they can keep in their heart. I look for respect, and I give respect. I don't care about nationality, color, or anything. I don't care if you don't like me, as long as you don't tell me to my face. The company pays me to work, not to get harassed. I'm going to do my job, and that's it.

A lot of people in this country don't like it if someone from another country has more than them. But anything you have here, you worked for it. Nobody gave it to you. And I think everyone could have the same if they wanted to.

When I was a kid growing up in Cuba, my dad was in charge of a farm. I went to trade school in the city to learn how to be a mechanic. The mechanics used to argue a lot about what was the best car. I was crazy about Ford. I would say that one day Ford will get ahead of General Motors. That was my dream, and now it has finally happened. I'll always love Ford vehicles. I would rather buy a Toyota than a General Motors car.

After I finished trade school in Cuba, I worked at the Guantanamo naval base. I decided to come to the United States because they were laying off civilians at the base and I was afraid I would get laid off. First I went to Chicago, where my brother works, but I didn't like it there. I moved to the Detroit area and tried to get a job at General Motors' Fisher Body Plant, but they weren't hiring. Finally a friend of mine told my brother he could get me a job at Ford, and he got me an application.

I started at the Michigan Truck Plant in August, 1965, when the plant was just opening up. I was put on the second shift. I had never worked on a line before. It was rough. But I just went to work, and the days started to go by, and then it was no problem. I was a welder in the body shop for seven years before I got into quality control.

My wife works for General Motors, at the Westland Trim Plant. I have a lot of consideration for women who work in the plant. They are working to make a decent living just like us. I respect them just like I respect the men.

If you don't have an education, the only way to make a decent living today is to work in the plant. I made close to $45,000 last year, plus all those fringe benefits. Where can you make that kind of money?

We deserve the money we make. I work hard. I do the best job I can. I'll even miss lunch sometimes if there's a problem. I do that because the quality control manager and the assistant manager give me respect and recognition for what I do. They care a lot about me, and I respect them, too. When I have a problem, I talk to them, and they solve it for me.

It's not like it was 15 years ago. Then, if you went to the plant manager's office for a problem, they would try to get rid of you. Now you can walk into any office and they'll tend to you.

Another example of the new respect in the plant is the program where some hourly employees are given new Bronco trucks to drive home overnight and check for defects. Before, only the supervisors could do that. The hourly employees can discover a lot more problems taking the trucks home because a lot of them have more knowledge than the supervisors. They are the ones fighting the problems every day."
This African-American woman was born in 1952 in Bessmer, Alabama. She came to work for Ford in 1976, hooking up electrical wires on the "final line."

"I wish I didn't have to pay union dues. Ford pays those union people, so they can only do what Ford tells them to do. I don't vote anymore because none of them help you. They're just getting out of running behind those trucks and cars on the line. All they want to do is lay back and smoke their cigarettes and drink their coffee and read their paper and wait for the checks on Friday, while you are out there doing all the damn work.

You don't need a union. What does the union do? Nothing. One time I was sick with the flu, and they wouldn't accept my doctor's excuse. The company-union review board decided they would let it stand on my record. The union people on the review board sit back on their ass and don't do a thing. They never worked on this production line a day in their life and they tell me they can't accept my excuse?

I'm tired of working hard. If I hit the lottery today, I would tell Ford that I appreciate what they did for me, but I don't want to stay there to get 30 years in. If I had to work the rest of my life, I will. But I don't want to.

I have six sisters and four brothers. My mother raised all of us herself. I never met my father until I was 18. We lived in two rooms, a living room and a kitchen. In the kitchen we had a bed, a stove, and an icebox, but no refrigerator. My mother used to pay $0.15 for a big cake of ice from the ice truck. It would last a couple of days. We had a table, but no chairs, so we would stand at the table to eat. There was no bathtub. We had to take baths on the back porch in a tub. In the living room we had a little closet with the toilet in it and a bed on one side and a baby bed. Me, my mother, and my two sisters slept in one bed. Later on my aunt and her boyfriend came to live with us, too.

We didn't even know what a lamp was. We had a socket with an extension cord, and we would screw the bulb in. We would move that socket, and that was our lamp. We used to make a fire when we got up in the morning, all year 'round, that would heat the house, and we'd cook on it.

My family got $150.00 a month from welfare. You weren't allowed to have radio or TV on welfare. But we got surplus cheese, butter, rice, and peanut butter. After my mother started work as a maid and making $20.00 a week, they cut her off welfare. Then it was rough.

Every afternoon, starting in the first grade, I would have to rush home from school. My mother and my two older brothers and one older sister were working, so I would cook dinner. When my mother came home, her kids would be sitting on the porch with their hair combed and clothes clean. Then everyone would eat dinner and clean up. The house was always clean. When my mother had someplace to go at night, I would watch the younger kids.

Food was no problem because my grandmother in Birmingham had a garden and raised chickens. She had pear trees and peach trees. She canned a lot of food. On Saturdays she would go to the grocery store and put groceries for us on the bus, and we would pick them up from the bus driver at the bus stop near our house."

1989 PROFILE

Carol Wasserman spends all her time balancing the pressures of school and work, the demands of being a minister's wife, and the need and desire to spend time with her husband and children.

Carol Wasserman's life is about balance.

Life at Home

- A woman in her early forties, Carol Wasserman is the wife of a United Methodist minister, mother of two children, ages 12 and 15, and guardian of a dog and a cat.
- On top of all these responsibilities, she works full-time as a family counselor and is going to school at a university.
- Her life is about finding and maintaining balance.
- She and her husband have been married 20 years.
- Four years ago, she decided to change careers from being a Christian educator to working as a family counselor; this meant adding a full 15-hour-a-semester college schedule to a 40-hour work week, not counting the travel time between home and her college, which is located 50 miles away.
- Between work and school, she is not home most evenings during the week.
- Despite these demands, she works hard to attend her daughter's band performances and her son's baseball games, as well as their other activities.
- Her husband's support is indispensable in making sure the kids get to school and activities during the day and have dinner in the evenings.
- Carol realizes that his flexible schedule, which allows him to help with the kids during the day, has made all the difference in keeping the family going.
- Her son, the younger child, is more affected by her absences.

- He had been very angry, and missed having his mom around, despite a full slate of friends and activities.
- To help him through this hard time, she sets aside one hour a week for the two of them to do something together.
- They go out for ice cream and talk to catch up.
- Since they started this routine, he has settled down and feels more secure.
- Another way that she set aside special time for him was for his birthday.
- She contacted his friends' parents and got permission for the kids to come over at 9:00 p.m. on a school night for a surprise party because that was when she could be at home.
- Her daughter, who is older, is more independent and does not seem to be as affected by her mother's busy schedule.
- She has close friends and more freedom because some of her older friends drive.
- She also has more activities with the band and theater at school, and her youth groups at church.
- Beyond Carol's obligations with work, school and family, the church also has expectations of her, as the minister's wife.
- Before Carol went back to school, she had worked as a Christian education professional in churches.
- Knowing this, members of the church expected that she would actively participate in the education programs of the church.
- She chairs the education committee, but graduate school prevents her from doing as much as is expected.
- She attends church and Sunday school, potlucks and Sunday school parties, and supports her children's activities in the church.

Carol works hard to attend her daughter's band events and son's baseball games.

One nuclear bomb can ruin your whole day.

- Because she is also a consecrated lay minister in her denomination, she often assists her husband with services and communion.
- Carol knows what it is like to be a social liberal in a conservative Southern town with a nuclear weapons plant nearby.
- She and her husband, along with their children, have been very active in peacemaking activities in the state.
- They are also part of a small group that meets on Friday afternoons to pray for peace in the world.
- These activities antagonize many people in the community and the church because much of the area's economy depends on the Savannah River Site,

Despite her schoolwork, Carol remains active in the church.

the nuclear weapons facility outside of town, where many members of the church are employed.
- Although she has good friendships with people in the church and has found some support there, it is not the church she would have chosen to attend, or the town she would have picked for raising a family.
- However, her work provides her with much satisfaction.

Life at Work
- It is important to Carol Wasserman that she is now seen as a professional in her own right.
- Unlike the many years employed as an educator, for the first time Carol is working in a different part of the community from her husband.
- She is still very much a part of her husband's professional life, but he is no longer part of hers.
- Currently, she works at Family Counseling Service, or FCS.
- FCS is a private, nonprofit United Way agency serving all strata of the population of Aiken County, South Carolina.
- The agency charges its clients on a sliding fee scale, so that persons with no insurance or little income can be seen and helped for as little as $5 per session.
- The agency plays an important role in the community.

- At any given time, the agency's board of directors has as its members the county solicitor, a bank vice president, the director of the county Department of Social Services, a school administrator and a variety of business people.
- Along with counseling children, adults and families, Carol writes grants to help fund programs to help victims of crime.
- One accomplishment she is very proud of is starting a treatment program for sexually abused children.
- She wrote the grant and the curriculum, led the groups, and then hired and trained others to lead groups.
- This program has become a successful model that receives referrals from the Department of Social Services.
- Carol is also involved in training teens to mentor kids.
- Carol earns $21,000 a year working 40 hours a week.
- Her school costs are $3,500 per semester, plus the cost of books; she has taken out student loans to pay for school.
- Carol has been back in school for three years, completing her master's degree in counseling and working on her doctorate.
- The Ph.D. program is three and a half years, and Carol intends to finish before her oldest child starts college.
- Being in the church, the family is always connected with work.
- This connection continues in Carol's new job so that her children know something about her work, as well.

Aiken, South Carolina, sponsors a wide range of activities for its youth.

- Her daughter works as an evening receptionist at her agency, which allows them to spend a little more time together.
- Her son has mentored a child that she counsels.

Life in the Community: Aiken, South Carolina

- The church Carol attends has a solid middle class congregation in Aiken, South Carolina.
- Many of the church members are in management at the Aiken nuclear production facility, recently renamed the Savannah River Site.
- The family lives in a house known as a parsonage, a home owned by the church and provided to the minister as part of his compensation.
- Aiken is a quiet Southern town near the Savannah River with a population of 20,000 in town and almost 120,000 in the county.
- The median household income in the county is $29,994 and 14 percent of the county population falls below the poverty level.
- Aiken is divided into four distinct economic communities: old Aiken money, the Savannah River Site, professional and manufacturing.
- Old Aiken money is connected with the horse community, golfing, and old houses and gardens.
- In the 1930s and 1940s, wealthy Northeast families would bring their horses on railroad cars to Aiken for the winter.
- A large section of Aiken near downtown is devoted to horses.
- Many horses still train at the race tracks in Aiken during the winter, and locals like to say that "every major race in the country has at least one Aiken-trained horse in it."
- Many of the secondary roads in this section of town are unpaved and covered in dirt to protect the horses' hooves.
- The Aiken Triple Crown in March is the big social event of the year.
- Tens of thousands of spectators come out on three consecutive Saturdays to watch the horses and their riders perform in the trials, the harness racing and the steeplechase.
- The Savannah River Site came to the area during the Cold War.
- The "bomb plant," as it is known by locals, was built in the early 1950s and has been a principal employer ever since.
- Thousands of high-paying jobs came to the area to produce the nation's only weapons-grade plutonium and tritium.
- The plant currently employs 12,000 people on its 300-square-mile complex.
- The operating budget this year is $1.3 billion.
- This year has been an important one for the SRS.
- Westinghouse Electric Corporation has taken over management of the plant from DuPont, which has managed the site for almost 40 years.
- The site was officially included on the National Priority List for environmental cleanup by the Environmental Protection Agency this year.
- Levels of contamination at the site have been found to pose a risk to the environment and human health, so the EPA will now regulate the site.
- Currently, all five reactors at the plant are shut down, either permanently or for maintenance.
- The professional community comprises teachers, bankers, attorneys, ministers and business owners.

Many community events are available for people of Aiken.

- The University of South Carolina has a campus in Aiken.
- Aiken Technical College provides training for manufacturing and other skilled jobs.
- The manufacturing community includes companies such as Owens Corning, American Switch Company, Kimberly Clark, and various textile mills.
- The people of Aiken have great civic pride.
- The downtown area is attractive and well kept.
- Hitchcock Woods is one of the largest urban forests in the country.
- The university hosts many events and a community theater provides local entertainment.
- Helping others is also important to the members of the community, and the United Way Campaign exceeds its goal every year.

- Many in Aiken have been occupied by the biggest event of the year, Hurricane Hugo hitting South Carolina.
- It was the strongest storm to strike the East Coast in almost 40 years.
- Although no damage occurred in Aiken from the storm, the state suffered tremendous damage.
- Twenty lives were lost in South Carolina and 24 counties were declared federal disaster areas.
- It has been labeled the costliest hurricane to date.
- When Carol's church sent work teams to the towns of Charleston and Sumter to participate in cleanup, she and her family participated in these work days.
- They cleaned debris from yards and helped cover roofs to protect homes until they could be repaired.

HISTORICAL SNAPSHOT
1989

- *The New York Times* reported that social service volunteerism was on the rise
- Demonstrations for democracy in China's Tiananmen Square were televised worldwide on CNN; more than a million Chinese protestors marched
- Americans became concerned about the growing economic power of Japan after Sony bought Columbia Pictures and a group of Japanese businessmen bought Rockefeller Center in New York
- Tanker *Exxon Valdez* spilled 11 million barrels of oil off the coast of Alaska
- Movie openings included *Born on the Fourth of July, When Harry Met Sally, Field of Dreams, Glory, Driving Miss Daisy, Dead Poet's Society, Roger and Me* and *My Left Foot*
- Publisher Malcolm Forbes flew hundreds of celebrities to his $3 million 70th birthday party in Morocco
- Fifty-seven percent of American households were linked to cable television
- Comedy cable TV, Michelob Dry, pregaphones to talk with fetuses, the Miata, female soldiers leading troops in battle and a girl in the Little League Baseball World Series all made their first appearance
- The term African American was introduced as a substitute for the racial designation "black"
- Pepsi fired Madonna after her video for "Like a Prayer" was released
- Cocaine use, including crack, was up 35 percent over 1985; an Illinois woman was charged with child abuse for cocaine use during pregnancy
- Hit songs included "Straight Up," "This Time I Know It's for Real," "Fight the Power" and "Cherish"
- America was in the 85th month of economic expansion; per capita income was up 19 percent since 1982
- The Berlin wall was torn down
- Pro-life groups demonstrated following the United States Supreme Court's decision on *Roe v. Wade* concerning a woman's right to an abortion
- The most popular shows on television included *Roseanne, The Cosby Show, Cheers, A Different World, Dear John* and *The Golden Girls*
- Women's advocacy groups charged that the Scholastic Aptitude Test was biased against women
- Jane Pauley was replaced by Deborah Norville on NBC's Today Show
- Soviet troops were withdrawn from Afghanistan
- Wendy Wasserstein won both the Pulitzer Prize and Tony Award for *The Heidi Chronicles*
- A long-acting contraceptive that protected women from pregnancy for up to five years when implanted under the skin was approved by the Food and Drug Administration
- Mothers Embracing Nuclear Disarmament sponsored a delegation of 10 Soviet women to the United States

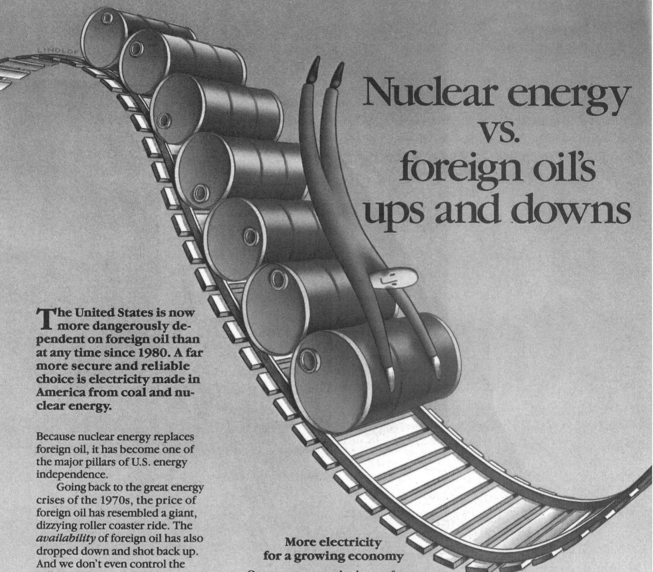

Nuclear energy vs. foreign oil's ups and downs

The United States is now more dangerously dependent on foreign oil than at any time since 1980. A far more secure and reliable choice is electricity made in America from coal and nuclear energy.

Because nuclear energy replaces foreign oil, it has become one of the major pillars of U.S. energy independence.

Going back to the great energy crises of the 1970s, the price of foreign oil has resembled a giant, dizzying roller coaster ride. The *availability* of foreign oil has also dropped down and shot back up. And we don't even control the roller coaster—others do.

Consider this ominous statistic: even though prices were low in 1986, America still had to pay about $30 billion for foreign oil. That's a lot of dollars leaving this country, adding to an already huge trade deficit.

Nuclear energy cuts oil imports

Clearly, the more energy we use in the form of electricity from coal and nuclear energy, the less oil we have to import.

Nuclear-generated electricity has already saved America over two billion barrels of oil, with billions more to be saved before the turn of the century. That's why it's so important for our energy self-reliance.

©USCEA, 1987.

More electricity for a growing economy

Our economy needs plenty of *new* electrical energy to keep on growing. Almost all of that new energy is coming from coal and nuclear electric plants.

The truth is that nuclear energy is an everyday fact of life in the U.S. It's been generating electricity here for nearly 30 years. Throughout the country are more than 100 nuclear plants, and they are our second largest source of electric power. As our economy grows, we'll need more of those plants to avoid even more dependence on foreign oil.

Safe energy for a secure future

Most important, nuclear energy is a safe, clean way to generate electric-

ity. U.S. nuclear plants have a whole series of multiple backup safety systems to prevent accidents. Plus superthick containment buildings designed to protect the public even if something goes wrong. (It's a "Safety in Depth" system.)

The simple fact is this: America's energy independence depends in part on America's nuclear energy.

For more information, write the U.S. Committee for Energy Awareness, P.O. Box 1537 (RC1), Ridgely, MD 21681. Please allow 4-6 weeks for delivery.

Information about energy
America can count on
U.S. COMMITTEE FOR ENERGY AWARENESS

Selected Prices

```
Camcorder, RCA ..................................................................$994.00
Car Seat...............................................................................$54.99
Cassette Player, Sony Walkman .......................................$19.95
Coffeemaker, Mr. Coffee ..................................................$36.00
Compact Disc Player, Technics ........................................$229.95
Compact Disc........................................................................$11.99
Computer Game...................................................................$149.00
Computer, Apple IIGS ........................................................$795.00
Floppy Disks, Fuji, per Box................................................$9.95
Liqueur, Kahlua, Bottle .......................................................$9.97
Printer, Epson......................................................................$425.00
Software, Lotus ....................................................................$339.00
```

"S. Carolina Challenges U.S. on Waste," by Ronald Smothers, *The New York Times*, March 9, 1989:

South Carolina, long a disposal site for hazardous waste from elsewhere, is striking back by banning waste from those states that do not allow disposal or treatment within their own borders.

The move, a clear challenge to the federal government's authority to regulate hazardous waste, came in an executive order by Gov. Carroll Campbell. The order, which went into effect last week, said South Carolina will no longer accept hazardous waste generated by industries in 23 states and Puerto Rico. The ban applies to industrial byproducts like arsenic and mercury, as well as waste oils, flammable chemicals, pesticides and highly corrosive chemicals . . . .

Some state officials and environmental leaders noted that the state's action, whether legal or illegal in the eyes of the Environmental Protection Agency, is forcing action in other states that the federal agency has long, but unsuccessfully, sought.

For example, the legislature in North Carolina, one of the states now banned from dumping wastes at Pinewood, last week lifted a four-year moratorium on hazardous waste dumps in the state. The legislature also began considering legislation to create a stronger executive-level commission to designate dump sites. North Carolina sent 45,000 tons of waste from 268 companies to Pinewood last year, nearly one-third of all the waste at the landfill.

"'Hugo Is a Killer' A deadly hurricane ravages South Carolina and leaves Caribbean islands prey to looters," *Newsweek*, October 2, 1989:

Hugo slammed into Charleston just before midnight, packing 135-mph winds and pushing a 12-to-17-foot wall of water that threatened to level everything before it. Over the next several hours, the worst hurricane to hit the South Carolina coast in 35 years wrecked selective havoc on the historic waterfront city and the coastal islands to the north and south. Chic beachfront communities were devastated. Fort Sumter, where the Civil War began, took a pounding reminiscent of the Confederate bombardment of 1861. Downtown, some 30 major office buildings were damaged and Charleston's 188-year-old city hall was flooded when the roof broke open. All told, Hugo left at least 21 persons dead in the Carolinas and Virginia, and caused untold millions of dollars in property damage. "This is the worst storm, the worst disaster, I've ever seen," South Carolina Gov. Carroll Campbell said. "We're going to be a long time digging out and rebuilding."

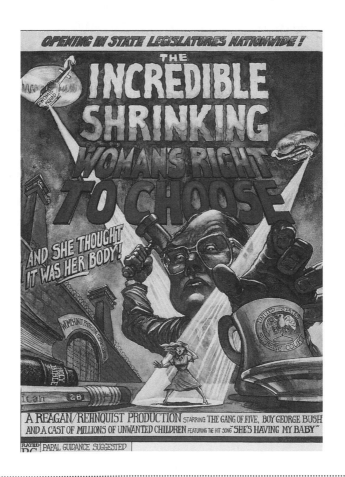

"DuPont Relinquishes Nuclear Plant," by Matthew L. Wald, *The New York Times*, April 1, 1989:

At midnight, control of one of the oldest, largest and most polluted nuclear complexes in the world will shift from E.I. DuPont de Nemours & Company, which designed and built it 38 years ago, to the Westinghouse Electric Corporation, which the government hopes will set it straight.

Most of the complex, the Savannah River Plant, is now shut down for safety reasons, but resumed operation is critical, because the plant is the nation's sole source of tritium, a perishable material vital to most nuclear weapons.

To resume production, Westinghouse is taking on a vast managerial challenge: 12,000 employees, many of them lifetime DuPont workers, spread over a 300-square-mile complex, running dozens of one-of-a-kind operations, and carrying out 1,400 repair and construction projects with a cost of $2.5 billion. The operating budget this year is $1.3 billion.

"It's a mixed bag," said James S. Moore, head of the Westinghouse subsidiary that is taking charge. "Some activities are absolutely first-class and modern, other parts are very aged and need work, and, everyone recognizes, the money has not been put into maintenance."

When the Westinghouse name is nailed to the sign board at 12:01 a.m. Saturday, it will be the first time the site is run under a contract that pays the operators more for doing a better job and less if there are accidents or unnecessary risks. It also makes explicit an assertion the Department of Energy has made in recent years: that it values safety above production goals.

But Westinghouse acknowledges that it faces a major challenge in changing the attitudes and procedures of workers and managers, virtually all of whom will be the same people doing the same jobs. Of 30 top managers, more than half will stay. Mr. Moore brought a team of 10 subordinates from Westinghouse's Pittsburgh headquarters, but Westinghouse has deliberately avoided making many changes in the ranks, because operations must continue....

DuPont is ingrained here. It built this place—invented it, admirers say, at the height of the Cold War, after Harry S. Truman told the company's chairman that the giant chemical concern, a military contractor since the time of the Revolution, was best qualified for the job. Describing the job at the time as "probably the largest industrial project ever attempted," DuPont agreed to do it for costs plus one dollar.

But for a decade, engineers and scientists have worried about the age of the reactors, and in recent months the Department of Energy has expressed dismay about worker attitudes, pollution and the condition of equipment.

"Fort Mill Sports a Hot Number for Friday Night's Entertainment," by Ken Garfield, *The Charlotte Observer*, September 1, 1989:

Fort Mill High senior Julie Youngblood, all of 5 feet 5 inches and she-won't-say-how-many pounds, tackles the comparison with the fury of a blitzing linebacker.

"Football players are jealous," said the color guard captain of the Yellow Jackets' marching band. "Everybody comes to the games to see the band. Band's big here."

Youngblood, 17, doesn't mean to put a hit on her school's football team, which is pretty hot stuff in its own right. But when it comes to what's cooking these days in Fort Mill, nothing sizzles like the high school marching band.

The band's 143 members (from a student body of 900) strutted onto their home field to a standing ovation last Friday when Fort Mill hosted Great Falls. When archrival Indian Land comes to town at 8 tonight, the home crowd will cheer for its football team—then save plenty of halftime whoops and hollers for the squad that has marched its way, double-time, into Fort Mill's heart.

"The band is the pride of this community," director Bob Cotter said before practice Wednesday afternoon. "This is the one thing they identify with, that sets them apart from every other community."

If high school football is king in South Carolina, marching bands ought to share the throne, adding a splash of color to the Friday night tradition that spices our lives....

It doesn't take a genius to walk into the band room at Fort Mill and realize nothing can hold a candle (or a trumpet) to the thrill that comes with being a marching Yellow Jacket.

All along the walls are banners and trophies signifying success, from winning state contests to marching in the Macy's Thanksgiving Day Parade in 1986, to copping a national championship last spring in St. Petersburg, Fla.

But the true reward of being in the band, said Cotter, doesn't just come from marching to glory.

"When the kids graduate out of this band, there's a lot they can use in life," said Cotter, who came to Fort Mill three years ago from Virginia Beach, Va. "They all get leadership roles. They have to use their brains every second they're out here."

How can you tell who builds America's best family wagons?

Put them to the test.

1989 PROFILE
INVASION OF PANAMA

Sergeant

Staff Sergeant Luella Sprague is part of a Military Police Battalion sent as part of the invasion of Panama, where the presence of women in combat captures headlines across the nation.

Life at Home

- Luella Sprague enlisted in the army right out of high school in order to help pay for college; her childhood dream was to become part of the Tennessee Bureau of Investigation.
- Luella grew up in the community of Alto, Tennessee, at the foot of the Cumberland plateau.
- In high school, her report card reflected more C's than A's, but her prowess as a lead-off-hitting softball shortstop earned her several partial scholarship offers to small colleges in the area.
- Her parents' persistent struggles with debt convinced her that she would not attend college on the "borrow now, pay back later" plan; money worries, she already knew, could be a huge burden.
- Besides, the army's offer to see the world and earn money toward college was appealing.
- Before she joined the army, Luella's longest journey from home had been to Graceland on the anniversary of Elvis Presley's death.
- She knew she had made the right decision almost immediately; the army assigned her to military police training and offered additional courses toward a degree in criminal justice.
- As an MP, she not only received police training, but also was qualified with an M-16 and all other basic combat tactics.

Luella Sprague joined the army to pay for college.

Traditionally, women were not allowed in combat units, but might see action as members of the 503rd Military Police Battalion.

- Luella enjoyed the day-to-day routine of police work in the 503rd Military Police Battalion at Fort Bragg, North Carolina, but she loved the idea that her unit could be assigned in a hostile situation to keep peace.
- Traditionally, women were not allowed in combat units; military police served a support function.
- Luella thought the prohibition against women in combat ridiculous, and though many of her fellow male soldiers agreed, few were willing to speak publicly.
- A quarter of the soldiers in her company were tough and aggressive—and female.
- She could out-arm-wrestle many of the men, and out-drink all of them.
- However, she was just as wary as the men when in the spring of 1989, after more than a decade in service, her platoon got a new female commanding officer, Second Lieutenant Alice Zayicek, a Chicago native straight out of ROTC.
- Zayicek was a rigid disciplinarian who expected respect, and conducted herself with a quiet confidence not always found in new officers.
- After a few months, Luella decided that Lt. Zayicek was the best officer she had served with in over 11 years of service.

Life at Work

- For much of 1988 and 1989, the country of Panama and its leader General Manuel Noriega had been in the headlines.

"Snap It, Scrap It," *Time*, March 2, 1987:

Disposable razors are one thing, but will anyone buy a throwaway camera? Fuji Photo Film and Eastman Kodak apparently think so. Their new rival models, both announced last week, combine film, plastic lens and shutter into one small box. After shooting pictures, users will take the entire camera to a photo lab for film processing. Kodak's Fling, which could be available by the summer, will sell for $6.95 and take 24 shots. It contains the 110 film used in Kodak's Instamatic cameras. Fuji will begin selling its Quick Snap this spring. It will cost less than $10 for 24 exposures and will use higher-quality 35-mm film.

These gadgets will sell for roughly two to three times the cost of comparable film for regular cameras. They are meant for use at the beach or other places where people might not want to bring more expensive cameras. They are not picture-perfect, though. Both models take outdoor shots only and cannot focus on objects that are less than three feet away.

- Despite nearly 12,000 American troops in Panama, Noriega and his Panama Defense Force were exercising nearly absolute control over the country.
- Since the Panama Canal Treaty was signed during the Carter Administration, the influence of the United States in Panama had been declining.
- The treaty, which was derided by many, called for the entire American military presence to be gone by the end of 1999—just a decade away.
- Currently, 12,700 American troops are assigned to Panama; the Central American country serves as the headquarters of the U.S. Southern Command.
- In May, a national election was held, with Noriega claiming victory even though neutral observers said he had lost in a landslide.
- In early October, a failed coup attempt increased tensions and exacerbated anti-American sentiment among Noriega supporters, particularly the Panama Defense Force.
- Word circulated around Fort Bragg that U.S. military involvement was imminent, although President Bush publicly denied any plans to invade Panama.
- In mid-December, Noriega's Panama Defense Force shot an American officer and tortured another while threatening to gang-rape the officer's wife.
- Bush ordered that Noriega be captured and his rogue government taken down.
- Seven thousand troops, including Ranger, airborne and infantry, were airlifted to Panama to join the forces on the ground.
- The operation was designated "Just Cause."
- Early on the morning of December 20, a multipronged attack—the largest force in the field since Vietnam—hit targets in Panama.
- As part of the assault, 3,000 members of the 82nd Airborne Division made the largest parachute drop since World War II.
- Noriega's defense forces provided token resistance before fading into the landscape to conduct guerrilla warfare.
- Luella's company was deployed early in the attack plan.

- Approximately 2,500 troops consisting primarily of MPs landed in Panama behind the air assault.
- Although for Luella, excitement had been building all week, some soldiers were visibly nervous, while others were in a panic about childcare, since both mother and father were deployed at the same time.
- The night before she shipped out, Luella wrote her family the longest letter of her life, describing her pride at being an American, her joy of being a female soldier, and her excitement that she would be allowed to fight for her country.
- Upon landing in Panama, the MPs were immediately immersed in the thick of the fray.
- Luella's squad was assigned to join a perimeter force around the Ministry of Foreign Affairs.
- Almost immediately, she was subjected to fire; as the day progressed, the sounds of war were persistent, but not heavy.
- One soldier in her unit was hit, and although the wound was not life-threatening, he screamed in pain and fear at seeing blood gushing out of his body.

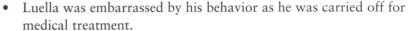

- Luella was embarrassed by his behavior as he was carried off for medical treatment.
- In the second of several firefights during the first day, she was sure she had taken down two of the enemy.
- What a rush!
- Late in the day, an exhausted Lt. Zayicek stopped at Luella's post, offering encouragement with a firm "Carry on, soldier," and moving on.
- Luella marveled at the maturity of the 22-year-old officer.
- Panamanian resistance collapsed quickly in the face of superior strength.
- In the days that followed, the MPs set up a police department, as well as a night court staffed by Panamanian magistrates.
- Luella had performed similar operations on the island of St. Croix after Hurricane Hugo struck the island in September.
- Her other concern was containing the looters trying to take advantage of the chaos; each day, she patrolled with several Panamanian policemen.

- A stickler for details, she kept those in her unit alert and aware of the dangers.
- Weapons were cleaned, oiled and on ready at all times, as the MPs were still subject to fire from burned-out buildings and looted storefronts.
- Rumors were bruited of sniper killings in the forbidding streets; every face and building were scanned for potential danger.
- Luella knew that she could die in seconds in these situations.
- She was amused that the stateside media was obsessed with the idea that women like her were in the line of fire, because in Panama, hundreds of women operated in the combat zone and had come under enemy fire.
- Also, for the first time, women led soldiers into action against an enemy.
- Official army policy still kept women from serving in units designated for combat; since the mid-1970s, women had served in support units such as the Military Police and the Signal Corps.
- The Panama invasion was now proving what military experts had said for years— in today's urban warfare, the line between combat and support is quickly blurred.
- Just as life began to fall into a routine—albeit still harrowing at times—word arrived that one of Noriega's chief lieutenants was hiding in a nearby apartment complex.
- Luella was beside herself with excitement as the entire unit piled in HMMWVs (high mobility multipurpose wheeled vehicles) and roared to the location.
- She leapt from the vehicle, her M-16 ready.
- As the building was quickly surrounded, a group led by Lt. Zayicek was the first inside, with Luella leading a group in right behind her.
- At each door, Lt. Zayicek knocked, producing a search warrant from the newly constituted Panamanian courts, then instructed Luella's team to fan quickly through the apartment from room to room with weapons highly visible.
- The Panamanian policemen watched in awe.

HOW FAR ARE YOU WILLING TO GO
TO MAKE A DIFFERENCE?

- Little was found until the fifth apartment search, where a soldier discovered a padlocked satchel from which, when slit open, tumbled out wads of U.S. bills.
- The three women occupying the apartment vehemently denied knowledge of the money as they were frisked and cuffed by Luella, who had little patience for their denials.
- She had even less patience with a soldier who began using the barrel of his gun to encourage one of the women to talk.
- "We're pros!" she barked, and the interrogation ended.
- She knew the prisoners would talk in good time.
- For the time being, it was her job to secure the money and wait for the women to be driven to the police station.
- Within weeks, she and her unit shifted from fighting to peacekeeping.
- Through a cash-for-weapons program, the U.S. paid out $60,000 for 75,000 guns collected by the police; one Panamanian received $5,000 for driving an armored personnel carrier up to the doorstep of the U.S. troops.

Life in the Community: Washington, DC and Panama
- Critics in Washington are condemning the invasion of Panama as a "throwback to the era of gunboat diplomacy."
- Others are saying it was simply a contrived, glorious moment in the "war against drugs" for a commander-in-chief who is still suspected of being wimpish.
- The United Nations did not approve the invasion, considering it an illegal, unilateral use of force.
- Approximately 23 American and 300 Panamanian soldiers died in the assault.
- Editorial writers generally agree with President Bush that the invasion of Panama was necessary as a crusade for a democratic and drug-free hemisphere.
- The president of the Panamanian Chamber of Commerce calculates that losses from looting and damage caused by the military invasion will top $1 billion.
- Millions more, it is believed, will be needed to refurbish streets, waterworks, public buildings and other facilities long neglected by a government more obsessed with power than governance.
- To help out in the crisis, the United States has asked Japan, which extensively uses the Panama Canal, to provide aid.

HISTORICAL SNAPSHOT
1989

- The longest peacetime period of economic expansion reached its eighty-fifth month in December; per-capita income was up 19 percent since 1982
- Congress passed a $166 billion legislation to bail out the savings and loan industry
- Cocaine and crack cocaine use was up 35 percent over 1985
- Sony purchased Columbia Pictures, sparking comments of Japan invading Hollywood
- Demonstrators at Tiananmen Square carried a Styrofoam Statue of Liberty as part of the protest against the Chinese government
- A private U.S. satellite, comedy cable TV, pregaphone to talk to the fetus and a girl in the Little League World Series drew national attention
- The movie *Batman* grossed $250 million, the fifth-highest-grossing film in movie history
- *Field of Dreams, When Harry Met Sally, Glory, Driving Miss Daisy, sex, lies and videotape* and *Roger and Me* premiered at movie theaters
- Baseball Commissioner Bart Giamatti banned ballplayer Pete Rose for life from the sport for allegedly betting on games
- *The Joy Luck Club by Amy Tan, The Satanic Verses by* Salman Rushdie, *The Temple of My Familiar* by Alice Walker, *The Oldest Living Confederate Widow Tells All* by Allan Gurganus and *A Brief History of Time* by Stephen Hawking were bestsellers
- In Chicago, U.S. veterans protested at the Art Institute where the American flag was draped on the floor
- "Wind Beneath My Wings" by Bette Midler won a Grammy Award for best song
- Americans watched live news coverage of the Chinese and Eastern European revolutions and the San Francisco earthquake
- Across America, 57 percent of households had cable TV, and 66 percent owned a VCR
- A piece of the fallen Berlin Wall could be purchased at Bloomingdale's for $12.50
- Van Cliburn made a successful comeback after 11 years, playing the Liszt and Tchaikovsky piano concertos in Philadelphia and Dallas
- Physicists agreed on three basic types of matter: up and down; charmed and strange; and top and bottom quarks
- AZT was shown to delay the onset of AIDS

Selected Prices

Azalea, Six-inch Pot	$3.99
Beer, Michelob, Case	$9.95
Car Phone	$995.00
Cereal, Kellogg's Corn Flakes	$1.59
Compact Disc	$11.99
Compact Disc Player	$229.95
Computer, Apple IIGS	$795.00
Glue Gun	$24.99
Gun Kit	$19.99
Light Bulb	$4.00
Microwave, Kenmore	$199.99
Panty Hose, Three Pairs	$8.07
Silk Azalea	$24.99
Soft Drink, Coke, Two-Liter	$1.00
Synthesizer, Yamaha	$188.88

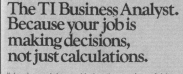

The TI Business Analyst. Because your job is making decisions, not just calculations.

1990–1999

The 1990s, called the "Era of Possibilities" by *Fortune* magazine, were dominated by an economic expansion that impacted every segment of society. For the first time, women filled half of all seats at the nation's law and medical schools. Fortune 500 companies boasted female presidents and CEOs, going beyond the token recognition of the abilities of women in previous decades. Increasingly, marketers focused their advertising on the millions of working women, understanding their tendency to exercise significant discretion over household spending. As wealth grew, possibilities flourished. Colleges became overcrowded, while the mini-baby boom of the 1980s swelled the attendance of elementary schools. Characterized by steady growth, low inflation, low unemployment and dramatic gains in technology-based productivity, the resulting expansion was particularly meaningful to computer companies and the emerging concept known as the Internet. This economy swelled the ranks of the upper class as Americans of all backgrounds invested in the soaring stock market and dreamed of capturing a dot-com fortune.

The decade opened in an economic recession, a ballooning national debt, and the economic hangover of the collapse of much of the savings and loan industry. The automobile industry produced record losses; household names like Bloomingdale's and Pan Am declared bankruptcy. Housing values plummeted and factory orders fell. Media headlines were dominated by issues such as rising drug use, crime in the cities, racial tensions, and the rise of personal bankruptcies. Family values ranked high on the conservative agenda, and despite efforts to limit Democrat Bill Clinton to one term as president, the strength of the economy played a critical role in his re-election in 1996.

Guided by Federal Reserve Chair Alan Greenspan's focus on inflation control and Clinton's early efforts to control the federal budget, the U.S. economy soared, producing its best economic indicators in three decades. By 1999, the stock market produced record returns, job creation was at a 10-year high, and the federal deficit was falling. Businesses nationwide hung "Help Wanted" signs outside their doors and even paid signing bonuses to acquire new workers. Crime rates, especially in urban areas, plummeted to levels unseen in three decades, illegitimacy rates fell, and every year business magazines marvelled at the length of the recovery, asking, "Can it last another year?"

The stock market set a succession of records throughout the period, attracting thousands of investors to stocks for the first time, including the so-called glamour offerings of high-technology companies. From 1990 to the dawn of the twenty-first century, the Dow Jones Industrial Average rose 318 percent. Growth stocks were the rage; of Standard and Poor's 500 tracked stocks, almost 100 did not pay dividends. This market boom eventually spawned unprecedented new wealth, encouraging early retirement to legions of aging baby boomers. The dramatic change in the cultural structure of corporations continued to threaten the job security of American workers, who had to be more willing to learn new skills, try new jobs, and move from project to project. Profit sharing, which allowed workers to benefit from increased productivity, become more common. Retirement programs and pension plans became more flexible and transferable, serving the needs of a highly mobile work force. The emerging gap of the 1990s was not always between the rich and the poor, but the computer literate and the technically deficient. To symbolize the changing role of women in the work force, cartoon character Blondie, wife of Dagwood Bumstead, opened her own catering business which, like so many small businesses in the 1990s, did extremely well. For the first time, a study of family household income concluded that 55 percent of women provided half or more of the household income.

During the decade, America debated limiting abortion, strengthening punishment for criminals, replacing welfare for work, ending Affirmative Action, dissolving bilingual education, elevating educational standards, curtailing the rights of legal immigrants, and imposing warnings on unsuitable material for children on the Internet. Nationwide, an estimated 15 million people, including smokers, cross-dressers, alcoholics, sexual compulsives, and gamblers, attended weekly self-help support groups; dieting became a $33 billion industry as Americans struggled with obesity.

The impact of the GI Bill's focus on education, rooted in the decade following World War II, flowered in the generation that followed. The number of adult Americans with a four-year college education rose from 6.2 percent in 1950 to 24 percent in 1997. Despite this impressive rise, the need for a more educated population, and the rapidly rising expectations of the technology sector, the century ended with a perception that the decline in public education was one of the most pressing problems of the decade. Throughout the decade, school violence escalated, capturing headlines year after year in widely dispersed locations across the nation.

The '90s gave birth to $150 tennis shoes, condom boutiques, pre-ripped jeans, Motorola 7.7-ounce cellular telephones, rollerblading, TV home shopping, the Java computer language, digital cameras, DVD players, and Internet shopping. And in fashion, a revival of the 1960s' style brought back miniskirts, pop art prints, pants suits, and the A-line. Black became a color worn at any time of day and for every purpose. The increasing role of consumer debt in driving the American economy also produced an increase in personal bankruptcy and a reduction in the overall savings rate. At the same time, mortgage interest rates hit 30-year lows during the decade, creating refinancing booms that pumped millions of dollars into the economy, further fueling a decade of consumerism.

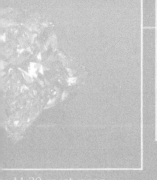

An extraordinary 7.35 carat F color, VS2 clarity Asscher-cut Diamond accented by 1.31 carats of white emerald-cut/bullet-cut Diamonds all set in a Platinum mounting. The famed Asscher cut, patented by Joseph Asscher in 1902, was inspired by the elegant table cuts of the Renaissance. #28-4462

A rare and spectacular 1.56 carat Brilliant Natural Fancy Orangy-Pink Diamond flanked by two trillion Diamonds (0.65 carats) and set in Platinum and 18K pink Gold. G.I.A. certified Natural Fancy Orangy-Pink. #28-1819

r 11.39 carat pear-
mond (J color, SI1
ted by 1.71ctw of
l Diamonds and set in
I.A. certified. #28-4723

*I*MPORTANT JEWELRY

1994 PROFILE

Joanne Binzen opened her own jewelry store and creates wonderful designs from old jewelry for her clients. In her spare time, she fulfills her other passion: doing fieldwork as a volunteer archeologist.

Life at Home

- Thirty-eight-year-old Chicago native Joanne Binzen dreamed of growing up in a happy home, attending college at a big name university and then opening an original-design jewelry store with her name out front.
- She settled for opening a jewelry store with her name out front.
- Her father's alcoholism dispelled the chances for a happy home, and her mother's early death ended any thoughts of college.
- An early marriage produced both a wonderful daughter and an acrimonious divorce.
- A second marriage, five years later, produced a deeper satisfaction; for Joanne, the phrase, "I married my best friend," has true meaning, after eight years.
- Currently, her husband is in Saudi Arabia working on a video project for a subcontactor for the military.
- He often writes that the days are hot, long and fascinating.
- He is making more than $70,000 a year; the couple plans to save his tax-free income and

Joanne Binzen loves being creative.

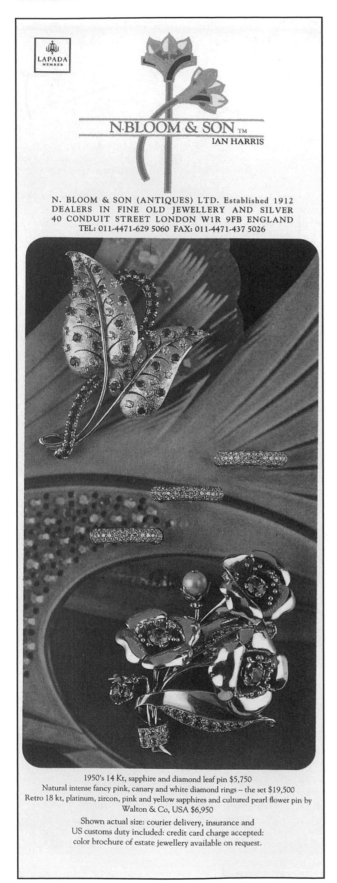

buy some property in uptown Chicago that will allow them to combine their lives and work.

- Besides, when her daughter Helen finishes her master's degree in human behavior at the University of Illinois at Chicago, Joanne believes she will be free to do anything—even go to college herself.
- Before she began working with jewelry, her first love was sculpture in wood, metal and ceramics.
- She fell in love with the details of working in sculpture; today, she derives enormous joy when customers finally discover, months later, the delicious, secret features she placed on their pieces..
- Joanne always believes that she gets paid three times for her work as a jeweler.
- The first time is when a customer trusts her to design something as personal as jewelry.
- The second payment comes in the form of cash or a check when the job is done.
- The third and most important payment arrives when a customer returns to the store both wearing a piece of jewelry and ushering in a friend who is "dying to meet the artist."
- Most of her business comes from word of mouth, the third payment frequently leading to the first.
- Her other passion is archeology.
- Once a month, whether or not time permits, Joanne serves as a volunteer Illinois archeologist doing fieldwork.
- Being outdoors scrubbing dirt off an artifact with a toothbrush opens her mind to endless questions.
- Who made this delicate arrowhead or served meals on this pottery fragment? What were they like? How did they plan their days? What did they dream about?
- If they wanted me to design jewelry for them, what would it look like?

Life at Work

- Unlike more conventional jewelry stores, Binzen Jewelers does not have a window display filled with gold and silver earrings, bracelets, necklaces, chains and rings.
- In fact, the only object in the window is Joanne Binzen herself, working on one of her original designs.
- Joanne is a recycler of nearly everything, capable of turning the old, the worn and the dented into new treasures.
- Clients bring her pieces of jewelry they no longer wear, and then rethinking begins immediately.
- Joanne makes drawings of how an old, misbegotten brooch might become a Binzen original using the existing gold, silver, platinum and gemstones.

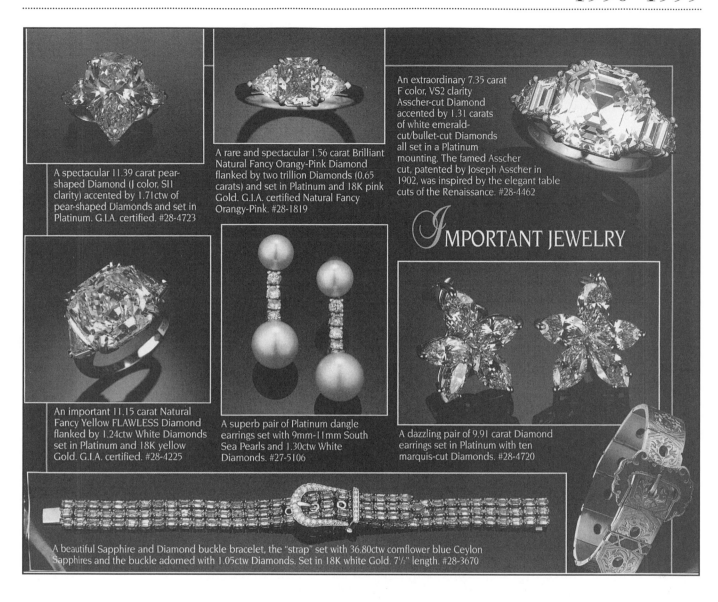

A spectacular 11.39 carat pear-shaped Diamond (I color, SI1 clarity) accented by 1.71ctw of pear-shaped Diamonds and set in Platinum. G.I.A. certified. #28-4723

A rare and spectacular 1.56 carat Brilliant Natural Fancy Orangy-Pink Diamond flanked by two trillion Diamonds (0.65 carats) and set in Platinum and 18K pink Gold. G.I.A. certified Natural Fancy Orangy-Pink. #28-1819

An extraordinary 7.35 carat F color, VS2 clarity Asscher-cut Diamond accented by 1.31 carats of white emerald-cut/bullet-cut Diamonds all set in a Platinum mounting. The famed Asscher cut, patented by Joseph Asscher in 1902, was inspired by the elegant table cuts of the Renaissance. #28-4462

IMPORTANT JEWELRY

An important 11.15 carat Natural Fancy Yellow FLAWLESS Diamond flanked by 1.24ctw White Diamonds set in Platinum and 18K yellow Gold. G.I.A. certified. #28-4225

A superb pair of Platinum dangle earrings set with 9mm-11mm South Sea Pearls and 1.30ctw White Diamonds. #27-5106

A dazzling pair of 9.91 carat Diamond earrings set in Platinum with ten marquis-cut Diamonds. #28-4720

A beautiful Sapphire and Diamond buckle bracelet, the "strap" set with 36.80ctw cornflower blue Ceylon Sapphires and the buckle adorned with 1.05ctw Diamonds. Set in 18K white Gold. 7½" length. #28-3670

- "A lot of other jewelers don't do this," she enjoys saying.
- "My customers save money because my labor is less expensive than new material, and I get to do original designs with some marvelous jewels that otherwise might never come my way."
- The process begins with each new client browsing through a gold-trimmed book of photos which eloquently displays Joanne's finest work during 14 years of jewelry designing.
- The next step takes place on paper.
- "This opens up each client to the possibilities," Joanne says. "We throw away the fences at the start and do a little dreaming."

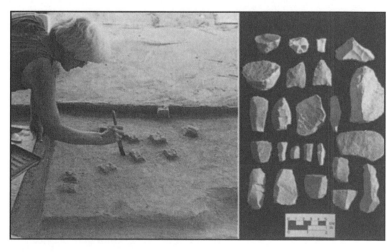

Once a month, Joanne works as a volunteer archeologist.

- At this stage, clients often recall other surplus jewelry that becomes another candidate for recycling.
- Then the fun really begins.
- And because the expense of the precious jewels is not included in the price, elaborate concepts can bubble to the surface at an affordable cost to the customer.
- Joanne is careful to explain that her prices include all phases of the process: the design, creation and construction.
- Joanne is not shy about charging ($35 an hour) for every phase of the process.
- Although many women dream about the spectacular, ultimately, most gravitate toward more traditional designs once they realize they will be wearing their Binzen original in public.
- Often, a trip through the history of art helps some women fall for the elaborateness of art nouveau, the strong lines of art deco or the zaniness of the 1960s.
- Once a look is created, Joanne always promises that a wax mold will be created within two weeks.
- The wax mold is necessary, Joanne believes, because most people can't really visualize the creation when looking at a two-dimensional drawing; the wax mold brings out the details.
- This means that Joanne is often locked in her shop late into the night, neglecting friends, her recently begun exercise program and the paperwork of running her business.
- To make sure that her cat Martha is never neglected, Joanne brings the big Persian to work with her.
- Repeat customers refer to Binzen Jewelers as the Persian Palace, insisting appropriately that Martha, not Joanne, actually runs the store.
- After the customer marvels over the wax design and makes minor changes, the final design is then created by hand at the store, often in sight of everyone passing by the store window.
- Recently, a customer asked Joanne to redesign her wedding band, using the original diamond as well as the gold from another ring she felt was dated.
- After talking for 10 minutes, Joanne had a vision of what the customer wanted, even though the woman was struggling to articulate it.
- As so often happens, Joanne was right on the mark.
- She has designed and made jewelry for 2,500 customers through the years.
- Many clients are now friends who love to stop by with a bagel, donut hole or coffee, so they will have an excuse to chat with the creator.

Life in the Community: Chicago, Illinois
- Joanne Binzen has been operating her business in uptown Chicago since 1980.
- When she relocated her shop to the neighborhood, it was hard times, but rents were cheap.
- For several years, she simply endured, often dreading the prospect of having to work late nights alone.
- The community hit rock-bottom around 1983, and then began to turn around approximately two years later.
- At its worst, it was entirely written off by city officials who saw the neighborhood as a blight, with halfway houses, slums, barred storefronts, liquor stores, highly transient immigrant populations, homelessness, panhandling, and dive bars—the works.

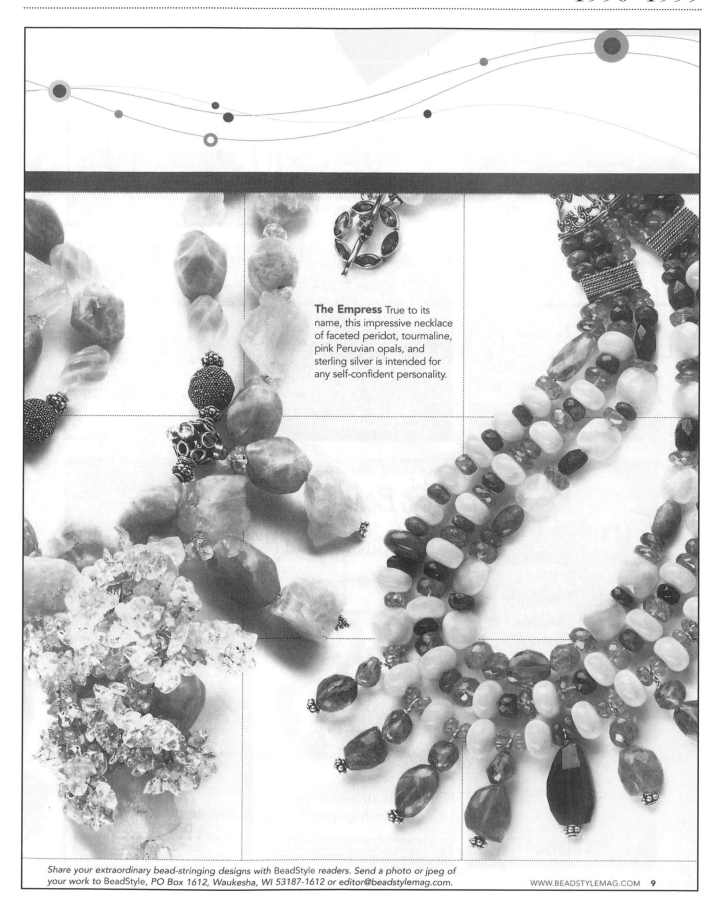

The Empress True to its name, this impressive necklace of faceted peridot, tourmaline, pink Peruvian opals, and sterling silver is intended for any self-confident personality.

WWW.BEADSTYLEMAG.COM **9**

- Then, the neighborhood began to gentrify.
- Apartment complexes were renovated properly after years of being poorly maintained with only quick fixes and secret bribes to building inspectors.
- Overnight, it seemed to Joanne, uptown became respectable, slum apartment buildings were converted into refurbished condos and new stores opened up.
- Stories appeared in the Chicago Tribune about the new uptown.
- With this injection of capital, people began to look at the neighborhood in a different light.
- Many discovered that the area possessed "good bones."
- Today, it boasts two theaters: the Aragon and the Riviera.
- When visitors ask, Joanne proudly tells them that her neighborhood abuts Lake Michigan and the northern reaches of Lincoln Park.
- Nowadays, sirens are still heard, but the number of poorly conditioned buildings is declining rapidly and only a couple of halfway houses remain.
- The Weiss Hospital is currently being renovated.
- Joanne no longer has bars covering her front windows, though most older front doors on her street still have metal gates.
- There is currently talk of several upscale bars and restaurants relocating into the better parts of the neighborhood.
- Joanne proudly tells potential customers that Al Capone and William Shakespeare are her neighbors.
- The Green Mill, a bar that gangster Capone made famous by frequenting, and perhaps "protecting," is on her street.
- A few doors north is Shake, Rattle, and Read, a small bookstore run for the last 20 years by the same family, that carries the sonnets of the Bard, the poetry of Lawrence Ferlinghetti and many other books.

HISTORICAL SNAPSHOT
1994

- The Ritz-Carlton in Virginia fired a woman for refusing to shave her mustache
- *Sex in America* reported that married people have more sex than single people do
- Newt Gingrich's "Contract with America" proposed a balanced budget amendment, term limits, orphanages for neglected children and cutting money for the arts
- Millions watched the television-broadcast trial of former professional football player O. J. Simpson, who was found not guilty of murdering his wife and her friend Ronald Goldman
- Hollywood madam Heidi Fleiss was sentenced to six months in prison for pandering
- The National Institute of Health was unable to find a single cause for the rising number of cases of "Gulf War Syndrome"
- Collectibles related to the movie *The Lion King* were a must-have in homes with children
- A jury awarded $2.9 million to a woman who was scalded by a cup of coffee purchased at McDonalds; the verdict was appealed
- The bald eagle and California gray whale were removed from the endangered species list
- AZT was found to reduce the transmission of AIDS to infants by two-thirds
- Television's top 10 were *Seinfeld, ER, Home Improvement, Grace Under Fire, NFL Monday Night Football, 60 Minutes, NYPD Blue, Friends, Roseanne* and *Murder, She Wrote*
- Organized protests against the use of fur in fashion clothing increased
- The words "information highway," "Internet," "e-mail" and "unplugged" all entered into common use
- Movie openings included *Forrest Gump, Pulp Fiction, Four Weddings and a Funeral* and *The Lion King*
- The CIA discovered that one of its own employees, Aldrich Ames, was a spy who had betrayed America for years
- Barbara Streisand made her first concert tour in 27 years; despite ticket prices as high as $350 each, 18 concerts sold out in one hour
- Tobacco advertisements featuring Joe Camel were censured because of their apparent appeal to underage smokers
- Sheryl Crow's "All I Wanna Do" won a Grammy for best record
- California voters approved a ballot initiative that barred illegal immigrants from public education and social services
- *The Stone Diaries* by Carol Shield won the Pulitzer Prize for fiction
- Doctors reported that babies were capable of recognizing their names at 4.5 months
- After rock star Kurt Cobain committed suicide, fans attending his memorial service hurled burning rolls of toilet paper

Selected Prices

Leggings $15.00
Running Shoes, Etonic $49.96
Pager, Motorola, per Month $7.95
CD/Cassette Player, Sony $166.00
VCR, JVC $399.00
Eggs, Dozen $0.89
Hotel Room, Sheraton, New York $169.00
Dishes, Corelle, 16 Pieces..$17.97
Dustbuster, Cordless Vacuum $17.99
Mattress, Sealy Queen Size..$324.00
Automobile, Toyota Previa..$20,893
Pistol, Smith & Wesson, 38-Caliber....................................$309.00

"True Gems, Partners Put a Gleaming Clasp on Business," by Jodie Jacobs, *Chicago Tribune*, October 9, 1994:

The $10,000 Etruscan Revival 18-karat gold choker made in France circa 1865 would not look out of place in a museum.

The $1,600 pin of delicate amethyst flowers in a quartz vase made in Lake Forest circa 1994 would not look out of place in the vault of, say, an Armour or McCormick or Walgreen.

Good jewelry, the really exceptional pieces, the kind that if you have to ask the price you might as well forget it, are the purview of gold-smith-gemologist Lise Bennett and antique jewelry collector-dealer Judy Rosenbloom.

The two have teamed up at Bennett's shop, Unicorn Designs on Bank Street in Lake Forest, to offer serious jewelry collectors the best of both of their worlds.

Bennett, a Lake Forest native, opened her display-front workshop 18 years ago after several years of study in England, including work at Medway College of Design in Rochester (Kent) and at the Sir John Cass College of Art in London.

"I was one of those kids who always knew what I wanted to do," said Bennett, 40. She had worked at a local antique furniture and accessory store during high school and took jewelry courses in England after graduating from high school.

Rosenbloom, 50, of Highland Park, found her jewelry career much later. After working in marketing for 20 years, the last several as a specialist in crisis communications at a Chicago public relations firm, she wanted to shift direction. She started the Treasure Chest, operated out of a Northfield office by appointment about four years ago.

Of her career, Rosenbloom said, "I was dealing with death and destruction. A product might be recalled because of poison. Jewelry is a happy business. The people giving jewelry are happy. The people getting jewelry are happy."

Holding a museum-quality gold Etruscan-styled bangle bracelet, she noted the lock of hair inside the back. "You know this was given in love," Rosenbloom said.

Pointing to the bracelet and choker, she said, "It's rare to find pieces on this level with this workmanship."

Rosenbloom speaks with the authority of a longtime collector and more recently, a student of jewelry history. She had a masters degree in marketing from Roosevelt University in Chicago. But when she embarked on her new career, she took classes offered by Sotheby's auction house with the University of Manchester in London.

Dealing in antique jewelry was a logical career switch. As a collector, Rosenbloom's search for fine antique pieces meant waiting until she and husband Jack traveled Europe, which was about once a year.

"I would really look forward to it so I could add to my collection. In Chicago you can find trinkets, but it's difficult to find the really fabulous museum-quality pieces here. For the really outstanding pieces, you have to go to Europe."

As an antique jeweler, Rosenbloom fills that gap for her customers by traveling to Europe about four times a year. "The best antique jewelry is found in England," she said. And given that her career switch came at midlife, she is doing all the traveling after her three children, Doug, Greg and Mary, all in their twenties, have left home.

Rosenbloom, who had used Bennett's skill in repairing antique jewelry, teamed with the goldsmith to do trunk shows (a designer's or dealer's special off-site showing) about three years ago. Explaining the delicate art of repairing antiques, Rosenbloom said, "You can't take these pieces to any jeweler. Lise shows a special appreciation of fine jewelry."

"Uncovering the Past, Amateur Archeologists Really Dig the Work," by Steve Stanek, *Chicago Tribune*, October 9, 1994:

While spending the better part of a warm and sunny Saturday with their hands in small tubs of chocolate-colored water, Beverly Rossman of Wheeling, Ellen McHugh of Rockford and Margaret Lindsey of Wheaton revealed something about themselves.

"We're committed, " said McHugh, 68, who was using a toothbrush to scrub dirt off what appeared to be a jawbone complete with teeth of a deer, or maybe an elk. "We're not doing this for pay. We're doing this because we love it."

A person must love it to spend hours washing centuries of dirt from bits of bone, chips of pottery and other refuse of primitive peoples. But for McHugh, Rossman, Lindsey and the nearly 70 other members of the Sauk Trail Chapter of the Illinois Association for the Advancement of Archeology, there's not much else they'd rather be doing—except, perhaps, digging up such items in the first place.

Sauk Trail, based in McHenry County, is a club for amateur archeologists. Many have worked with college professors and professional archeologists at some of the most important archeological sites in the Midwest and beyond.

"We're not armchair archeologists," said Rossman, a fiftyish woman who works at a Wheeling Kmart when she isn't indulging her interest in archeology. "We love field work."

They love it so much, in fact, that they often pay to do it. Rossman smiles at the thought of her two trips to the Sand Canyon archeological site near Cortez, Colo. She paid $1,000 both times to spend a week on her hands and knees, scratching away paper-thin layers of hard dirt in the search for artifacts from Native Americans.

"For an amateur archeologist, those trips were the ultimate," she said.

For the most part, though, group members do their work closer to home. The artifacts the club members were cleaning that day came from a site in New Lenox. Club members and Midwest Archeological Research Services, a professional archeological firm run by Rochelle Lurie of Harvard, recovered them from New Lenox Park District property. The district is building a golf course and parking lot and hired Lurie's firm to excavate some of the property after finding evidence of an extensive Native American village.

The New Lenox job is one of many Lurie has invited Sauk Trail members to work on. The excavation of the 20-acre site began last year and must be completed this year. So she welcomes help from Sauk Trail.

"It takes a lot of hands to do this kind of work," she said. "Professionals often don't have the chance to get out and record sites that people in developing areas know about. Groups like Sauk Trail can do a lot of good by identifying such sites and helping to record them.

Lurie said the New Lenox project "is a large and complicated site." She said it appears that several distinct groups of people occupied the area over a 600-year period, starting at 1000 A.D. The archeologists have found lots of pottery, stone tools, animal bones, charcoal, and some plant fibers, even European beads and brass.

"Academic Research Far from Dry," by Pam Kassner, *Chicago Tribune*, October 9, 1994:

Beverly Dow studies tree sex. A doctoral student, she has spent five years trying to find the father trees of nearly 300 acorns. In technical terms, she's studying wind pollution.

David Crewe's doctoral research sounds like something from the 1989 movie Honey, I Shrunk the Kids. Crewe and 50 other students at the University of Illinois at Chicago are studying how to make things smaller.

For her master's work, Diane Lockwood researched the consequences of professional women using humor. And for his master's degree, Michael Erickson studied bicycle commuting.

To non-academics, these study topics and others might seem unusual, but most graduate and postgraduate research topics do seem a little strange, said Jeff Slovak, the University of Chicago's deputy dean of students in graduate programs. That's because the work is so narrowly focused, he said.

"You can't stay at a general level and make a contribution," he said. "You have to set out to answer a specific question or topic. But the answer to that specific issue might very well lead you to form a more general perspective on a topic."

1994 NEWS PROFILE

The single mother emerged in the later part of the 20th century as the new poor, or as one author said, the "feminization of poverty." Marilyn is the divorced mother of two teenagers and a young boy with mental problems. She left school after completing the 10th grade and has worked a variety of jobs ever since.

"I worked for four years in a foundry. They made anything from cast-iron doorstops to manhole covers. It's good money. I made $8.45 an hour and I went from $7.02 to $8.45 in three months. That's good money. Normally I would work from three in the afternoon until midnight. But sometimes you had to work a lot more. It is non-union so you have to do it. Many times we worked from one in the afternoon until three in the morning. And that was six days a week.

I worked on the sorting line. You had to break castings off the molds. Like, if it's a barbell, we made barbells, you pick the weight up, slam on the side of the line to break the mold casting off. You take an air gun, sort of like a dentist's drill with a sander on it, and sand the barbell down smooth. Then you take it over and slide it down a chute. I would do like three or four of these a minute. That would be hard, lifting all night. I got tendinitis in both of my arms.

There are about five people on the sorting line. It's very noisy and very dirty. You have to take a shower before you leave there. It's black sand and oil, pieces of cast-iron metal. You get it in your hair. You are all black. You look like you came out of the coal mine.

They really don't train you. You just put your ear cuffs on, you wear your safety glasses and steel-tip shoes, and go down the stairs. I had a super boss. His boss would come out and yell at him. Then he would come and say, 'Hey, look, you did this wrong but I am supposed to really yell at you, so bear with me.' Then he would scream at the top of his lungs at you, so the big guys would understand that he was yelling at you. Then he would say, 'I'm sorry I had to do that.'

You get two 15-minute breaks and 35 minutes for lunch. They shut down two weeks in the summer. Once you've been there a year, you get paid one week, and the other you don't get paid. After five years you get a whole whopping two weeks. That's still during the shutdown weeks.

I don't know if I could have gone any further. You work there. That's it. That's as far as you go. After five or six months you might get a quarter raise. But I started to get more raises, almost up to $2.80 through my work. I probably would have worked my way up, probably to the weighing scale. They bring the parts over, you weigh them, and that's how they can determine how many parts are in or how many parts are missing."

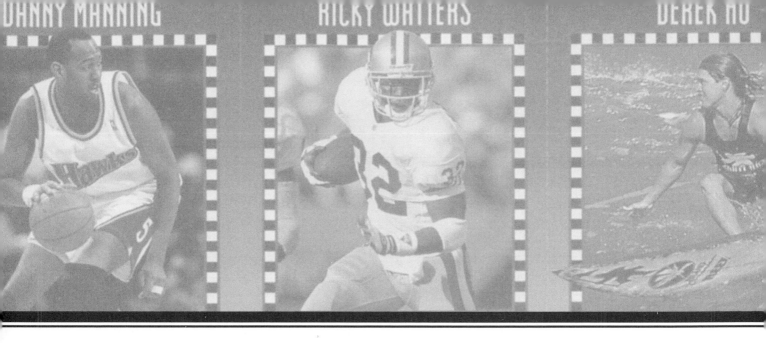

1995 FAMILY PROFILE

Paula Langone, a single, White schoolteacher from Omaha, Nebraska, lives in New York City, where she teaches in the south Bronx, one of the poorest sections of the city; her life revolves around her students.

Annual Income: $27,000

Annual Budget

Clothing $600.00
Educational Expenses $4,500.00
Electricity $288.00
Food $6,200.00
Food away from Home $600.00
Heat $0.00
Intercity Transportation $1,250.00
Personal Care $250.00
Rent $5,780.00
School Supplies $1,000.00
Telephone $960.00
Transportation $1,200.00

Life at Home

- For the past three years, Paula has been living in the Italian Williamsburg section of Brooklyn, New York.
- Her apartment, which sits right on the street, was built at the turn of the century to house immigrant dock workers.
- Later the building became a prosperous bar and brothel.

- Paula's third-floor, 900-square-foot apartment was created by combining two rooms.
- The apartment includes a living room, bedroom, kitchen, and bathroom.
- The bathroom was added in the 1940s when outhouses were removed from the area; the space occupied by the toilet and bathtub was once a closet. There is no room for a sink, so she washes her long hair in the kitchen sink.
- Heat, the cost of which is included in the $480.00 monthly rent, is provided by steam radiators, which can be very noisy.
- Paula lives with her cat and hundreds of books, most concerning teaching, education, or art—her first love.
- The television set is eight years old and stays unplugged.
- Her food expenses include eating at a deli twice a week near Columbia Teacher's College, where she is working on her master's degree in education.
- Her food consists of vegetables from the Korean market, rice, pasta, and chicken; she spends $4.00 a week on cat food.
- Pork, beef, and fish are generally prepared and eaten only on special occasions.
- A pack-a-day smoker, her tobacco bill runs $18.00 a week; she also occasionally buys beer and wine.
- She does not own a car, but she rides the subway to work and home every day and twice a week to night classes at Columbia Teacher's College; she receives some scholarship money to attend the school.
- The subway stop is three blocks from her apartment; she does not hesitate to ride the subway late at night by herself.
- Paula is currently building her teacher wardrobe; a friend in Omaha, Nebraska, who works at a major department store puts away clothing for her all year; she spends $600.00 on clothing that would have cost twice that in New York City.
- During her flight across country to Nebraska to see her parents, she buys the clothes her friend has collected for her; she normally spends a total of $1,200 on trips out West.

- The bulk of her discretionary money goes to buy supplies for her classroom; the $125.00 "teacher's choice" supply allowance covers about one-third of her needs. In addition she buys books and magazines for her use in the classroom.
- School supply buying trips include a visit to the New York City Library where she buys used paperback books for $0.25 and hardbacks for $0.50; friends often donate art supplies and magazines for her use in the classroom.
- Her personal care budget includes perfume and normal toiletries; she does her own hair.
- On major holidays such as Easter, Christmas, and summer she escapes the city by travelling to a monastery in upstate New York where her uncle is a monk.
- On Thanksgiving she often sleeps late and eats Chinese takeout.

Life at Work: Education

- Her fifth grade class in the south Bronx includes 20 children.
- Approximately 40 percent are African-American and 60 percent are Spanish, mostly from Puerto Rico.
- She earnestly believes, "If I can help them, I can save the world."
- She now believes that she has been called to be a teacher of the disadvantaged.
- The parents of more than half the class are on welfare. Most have been in the United States all of their lives, as few new immigrants are moving into the area.
- Three of the 20 children have both a mother and father in the home.

- The school where she teaches was built in 1960 with sleek, modern lines; the janitorial service has worked hard to maintain the facilities despite declining funds.
- Most of her children have serious deficiencies in reading and English, since many speak only Spanish at home.
- Paula often buys with her own money hands-on materials, such as puzzles, to help the children with their reading skills.
- Typically the children are closer to their expected age group in math.
- The school provides both breakfast and lunch; for most of the children in her class these meals are important because they guarantee the children will eat, and are often the biggest meals of the day for them.
- A typical day includes reading, writing exercises, diagramming of sentences, and extensive work with grammar and math through applied science exercises.
- The class also takes a field trip once a month to art museums, zoos, the ballet, and parks.
- In the spring much of the school curriculum revolves around teaching for the annual city and state tests that measure performance and determine funding.
- Test scores are declining; Paula believes it is a "forgotten school."
- Currently, the increasing use of crack is invading her classroom; children come to school exhausted because their parents have gotten and stayed high the night before.
- Some of her best students have the most isolated lives, she says.
- To protect their children from gangs and drugs, parents keep the children inside on weekends, often renting three or four movie videos on Friday afternoon and watching them continuously until Sunday evening.
- Many of the children do attend church on weekends, especially Jehovah's Witness and fundamental Baptist; many of the Spanish families were once Catholic.
- By her own description Paula fell into teaching backwards after two decades in theater and set design.
- Originally from Omaha, Nebraska, while attending an all girl's Catholic high school, her life revolved around the community theater where she both acted and worked in the make-up crew.
- After attending colleges in Nebraska, Florida, and New York, she went to work in theater in 1978.
- She worked primarily in set design and finally left at age 38 to begin substitute teaching in 1991 because "I didn't want to paint scenery anymore."

"Education Transfers and Stops—Public Schools Are Struggling with High Student Turnover," *The New York Times*, March 1995:

"It is March, and Marie Pompeo-Melone, the nurse at Public School 8, is still registering new students—25 in the first eight days of the month alone.

The students keep coming, but the seams of the school do not burst because others are leaving just as fast. In 1993, the school had a mobility rate of 89 percent according to the Education Department, meaning that 89 percent of the children spend part of the year elsewhere. Ms. Pompeo-Melone's file cabinets are crammed with their transfer papers, and her head swims with their faces and names.

'I can't tell you the last time there was a day when I had no transfers,' Ms. Pompeo-Melone said. 'It's just all the time. Words cannot describe how mobile it's become.'

P.S. 8 is not alone. Throughout the county, especially in poor areas, schools are struggling with student turnover rates of 70, 80, and 90 percent. A 1994 report by the General Accounting Office found that nationwide, 17 percent of third graders had attended three or more schools since first grade. At many urban schools, that third-grade percentage is often double.

The consequences can be troubling for both schools and students. Children who move often are more likely to fail a grade and have behavioral problems than those who do not, according to a 1993 study published in *The Journal of the American Medical Association*. 'Even a short move is often stressful,' said David Wood, an author of the study and a pediatrician at Cedars-Sinai Medical Center in Los Angeles.

Lillian Soto was in first grade in Puerto Rico, split the second grade between schools in Hoboken and Jersey City, attended P.S. 8 for third, fourth, and fifth grades, transferred to another Jersey City school for sixth grade and now, as an eighth grader, is back at P.S. 8. Lillian said she did not know why her family had moved so much. But recently, she said, her mother has been thinking about returning to Puerto Rico. Lillian, 13, said her brothers all wanted to go. But she will resist.

'She didn't want to let me finish the eighth grade,' she said. 'I don't want to keep moving to different places. I'm tired already.'

The question, educational experts say, is this: Can any effort to improve public schools succeed if the schoolhouse door is a turnstile?

'Do we really have a prayer of educating these kids?' said L. Scott Miller, author of a study of student mobility, for the Council for Aid to Education. 'I say no.'

Education experts say they have only started examining the problem in recent years, and as a result there are few data, making it difficult to know if the mobility rate is growing worse. But at P.S. 8, the teachers have no doubt.

'Years ago I could see a little kid in the first grade and that kid was here at graduation,' said Linda Herman, who has taught at P.S. 8 for 30 years. 'That was most. Now it's a handful. Everything has just changed so.'

For some families, moving means enhanced fortunes as a parent takes a better job or buys a larger home. But among the nation's most transient families, it is often poverty and its complications that lead to a change in address. A parent loses a job and is evicted. An unemployed mother bounces from the house of one relative to another. An immigrant gives up on his dreams and returns to his homeland.

Poor families move twice as often as those that are not poor, according to a report by the Bureau of the Census. A study by the Council for the Aid to Education linked frequent moving to unemployment, immigrant status, the shortage of low-income housing and problems like drug use, violence, and child neglect.

'Mobility is both a cause and a symptom,' said Mr. Miller, author of the study."."

Life in the Community: New York City

- The two most secure institutions in the south Bronx community are the police station and the school; the community includes few banks, grocery stores, or movie houses.
- Most services available within the community are more expensive than those in other sections of New York; many of the families have cars, often nice cars.

HISTORICAL SNAPSHOT
1995–1996

- Chevron settled harassment charges concerning offensive jokes and comments for $2.2 million
- Michael Jordan left baseball, returning to professional basketball
- The longest Major League Baseball strike in history, 234 days, ended
- The Supreme Court ruled that only a constitutional amendment can enforce term limits on Congress
- 40,000 African-American men met in Washington, D.C.
- 25 percent of Americans continued to smoke cigarettes despite health warnings
- The Dow Jones Industrial Average peaked at 5,216; unemployment was at 5.6 percent
- The pushup bra gained enormous popularity
- Casual Fridays were introduced at the workplace
- After 130 years, Mississippi lawmakers ratified the 13th Amendment abolishing slavery
- The nation was divided over the not guilty verdict for O.J. Simpson, accused of killing his wife; polls indicated that 65 percent of Whites believed he was guilty, while 65 percent of Blacks thought he was innocent
- The FBI reported another sharp decline in crime rates
- President Bill Clinton's approval rating surpassed 50 percent for the first time
- About 55 percent of women provided half or more of household income
- The Centers for Disease Control reported a leveling-off of teen sexual activity; 52.8 percent used condoms
- New York became the 38th state to reinstate capital punishment
- For the first time, Ford sold more trucks than cars; demand for light trucks, like minivans and sports utility vehicles, increased in urban and rural areas
- Mars released a blue M&M candy for the first time
- The Minnesota Aid Project for Condoms advertised: "When you give the gift of love, make sure it's wrapped properly."
- The 25th anniversary of Earth Day was celebrated
- Dow Corning declared bankruptcy after failure of its silicone breast device

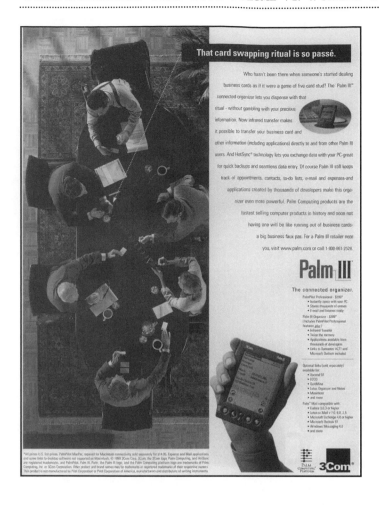

1995 ECONOMIC PROFILE

Income, Standard Jobs

Bituminous Coal Mining $42,711.00
Building Trades $28,465.00
Domestics $10,854.00
Farm Labor $15,863.00
Finance, Insurance,
  and Real Estate $38,577.00
Gas, Electricity, and
  Sanitation Workers $38,936.00
Manufacturing, Durable Goods . . .$28,507.00
Manufacturing, Nondurable
  Goods $24,387.00
Medical/Health Services
  Workers $21,234.00
Miscellaneous Manufacturing $21,798.00
Motion Picture Services $39,585.00
Nonprofit Organization
  Workers $15,016.00
Passenger Transportation
  Workers, Local and Highway . . .$18,525.00
Postal Employees $35,797.00
Public School Teachers $27,130.00
Radio Broadcasting and
  Television Workers $32,223.00
Railroads $42,175.00
State and Local Government
  Workers $29,023.00
Telephone and Telegraph
  Workers $35,844.00
Wholesale and Retail Trade
  Workers $14,412.00

Selected Prices

Bridgestone High Performance
  65 HR Tire $85.00
Cashmere-Blend Jacket $69.99
Crest Gel Tartar Control
  Toothpaste, 6.4 Ounces $2.00
Disney's Lion King Video $29.97
Everyday Battery, D-Size, Two-Pack $6.00
Hotel Room at The Talbot Hotel $160.00
Kirium Chronometer Men's Watch . .$1,695.00
Lubriderm Lotion, 16 Ounces $7.00
Pink/White Lily Flowering Tulip
  Bulbs, 100 . . . .$43.00
Rand Barbie 12" Girl's Bicycle $49.97

Robitussin DM Cough
   Suppressant, Four Ounces $3.00
Secret Deodorant, 1.7 Ounces $1.50
Sierra Four-Piece Setting; Bakelite
   Handles $40.00
Sofa, Green Stripe Cover $999.00

SOLO Radar and Laser
Cordless Detector $199.00
Ultra-Downy, 20 Ounces $2.00
Variflex Rollerblades $34.97
Wing Chair, Floral Cover $699.00
Zenith 19" Color Television $139.00
Zinsser's Blend & Glaze
Decorative Paint, Gallon $25.00

"Despite Higher Rates, Miles Wear on Trucker," *The New York Times:*

"Charles Holman had no time to clean out the mud and the dung from his livestock trailer because he had to drive 760 miles after delivering a truckload of cattle in Colorado the day before.

Now, on a west Texas ranch, he was coaxing and prodding 111 terrified calves into the trailer, a double-decker aluminum labyrinth of cramped compartments.

They kicked, they scrambled, they bellowed. They added to the malodorous mess and they splattered it on his jeans, his shirt, and his face.

To stomp around in this slop day after day 'you've got to have diesel fuel for blood,' Mr. Holman said, 'and manure for brains.'

An an independent trucker with his own rig, he also has to have the financial savvy of a corporate treasurer to turn a profit when the industry he depends on—ranching—is in a slump.

Judged by one important number, his business is picking up. Mr. Holman managed to negotiate a nine percent increase in his rates this year, to $2.40 a loaded mile from $2.20. That's three times the three percent consumer price inflation rate that most economists are predicting for the United States for all of 1995.

But Mr. Holman is not celebrating. For one thing, his bottom line still looks pretty weak. He says his income this year—after expenses but before taxes—from the truck he operates and a second trailer that he rents out will total $18,000 at most. And if ranchers keep cutting back their herds, he adds, he might have to go out hustling for business again. 'I read where the economy is getting better every day,' he said. 'But live in a farming and ranch area. It doesn't look like it's getting better here.'

The biggest threat to his prosperity at the moment, though, probably isn't economic uncertainty. It is his age. At 56, he can still bound up into his cab without a grunt and, brandishing his yellow electric prod, can still let the cattle know who's boss. But his beard has turned white and he is less willing to sleep in an upholstered sleeping compartment instead of at home with his wife in Childress, in the Texas panhandle. After almost four decades of driving, he said, 'The old miles just kind of wear me down.'

As he drives less, with the gross income from his truck falling to a projected $70,000 this year, from $102,000 in 1994, Mr. Holman is taking no chances. Instead of buying a shiny new rig, he has stayed with a 1985 Autocar that he found for $30,000 in 1990, less than half the original price. It has now been driven 1.2 million miles.

His son got a nearly new truck last year just by agreeing to assume someone else's payments. After five months, Mr. Holman recounts, the bank had the truck and his son was calling him for leads on a new job."

Time Magazine, December 21, 1998:

"The story was a headshaker. Ruth Sherman, a White Brooklyn, New York, elementary school teacher, assigned her class a book called Nappy Hair, about a little girl's proud acceptance of her coily mane, in order to bolster the self-esteem of her Black and Latino charges. But some parents, after seeing only a few photocopied pages, assumed the book was a racist put-down and essentially ran Sherman out of the school. Most New Yorkers were torn between amazement at the brouhaha and pity for the children, who have lost a good teacher. But for Trevelyn Jones, book-review editor of the School Library Journal, the real surprise was that the book made it into Sherman's classroom at all. 'Many teachers find it easier to stick with the tried and true,' she says. 'That Sherman even knew about this book is unusual.'

Reading, so we're told, is fundamental to a child's education. But trying to get good books—not just the classics but also worthy contemporary works—into young hands is increasingly providing a pit of problems. Spotty teacher training, lack of library assistance (if not lack of libraries themselves), and fear of controversy all help push teachers toward outdated or bland book choices. Those who fight back with verve risk being drummed out of a job or even chased into court . . .

. . . According to the National Children's Book and Literacy Alliance (N.C.B.L.A.), 48 states don't require children's literature training for state certification. What's more, the budget cuts of the 1980s left a quarter of all American schools without libraries and many of those remaining are manned by untrained volunteers."

Economics and Education
- Income is not the sole determinant of how children turn out, but many believe parental income is the single most important influence on a child's chances.
- Poor children weigh less than rich children at birth and die more often in their first year of life.
- When they enter school, poor children score lower on standardized tests.
- Poor children are absent more often from school and have more behavior problems.
- Poor teenagers are more likely than teenagers of affluent families to have a baby, drop out of school, and get in trouble with the law.
- Children raised in poverty are more likely to end up poor and in need of public assistance.
- From the Great Depression to the 1970s, U.S. policy was dominated by the theory that income support can cure many of the problems of poor children.
- Prior to the Great Depression, poverty was viewed as a sign of weak character.
- Aid to families with dependent children grew from 3.1 million families in 1960 to 6.1 million in 1969.

"To End Pog Fights, Schools Ban Game," *The New York Times*, March 22, 1995:

"Schools around the country are finding that it is easier to ban Pogs, the Hawaiian disk game that is supplanting children's pastimes like marbles, than to spend hours straightening out schoolyard fights.

In Wormleysburg, Pennsylvania, the raucous recess game is no longer permitted. 'We have to put them away or we get sent to the principal's office,' said Laura Arter, 10.

'Pogs is often played for keeps, with the winners taking home the pog disks as spoils, a situation ripe for conflicts,' said Mary Larcome, a fourth-grade teacher in Haverhill, Massachusetts. 'It takes away from your teaching time when you're trying to settle the problems,' she said.

The game has also been discouraged or banned in schools from Windham, New Hampshire, to Spokane, Washington.

There are various ways to play Pogs, also known as 'milk caps,' but generally each player has some of the waferlike cardboard disks and a heavier disk, usually made of plastic, called a 'slammer.' The disks are stacked and a player throws the slammer on them; in one version of the game, he keeps all the ones that flip over.

Pogs started taking off in Hawaii in 1992. The name comes from the abbreviation on the caps of a popular Hawaiian drink containing passion fruit, orange, and guava juice.

The game is now a multimillion-dollar industry, with fancier caps that carry designs like cartoon and movie characters. The disks cost from a few pennies to about $7.00.

At Thompson Middle School in St. Charles, Illinois, 'they became a pretty hot item to steal as well as the cause of arguments,' said Kurt Anderson, the principal. 'We just ask the kids not to bring them.'"

AMANDA BURNS

MANDA BURNS HOLDS A MARBLE called a shooter in the curl of her right index finger. She "knuckles down" by placing the knuckles of her right hand just outside a 10-foot circle. In the middle of the circle are 13 marbles set in the shape of a cross.

"The idea is to knock a marble out of the circle," says Amanda, the 1993 girls' national marbles champion. "If you knock a marble out and your shooter stays in, you get another shot."

Amanda flicks her shooter into the circle. *Whack!* A marble skips out of the ring.

Amanda is playing "ringer." The first person to knock seven marbles out of the ring wins.

Amanda has played marbles since age 10.

"I don't know if I'm going to play in any more tournaments," she says. "I'm sort of afraid to play. I'm the champion now, but if somebody beats me, then I'm not the champ anymore."

AGE: 13 **GRADE:** 7th
HOMETOWN: Moss, Tennessee
OTHER SPORT: Basketball
FAVORITE TEAM: Dallas Cowboys
PETS: "I have 10 cows and five goats. I'm lookin' to get me another goat."
SOMEDAY: "I want to go to college and then live on a farm in Tennessee."

AMANDA "KNUCKLED DOWN" TO WIN THE NATIONAL CHAMPIONSHIP IN MARBLES

What Money Can't Buy, Family Income and Children's Life Changes:

"An assistant principal in a school in which nearly all the students are economically disadvantaged described it this way: 'A lot of time the parents want to have expectations for their kids. But they think it doesn't do any good to have expectations if you don't think it's ever going to be in the reach of the child. So they don't follow through. Lack of hope. That is one of the most profound things. Simply the lack of hope. You take most of the parents that we work with and they would like to hope that their child will go to college, but they don't really see a way that they are going to make that happen.'"

"A Happier Twist on Housing: From Bad Landlords to Co-ops," *The New York Times*, September 17, 1995:

"When Robert Santiago moved into his apartment on Division Avenue in Williamsburg 20 years ago, it had no boiler, no heat, and few tenants, and the landlord did not pay property taxes. The city took over the building in the mid-1980s.

Now, Mr. Santiago and the other tenants won the building: They bought it four years ago from the city for $250.00 an apartment to form a co-op. Every month, they meet to pay bills and discuss repairs. 'When I came here, it was the *Twilight Zone*,' said Mr. Santiago, 38. 'I can sleep now. I couldn't sleep before.'

Weighed down by the costs of maintaining buildings it has seized, the city has increased its efforts to sell them—to private landlords, non-profit groups, and tenant co-ops. And a survey released last week indicates that, among Brooklyn residents in current and former city-owned housing, tenant co-ops are by far the most popular. The co-ops scored highest in terms of services like heat and hot water, management, and safety; city-owned units came out last. The city owns 2,885 occupied buildings seized for tax delinquency, 1,054 of them in Brooklyn.

The survey, sponsored by a group of housing organizations, polled 3,000 residents in 500 Brooklyn buildings.

Deborah C. Wright, Commissioner of the Department of Housing Preservation and Development, which oversees city-owned housing, said that when the city sells a building, tenants are given the option to form co-ops. But 60 percent of the residents must agree to do so and must take classes in management, budgets, and repairs. 'Some people are highly motivated and want to own and take responsibility for every aspect of their buildings,' she said. 'Other people just want to rent.'

Ms. Wright said that she thought the survey's conclusions did not reflect recent changes in housing programs under the Giuliani administration. 'The one thing we agree on 100 percent is that the city is the worst landlord in the city,' she said.

Standing in a newly painted hallway of his tenant co-op on Division Avenue, Santana Rosendo said taking on the responsibility was worth the effort. 'Everyone owns their apartment,' said Mr. Rosendo, 74. 'Everything is better because it is our own.'"

1998 Profile

Middle Class

It's been quite a year for Robin Lye. As a high school sophomore, she played on a basketball team that emerged second in the state, a soccer team that was state champion, and she was named player of the year; best yet, she is making all A's in advanced classes and has a boyfriend.

Life at Home

- The past year has been rewarding.
- It began with the high school cross-county season last fall, when Robin finished eighth in the state of Georgia and fifth in Atlanta.
- But soccer is her real passion.
- During the same season, Robin played "club" soccer with girls aged 17 years and under, many actively recruited for the team from seven other high schools in the area.
- Each weekend they would travel to locations as distant as Jacksonville, Florida; Columbia, South Carolina; Washington, DC; or Raleigh, North Carolina, to play soccer against the region's best teams.
- They won more than half their games and were seen by a wide range of college recruiting coaches; because Robin is a sophomore, no coach was allowed to talk with her, but many asked questions of her coach.
- When basketball season arrived, the high school coach asked her if she would try out, and she became the only white girl on the squad.
- Her school, which is 50 percent African-American, generally observes clear dividing lines—black girls play basketball and white girls play soccer.

Robin Lye is having a great year.

Robin travels throughout the South playing soccer on weekends.

- Most of the teams they play reflect the same racial makeup; at most basketball games, 90 percent of the fans are African-American, while at the soccer games, less than five percent are black.
- Her primary job on the basketball team was playing defense, and she was only occasionally called upon for her skills.
- Her jump shot is awkward and the source of great amusement for her more experienced teammates.
- Before one important game, when the other members of the team decided to fashion their hair in cornrows, Robin wove her hair into French braids in a show of unity.
- Spanning two seasons, the team won 40 games in a row before losing in the state finals.
- Because she never left the bench in the final game, she is unsure whether she will rejoin the basketball team next year or simply concentrate her junior year on visiting colleges, rock climbing, water sports and soccer.
- Rock climbing is a particular attraction because her fellow athletes are so laid-back and supportive.
- She believes she can be less self-conscious while rock climbing than in any of the team sports she plays.
- She especially enjoys the fact that many of the indoor climbing walls in the area provide both physical and mental challenges.
- Several times, her athletic skills allowed her to reach places that turned into dead ends, but now she is learning to combine her strength with excellent planning.
- The highlight of the year has been high school soccer, where she played with many of her best friends.
- Entering the season, she and her teammates knew the coach would be leaving in the fall to attend law school, so they wanted the year to be special.
- He delayed his entry into law school for one year so he could coach the team; he, too, wanted the year to be special.

The fans were enthusiastic at the championship game.

- Robin plays center forward and is the leading scorer on the team.
- She believes her greatest skill is passing and creating good ball movement, and dreams of taking a leadership role in life.
- The two-week buildup to the game was exciting and agonizingly slow as they worked their way through the playoffs.
- On the day of the championship, played at her high school's highly manicured, natural-grass stadium, the student body arrived in force.
- For the first time all season, all seats were filled an hour before the game, and many of the fans had brought giant banners and horns.
- Having lived with the embarrassment of the basketball team's loss of its state championship game, Robin was focused on winning.
- The first half ended in a scoreless tie, and then the other team scored first to break the deadlock, 1-0.
- Late in the game, Robin sprinted past two defenders and drove the tying goal into the upper corner of the net, forcing the game into overtime.
- During the extra time period, with the crowd screaming, she contributed two additional assists, resulting in a 3-1 victory; it was the school's first state championship in women's soccer.
- Pandemonium reigned afterward.
- Following the game, a panel of coaches named her player of the year, even though she was only a sophomore, and the local sportswriters then bestowed on her the same honor, earning her a picture in the newspaper.
- The three local television stations showed her goal and assists over and over.
- She realizes that the quality of her coaches, uniforms, fields and referees are a direct result of the 1972 Title IX law that required schools to provide equal opportunities for men and women.

Robin scored during the championship game.

- In 1972, females represented seven percent of high school varsity athletes, while today, they represent 42 percent.
- At the college level, the number of women athletes has risen from 15 percent to 42 percent during the same period.
- Now that school is over, Robin is working at a summer camp in the mountains of North Carolina as a junior counselor.
- Her cabin is populated with nine-year-olds who have a fascination with her personal life, especially her boyfriend.
- Even the slightest tidbit of information will keep them up for hours giggling with each other.
- When the year began, she was dating a senior from a neighboring school, whom she could only see after school and on weekends.
- The relationship ended when she caught him with another girl.
- Within two months, she met a guy at a local gym, a college sophomore who is working his way through school.
- Her parents, who divorced eight years ago, are unsettled by the four-year age difference.
- Robin's mother, in particular, is concerned about the relationship, but her father makes very few negative comments, and even invites her boyfriend to the house for meals and conversation.
- Since the divorce, Robin has lived with her mother, even though her parents have joint custody.
- Her parents live only a few miles apart; she spends Wednesdays, Thursdays and every other weekend with her father, who remarried several years ago.
- Recently, as part of the divorce settlement, her mother sold the home in which Robin had grown up to help pay college tuition for her older brother.
- Robin still does not think it's fair that her mother and father waited six years until her brother graduated from high school to sell the family house, but could not wait three more years for her graduation.
- One of the hardest parts of living between two houses is telling friends where to find her on any given day.
- She also worries that if she leaves schoolbooks and notes she needs for homework at one house, someone will get mad.
- When she was in middle school, she felt different from other kids because of the divorce; everyone else's parents were married and many had stay-at-home moms who could help with school projects.

Atlanta is known for its innovative educational programs.

Following the championship victory, pandemonium reigned.

- Now, though, it bothers her less, especially since she has a car and can drive where she needs to be.

Life at School

- Last year, in an attempt to raise standards and test scores, Robin's school adopted block scheduling, in which all classes are 93 minutes long and last for only one semester.
- Robin takes four classes per semester, 2 of which are AAP, or Advanced Academic Placement classes for college.
- She is also taking two AP, or advanced placement, classes, allowing her to earn college credit if she passes a nationally sanctioned exam at the end of the semester.
- She thinks the longer classes are stupid, believing that the absorption rate of high school students—even smart ones—ends long before the 93 minutes are up.
- Besides, most of the teachers gear their lesson plans to 50-minute classes, and most have had difficulty shifting to the longer format, resulting in wasted time.
- Last semester, she took Spanish 4, U.S. history, chemistry, and business computer applications.
- Her favorite was chemistry, because of both the subject and the entertaining way the teacher presented the material.
- This semester, she is taking anatomy and physiology, precalculus, history and English.
- Her English class, which includes an intensive unit on writing, is taught by her favorite teacher.
- Unlike many of her other teachers, Ms. Haggett provides the freedom to learn; if you know the material and don't want to pay attention all the time, it's okay.
- Robin is currently preparing to take the SAT exam; her PSAT came in at 1260, but she wants to break 1400 to ensure a good choice of colleges.

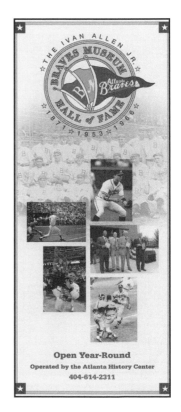

THE IVAN ALLEN JR.
BRAVES MUSEUM
HALL OF FAME
1871 · 1953 · 1966

Open Year-Round
Operated by the Atlanta History Center
404-614-2311

Atlanta was the home of the 1996 Olympics.

- Friends have repeatedly said she is a shoo-in to get a college soccer scholarship, but, having heard that college soccer is all-consuming and will dominate her life, she is unsure if she wants to play in college.
- She has too many interests for that, she thinks.
- Besides, she dreams of attending a college that will prepare her for a career in medicine, and though she has not yet chosen a school, her criteria include an out-of-state location and a premed course.
- A current favorite is Wake Forest University in Winston-Salem, North Carolina, even though she has never been on the campus.
- In class rank, she is now number five overall in a class of 350, having moved from the number eight slot as a freshman; in her high school career she has made one B out of all A's.
- She is also trying to decide how active she would like to be in her high school sorority.
- As a freshman, she was honored to be invited by the popular girls into the social club, which is banned by the school because of its exclusivity, but she is now wondering how much time she wants to devote to it.
- Athletics and schoolwork allowed her only occasionally to attend the parties thrown by the group most of the year.
- Currently, the newspapers are replete with stories about high school drug use; when her father asks about marijuana, she readily admits that a lot of people "smoke up" in the mornings.
- Acid and cocaine, she believes, are used primarily by the rich kids in school who can afford a more expensive high.
- Alcohol, especially beer, is the drug of choice at her school; it's readily available at parties, especially those that form almost spontaneously at homes where parents have left for a weekend, trusting their children to do the right thing.

The dynamics of the Atlanta economy electrify the state.

Life in the Community: Atlanta, Georgia

- The city of Atlanta, where the 1996 Olympics were held, is struggling with what to do with the Olympic caldron, the symbol of the summer games.

- Atlanta media mogul and billionaire Ted Turner, who recently pledged $1 billion to the United Nations, is being criticized because his foundation has only given $2.7 million to Atlanta-based charities.

- Atlanta ranks fifth among major American cities in the percentage of people living in poverty.

- The latest FBI statistics show that the city's murder rate plunged to 36 murders per 100,000 residents, the lowest level in a decade.

- An intensive manhunt continues for Eric Rudolph, accused of three bombings in Atlanta, including a blast at Centennial Olympic Park during the Olympics.

HISTORICAL SNAPSHOT
1998

- The movie *Titanic* became the highest-grossing film in history at $850 million
- Studies indicated that 50 percent of all Americans were overweight
- Seventeen major newspapers called for President Bill Clinton's resignation following his admission to a grand jury that he had engaged in an extramarital affair and lied about the relationship
- Online birth, surgical glue, vaccines for Lyme disease, drive-through cigar stores, nanotubes, iris-scanning ID systems and a quantum computer network made their first appearance
- Georgia Governor Zell Miller proposed that newborns be sent home with a recording of Mozart and Bach to stimulate brain development
- Births to unwed mothers and infant mortality fell to 25-year lows
- Popular books included *Confederates in the Attic* by Tony Horwitz, *Pillar of Fire: America in the King Years* by Taylor Branch, *Slaves in the Family* by Edward Ball, *A Man in Full* by Tom Wolfe, *The Street Lawyer* by John Grisham, *Rainbow Six* by Tom Clancy, and *Tuesdays with Morrie* by Mitch Albom
- The Pulitzer Prize for U.S. history went to Edwin G. Burrows and Mike Wallace for *Gotham: A History of New York City to 1898*
- Nineteen students were killed as a result of several small-town shootings by teenagers at their schools
- A New Jersey fertility clinic doubled its stipend to egg donors to $5,000 for a month's supply, igniting fears of a bidding war for human eggs
- Fads for the year included the use of ginkgo, Internet shopping, "Teletubbies" and techno
- The Dow-Jones Industrial Average peaked at 9,374, while unemployment was at its lowest since 1970
- The undergraduate tuition at Princeton reached $22,820 a year, plus $6,711 for room and board
- U.S. rockets were fired at Osama Bin Laden's terrorist network in Afghanistan and Sudan
- President Clinton ordered air attacks against Iraq's Saddam Hussein for obstructing the work of UN inspectors
- The United States budget showed a $70 billion surplus, the first time it had been positive since 1969
- On television, *Sports Night, Jesse, That '70s Show* and Felicity premiered
- Geraldo Rivera signed a six-year, $30 million contract with CNBC
- Dr. Jack Kevorkian demonstrated patient-assisted death on the television program *60 Minutes* and was arrested for first-degree murder
- *Shakespeare in Love, Saving Private Ryan, Life Is Beautiful, A Bug's Life and Out of Sight* opened at movie theaters
- Top albums of the year included the soundtrack from *Titanic,* Celine Dion's "Let's Talk about Love," "Come On Over" by Shania Twain and "The Backstreet Boys" by the Backstreet Boys

1998 ECONOMIC PROFILE

Selected Prices

Book, Mediterranean Cooking
Kitchen Library $14.95
Bulbs, 100 Tulips $43.00
Breadmaker, Welbilt $129.99
Chair, La-Z-Boy $332.99
Comforter, Quallowarm II,
King Size $160.00
Cookware, All-Clad Soup Pot $230.00
Envelopes, 100 9 x 12 Brown Kraft . . .$4.65
Jacket, Adidas Polar Fleece $69.95
Museum Admission, New York,
Museum for African Art $8.00
Purse, Kenneth Cole, Leather $148.50
Soccer Ball $69.95
Soccer Cleats $129.95
Suit, Man's Hickey-Freeman $760.00
Tea, Tetley Ice Tea Mix,
42 Servings $0.99
Videotape, Disney's
The Lion King $29.99

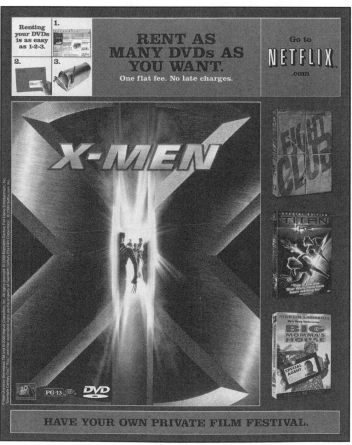

Robin often hikes with friends in the Appalachian Mountains.

Changing America

- The typical tire for a large automobile weighed 25 pounds, down from 32 pounds in the late 1960s.
- America's Hispanic population jumped by 58 percent during the past decade to 35.3 million people.
- The number of corporate pension plans fell from 112,200 in 1985 to 42,300.
- Viagra, for male erectile dysfunction, captured national attention and sold at a record rate, despite its cost of $10 a pill.
- The per capita consumption of food by Americans had increased eight percent during the past decade, or approximately 140 pounds of food a year per person.
- Roughly one-half of the average household food budget was spent outside the home, up from one-quarter in 1970.
- Ku Klux Klan leader Samuel Bowers was convicted in Mississippi for the 1966 murder of civil rights leader Vernon Dahmer.
- AIDS deaths fell nearly 50 percent from the previous year.
- DNA evidence proved that Thomas Jefferson fathered a child with his slave/mistress Sally Hemings.
- The number of welfare recipients dropped below four percent, the lowest in 25 years.
- A study reported that PMS was a biological, not a psychological, syndrome.
- The New York Philharmonic toured Asia, performing in Beijing for the first time.

"Practice Makes Perfect (and Poorer Parents)," by James Schembari, The New York Times, January 27, 2002:

Has so little changed since Allan Sherman, the late comedic songwriter, recorded these lyrics in 1966 (sung to "Makin' Whoopee")?

"My daughter, Linda, she takes ballet.
Her first recital was yesterday.
She dropped her tutu, her left shoe, too.
She needs more lessons.
Then there's my daughter, Dottie,
She takes guitar, that's true.
Junior, he takes karate.
Smashed her guitar in two.
For all these lessons, I have to pay.
I must raise money. I found a way.
Read my brochure folks, learn how to be poor, folks.
I'm giving lessons."

Parents seem to have been as crazed then about training their children as baby boomers are now.

My three sons, ages seven to 11, play on community baseball and T-ball teams, and once played organized soccer and basketball. They have taken trumpet lessons and chess lessons.

My daughter, Marian, 14, has been a member of the Brownies, has played the violin and is now taking piano lessons. She has also joined the drama department and the choir at her high school, a step that means buying costumes and show tickets. This spring, the choir is taking a $400 field trip to Virginia. Before Thanksgiving, she announced that she wanted to try out for the highly competitive regional chorus. I encouraged her.

"But if I'm going to make it, I need to take voice lessons," she said.

That was $40 a week for several weeks, but she made the cut, and her concert this month was a delight.

That explains, of course, why we say yes to our children. We want them to find their passion—and what if they are really talented and just need a bit of coaching? So even before they go off to college, we've spent a fortune on them.

Actually, we may be a bit more obsessed about this than our parents were. According to figures from the Agriculture Department, which tracks family expenditures, parents with incomes of $38,000 to $64,000 spent $18,510 on miscellaneous items for the average child from birth through age 18. That is up from $17,600 in 1960, adjusted for inflation. The category includes entertainment, reading material, VCRs, summer camp, and lessons. A study by Child Trends, a nonpartisan research group in Washington, found that about 82 percent of American children had participated in at least one extracurricular activity in 1998.

One? How about five or six? Bugs Peterschmidt, 44, of Plymouth, Minnesota, said her two children were involved in piano, trumpet, soccer, scouting, after-school math classes, swimming and summer enrichment programs. She said she was spending about $3,000 a year on all the activities.

"I was working part-time, and once one of my paychecks went to all of this stuff," she said. "The thing is, I was bummed."

Susan Kakuk, 42, also of Plymouth, said she was also spending about $3,000 a year on her two children. Barbara Carlson, 53, of Greenfield, Minnesota, put the total for her four children at a few thousand dollars. Mark Lino, an economist for the Agriculture Department, said parents found ways to pay for all of this.

"People seem to be purchasing more of this for their children since 1960," he said. "I think it is one of the reasons more women have joined the workforce. Parents are also cutting back expenditures on themselves. They are not cutting back on their children; they are spending more on their children."

Kristin A. Moore, the president of Child Trends, said that there was a downside to all this. "They are good for children until you get past the midpoint and everyone is overwhelmed by sheer quantity," she said. "At some point families can get too busy, but no one knows how much is too much."

"Were You Born That Way? It's not just brown eyes. Your inheritance could also include insomnia, obesity and optimism. Yet scientists are saying that genes are not—quite—destiny," by George Howe Colt and Anne Hollister, *Life*, April 1998:

In the debate over the relative power of nature and nurture, there may be no more devout believers than new parents. As my wife and I, suffused with a potent mix of awe, exhaustion and ego, gazed down at our newborn daughter in the hospital, it has hard not to feel like miniature gods with a squirming lump of figurative putty in our hands. We had long believed that people could make the world a better place, and now we firmly believed that we could make this a better baby. At home our bedside tables are swaybacked by towers of well-thumbed parents' manuals. A black-and-white Stim-Mobile, designed to sharpen visual acuity, hung over the crib. The shelves were lined with books, educational puzzles and IQ-boosting rattles. Down the line we envisioned museum visits, art lessons, ballet. And if someone had tapped us on the shoulder and told us that none of this would matter—that, in fact, if we could switch babies in the nursery and send our precious darling home with any other new parents in the hospital, as long as these parents weren't penniless, violent or drug addicted, our daughter would turn out pretty much the same . . . well, we would have thwacked that someone with a Stim-Mobile.

Does the key to who we are lie in our genes or in our family, friends and experiences? In one of the most bitter controversies of the twentieth century—the battle over nature and nurture—a wealth of new research has tipped the scales overwhelmingly toward nature. Studies of twins and advances in molecular biology have uncovered a more significant genetic component to personality than was previously known. Far from a piece of putty, say biologists, my daughter is more like a computer's motherboard, her basic personality hardwired into infinitesimal squiggles of DNA. As parents, we would have no more influence on some aspects of her behav-

ior than we had on the color of her hair. And yet, new findings are also shedding light on how heredity and environment interact. Psychiatrists are using these findings to help patients overcome their genetic predispositions. Meanwhile, advances in genetic research and reproductive technology are leading us to the brink of some extraordinary—and terrifying—possibilities.

The moment the scales began to tip can be traced to a 1979 meeting between a steelworker named Jim Lewis and a clerical worker named Jim Springer. Identical twins separated five weeks after birth, they were raised by families 80 miles apart in Ohio. Reunited 39 years later, they would have strained the credulity of the editors of Ripley's Believe It or Not. Not only did both have dark hair, stand six feet tall and weigh 180 pounds, they spoke with the same inflections, moved with the same gait and made the same gestures. Both loved stock-car racing and hated baseball. Both married women named Linda, divorced them and married women named Betty. Both drove Chevrolets, drank Miller Lite, chain-smoked Salems and vacationed on the same half-mile stretch of a Florida beach. Both had elevated blood pressure, severe migraines and had undergone vasectomies. Both bit their nails. Their heart rates, brain waves and IQs were nearly identical. Their scores on personality tests were as close as if one person had taken the same test twice.

Identical twins raised in different families are a built-in research lab for measuring the relative contributions of nature and nurture. The Jims became one of 7,000 sets of twins studied by the Minnesota Center for Twin and Adoption Research, one of a half-dozen such centers in this country. Using psychological and physiological tests to compare the relative similarities of identical and fraternal twins, these centers calculate the "inheritability" of behavioral traits—the degree

2000–2005

History will record that the twenty-first century began in the United States on September 11, 2001, when four American commercial airliners were hijacked and used as weapons of terror. After the tragedies at the World Trade Center in New York; Shanksville, Pennsylvania; and the Pentagon in Washington, DC, Americans felt vulnerable to a foreign invasion for the first time in decades. Citizens in every part of the nation, even those thousands of miles from the targets, immediately began to question what was important in their lives. Church attendance increased; sales of home improvement products or garden supplies soared. International travel by Americans declined, while shopping via the Internet exploded. Surveys showed that "security" had become a cherished value particularly among women in a nation where half of all marriages resulted in divorce and the much bally-hooed dot-com boom had turned into a bust.

America's response to the attacks was to dispatch U.S. forces around the world in a War on Terror. United in grief and outrage, the nation mobilized its military, intelligence, law enforcement, and diplomatic and financial resources. The first stop was the mountains of Afghanistan, where a new breed of suicidal terrorists, al-Qaeda, were collected into an army of angry, self-styled Islamic warriors determined to destroy America. Under the protection of the ruling Taliban party, al-Qaeda had built as many as 60 terrorist cells. America's military response was swift and uncompromising. The goal was to hunt down the al-Qaeda leadership and free Afghanistan from Taliban rule. The initial fighting force combined billion-dollar U.S. technology, which struck targets from the air using laser-guided missiles, with the skills of the15,000-strong rag-tag Northern Alliance. The Taliban was quickly routed, although al-Qaeda leader Osama Bin Laden and several of his top aides escaped capture. Within months of the invasion, more than 2,400 suspected terrorists in 90 countries were detained in the War on Terror, followed by popular elections throughout Afghanistan that included women as voting members of the citizenry. In the U.S., the widows of several of the men killed in the World Trade Center employed significant media and political savvy to force the government to conduct an aggressive and comprehensive inquiry into the events surrounding the 9/11 attacks that led to a reordering of the intelligence agencies protecting America.

With the economy in an overall decline and national debt increasing at a record pace, the United States rapidly shifted from war in Afghanistan to Iraq, home of leader Saddam Hussein. Despite vocal opposition from allies such as Germany and France, President George W. Bush launched Operation Iraqi Freedom to eliminate Saddam Hussein and the possibility of his employing weapons of mass destruction. This decision resulted in worldwide demonstrations against the invasion, including some of the largest U.S. protest marches since the Vietnam War in the late 1960s and early 1970s. As in the invasion of Afghanistan, the U.S. achieved a rapid victory, including the capture of the Iraq capital of Baghdad and subsequently the capture of Saddam Hussein himself. The weapons of mass destruction proved to be more elusive, sparking political debate concerning both the quality and goals of American intelligence. Waging peace and establishing stability were far more complex and expensive than fighting the Iraqi army, although elections were held in the opening days of 2005, igniting hope for a long-term solution.

Despite the cost of the war, the falling value of the dollar and record high oil prices, the American economy began to recover by 2004. Unemployment declined, new home purchases continued to surge, and the full potential of previous computer innovation and investment impacted businesses large and small. Men and women of all ages began to buy and sell their products on the Internet. Ebay created the world's largest yard sale; Amazon demonstrated, despite the sneering of critics, that it could be the bookstore to the world. And everyone, it seemed, learned to Google, whether the need was the exact wording of a Shakespearian sonnet or the menu at Sarah's Pizza Parlor two blocks away. At the same time, globalization took on new meaning and political import as jobs—thanks to computerization—moved to India, China or the Philippines, where college-educated workers were both cheap and eager. American manufacturing companies that once were the centerpiece of their community's economy closed their U.S. factories to become distributors of furniture made in China, lawn mowers made in Mexico or skirts from Peru. The resulting structural change that pitted global profits and innovation against aging textile workers unable to support their families resulted in a renewed emphasis in America on education and innovation. If the U.S. was to maintain its economic dominance, the pundits said, innovative ideas and research would lead the way.

Professional women, who for decades had struggled to rise past the glass ceiling in their companies, began to find bigger opportunities in the 2000s. Significantly, the promotion of a woman to a top slot in a Fortune 500 company ceased to make headlines. Some top female CEOs even began to boldly discuss the need for more balance in the workplace. Yet, surveys done at mid-decade showed that more Americans were working longer hours than ever before to satisfy the increasing demands of the marketplace and their own desire for more plentiful material goods. In some urban markets the average home sales price passed $400,000; average credit card debt continued to rise and the price of an average new car, with typical extras, passed $20,000.

The

conomist

APRIL 8TH - 14TH 2000

MICROSOFT
AND THE
MARKETS
pages 18, 63 and 79

Who owns the

2000 PROFILE

Elizabeth Harris, married and a mother of three, is a publisher who has lived in Bath, Connecticut, for 19 years; her office is just over the state line in Millington, New York.

Life at Home

- Since 1981, Elizabeth and her husband Michael have lived in the center of the town of Bath, Connecticut; their three children are all away at college or boarding school.

- Their traditional colonial-style home, built in 1780, overlooks the town green, an area that was used as a common grazing area during colonial times and is now a park.

- The original front section of the house was done in a four-over-four colonial style, in which the first and second floors of the house were divided into four relatively equal-size rooms.

- The exterior is painted white and has black shutters that frame the centuries-old colonial glass windows.

- The front of the house has a large porch that has two benches on opposite ends that face each other; the structure of the porch, with its opposing benches, is known as the "Bath stoop," and is unique to the 250-year-old village.

- There is also a large side lawn.

- In the 1800s, an addition was built onto the back of the house, creating a kitchen area on the first floor and servants' quarters on the second floor.

- The house was occupied for almost 150 years by the Sedgwick family, early members of whom were close relations to General Charles Sedgwick, the famous Civil War general who fought at Gettysburg and the highest-ranking general killed in combat.

Elizabeth Harris is a successful publisher of reference directories.

A healthy outdoor environment for her children is important to Elizabeth.

- After the Sedgwick family moved out in the mid-1900s, several different families occupied the house.
- Elizabeth likes to say that the last wealthy family to live in the house moved out in the 1950s.
- When Elizabeth, her husband and their two young sons arrived in 1981, the large house had been chopped into several rental apartments.
- They occupied the old front section of the Sedgwick House, which was larger than their apartment in New York City.
- The area had a strong school system and a healthy outdoor environment, creating an ideal setting for raising their children.
- They shared the house with another family of four who lived in the back addition.
- Elizabeth and Michael used two of the front rooms to operate their startup publishing business, Pocket Knife Publishing.
- In 1984, the family welcomed a baby girl, Victoria, who was born across the street in Bath Hospital.
- Only a few days after the birth, Elizabeth went back to work at their new office, located above a bank in downtown Bath
- The 200-year-old house, which they had by this time taken over completely, desperately needed repairs.
- The Harrises needed to spend a part of their yearly budget keeping the huge old house standing.
- The children are very athletic; all of them from the age of four played for a local youth hockey league, and also participated in baseball and basketball.
- Starting in 1990, Elizabeth hired summer baby sitters to look after the three children while she and her partner-husband put in long hours at the office.
- The baby sitters shuffled the children around to the beach, to different sports events and to friends.
- The children grew very close to them, and thought of them more as friends than as adults.
- Elizabeth and Michael come from different religious backgrounds, but are not attached to their faiths.
- All of the children have attended the local public elementary school, then transferred to private high schools.
- Currently, Mac is attending Wesleyan College, a small liberal arts college near Hartford, Connecticut; Chris is in his sophomore year at Tulane University, and Victoria is in her junior year at an all girls' prep school.
- Elizabeth is still adjusting to the empty nest, and speaks to her daughter every day
- The children come home every few weekends, on holidays, and sometimes for the summer.

- When it's only Elizabeth and Michael, Elizabeth spends about $60 a week on groceries; when the children are there, she spends over $100 a week.
- It takes about 10 minutes for the couple to drive to their offices in New York State.
- On weekends, they make the two-hour drive to their apartment in New York City, or occasionally take the commuter train, which costs $20 for a round trip.
- Elizabeth and Michael love their downtown New York City apartment, and use it on weekends to relax.
- From there, they can go out to eat, meet with friends and attend the theater or opera.

Life at Work

- Elizabeth Harris attended college at the University of Michigan, where she earned a degree in art history.
- Her husband Michael went to Dartmouth, where he studied political science.
- After working in Chicago for several years, Elizabeth moved to New York City, where she worked for Scholastic Publishing.
- She left Scholastic in 1981 to stay home with her two young sons.
- Elizabeth and Michael created Pocket Knife Publishing that same year.
- They started with one title, a directory of mail order catalog companies—the first of its kind.
- The same year they started the company, the family moved into their house in Bath, which served as both a place to raise their children and, with its ample office space, for working at home.
- After only a couple of years, the business grew too big for the house; Pocket Knife Publishing was moved to an office space above the local bank, and later to larger offices nearby.
- Every year the sales improved on the one directory, but producing a single book required tremendous energy.
- The process, including the data entry, proofreading, and getting the directory set in type, took months.
- In 1981, a printer would take six weeks to print a book for a publisher; currently, it takes two weeks.
- By the 1980s, the personal computer allowed small companies that performed research to do typesetting "in-house," transforming the process and time requirements.
- Now, in 2000, getting books set in type is almost instantaneous.
- Yet the actual printing for the Pocket Knife books is still done by printers as far away as Nebraska.

The Harris home, built in 1780, sports a porch with facing benches — an architectural detail unique to the 250-year-old village.

All of the Harris children attend private high school.

Bath, Connecticut, sponsors many fun, family events.

- From 1988 to 1997, Pocket Knife created about two new titles a year, with minimal addition of staff.
- Some of its employees are linked electronically, working off-site in their homes, and have never been to the office except for a visit.
- In the 1990s, the economy was strong enough to allow the company to grow 20-25 percent a year and the company opened satellite offices in nearby Putnam and Fairfield, Connecticut.
- In the late 1990s, Pocket Knife began to expand the business by buying reference works from other publishers, growing through acquisition.
- Around the same time, Pocket Knife began to publish reference books for the high school market.
- They also expanded their product line into statistical information, developing powerful databases that allowed them to sort and rank important statistical data and provide comparisons and rankings.
- Not only did Pocket Knife acquire directories, but they also bought a couple of small companies.
- Right now, Elizabeth is worried about the economy.
- For the first time, Pocket Knife is not experiencing the 20 percent annual growth it had been enjoying in recent years.
- Schools and libraries are beginning to cut back on their budgets, and moving some of the readers' research activity to the Internet.
- To combat the threat of the Internet, Elizabeth put her energy into developing a strong Web site, and began allowing the directories to be sold by Internet distributors such as Amazon.com.
- Elizabeth worked with the search engines so that Pocket Knife would come up easily when people searched for a product on the Web.
- They also began to offer the directories and reference books on the Internet by subscription.
- Although Pocket Knife is putting intense effort into becoming more Internet-compatible, their main focus is on the day-to-day challenges of a publishing company.
- Earlier in the year, as the new millennium approached, newspapers were filled with concerns that computers would not be able to adapt to the changing decade, causing massive data loss in what was dubbed the "Y2K bug."
- Elizabeth took the "wait and see" approach to Y2K threats after testing her company's programs.
- She was correct: The new year passed in cyberspace without incident.
- Elizabeth and Michael have internally divided up the responsibilities of running Pocket Knife.
- Elizabeth is focused on the internal operations of the company, its finances, the databases and the editorial operations.
- Michael is focused on planning the budgets, sales, and marketing, and is the external face of the company.
- Elizabeth's workday starts at 8:30 when she arrives at the offices in Millington.
- During the day, Elizabeth helps develop the database file structures for any new products, and also works on composition problems with the books.
- She attends at least one meeting a day with department managers to review department operations and progress on current projects.
- She checks the outstanding bills, approves payments and signs checks.
- Since she is a hands-on manager, many issues from a variety of departments are addressed throughout each day.

THE CHANGING OF THE GUARD
"THE OLD BOY NETWORK IS
BEING REPLACED BY THE
COMPUTER NETWORK."
—ANDREW LO, PROFESSOR,
MIT'S SLOAN SCHOOL

ILLUSTRATION
ROBERT DE MICHIELL

BACK IN THE OLD DAYS....

Remember talking to your parents or grandparents about what life was like before television? In decades to come, you may find yourself having to describe to incredulous kids and grandkids what it was like to scrounge around for coins or reasonably crisp dollar bills when you wanted to buy something from a vending machine. The reason: Technology from TeleVend is making it possible to purchase an ice-cold soda simply by tapping a code into your cell phone or beaming credit-card information to the machine from your Palm Pilot.

- Because of her busy schedule, Elizabeth prefers to have a sandwich at her desk instead of going out for lunch.
- The day runs down at five, but she will work until six or seven, getting a couple of quiet hours of work in at the end of the day.

Life in the Community: Bath, Connecticut
- Bath is a small town with a population of about 3,000.
- According to the 2000 census, 96.9 percent of the town is white, 0.6 percent is black, 0.5 percent is American Indian and Alaskan Native, 1.0 percent is Hispanic of any race, 1.0 percent is two or more races.
- The median income for the area is $53,000.
- The high school graduation rate is 90.2 percent and the college graduation rate is 36.3 percent.

With savings like this, who needs to be subtle?

Fiction, non-fiction, paperback or hardcover, every book on the list is now 50% off everyday.

Earth's biggest selection.

books | video | dvd | music | gifts | auctions | e-cards

This historical building housed Pocket Knife Publishing for 16 years.

- The median home value is $179,400.
- When the children were at the local elementary school, Elizabeth was very active in the PTA, where she helped organize the sale of gift wrap paper in order to raise funds for the school.
- Elizabeth is on the volunteer board of the regional mental health organization.
- Michael is a paramedic with the local fire department and has served on various town boards.
- He is also a justice of the peace, and enjoys performing marriages.
- Pocket Knife Publishing is one of the largest employers in the region.

Elizabeth and Michael enjoy when all three children are home at the same time.

- Because the town is the site of the regional hospital, a high number of the doctors and lawyers in the area have their offices in Bath.
- As recently as the 1950s, Bath was a predominantly agricultural community, with a focus on dairy farming.
- In recent years, the town has seen a significant portion of the housing stock purchased by wealthy New Yorkers buying second homes and vacation houses.

"IF MEN WERE THE HUNTERS, AND WOMEN WERE THE GATHERERS, WHO WERE THE GRILLERS?"

HISTORICAL SNAPSHOT
2000

- As a result of increased online purchasing, one in 20 packages delivered in the United States was the result of an Ebay auction
- Since 1963, when the Equal Pay Act was signed, the closing of the wage gap between men and women had been at a rate of less than half a penny a year; currently, women make 76 percent of the wages paid to men
- CBS Broadcasting agreed to pay $8 million to settle a sex discrimination lawsuit by the Equal Employment Opportunity Commission on behalf of 200 women
- The U.S. Supreme Court invalidated those portions of the Violence Against Women Act permitting victims of rape, domestic violence, etc., to sue their attackers in federal court
- Thanks to extensive planning, preparation, and plain luck, the "Y2K bug" fizzled
- The Hubble space telescope captured an image of the death of a star
- Free/low-cost open-source software, particularly the Linux operating system, gained momentum among computer users and began to offer a serious alternative to proprietary software
- George W. Bush was declared the winner of the presidential campaign after the U.S. Supreme Court rendered a complex decision to overturn the Florida Supreme Court ruling that called for manual recounts
- Although females outnumbered males nationally, four states recorded that females were in the minority: Alaska, Hawaii, Nevada and Wyoming
- The estimated median age for women at first marriage was 25 years, up almost a full five years since the early 1960s
- According to the census, the nation's population numbers topped more than 280 million
- Development of a new hard contact lens was announced; designed to be worn it night, it reshaped the cornea so people with mild nearsightedness could have normal vision during the day
- Music industry executives, angry about companies offering free music over the Internet, brought a court action to stop the company Napster from distributing copyrighted music for free
- The number of unmarried couples heading U.S. households increased from 3.2 million in 1990 to 5.5 million in 2000
- Scientists announced that they had constructed a rough draft of the human genome, the complete set of human DNA

Selected Prices

Bath Towel, Long Cotton Terry $24.00
Bird Bath, Cast Stone...$236.00
Camera, Canon 35 mm..$1,900.00
Cat Food, Purina, 20 Pounds..$7.99
Cookies, Amaretti, One Tin $18.00
Exercise Machine, Pro-Form Cage $299.99
Magazine, Annual Subscription, *People Weekly* $103.98
Necklace, Cultured Pearl, 18 Inches..$425.00
Rollerblades $34.97
Salt, Brittany Sea Salt, Two Pounds $10.50
Telescope, Bushnell $225.00
Tire, Bridgestone $85.00

"Your Salary, What New Yorkers Make," *New York*, November 20, 2000:

Publishing: Old media, old salaries. "It's not so bad as it used to be," says Lorraine Shanley, a publishing recruiter, "before Harry Potter." Publishers have been suffering brain drain, with promising talent defecting to the Internet or other, more glamorous businesses. Random House's recent move to a $30,000 starting salary may have turned the tide, but Shanley suggested that some sex appeal comes from a renewed focus on electronic publishing, big advances, and the presence of world-straddling media conglomerates like Viacom, Time Warner, and Bertelsmann in the book business. Once you get in the door, the real salary escalators are in marketing, and especially publicity, where the promotions come fast and furious and a decent publicist should make $65,000. A marketing director should make $85,000 to $100,000 or more. In editorial, where everyone seems to want to work, the salaries start low and stay there until you get a big job offer across town or have a hit author. Senior editors make $55,000 to $90,000; executive editors pull down closer to $100,000 or more. Establish a list and make your name in the business, and you should be able to make in the low six figures; the editor-in-chief of a good mid-size imprint makes $175,000, and the publisher of a larger imprint should make $250,000 or more.

"Down-word Spiral," *Seventeen*, June 2000:

In the age of cell phones and e-mail, it's hard to believe that teens should be at a loss for words. But according to *World Watch* magazine, the vocabulary of the average American 14-year-old has dropped from 25,000 words in 1950 to 10,000 words in 1999. Scrabble anyone?

"The Elephant and the Flea, an interview with Charles Handy," *Context*, **June/July 2001:**

CONTEXT: While writing your latest book, you've thought a lot about the future of business. What changes do you see in the next few years?

CHARLES HANDY: The world is increasingly dividing into elephants and fleas—big organizations and small organizations or self-employed independents.

One reason that so many people are choosing to be a flea, rather than work for elephants, is that ideas have become very important in the knowledge economy. It's a very bad exchange to hand over the ownership of intellectual property in return for an employment contract.

Though I spent 25 years working for an elephant, today I am an independent, as an author. There is no way that I would give up my royalty status for an employment contract. Why should people in companies who have all the great ideas do that either? I expect more people are going to think like authors and say, "My intellectual property is mine". . .

Another reason for the rise of fleas is that big companies are operating more efficiently. I have a formula for productivity: _ x 2 x 3. It means that there will be half as many people working twice as hard and making three times as much money. The other half will be pushed out into small organizations or become independents.

It seems to me that large organizations are increasingly going to be young places. Starting out, people will have apprenticeships in large organizations. After 10 or 20 years, they will either jump or be pushed out of large organizations and live a more independent life. . . .

CONTEXT: Can you talk more about the life of a flea?

HANDY: Being a flea isn't all bliss. Adapting to life as a flea is dramatic.

You need to belong to something. If other people don't matter to you, you don't matter to them. So, you have to build your community of mattering with friends and colleagues. But if it becomes too formal you constrict yourself....

One great thing about being a flea is the freedom to allocate your time. But with that freedom comes the conflict between money and time. Because you aren't guaranteed that there's going to be money coming in, you take on more than you should. Suddenly you have freedom but no free time. You have to overcome that.

It's terribly important that you end up with some concept of what's enough in terms of money. If you don't, you'll never have any time. . . .

The other complication is that you have to sell yourself. You've never had to do this in an organization. Elephants buy your time and then market your contribution in some way. When you are on your own, you have to decide on pricing. It's very difficult. Typically, talented people get someone else—an agent—to do it for them. In the future, more and more of us will have agents.

I don't think you can do it on your own. You'll overprice or underprice yourself.

"The Year of the Genome, The End of a Great Mystery, The Real Beginning of Biology," by Matt Ridley, *Discover*, January 2001:

Imagine that one day there lands upon Earth an alien spacecraft stuffed with a million crumpled pieces of paper, each covered in text written in an unknown script. The best brains in the world are put to the task of deciphering the code, which takes 10 years. But it takes another 40 years to smooth out all the pages, translate them into English, sort them and publish them in a vast book. Then, at long last, the task is done, and we sit down to read the book from beginning to end. It contains thousands of stories about the past, the present, and the future of humankind, from the origin of life to the recipe for curing cancer.

What an extraordinary and unlikely tale. And it is essentially what happened this year. After 50 years of preparation, we have suddenly been placed in the position of being able to read the entire genetic story of human beings, the genome.

On June 26 Francis Collins, head of the Human Genome Project, and Craig Venter, head of Celera Genomics, jointly announced that they had completed the reading of a "rough draft" of the human genome—the complete set of human DNA. The announcement came at least two years earlier than expected and marked a dead heat in a fiercely contested scientific marathon....

This announcement was the beginning of a whole new way of understanding human biology. Everything we have laboriously discovered hitherto about how our bodies work will be dwarfed by the knowledge tumbling from the genome.

Internet postings suggest that, come New Year's Day, computers the world over will send out memos like the one that follows…

"Our records indicate that you have not used any vacation time over the past 100 years. Please either take 9,400 days off work, or notify our office and your next paycheck will reflect payment of $8,277,432.22."

—*Context*, September/October 1999

Women's Work

2002 PROFILE

Stacey Kruger is a dynamo when it comes to organizing charities; she has worked to help underprivileged children have access to computers and has recently begun an enterprise that helps women acquire interview outfits and the confidence to wear them.

Life at Home

- Stacey Kruger is a perpetual motion machine who lives to help others.
- The daughter of a Marine captain who loved the nomadic life of the military, Stacey grew up knowing how to say "hello," "good-bye," and phrases such as "you are a crazy, fat pig" in five languages.
- Her mother, who was born in Costa Rica, met her American husband at a coffee shop near the post at Parris Island, South Carolina, where he was a drill instructor.
- He was attracted by her refusal to back down during a disagreement.
- Stacey struggled to win his approval; his love was conditional based on her behavior, which was not always stellar.
- School served up its own set of problems.
- Mildly dyslexic and determined to earn top grades, Stacey remembers throwing up before every math test.
- But she fould real freedom in her English and drama classes where she won praise and even admiration.
- Now that her daughter has hit the awkward age of 13, Stacey works hard to make sure she feels loved.

Stacey Kruger creates jobs out of her desire to help people.

I HAVE TO START SAVING FOR MY KID'S COLLEGE.
I HAVE TO START SAVING FOR MY KID'S COLLEGE.
I HAVE TO START SAVING FOR MY KID'S COLLEGE.

You know what you have to do. And it's never been easier to get started. Because now the State Farm agent who helped you plan for "just in case" can help you with "what could be." With college savings plans that'll help you be ready when your child is ready. You can choose from a variety of education funding options—many with tax advantages. So listen to that little voice in your head. And talk to your State Farm agent about getting started today. WE LIVE WHERE YOU LIVE.

LIKE A GOOD NEIGHBOR STATE FARM IS THERE.®

Providing Insurance and Financial Services

Consult your tax or legal advisor for specific advice. State Farm • Home Offices: Bloomington, IL • statefarm.com®

- Olivia, who arrived when Stacey was 32 and just starting her third marriage, is a precocious, mother-pleasing ugly duckling.
- Her skills range from voluminous creative writing endeavors and imaginative science projects to a willingness to participate in each and every new charity cause her mother undertakes.
- Olivia has attended so many city council and charity board meetings with her mother that she now fully understands Robert's Rules of Order, and on one occasion, when only 11 years old, raised a point of order from the audience.

LET'S BUCK THE TREND, GET MARRIED, LIVE TOGETHER, HAVE A FAMILY...

CENSUS REPORT: UNWED COUPLES SURGE

- Stacey could not have been prouder.
- She is enormously worried about how she will pay for Olivia's college tuition; husband number three is a great father and an even better fisherman, but a lousy provider.
- Currently, he works for a major law firm supervising its photo copying operations—a time-consuming, but hardly lucrative position.
- Despite their struggles, Stacey likes being married and has no desire to raise Olivia as a single mother.
- For most of her married life, Stacey lived in Knoxville, Tennessee, where the needs were great and the charity leadership erratic.
- When she began a clothing bank in her garage, city officials first laughed at her work, ignored her requests for help, and tried to close her operation because of her success and the traffic it caused in the neighborhood.
- Finally, backed by community leaders, they found her a building and provided a grant.
- Once she had space and funding, Stacey expanded her clothing bank network to help families whose homes had burned, including everything they needed to start again, from furniture and cleaning supplies to underwear for their children.
- Then she sought out children who needed school clothes; after that it was an annual citywide drive, cosponsored by a local TV station, to offer school supplies for every underprivileged child preparing to start school each fall.
- The poor of the community viewed her as an eccentric Mother Teresa, charity boards thought her a genius, and administrators invariably considered her a pain to work with.
- She is now living in Oak Ridge, Tennessee, where the schools are good, employment is available for her husband, and the community is eager for new ideas.
- She and her daughter love visiting the American Museum of Atomic Energy at the National Laboratory.
- Stacey hopes the National Lab, with its extensive outreach programs, will be one of her funding sources in the future.
- She knows from experience that once she gets these smart, flexible professional people to click into her ideas, they will become staunch supporters.
- Workers at the National Laboratory explore alternatives to America's oil dependency, environmental solutions to burning fossil fuels, and ways to make America more secure in the shadow of the 9/11 tragedy.

Oak Ridge, Tennessee, has attracted a prosperous retirement community.

- Many believe it is their social responsibility not only to research the possibilities of tomorrow, but improve the world around them today.
- Stacey is determined to make everything work smoothly this time.
- Currently, she is doing something she has avoided most of her life—watching television.
- Starting with the 9/11 attack on America, Stacey and Olivia have become addicted to news programs featuring America's War on Terror, including the invasion of Afghanistan.
- Stacey believes the threat is real and imminent; Osama bin Laden must be hunted down and brought back "dead or alive," just as the president proposed, if America is to achieve justice.

Life at Work
- Stacey is focused on transforming the looks and lives of individual women in her new community.
- Thanks to the needs of the nuclear age and the federal government's consistent 60-year track record of funding the Oak Ridge National Laboratory, opportunities abound in the Oak Ridge, Tennessee.
- But lack of confidence or polished speaking hold these women back.
- For Stacey, getting these women real opportunities fits well with her quixotic past.

- After she left her clothing bank operation in Knoxville, she worked through the Knoxville churches of her suburban neighborhood to establish a day-care center where welfare-to-work mothers could safely leave their children.
- Once that was up and running, and largely funded by two local charities, she moved on to battling one of the root causes of poverty—an uneven playing field in society.
- To provide poor children with a chance to compete educationally, she looked to computers as the equal opportunity tool of 1996.
- Initially, she viewed hardware as the most critical component, and proposed installing home computers in the subsidized housing projects so that African-American kids, too, could turn in typewritten papers.
- After thousands of working, rehabilitated computers were distributed, and families educated in their use, Stacey turned her attention to computer software.
- Using her considerable grant-writing skills, Stacey obtained a $450,000 computer technology grant from the federal government to teach underprivileged African-American kids how to use software applications.

Equal access to computers can provide a more equal society.

- Stacey knew from experience that when exposed to early enough, computers could become partners in creativity, becoming tools for dreaming rather than merely machines.
- The local television media turned out in droves when the then six-year-old Olivia demonstrated how to use plastic LEGOs to build robots wired to animation software on the computer.
- As a final touch, the children used minicams to create their own videos.
- The animation videos created by the boys all ended in dramatic fights between two or more robots; the girls usually choreographed the robots forming some kind of friendship.
- Stacey did not hold her tongue when the TV cameras focused most on the battling boy robots and ignored the girls.
- After she complained, the cameramen also interviewed the girls, but used little of the footage.
- The charity board that had been formed to administer the grant insisted that Stacey take a salary of $45,000 a year, but she pleaded for $35,000 so more money could be put into computer equipment.
- Besides, she told the board, her paycheck included health insurance for her family for the first time, which in many ways was payment enough.
- This foray into computer technology earned Stacey numerous national speaking engagements, several prestigious awards and a bad case of burnout.
- The creation of an Internet café for high school students, complete with lattes, lots of teenage angst and too many hassles, pushed her over the edge.
- Instead of quietly requesting time off, Stacey imploded in the middle of a city council meeting.
- The newspapers reported that she called the city officials, "fools and children" for failing to fully support her budget.
- Eventually, security had to be called.
- Now, Stacey is taking a less visible path of helping by returning to her clothing store roots, and helping one woman at a time with makeovers.

Stacey uses quality clothing to build confidence.

- Through the years, Stacey has lost count of the number of times strong, capable women failed to get job opportunities because they did not present themselves with confidence.
- Confidence, Stacey believes, begins with looking and feeling good.
- Applicants in jobs as diverse as nursing assistant, marketing director, lawyer, and fast food manager have been trained in Stacey's living room school of self-improvement.
- She learned early that clothes often make the woman.
- Using long-established contacts in the retail clothing industry, Stacey has access to last year's fashion clothing for free as long as she will take a vanload at a time.
- Thus was created an impressive businesswoman's clothing closet, including all types of nursing uniforms and professional suits hanging in the tiny, five-room rented home that her family now occupies.
- Stacey starts by allowing aspiring job seekers to select their own clothing, including shoes and accessories.
- Then the negotiations begin.
- While they are trying on different clothes and evaluating various accessories, Stacey and her clients talk about goals, fears and options.
- Often through this process, they find the outfit and the attitude that meet those job goals.
- After that, it is easy to talk about hurdles, issues and deep hurts.
- Coaching often becomes life-changing.
- Recently, halfway through a haircut, an attractive, self-assured woman in her fifties began to weep.
- For the past five years, all the attention she had been paid was negative, she said.
- She had lost her job, had a double mastectomy, and frequently fought with her grown children.
- Stacey's payment comes in moments like that; to pay the rent, she asks that clients who find a job turn over to her their fifth paycheck, whatever it might be.
- For most, the fifth week on the job marks a transition from underachiever to successful woman.
- Stacey will make $21,000 this year by helping others, and has a waiting list of women eager for Stacey's help.

Life in the Community: Oak Ridge, Tennessee
- The City of Oak Ridge was created in 1942 for a single purpose—secret production of the atomic bomb for World War II.
- Oak Ridge was founded by the U.S. Government to house the workers who developed the uranium-235 and plutonium-239 for the bomb.
- The community's existence was kept secret from most of the country until the summer of 1945.
- The "secret city" quickly became one of the world's foremost centers of research and development, and the advanced applications of high technology.
- Work in Oak Ridge remained under the control of the Atomic Energy Commission, but in 1955 the city was turned over to its residents.
- In the 1990s, the federal government began decontaminating and leasing much of the complex to private industry, and one section was renamed the East Tennessee Technology Park.

- The Oak Ridge Institute of Nuclear Studies, sponsored by many educational institutions, and the University of Tennessee Biomedical Science graduate school are also part of the community.

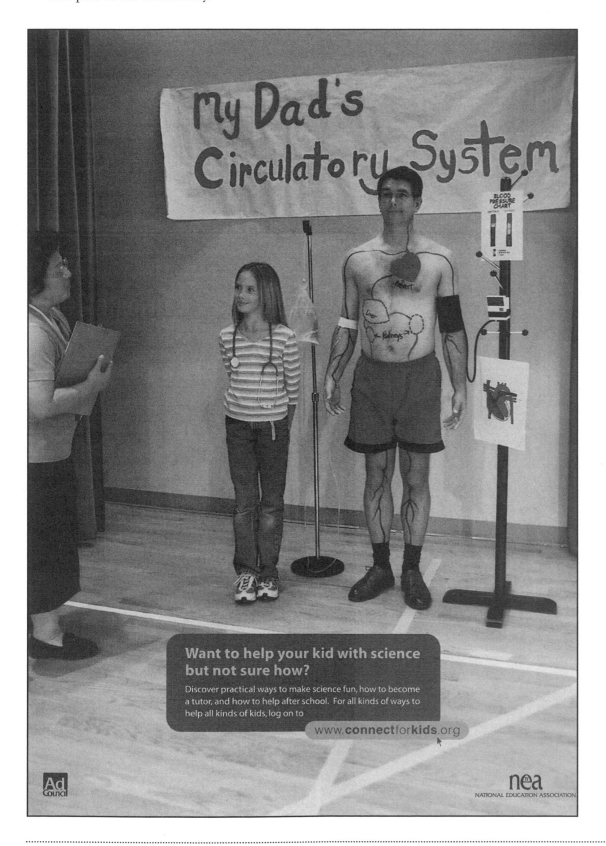

HISTORICAL SNAPSHOT
2002

- The euro was introduced as a cash currency in 12 counties: The Netherlands, Ireland, France, Austria, Belgium, Finland, Germany, Greece, Italy, Luxembourg, Portugal and Spain
- The Nobel Prize for Peace was awarded to Jimmy Carter
- Former Ku Klux Klansman Bobby Frank Cherry was found guilty on murder charges in the 1963 Birmingham church bombing that killed four black girls
- The U.S. Postal Service increased the price of a first-class stamp from $0.34 to $0.37
- U.S. Army Special Forces Sgt. Ross Chapman (31) was killed by enemy fire near Khost, Afghanistan, becoming the first U.S. soldier to die by enemy fire during the assault on that country
- Scientists reported that symptoms of Parkinson's disease were relieved in rats when stem cells were injected into their brains
- President George W. Bush signed a far-reaching federal education bill that tied federal aid to test performance
- The Bush administration and the auto industry agreed to promote development of pollution-free cars and trucks powered by hydrogen fuel cells, pledging more than $1 billion toward research
- The off-Broadway musical *The Fantasticks* was performed for the last time, ending a run of nearly 42 years and 17,162 shows
- Enron fired accounting firm Arthur Andersen, citing its destruction of thousands of documents and its accounting advice; for its part, Andersen said its relationship with Enron ended in early December 2001 when the company slid into the biggest corporate bankruptcy in U.S. history
- At the 59th Annual Golden Globe Awards, Ron Howard's *A Beautiful Mind* was named best drama and its star, Russell Crowe, the top dramatic actor; Sissy Spacek was named best dramatic actress for *In the Bedroom*
- Kmart, the third-largest discount retailer in the U.S., filed for bankruptcy protection
- Daniel Pearl, *Wall Street Journal* reporter, was kidnapped in Karachi, Pakistan, by the "National Movement for the Restoration of Pakistani Sovereignty" and was later murdered
- After an absence in our solar system of nearly 350 years, comet Ikeya-Zhang was sighted by two amateur astronomers in Japan and China
- The Bush administration approved a $700 million grant to help rebuild the part of lower Manhattan devastated by the September 11 terrorist attacks
- A U.S. federal court ruled that it is unconstitutional to sentence a felon to 25 years to life for shoplifting, which was allowed under the California "three strikes law"
- Paula Radcliffe set a new record in the Chicago Marathon, finishing the 26.2-mile race in 2 hours, 17 minutes and 18 seconds
- *The Lord of the Rings: The Fellowship of the Ring* received 13 Academy Award nominations
- Geological expert Mark Meier predicted that oceans would rise 7-11 inches by the end of this century due to polar warming

Selected Prices

Armoire, Entertainment $899.00
Ceiling Fan, Hunter Sojourn $190.00
Chair, La-Z-Boy $322.99
Computer, Sony Laptop $2,300.00
Crib, Oak Finish $190.00
Digital Camera, Nikon Coolpix...$800.00
Fax Machine, Sharp..$150.00
Paper Shredder..$34.00
Silverware, Sterling, 46-piece $2,999.00
Tapes, Audio, Seven-pack $5.00
Tennis Shoes, Brooks Paragon...$55.00
Water, 1.5 Liters..$0.49

The new PowerBooks. Now available in three sizes. Meet the PowerBook® G4 family. The 12" PowerBook is the only ultra-compact portable with a slot-loading CD/DVD-burning SuperDrive.™ The 17" PowerBook offers the largest, most stunning display to ever grace a notebook. And the family is now joined by the all-new 15" PowerBook.

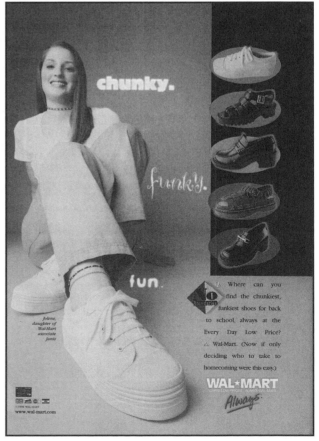

"Taunts from the Border, U.S. forces are itching to pursue al-Qaeda hiding out in Pakistan," by Michael Ware, *Time*, October 28, 2002:

It was an impressive show of force. Under the cloak of darkness last week, Chinook and Black Hawk choppers dropped an entire battalion of 520 U.S. paratroopers into a remote valley in Afghanistan, just across the border from the rugged mountains of Pakistan, where al-Qaeda has established training camps. With dogs barking, cows chewing and a watchful camel resting, the heavily armed U.S. force trudged through irrigated fields and muddy Pashtun villages, cordoning off a 3.5-mile-long area and searching each of 150 residential compounds that dangle off the nosebleed hillsides by the Kakh and Khardala rivers. "We aim to get the maximum number of people on the ground at once," says Major Mike Richardson, paratroops operations officer. "It gives us shock value."

But on this particular occasion, the value was limited. Two complexes suspected of being al-Qaeda staging posts were discovered with caches of hundreds of rocket-propelled grenade rounds, mines and ammunition, but the enemy was nowhere to be found; the most threatening local seemed to be an old woman carrying a hatchet over her shoulder and complaining about her uninvited guests.

For the battle-ready members of the army's 82nd Airborne Division, such small victories, as frustrating as they may be, will have to suffice. That's because the troops are confined behind Afghanistan's border with Pakistan, unable to reach the concentrations of al-Qaeda survivors safely ensconced in camps in the mountains surrounding the town of Mirim Shah. From these retreats in Pakistan, al-Qaeda commanders can send out specially trained teams to lob rockets at U.S. bases and air fields. The most U.S. forces can do is disrupt the endless teams of terrorists popping into Afghanistan, closing off their transport routes and seizing weapons and equipment stashed for them by abettors inside the country. "This is the type of warfare that many folks don't have the patience to fight. Hell, I don't know if I'm patient enough," says Lieut. Colonel Martin Schweitzer, battalion commander.

"Modern Etiquette: Treat Them Right," by Desa Philadelphia,
***Time*, October 28, 2002:**

For parents, the scariest part of Halloween can be the amount of cavity-inducing sweets their kids consume after returning home. Since home-baked goods are frowned on these days and kids don't get too excited about pretzels, what treats can you substitute for candy? These might do the trick:

Cold Cash: Roll up those unwanted pennies in papers, or put a dozen or two in drawstring bags. With any luck, the kids will use them for something other than candy shopping—maybe even give them to UNICEF.

Petrifying Pencils: Halloween-theme pencils, erasers, sharpeners or key rings make for scary-but-good fun. You can get them at party stores that sell costumes and decorations.

Terrifying Trading Cards: Give them their favorite sports stars. Or put them a Monster ahead of the pack with Yu-Gi-Oh! Cards, current playground favorites. They're at most toy stores and discount chains.

(SHHH!) Sugarless Candy: Jolly Rancher, Bubble Yum and Bazooka all make sugarless batches of their delicacies, some sweetened with fruit juice. They're hard to find at supermarkets; try your local candy store.

"At Camp, Survival Skills Include a Solid Resume," by Arthur Bovino, *The New York Times*, May 26, 2002:

At a camp in Fishkill, NY, a group of teenagers were surrounded by woods and wildlife. But an assistant camp counselor was rehearsing them in survival skills that had little to do with nature unless it was the nature of growing up.

As six of the teenagers sat in a circle inside a pine-scented cabin, the counselor, Tony Fong, posed a question: "What will you have to pay for if you live on your own?"

"Interview clothes," offered Brandon Ankle, a tenth-grader at Rice High School in Harlem.

"Student loans, but I'm going to get financial aid," said Christopher Medina, 15, a tenth-grader at Manhattan Village Academy.

"Your hair, $200," said Kenyatta Legree, 17, an eleventh-grader at Grace Dodge Vocational High School in the Bronx.

"Two hundred dollars!" the counselor said.

During a weekend retreat earlier this month, the teenagers spent a lot of time learning how to survive, not in the wilderness, but in the real world. They are members of the Pre-Occupations Club, who were on a visit in connection with the Fresh Air Fund's Career Awareness Program.

The Fresh Air Fund is a nonprofit agency that provides children from low income neighborhoods in New York City with a chance to enjoy free vacations in the country. Many of the youngsters are matched with volunteer families. Others visit the fund's five camps in Fishkill.

Camp Mariah is unique among those camps because of its strong focus on continuing education, careers and decision-making. It is

named for the singer Mariah Carey, who attended a publicly funded camp when she was young and donated $1 million to establish the site in 1994 and 1995. Boys and girls ages 12 to 14 attend for three summers, three and a half weeks each visit, to learn about things like computer skills, fashion design, journalism or TV production. During the school year, they tour workplaces like hospitals, newspapers and law firms, where they follow professionals and try to zero in on their own career interests.

"We looked at what the pressing need was and I was concerned about youth unemployment," said Jenny Morgenthau, executive director of the Fresh Air Fund. "I thought we should help prepare kids for careers."

"We want to make children aware of different careers," she added. "With that, the most important thing is for them to stay in school. Kids would say, 'I want to be a doctor,' but they wouldn't know what to do." The fund helps students with the college application process, with the college boards and with seeking financial aid. "We help them find out what interests them and what they need to do. It empowers them."

ed through two World Wars
here, determined
re'll never be a Third!

2003 Profile

To most who know her, it is not surprising that Erika Durst ended up taking time from her position as a test engineer at the University of North Carolina to travel to Washington, DC, protest the Bush administration's push to go to war with Iraq.

Life at Home

* Erika Durst was born in the early 1970s in California.
* Her parents became involved in working for racial and social justice while they lived in California, continuing that involvement throughout Erika's childhood in South Carolina and passing these ideas and values on to Erika as she was growing up.
* Erika's experiences over the years, and especially the influence of her parents and the church, led her to believe that war is wrong and that it does not solve problems.
* She thinks that war only causes more problems and brings great heartache to those who lose loved ones on both sides.
* Erika's father was a minister in the United Methodist Church, so she was always the "preacher's kid."
* This meant she moved around every three to five years and never completely felt like she belonged anywhere.
* She sensed that people were always watching what she did and how she behaved, and that she was held to a higher standard of behavior than were the other kids.

Erika Durst, a test engineer at the University of North Carolina, joins the protest against the Iraq war.

449

The war attracts a diverse audience.

- This was especially hard, as she was not the kind of kid who sat quietly when she felt she was not being treated fairly.
- In 1985, Erika and her family moved to Columbia, South Carolina, to a neighborhood of old mill houses.
- Most people in the area were poor families living in dirty, overcrowded conditions.
- Because her family lived next to the church, people were often knocking on the family's door for help.
- Erika helped with the social services department's food distribution at the church; in the eighth grade she wrote a paper on homelessness based on her experiences in this community.
- During this time, Erika's parents became very involved in the Carolina Peace Resource Center, which works for peace and justice in the world through education.
- Erika and her younger brother were included in these activities.
- During her middle and high school years, Erika participated in protests and vigils against the manufacturing of nuclear weapons, the death penalty, domestic violence, the American policies in Central America, and war in general.
- She also attended a peacemaking conference with her parents that included a workshop for young people.
- Erika generally felt out of place as a liberal thinker in South Carolina.
- This became even more of a problem in high school when living in an especially conservative community; she discovered that she could not even discuss politics with her best friend.
- During the Gulf War, Erika felt very alone being against the war when all of her friends were supporting it.
- She was very angry and frustrated during her graduation when the valedictorian spoke about the great things that had happened during their years in high school—including the winning of the Gulf War.
- Erika attended a small liberal arts college in South Carolina.
- During the 1992 election, she and a handful of friends and two teachers watching the results together celebrated the election of Bill Clinton.
- The rest of the campus was disappointedly quiet.
- During her college years, Erika traveled to Brazil, Ghana and Kenya with school- and church-sponsored programs.
- Those experiences nurtured her belief that it is good for young people to travel and meet people of different cultures, races and economic backgrounds, and to realize how much they have in common.

- She feels that these interactions among young people will help bring peace in the future.

Life at Work

- After college, she moved to Colorado for graduate school and stayed there for six years.
- She spent one of those years working for Habitat for Humanity as an AmeriCorps VISTA volunteer.
- Her experience of working to help people with limited incomes achieve home ownership in a wealthy community educated her further on the disparity of wealth in the United States.
- She moved to Chapel Hill, North Carolina, a year ago with her husband.
- She is now in her late twenties and works in the School of Public Heath at the University of North Carolina.
- A friend from work told Erika about an antiwar demonstration planned for October 24 in Washington, DC.
- She and her friend had talked about their frustrations with President Bush's policies and actions.
- They were angry that he insisted that the American people speak with one voice—his voice.
- They also feared the precedent that would be set if the United States acted preemptively, especially if there was no international or United Nations support.

Erika is unsure of what to expect during the march.

More than 500,000 show up in Washington to protest the invasion of Iraq.

- The friend encouraged her to join a group of protestors traveling from Chapel Hill, North Carolina.
- Still uncertain about her real plans, Erika went to the bookstore near the University of North Carolina campus that was organizing the group and purchased a roundtrip ticket by bus for $30.
- Later, she learned her parents were going to be at the protest march, as well, and they all agreed to try to meet in Washington.
- On the day of the march, Erika got up at 5 a.m. and made her way to the meeting place.
- Not knowing anyone except her friend and her friend's boyfriend, she was very nervous and unsure of what to expect.
- She had been told that lawyers had volunteered their services if people were arrested, and that, too, made her a bit nervous.
- In Washington, Erika discovered thousands of sincere, passionate people like herself, all there to spend the day marching for peace.
- The weather was warm and sunny, and the atmosphere was festive, and the demonstration peaceful.
- Erika felt as if she was finally able to voice her opinion in a way that just might make a difference, surrounded by thousands of people who felt as she did; she was especially pleased to see a group of veterans joining in the protest.
- When plans for a second march were finalized in January 2003, Erika was better prepared.
- This time, the country looked even closer to going to war.
- She is very frustrated by her inability to stop the war and is angered by the administration's rationale for going to war, which she feels are not the real reasons.

- She thinks that President Bush wants to finish what his father started with the Gulf War and to increase America's control over Middle Eastern oil.
- She believes the rush to war is much more about economics than humanitarianism.
- This time, her mother was unable to go, but Erika drove with her father rather than taking a bus.
- They drove to suburban Washington on Friday and stayed for the weekend with her aunt and uncle, who were very hospitable, despite their obvious political differences.
- On Saturday morning, Erika and her father took the Metro into DC.
- It was very cold, and her dad had a bad cold and cough, but they decided it was important to attend the march anyway.
- They wanted the world to know that there were Americans who did not support what their country was doing.
- As they walked from the Metro station to the rally, they were treated to free Ben and Jerry's ice cream bars.
- After years of living on a tight budget as a graduate student and a VISTA volunteer, Erika always enjoys getting free food, especially dessert.
- As they tried to eat the bars, though, they realized that the weather was so cold the bars were frozen solid and they had to warm them in their pockets first before taking a bite.
- Erika and her dad were impressed with the number of people at the rally, despite the bone-chilling cold.
- Like the rally in October, the people involved were very diverse.
- Erika was pleased to see more than just hippie leftovers from the Vietnam protests.
- The protesters included infants, children, students, thirty-somethings, baby boomers, and even the elderly.
- Republicans and Democrats, veterans, moms and dads, teachers, church groups, scientists, among others, all seemed to be there.
- Whites, blacks, Latinos and Arabs, Christians, Jews and Muslims all joined together to protest the plans for war in Iraq.
- Even a few dogs were there with their own protest signs.
- Erika found it more difficult to be there this time, partly because of the weather, partly because she was not a part of a group, and finally, because it felt even more hopeless.
- President Bush was expected to declare war within days.
- Erika was also worried that being in the cold made her dad's cough feel worse.
- They joined the rally for a while, but it was hard to hear the speakers, so they decided to join the march to help them warm themselves up.
- As they looked back, they were amazed to see how far the crowd stretched behind them.
- Halfway along the route, they stopped for some coffee.
- Cold and tired, they decided to go back to her aunt and uncle's house to get warm and rest so her dad would stop coughing.
- When they hopped onto the Metro, and they noticed that many other marchers were being driven indoors by the cold.
- Erika felt that she had done what she could, but like the march in October, she was aware that President Bush was not in Washington to "hear" what they had to say, which was disappointing.
- Once they were warm, their attention turned to soccer.
- The U.S. men's soccer team was playing a friendly game against Canada that night, and the "best soccer bar in the U.S.," Summers Restaurant in Arlington, was showing the game.

- Summers is well-known in the soccer community for always having soccer games on, and the crowds were overflowing for U.S. games during the 2002 World Cup.
- Erika is a huge soccer fan.
- She was at a World Cup Qualifier in Boston when the U.S. started bombing Afghanistan.
- For Erika, the bombing put a damper on the U.S. Men's win over Jamaica and its qualification for the World Cup.
- The bar was crowded and they had to stand for the first half, but Erika was still happy to be there.
- In contrast to the march, this experience was at least warm.
- Two former National Team players were at the bar watching the game, which was exciting to Erika.

Life in the Community: Washington, DC

- The January March on Washington and the one on October 24 were the largest antiwar protests since the Vietnam War.
- Organizers estimate that 200,000 people attended the October rally and that 500,000 marched on January 19.
- Rallies were also being held in San Francisco, Tampa and in 30 other countries across Europe, the Middle East, and Asia.
- Organizers of the events chose January 19 partly because of the imminent deadline for a report from the weapons inspectors in Iraq, and partly to mark the Martin Luther King Jr. holiday.
- Many speakers at the rallies invoked King's spirit of nonviolence, agreeing with his statement, "The greatest purveyor of violence on Earth is my own government."
- International ANSWER (Act Now to Stop War and End Racism) organized this march to protest the Bush administration's reorganization of U.S. military doctrine and strategy.
- The U.S. has spent $7 trillion on the development of nuclear weapons and has an arsenal of more than 10,000 nuclear weapons.
- President Bush and Congress just signed a new defense budget at a cost of a billion dollars a day.
- ANSWER is calling for this money to be redirected toward jobs, education, housing and healthcare for Americans.
- Although the preliminary report from the United Nations arms inspectors in Iraq is not due until January 27, the Pentagon is continuing to prepare for war.
- These preparations include ordering more carriers to the Persian Gulf.
- Most protestors are calling January 27 a deadline for war.
- They fear that once the report comes in, Bush will declare war with or without the approval of the UN Security Council.
- The president is at Camp David this weekend, and many members of Congress are out of town for the holiday weekend, so they are not here to see the protest.
- Ari Fleischer, a White House spokesman, has stated that President Bush does not see the growing protests as evidence that support is fading for his Iraq policy.
- Newsweek released polls on January 18 that show 60 percent of those polled want the administration to take more time to seek an alternative to war, compared with 35 percent who think the time for war has come.
- Also, 80 percent polled would back a military campaign if it had the full backing of U.S. allies and the UN Security Council.

- International ANSWER was formed three days after 9/11 in response to the Bush administration's "war on terrorism."
- The coalition grieves for those lost or injured on September 11, but its members join together to say that war is not the answer.
- They believe that "Anti-Arab and Anti-Muslim racism is a poison that should be repudiated."
- The members also think that the government is using the country's grief and fear to curb civil liberties and expand police powers, thus restricting basic democratic rights.
- Other organizations supporting the rally include Move On, True Majority and the Campaign to End the Cycle of Violence.

American Red Cross

Together, we can save a life

"Thank you for making our country a better place."

Since September 11, our world has changed.
And Americans of all ages have changed with it, coming together with purpose and hope.
Your caring and concern has led the way. Because of your continued support,
our nation has become a safer place for our families.

To everyone who has helped another person during a time of need,
we salute you.

HISTORICAL SNAPSHOT
2003

- The Supreme Court upheld a copyright extension, lengthening existing copyrights by 20 years in a decision considered a victory for Hollywood studios
- The former governor of Pennsylvania, Tom Ridge, became the nation's first secretary of Homeland Security, uniting 22 agencies and 170,000 employees
- Scientists reported that the fossil discovery of a four-winged bird in China was advancing the explanation of evolution of birds and flight
- The Space Shuttle *Columbia* exploded as it reentered Earth's atmosphere on its way to Kennedy Space Center, killing all seven crew members
- A satellite called the Wilkinson Microwave Anisotropy Probe produced a detailed map of the universe, revealing that it is 13.7 billion years old, is rapidly expanding, and that its weight is 4 percent atoms, 23 percent dark matter, and 73 percent dark energy
- U.S. forces launched Operation Iraqi Freedom designed to end the reign of Saddam Hussein
- Broadway theaters went dark when stagehands and actors voted to support the musicians' strike
- Congress approved the Amber Alert Bill to create a national system to promptly alert the public of kidnappings, particularly of children
- Virginia passed a law to end the sending or receiving of unsolicited commercial e-mail to or from the state
- Congress passed a 10-year $350 billion tax package, the third-largest tax cut in U.S. history, eliminating dividend taxes, reducing capital gains taxes, and increasing child credit for most taxpayers
- Eric Rudolph, accused in the bomb attack at the 1996 Atlanta Olympics, was apprehended in North Carolina after spending five years on the lam
- The journal *Nature* reported that players of first-person action games scored 30 to 50 percent higher in visual attention skills tests
- Maine approved universal health care, announcing plans to offer low-cost coverage to all residents by 2009
- Businesswoman Martha Stewart was charged with conspiracy, obstruction of justice, and securities fraud from the December 2001 sale of shares in ImClone Systems
- McDonalds, the world's largest restaurant chain, asked its meat suppliers to phase out the use of some growth-producing antibiotics in animals
- The fifth installment of the Harry Potter series, *Harry Potter and the Order of the Phoenix*, tallied record sales
- A massive blackout that darkened the Northeast and Midwest was considered the country's largest power failure in history, impacting 50 million people in eight U.S. states and parts of Canada
- The diocesan bishops of the Episcopal Church voted to confirm V. Gene Robinson as church's first openly gay bishop on a vote of 62–45, sparking worldwide controversy
- The Census Bureau reported that the number of U.S. residents who were born in other countries grew to more than 33 million in 2002, a number slightly larger than the entire population of Canada
- The Pope beatified Mother Teresa, calling her an "icon of the Good Samaritan"
- Alabama Chief Justice Roy S. Moore was removed from office for his refusal to comply with a federal court order to remove from the Alabama State Courthouse rotunda a 5,280-pound monument of the Ten Commandments that had been on display since 2001

Selected Prices

Brassiere, Olga Push-up $20.63
Breadmaker, Welbilt...$129.99
Cell Phone, Motorola..$199.00
Computer, Compaq Presario Notebook $1,199.00
Cookware, Williams-Sonoma Soup Pot $230.00
Knife, Schaak 5-Inch Tomato Knife $44.95
Luggage, Willis & Geiger Leather Case $470.00
Olive Oil, 23 Ounces $32.00
Palm Pilot $369.00
Printer, Epson Stylus $279.00
Toilet, Low Flush $270.00
Wine Rack $150.00

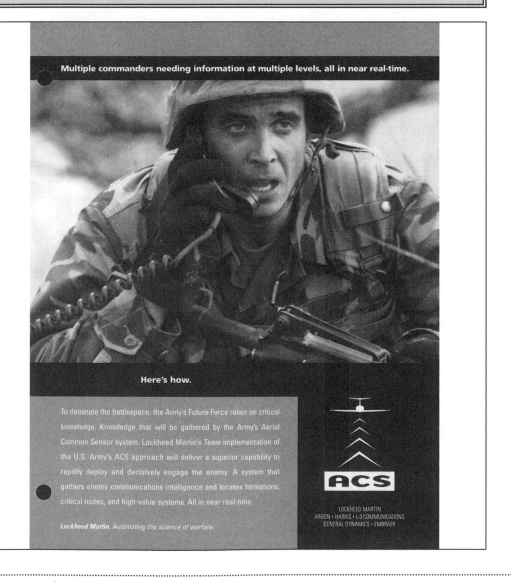

"Working Women," *Ms.*, September 2004:

Results from the first American Time Use Survey are in, and the big surprise may be that there isn't much of a surprise.

As *The New York Times'* Edmund Andrews writes: It may fall into the category of Things You Knew but Could Never Prove, but a new survey by the Department of Labor shows that the average working woman spends about twice as much time as the average working man on household chores and the care of children.

The average working woman also gets about an hour's less sleep each night than the average stay-at-home mom. And men spend more time than women both at their jobs and on leisure and sports.

According to the survey of 21,000 people, all of whom recorded how they spent every hour in a 24-hour period, employed men worked about an hour more than employed women, though the difference is partly due to the number of women working part-time. Among full-time employees, men worked 8.3 hours vs. 7.7 hours for women.

"We've been measuring work for a long time, but we didn't understand the context for work," the survey's project manager, Diane Herz of the Bureau of Labor Statistics, told the *Times*. "How do people fit work into their lives? Are they doing it Monday through Friday? Is work becoming more or less prevalent on the weekends? What trade-offs are people making?"

Some findings reported in the *Times*:

The average working woman, for example, spends about an hour and a half a day caring for other members of the family, the average working man barely 50 minutes. Likewise, the average working woman spends more than 1 hour 20 minutes on household chores, the average working man less than 45 minutes.

Almost as many women as men hold jobs, the Labor Department said: about 78 percent of women, compared with 85 percent of men. But two-thirds of all women said they prepared meals and did housework on an average day, compared with only 19 percent of men who said they did housework and 34 percent who said they helped with meals or cleanup.

"We got two different reactions from people to these results," Ms. Herz said. "Some said it proved that nothing had changed between men and women. Others were surprised that the differences weren't greater."

Here's the specific breakdown of average hours per day spent by persons 18 years and over caring for household children under 18 years, and the average hours per day spent by persons 18 years and over caring for household children under 13 as a secondary activity (the child was in his or her care while the person was doing something else, like grocery shopping).

"Activists March for Peace," by John Byrne, *The News & Observer* (Raleigh, NC), January 19, 2003:

WASHINGTON—As hundreds of Triangle residents swarmed the streets of the nation's capital for Saturday's anti-war rally, first-time protesters joined hands with veteran demonstrators for a song of peace at a subway station.

"People are really afraid with the Jan. 27 deadline, it will be literally weeks [before war]," said Heide Kober, a Durham organizer. "With all the deployment, it has become real.

"It's not a video game anymore. As a mother and grandmother, the lives of our children are just too precious to be sacrificed for a needless war."

Organizers estimated that about 3,000 North Carolinians attended Saturday's anti-war rally, traveling on 35 buses from 13 cities. Arriving bundled in colorful jackets, mittens and gloves, frigid but enthusiastic demonstrators marched from the National Mall to the Washington Navy Yard in hopes of preventing war.

A dozen busloads, seven from Chapel Hill, three from Raleigh and two from Durham, represented the Triangle. Despite the icy weather and a flat tire on one of the buses, the Tar Heel anti-war demonstrators seemed charged and relatively cheery upon their arrival.

Taking a line from the protest's organizer, International ANSWER (Act Now to Stop War and End Racism), many said the war may be more about the United States' need for oil than it is about disarming Iraqi leader Saddam Hussein. "Our government says that it is about weapons of mass destruction, but I think it's clear it's about oil and access to oil," said Paul Dowds, 30, who works with a literacy organization in Chapel Hill.

Others, like Mandy Carter, co-founder of Southerners on New Ground, a multiracial social justice group in Durham, said that they came out of concern for North Carolina's service members.

"We have four key military bases that are sending troops over by the thousands," Carter said. "And so, as North Carolinians, why we're here is to say not everyone is in support of the war."

She also expressed frustration that congressional leaders who were pushing for war didn't have sons and daughters who were going off to fight.

"None of their kids are going over, and these young men and women are going to kill or be killed," she said. "Let the people who want to do these wars go and fight, the ones who are saying they'll vote for it."

Activists planned the event on Martin Luther King Jr. weekend, seeking to invoke the nonviolent spirit of the legendary civil rights leader. Some, like Asheville native Danny Wolverton, carried signs with quotations from King. Wolverton's read: "The greatest purveyor of violence on Earth is my own government."

While most decried the administration's stance, some were careful to voice their support for the armed forces.

"I feel like it's important to be in support of people in the armed forces at the same time we're speaking out for peace," said Gib Barrus, a 44-year-old Celo camp director who came with his wife and two young daughters.

Chris Kromm, a Triangle organizer and director of the Institute for Southern Studies, said that he was awed by the diversity of the movement. While Vietnam protesters were characterized as young hippies, he said, Saturday's movement was far more encompassing.

"The movement from the get-go has been churchgoers, teachers, engineers, Republicans and Democrats," Kromm said. "It's broad and deep."

He believes that while Southerners may be quick to jump on the pro-war bandwagon, many will become more reticent if their friends,

(continued)

(continued)

sons and daughters see combat. He said 42 percent of the U.S. Armed Services are stationed in the South.

Triangle residents who couldn't make the trip to Washington made their feelings heard in Durham. About 350 adults and children, bundled in winter coats and hats, held signs, drums and flags as they lined up along the intersection of Main and Gregson streets, all the way to Morgan and Duke streets, in a protest of the possible war.

"No War, Yes Jobs," one sign said, while another stated, "Bush's War = Al Qaeda's Recruitment Program." Others proclaimed, "Jews Against the Occupation," "Impeach the Moron," "Jobs Not War," and "Stop WWIII."

Kathy Kling of Chapel Hill, 61, who has lived in Saudi Arabia and worked in five Muslim countries, said there were other solutions. "We can find alternatives to get along," she said, holding a sign that said, "Why War?"

Steve Bocckino, 51, an organizer and participant from the People's Alliance in Durham, complained that the media haven't done enough to cover Americans' antiwar attitude. "A lot of people are frustrated by the drive toward war," he said. "This gives them a direction to show it."

For Cathy Kielar, 53, of Durham, another organizer, war means her two sons, ages 21 and 23, could be sent overseas. "I'm a mother," she said. "This is very important to me."

No War Toys

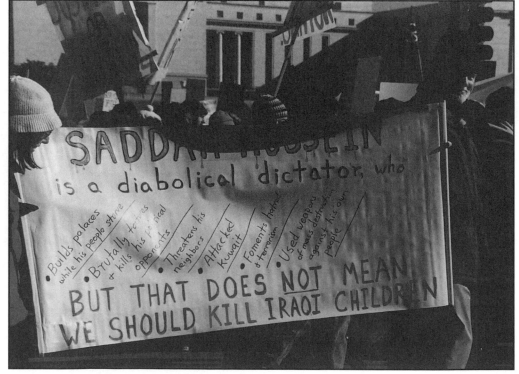

"A Stirring in the Nation," editorial, *The New York Times*, January 20, 2003:

A largely missing ingredient in the nascent debate about invading Iraq showed up on the streets of major cities over the weekend as crowds of peaceable protesters marched in a demand to be heard. They represented what appears to be a large segment of the American public that remains unconvinced that the Iraqi threat warrants the use of military force at this juncture.

Denouncing the war plan as an administration idée fixe that will undermine America's standing in the world, stir unrest in the Mideast and damage the American economy, the protesters in Washington massed on Saturday for what police described as the largest antiwar rally at the Capitol since the Vietnam era. It was impressive for the obvious mainstream roots of the marchers from young college students to grayheads with vivid protest memories of the 60s. They gathered from near and far by the tens of thousands, galvanized by the possibility that President Bush will soon order American forces to attack Iraq even without the approval of the United Nations Security Council.

Mr. Bush and his war cabinet would be wise to see the demonstrators as a clear sign that noticeable numbers of Americans no longer feel obliged to salute the administration's plans because of the shock of Sept. 11, and that many harbor serious doubts about his march toward war. The protesters are raising some nuanced questions in the name of patriotism about the premises, cost and aftermath of the war the president is contemplating. Millions of Americans who did not march share the concerns and have yet to hear Mr. Bush make a persuasive case that combat operations are the only way to respond to Saddam Hussein.

Other protests will be emphasizing civil disobedience in the name of Martin Luther King Jr. But any graphic moments to come of confrontation and arrest should be seen in the far broader context of the Capitol scene: Peaceable throngs of mainstream Americans came forward demanding more of a dialogue from political leaders. Mr. Bush and his aides, to their credit, welcomed the demonstrations as a healthy manifestation of American democracy at work. We hope that spirit will endure in the weeks ahead if differences deepen and a noisier antiwar movement develops. These protests are the tip of a far broader sense of concern and lack of confidence in the path to war that seems to lie ahead.

2004 News Feature

"After some intervention, Pat Dillard got to work; after 13 years running the Presbyterian Community Center, she plans to retire," by Kathy Lu, *The Roanoke Times* **(Virginia), December 2004:**

Here first instinct was to turn down the job.

"I thought it was a little more than I could have handled or wanted," said Pat Dillard, executive director of the Presbyterian Community Center in Southeast Roanoke. "But God intervened and had other plans."

The day was July 19, 1991. Dillard, who by then had spent nine years as a volunteer at the center and five years heading the board of directors, was approached by outgoing director George Pollash about taking the job. Dillard declined after a long conversation with Pollash and praying about the opportunity.

Then, that afternoon, Dillard opened her Bible—something she had done every day for about 25 years as part of her personal devotion to read the Bible through annually. The scripture she fell upon, 1 Chronicles 28:20, practically grabbed her by the collar.

"Be strong and courageous and get to work. Don't be frightened by the size of the task, for the Lord my God is with you; he will not forsake you."

So Dillard obeyed and took the job. Now 13 years later, she is preparing to retire. Her last day will be Dec. 30.

"It's been an amazing adventure," said Dillard, 64. "I'm privileged to be part of the effort."

Dillard was born in Norfolk but raised in Detroit. She graduated a history major from

Detroit's Wayne State University and had planned on joining the navy, following in her father's footsteps.

But she also had to think about a future with Bob Dillard, the man she was dating at the time and who would become her husband in 1963. Bob Dillard is from Botetourt County, and the two have known each other since they were children, having met through family. Her aunt is married to his uncle.

Pat Dillard said she came to the Roanoke Valley—"I thought this was the boonies"—to visit family one summer and decided to see if she could find a job in the area. She was soon offered a job as a probation officer for Roanoke's juvenile court and worked there for seven years, until she was pregnant with her second son. Then she became a full-time mom for 20 years while her husband ran Southwest TV & Appliance Co. on Brambleton Avenue, the store he opened in the early 1970s.

In 1981, Dillard's eldest son, John, died at the age of 15 from a congenital heart malfunction. The year after that, a visitor to her church talked about a need for volunteers at the center. Dillard took note and started volunteering. The visitor was Pollash.

Dillard started by working the front desk before moving on to interviewing clients for eligibility. The nonprofit center provides emergency services to families, such as food and financial aid for rent or utilities.

When Dillard became director, there were no computers at the agency. Now, she has a laptop computer on her desk and there are separate computer labs for the

elementary and middle school students who come to the agency's after-school program.

Having come through the ranks at the center, Dillard is quick to fill in where she's needed, said Tom MacMichael, director of family programs.

"If a volunteer can't make it, she'll step right in and do interviewing or work the reception desk," MacMichael said. "She tries to see what's going on with kids in the after-school program. She's just very interested in what the center is doing and what it needs to do to improve the community."

During her tenure, Dillard has helped the agency grow physically and financially. There were just three full-time employees when she started, including herself. Now there are four full-time and five part-time employees. The agency also now owns the entire corner of Jamison Avenue and 13th Street, occupying space that once belonged to the Rendezvous Bar and Grill and Garland's Drug Store. The agency's retro front counter is a remnant of Garland's.

The center's budget has more than quadrupled—from about $100,000 to $469,000—during Dillard's watch. It also launched the Pathways for Youth program about 10 years ago when the agency wanted to look at ways to address the root causes of poverty. So it hired MacMichael, who conducted a study to determine community needs and find out what the center could do to keep people from having to come back. The results focused on improving family literacy through adult tutoring and after-school programs.

Pathways for Youth started with eight children. It now has 47. MacMichael said the program maintains a constant waiting list, despite the fact that it never officially recruited participants.

The agency has also invested a $20,000 venture grant from the United Way of Roanoke Valley into an initiative that will pay for two years of tuition at Virginia Western Community College for any Pathways student who graduates from high school.

"We won't see the results from that for many, many years," Dillard said. "But anything good takes time to build on."

To give the center more presence in the community, she has also participated in the Southeast by Design project and is a member of the board of directors for the new community health center being developed in Southeast Roanoke.

But as passionate as Dillard is about her work, she realized in July that something in her life had to give. Every day, she visits her 91-year-old mother, who is ill and living at a nursing home. And her 69-year-old husband is dealing with diabetes.

"It had gotten to the point where I was tired all the time," Dillard said. "When I finally made the decision [to retire], it was a great relief."

She said she'll miss the people at the center—"I feel like it's my extended church family"—but will be spending more time with her family, which includes two grandchildren. She will also help out at her husband's business, where her son Rob also works.

As for the center's future, Dillard said she hopes to see more support for it from private donors.

"We have such a great program and yet there are limited monetary resources for it," she said. "We can't rely on grants."

The tentative plan is to hire a new director by February. And she asks just one thing from that person.

"Just keep making people's lives cheerier and happier," Dillard said.

THE PRESBYTERIAN COMMUNITY CENTER

- The Presbyterian Community Center was founded in 1968 as an inner-city ministry to address community needs.
- A majority of the clients are from southeast and northeast Roanoke and the Vinton area.
- The center's clients typically live in subsidized housing and have annual incomes that are at or below poverty level.

QUICK FACTS:

- In 1982, the center gave $18,635 to 493 families.
- In 2003, the center gave $94,705 to 1,374 families.
- The center filled 3,018 food orders in 2003.
- The center has approximately 400 volunteers, about 80 of whom tutor students in the Pathways for Youth program.

2005 News Feature

"Old Law Shielding a Woman's Virtue Faces an Updating," by Sarah Kershaw, *The New York Times*, January 26, 2005:

It is about time, politicians here are saying, for the state of Washington to catch up with the rest of the world.

Florida has struck down a law forbidding unmarried women from parachuting on Sundays. Michigan has done away with a law making it illegal to swear in front of women and children. Texas women no longer face 12 months in prison for adjusting their stockings in public. And the ladies of Maine can now legally tickle a man under the chin with a feather duster.

But here in Washington, in 2005, it is still illegal, under a 1909 law, to bring a woman's virtue into question publicly, to call her a hussy or a strumpet.

And now, a state senator from Seattle—who is not saying she supports attacking the chastity of Washington women—is, nevertheless, trying to overturn the state's "Slander of a Woman" law.

The law was enacted here at a time when women could not vote, when they were viewed by society as delicate flowers to be kept in the kitchen, tending to wood-burning stoves for their genteel gentlemen, vulnerable maidens in need of legal protection from verbal assaults on their purity. It was upheld by the State Supreme Court in 1914, which researchers say was apparently the last time it was before the courts.

Now, Senate Bill 5148, introduced this month by Senator Jeanne Kohl-Welles, a Democrat, would repeal the law, which makes it a misdemeanor to slander any female older than 12—other than prostitutes—by uttering "any false or defamatory words or language which shall injure or impair the reputation of any such female for virtue or chastity or which shall expose her to hatred, contempt or ridicule."

If the bill becomes law, women will have the same protection as men under the other slander laws, which will remain in effect.

Ms. Kohl-Welles—who lectures on women's studies at the University of Washington and admits there are more pressing priorities facing a state with a $1.8 billion deficit—said the old law was nonetheless a vestige of sexism, a "double standard" and an unconstitutional affront to free speech.

"Even though one type of treatment can appear on the surface to be positive and complimentary, it's also being protective and patronizing," said Ms. Kohl-Welles, who has researched other old-fashioned laws and found that many states have done away with them.

But Washington women are not the only ones who have such legal protections against dastardly assaults on their integrity. Eight other states, including New York, still have similar laws on their books, according to the National Conference of State Legislatures, even if they have been rarely used since the days of horse-drawn carriages.

Michigan is one of those states. But in 2002, an appeals court there did strike down a separate 105-year-old law that made it illegal to swear in front of women and children, after a man dubbed by local media as the "cussing canoeist" was punished with a $75 fine and ordered to perform four days of community service. His offense was uttering profanities in front of women and children in 1999, after he fell out of his canoe.

Here in Washington, where Republicans and Democrats are deeply divided over a contested governor's election, the bill to repeal the law against slandering a woman seems to have unusual support from both sides of the aisle, from both Venus and Mars, with three Democrats and one Republican, two men and two women, sponsoring the bill.

Ms. Kohl-Welles introduced the bill two years ago, but it died a fast death in the Republican-controlled Senate. This year, Democrats control both houses of the Legislature, and the head of the Senate Judiciary Committee, Adam Kline, is a Democrat and a co-sponsor of the bill, leading to optimism that impugning a woman's virtue could become legal here.

Mr. Kline said his interest in the bill was less about women's rights and more about purging the law books of anachronisms.

"This was a simply an attempt to get rid of an anomaly, something that was enacted in 1909," he said. "It's archaic. It has no business being in the law in the year 2005." While most of the nation's laws prohibiting impugning a woman's chastity have not been used for decades—or longer—New York's law was cited in a lawsuit filed in 1996 by a Harlem teacher against Joe Klein, author of the 1995 novel *Primary Colors,* and his publisher, Random House. The teacher said she was the basis for a character that had a sexual relationship with a fictional Southern governor. She claimed a violation of New York State Civil Rights Law, Article 7, Section 77, relating to "action of slander of a woman imputing unchastity to her." The case was dismissed in 2003.

With all of Washington's political and financial troubles, Ms. Kohl-Welles's effort to strike down the 1909 law has drawn some criticism.

"The last record of an appeal related to the crime was nine decades ago," said an editorial in the *Seattle Times* last Saturday, "which makes you wonder what is Senate Bill 5148's urgency, given the daunting challenges facing the Legislature."

Ms. Kohl-Welles acknowledged that as the Legislature, torn apart by the tumultuous governor's race here, is tackling so many other things, the bill is not a high priority. Republicans have filed a lawsuit contesting the election won by only 129 votes of Christine O. Gregoire, the Democrat, who was sworn in this month.

"On first blush, this could sound silly," she said. "I'm not fearful that women or men are going to be arrested and this has to be a big case for violations of this law. But let's just get rid of it."

INDEX

Universal Reference Publications
Statistical & Demographic Reference Books

The Value of a Dollar 1860-2004, Third Edition

A guide to practical economy, *The Value of a Dollar* records the actual prices of thousands of items that consumers purchased from th Civil War to the present, along with facts about investment options and income opportunities. This brand new Third Edition boasts brand new addition to each five-year chapter, a section on Trends. This informative section charts the change in price over time and provides added detail on the reasons prices changed within the time period, including industry developments, changes in consumer attitudes and important historical facts. Plus, a brand new chapter for 2000-2004 has been added. Each 5-year chapter includes a Historical Snapshot, Consumer Expenditures, Investments, Selected Income, Income/Standard Jobs, Food Basket, Standard Prices a Miscellany. This interesting and useful publication will be widely used in any reference collection.

600 pages; Hardcover ISBN 1-59237-074-8, $135.00   *"Recommended for high school, college and public libraries." —ARB*

Working Americans 1880-1999
Volume I: The Working Class, Volume II: The Middle Class, Volume III: The Upper Class

Each of the volumes in the *Working Americans 1880-1999* series focuses on a particular class of Americans, The Working Class, The Middle Class and The Upper Class over the last 120 years. Chapters in each volume focus on one decade and profile three to five families. Family Profiles include real data on Income & Job Descriptions, Selected Prices of the Times, Annual Income, Annual Budgets, Family Finances, Life at Work, Life at Home, Life in the Community, Working Conditions, Cost of Living, Amusements a much more. Each chapter also contains an Economic Profile with Average Wages of other Professions, a selection of Typical Pricin Key Events & Inventions, News Profiles, Articles from Local Media and Illustrations. The *Working Americans* series captures the lifestyles of each of the classes from the last twelve decades, covers a vast array of occupations and ethnic backgrounds and travels th entire nation. These interesting and useful compilations of portraits of the American Working, Middle and Upper Classes during th last 120 years will be an important addition to any high school, public or academic library reference collection.

"These interesting, unique compilations of economic and social facts, figures and graphs will support multiple research ne They will engage and enlighten patrons in high school, public and academic library collections." —Bo

Volume I: The Working Class ♦ 558 pages; Hardcover ISBN 1-891482-81-5, $145.00 ♦ Volume II: The Middle Class ♦ 591 pages; Hardcover ISBN 1-891482-72-6; $145.00 ♦ Volume III: The Upper Class ♦ 567 pages; Hardcover ISBN 1-930956-38-X, $145.00

Working Americans 1880-1999 Volume IV: Their Children

This Fourth Volume in the highly successful *Working Americans 1880-1999* series focuses on American children, decade by decade fr 1880 to 1999. This interesting and useful volume introduces the reader to three children in each decade, one from each of the Work Middle and Upper classes. Like the first three volumes in the series, the individual profiles are created from interviews, diaries, statistical studies, biographies and news reports. Profiles cover a broad range of ethnic backgrounds, geographic area and lifestyles everything from an orphan in Memphis in 1882, following the Yellow Fever epidemic of 1878 to an eleven-year-old nephew of a bee baron and owner of the New York Yankees in New York City in 1921. Chapters also contain important supplementary materials including News Features as well as information on everything from Schools to Parks, Infectious Diseases to Childhood Fears along with Entertainment, Family Life and much more to provide an informative overview of the lifestyles of children from each decade. This interesting account of what life was like for Children in the Working, Middle and Upper Classes will be a welcome addition to reference collection of any high school, public or academic library.

600 pages; Hardcover ISBN 1-930956-35-5, $145.00

Working Americans 1880-2003 Volume V: Americans At War

Working Americans 1880-2003 Volume V: Americans At War is divided into 11 chapters, each covering a decade from 1880-2003 and examines the lives of Americans during the time of war, including declared conflicts, one-time military actions, protests, and preparations for war. Each decade includes several personal profiles, whether on the battlefield or on the homefront, that tell the sto of civilians, soldiers, and officers during the decade. The profiles examine: Life at Home; Life at Work; and Life in the Community. Each decade also includes an Economic Profile with statistical comparisons, a Historical Snapshot, News Profiles, local News Article and Illustrations that provide a solid historical background to the decade being examined. Profiles range widely not only geographically, but also emotionally, from that of a girl whose leg was torn off in a blast during WWI, to the boredom of being stationed in the Dakotas as the Indian Wars were drawing to a close. For easy reference, *Working Americans 1880-2003 Volume V: Americans At War* includes an in-depth Subject Index. The *Working Americans* series has become an important reference for public libraries, academic libraries and high school libraries. This fifth volume will be a welcome addition to all of these types of reference collections.

600 pages; Hardcover ISBN 1-59237-024-1; $145.00 ♦ Five Volume Set (Volumes I-V), Hardcover ISBN 1-59237-034-9, $675.00

To preview any of our Directories Risk-Free for 30 days, call (800) 562-2139 or fax to (518) 789-05

e Asian Databook: Statistics for all US Counties & Cities with Over 10,000 Population

is the first-ever resource that compiles statistics and rankings on the US Asian population. *The Asian Databook* presents over 20 stical data points for each city and county, arranged alphabetically by state, then alphabetically by place name. Data reported for place includes Population, Languages Spoken at Home, Foreign-Born, Educational Attainment, Income Figures, Poverty Status, neownership, Home Values & Rent, and more. Next, in the Rankings Section, the top 75 places are listed for each data element. se easy-to-access ranking tables allow the user to quickly determine trends and population characteristics. This kind of comparative can not be found elsewhere, in print or on the web, in a format that's as easy-to-use or more concise. A useful resource for those ching for demographics data, career search and relocation information and also for market research. With data ranging from stry to Education, *The Asian Databook* presents a useful compilation of information that will be a much-needed resource in the rence collection of any public or academic library along with the marketing collection of any company whose primary focus in on Asian population.

0 pages; Softcover ISBN 1-59237-044-6 $150.00

e Hispanic Databook: Statistics for all US Counties & Cities with Over 10,000 Population

iously published by Toucan Valley Publications, this second edition has been completely updated with figures from the latest us and has been broadly expanded to include dozens of new data elements and a brand new Rankings section. The Hispanic ilation in the United States has increased over 42% in the last 10 years and accounts for 12.5% of the total US population. For ease-se, *The Hispanic Databook* presents over 20 statistical data points for each city and county, arranged alphabetically by state, then abetically by place name. Data reported for each place includes Population, Languages Spoken at Home, Foreign-Born, Educational inment, Income Figures, Poverty Status, Homeownership, Home Values & Rent, and more. Next, in the Rankings Section, the top laces are listed for each data element. These easy-to-access ranking tables allow the user to quickly determine trends and ilation characteristics. This kind of comparative data can not be found elsewhere, in print or on the web, in a format that's as easy-se or more concise. A useful resource for those searching for demographics data, career search and relocation information and also narket research. With data ranging from Ancestry to Education, *The Hispanic Databook* presents a useful compilation of information will be a much-needed resource in the reference collection of any public or academic library along with the marketing collection of company whose primary focus in on the Hispanic population.

"This accurate, clearly presented volume of selected Hispanic demographics is recommended for large public libraries and research collections."-Library Journal

0 pages; Softcover ISBN 1-59237-008-X, $150.00

cestry in America: A Comparative Guide to Over 200 Ethnic Backgrounds

brand new reference work pulls together thousands of comparative statistics on the Ethnic Backgrounds of all populated places in United States with populations over 10,000. Never before has this kind of information been reported in a single volume. Section , Statistics by Place, is made up of a list of over 200 ancestry and race categories arranged alphabetically by each of the 5,000 rent places with populations over 10,000. The population number of the ancestry group in that city or town is provided along with ercent that group represents of the total population. This informative city-by-city section allows the user to quickly and easily ore the ethnic makeup of all major population bases in the United States. Section Two, Comparative Rankings, contains three tables ach ethnicity and race. In the first table, the top 150 populated places are ranked by population number for that particular ancestry p, regardless of population. In the second table, the top 150 populated places are ranked by the percent of the total population for ancestry group. In the third table, those top 150 populated places with 10,000 population are ranked by population number for each stry group. These easy-to-navigate tables allow users to see ancestry population patterns and make city-by-city comparisons as . Plus, as an added bonus with the purchase of *Ancestry in America*, a free companion CD-ROM is available that lists statistics and ings for all of the 35,000 populated places in the United States. This brand new, information-packed resource will serve a wide-e or research requests for demographics, population characteristics, relocation information and much more. *Ancestry in America: A parative Guide to Over 200 Ethnic Backgrounds* will be an important acquisition to all reference collections.

"This compilation will serve a wide range of research requests for population characteristics … it offers much more detail than other sources." –Booklist

0 pages; Softcover ISBN 1-59237-029-2, $225.00

Profiles of America: Facts, Figures & Statistics for Every Populated Place in the United States

Profiles of America is the only source that pulls together, in one place, statistical, historical and descriptive information about every pl. in the United States in an easy-to-use format. This award winning reference set, now in its second edition, compiles statistics and da. from over 20 different sources – the latest census information has been included along with more than nine brand new statistical topi. This Four-Volume Set details over 40,000 places, from the biggest metropolis to the smallest unincorporated hamlet, and provides statistical details and information on over 50 different topics including Geography, Climate, Population, Vital Statistics, Economy, Income, Taxes, Education, Housing, Health & Environment, Public Safety, Newspapers, Transportation, Presidential Election Resul. and Information Contacts or Chambers of Commerce. Profiles are arranged, for ease-of-use, by state and then by county. Each coun. begins with a County-Wide Overview and is followed by information for each Community in that particular county. The Communit. Profiles within the county are arranged alphabetically. *Profiles of America* is a virtual snapshot of America at your fingertips and a unique compilation of information that will be widely used in any reference collection.

A Library Journal Best Reference Book "*An outstanding compilation.*" *–Library Jou.*

10,000 pages; Four Volume Set; Softcover ISBN 1-891482-80-7, $595.00

The Comparative Guide to American Suburbs, 2005

The Comparative Guide to American Suburbs is a one-stop source for Statistics on the 2,000+ suburban communities surrounding the 5C. largest metropolitan areas – their population characteristics, income levels, economy, school system and important data on how they compare to one another. Organized into 50 Metropolitan Area chapters, each chapter contains an overview of the Metropolitan Area. detailed Map followed by a comprehensive Statistical Profile of each Suburban Community, including Contact Information, Physical Characteristics, Population Characteristics, Income, Economy, Unemployment Rate, Cost of Living, Education, Chambers of Comme. and more. Next, statistical data is sorted into Ranking Tables that rank the suburbs by twenty different criteria, including Populatio. Per Capita Income, Unemployment Rate, Crime Rate, Cost of Living and more. *The Comparative Guide to American Suburbs* is the best source for locating data on suburbs. Those looking to relocate, as well as those doing preliminary market research, will find this an invaluable timesaving resource.

"*Public and academic libraries will find this compilation useful…The work draws toget. figures from many sources and will be especially helpful for job relocation decisions.*" *– Book.*

1,700 pages; Softcover ISBN 1-59237-004-7, $130.00

The Environmental Resource Handbook, 2004

The Environmental Resource Handbook, now in its second edition, is the most up-to-date and comprehensive source for Environmental Resources and Statistics. Section I: Resources provides detailed contact information for thousands of information sources, including Associations & Organizations, Awards & Honors, Conferences, Foundations & Grants, Environmental Health, Government Agencie. National Parks & Wildlife Refuges, Publications, Research Centers, Educational Programs, Green Product Catalogs, Consultants an. much more. Section II: Statistics, provides statistics and rankings on hundreds of important topics, including Children's Environmen. Index, Municipal Finances, Toxic Chemicals, Recycling, Climate, Air & Water Quality and more. This kind of up-to-date environmental data, all in one place, is not available anywhere else on the market place today. This vast compilation of resources an. statistics is a must-have for all public and academic libraries as well as any organization with a primary focus on the environment.

"*…the intrinsic value of the information make it worth consideration by libraries u. environmental collections and environmentally concerned users.*" *–Boo.*

1,000 pages; Softcover ISBN 1-59237-030-6, $155.00 ♦ Online Database $300.00

Weather America, A Thirty-Year Summary of Statistical Weather Data and Rankings

This valuable resource provides extensive climatological data for over 4,000 National and Cooperative Weather Stations throughout the United States. *Weather America* begins with a new Major Storms section that details major storm events of the nation and a National Rankings section that details rankings for several data elements, such as Maximum Temperature and Precipitation. The m. body of *Weather America* is organized into 50 state sections. Each section provides a Data Table on each Weather Station, organized alphabetically, that provides statistics on Maximum and Minimum Temperatures, Precipitation, Snowfall, Extreme Temperatures, Foggy Days, Humidity and more. State sections contain two brand new features in this edition – a City Index and a narrative Description of the climatic conditions of the state. Each section also includes a revised Map of the State that includes not only weath. stations, but cities and towns.

"*Best Reference Book of the Year.*" *–Library Jou.*

2,013 pages; Softcover ISBN 1-891482-29-7, $175.00

erica's Top-Rated Cities, 2004

ica's Top-Rated Cities provides current, comprehensive statistical information and other essential data in one easy-to-use source on
00 "top" cities that have been cited as the best for business and living in the U.S. This handbook allows readers to see, at a glance,
cise social, business, economic, demographic and environmental profile of each city, including brief evaluative comments. In
ion to detailed data on Cost of Living, Finances, Real Estate, Education, Major Employers, Media, Crime and Climate, city reports
include Housing Vacancies, Tax Audits, Bankruptcy, Presidential Election Results and more. This outstanding source of
mation will be widely used in any reference collection.

"The only source of its kind that brings together all of this information into one
easy-to-use source. It will be beneficial to many business and public libraries." –ARBA

pages, 4 Volume Set; Softcover ISBN 1-59237-038-1, $195.00

erica's Top-Rated Smaller Cities, 2004

fect companion to *America's Top-Rated Cities*, *America's Top-Rated Smaller Cities* provides current, comprehensive business and
; profiles of smaller cities (population 25,000-99,999) that have been cited as the best for business and living in the United States.
cities make up this 2004 edition of *America's Top-Rated Smaller Cities*, all are top-ranked by Population Growth, Median Income,
nployment Rate and Crime Rate. City reports reflect the most current data available on a wide-range of statistics, including
loyment & Earnings, Household Income, Unemployment Rate, Population Characteristics, Taxes, Cost of Living, Education,
h Care, Public Safety, Recreation, Media, Air & Water Quality and much more. Plus, each city report contains a Background of
ity, and an Overview of the State Finances. *America's Top-Rated Smaller Cities* offers a reliable, one-stop source for statistical data
before now, could only be found scattered in hundreds of sources. This volume is designed for a wide range of readers: individuals
dering relocating a residence or business; professionals considering expanding their business or changing careers; general and
et researchers; real estate consultants; human resource personnel; urban planners and investors.

"Provides current, comprehensive statistical information in one easy-to-use source…
Recommended for public and academic libraries and specialized collections." –Library Journal

pages; Softcover ISBN 1-59237-043-8, $160.00

me in America's Top-Rated Cities, 2000

volume includes over 20 years of crime statistics in all major crime categories: violent crimes, property crimes and total crime.
e in America's Top-Rated Cities is conveniently arranged by city and covers 76 top-rated cities. *Crime in America's Top-Rated Cities*
details that compare the number of crimes and crime rates for the city, suburbs and metro area along with national crime trends
olent, property and total crimes. Also, this handbook contains important information and statistics on Anti-Crime Programs,
e Risk, Hate Crimes, Illegal Drugs, Law Enforcement, Correctional Facilities, Death Penalty Laws and much more. A much-
d resource for people who are relocating, business professionals, general researchers, the press, law enforcement officials and
nts of criminal justice.

"Data is easy to access and will save hours of searching." –Global Enforcement Review

ages; Softcover ISBN 1-891482-84-X, $155.00

American Tally, 2003/04 Statistics & Comparative Rankings for U.S. Cities with Populations over 10,000

important statistical handbook compiles, all in one place, comparative statistics on all U.S. cities and towns with a 10,000+
lation. *The American Tally* provides statistical details on over 4,000 cities and towns and profiles how they compare with one
er in Population Characteristics, Education, Language & Immigration, Income & Employment and Housing. Each section begins
an alphabetical listing of cities by state, allowing for quick access to both the statistics and relative rankings of any city. Next, the
st and lowest cities are listed in each statistic. These important, informative lists provide quick reference to which cities are at
extremes of the spectrum for each statistic. Unlike any other reference, *The American Tally* provides quick, easy access to
arative statistics – a must-have for any reference collection.

"A solid library reference." -Bookwatch

ages; Softcover ISBN 1-930956-29-0, $125.00

preview any of our Directories Risk-Free for 30 days, call (800) 562-2139 or fax to (518) 789-0556

The Comparative Guide to American Elementary & Secondary Schools, 2004/05

The only guide of its kind, this award winning compilation offers a snapshot profile of every public school district in the United Stat serving 1,500 or more students – more than 5,900 districts are covered. Organized alphabetically by district within state, each chap begins with a Statistical Overview of the state. Each district listing includes contact information (name, address, phone number and web site) plus Grades Served, the Numbers of Students and Teachers and the Number of Regular, Special Education, Alternative an Vocational Schools in the district along with statistics on Student/Classroom Teacher Ratios, Drop Out Rates, Ethnicity, the Numb of Librarians and Guidance Counselors and District Expenditures per student. As an added bonus, *The Comparative Guide to America Elementary and Secondary Schools* provides important ranking tables, both by state and nationally, for each data element. For easy navigation through this wealth of information, this handbook contains a useful City Index that lists all districts that operate schools within a city. These important comparative statistics are necessary for anyone considering relocation or doing comparative researc their own district and would be a perfect acquisition for any public library or school district library.

"This straightforward guide is an easy way to find general information. Valuable for academic and large public library collections." –A

2,400 pages; Softcover ISBN 1-59237-047-0, $125.00

Sedgwick Press
Health & Education Directories

Educators Resource Directory, 2005/06

Educators Resource Directory is a comprehensive resource that provides the educational professional with thousands of resources and statistical data for professional development. This directory saves hours of research time by providing immediate access to Associat & Organizations, Conferences & Trade Shows, Educational Research Centers, Employment Opportunities & Teaching Abroad, Scho Library Services, Scholarships, Financial Resources, Professional Consultants, Computer Software & Testing Resources and much more. Plus, this comprehensive directory also includes a section on Statistics and Rankings with over 100 tables, including statistics Average Teacher Salaries, SAT/ACT scores, Revenues & Expenditures and more. These important statistics will allow the user to how their school rates among others, make relocation decisions and so much more. For quick access to information, this directory contains four indexes: Entry & Publisher Index, Geographic Index, a Subject & Grade Index and Web Sites Index. *Educators Resour Directory* will be a well-used addition to the reference collection of any school district, education department or public library.

"Recommended for all collections that serve elementary and secondary school professionals." –C

1,000 pages; Softcover ISBN 1-59237-080-2, $145.00 ◆ Online Database $195.00 ◆ Online Database & Directory Combo $280.00

The Complete Learning Disabilities Directory, 2005/06

The Complete Learning Disabilities Directory is the most comprehensive database of Programs, Services, Curriculum Materials, Professional Meetings & Resources, Camps, Newsletters and Support Groups for teachers, students and families concerned with learning disabilities. This information-packed directory includes information about Associations & Organizations, Schools, College: Testing Materials, Government Agencies, Legal Resources and much more. For quick, easy access to information, this directory contains four indexes: Entry Name Index, Subject Index and Geographic Index. With every passing year, the field of learning disabilities attracts more attention and the network of caring, committed and knowledgeable professionals grows every day. This directory is an invaluable research tool for these parents, students and professionals.

"Due to its wealth and depth of coverage, parents, teachers and others… should find this an invaluable resource." –Bo

900 pages; Softcover ISBN 1-59237-092-6, $145.00 ◆ Online Database $195.00 ◆ Online Database & Directory Combo $280.00

The Complete Directory for People with Disabilities, 2005

A wealth of information, now in one comprehensive sourcebook. Completely updated for 2005, this edition contains more informatio than ever before, including thousands of new entries and enhancements to existing entries and thousands of additional web sites and mail addresses. This up-to-date directory is the most comprehensive resource available for people with disabilities, detailing Independent Living Centers, Rehabilitation Facilities, State & Federal Agencies, Associations, Support Groups, Periodicals & Books Assistive Devices, Employment & Education Programs, Camps and Travel Groups. Each year, more libraries, schools, colleges, hospitals, rehabilitation centers and individuals add *The Complete Directory for People with Disabilities* to their collections, making sur that this information is readily available to the families, individuals and professionals who can benefit most from the amazing wealth resources cataloged here.

"No other reference tool exists to meet the special needs of the disabled in one convenient resource for information." –Library Jo

1,200 pages; Softcover ISBN 1-59237-054-3, $165.00 ◆ Online Database $215.00 ◆ Online Database & Directory Combo $300.00

To preview any of our Directories Risk-Free for 30 days, call (800) 562-2139 or fax to (518) 789-05!

Complete Directory for People with Chronic Illness, 2005/06

...usands of hours of research have gone into this completely updated 2005/06 edition – several new chapters have been added along ... thousands of new entries and enhancements to existing entries. Plus, each chronic illness chapter has been reviewed by an medical ...ert in the field. This widely-hailed directory is structured around the 90 most prevalent chronic illnesses – from Asthma to Cancer ...Wilson's Disease – and provides a comprehensive overview of the support services and information resources available for people ...nosed with a chronic illness. Each chronic illness has its own chapter and contains a brief description in layman's language, ...wed by important resources for National & Local Organizations, State Agencies, Newsletters, Books & Periodicals, Libraries & ...earch Centers, Support Groups & Hotlines, Web Sites and much more. This directory is an important resource for health care ...essionals, the collections of hospital and health care libraries, as well as an invaluable tool for people with a chronic illness and their ...oort network.

"A must purchase for all hospital and health care libraries and is strongly recommended for all public library reference departments." –ARBA

...0 pages; Softcover ISBN 1-59237-081-0, $165.00 ◆ Online Database $215.00 ◆ Online Database & Directory Combo $300.00

Complete Mental Health Directory, 2004

... is the most comprehensive resource covering the field of behavioral health, with critical information for both the layman and the ...tal health professional. For the layman, this directory offers understandable descriptions of 25 Mental Health Disorders as well as ...iled information on Associations, Media, Support Groups and Mental Health Facilities. For the professional, *The Complete Mental* ...*lth Directory* offers critical and comprehensive information on Managed Care Organizations, Information Systems, Government ...ncies and Provider Organizations. This comprehensive volume of needed information will be widely used in any reference ...ction.

"... the strength of this directory is that it consolidates widely dispersed information into a single volume." –Booklist

...pages; Softcover ISBN 1-59237-046-2, $165.00 ◆ Online Database $215.00 ◆ Online & Directory Combo $300.00

...der Americans Information Directory, 2004/05

...apletely updated for 2004/05, this Fifth Edition has been completely revised and now contains 1,000 new listings, over 8,000 ...ates to existing listings and over 3,000 brand new e-mail addresses and web sites. You'll find important resources for Older ...ericans including National, Regional, State & Local Organizations, Government Agencies, Research Centers, Libraries & ...rmation Centers, Legal Resources, Discount Travel Information, Continuing Education Programs, Disability Aids & Assistive ...ices, Health, Print Media and Electronic Media. Three indexes: Entry Index, Subject Index and Geographic Index make it easy to ...just the right source of information. This comprehensive guide to resources for Older Americans will be a welcome addition to any ...rence collection.

"Highly recommended for academic, public, health science and consumer libraries..." –Choice

...0 pages; Softcover ISBN 1-59237-037-3, $165.00 ◆ Online Database $215.00 ◆ Online Database & Directory Combo $300.00

...e Complete Directory for Pediatric Disorders, 2004/05

... important directory provides parents and caregivers with information about Pediatric Conditions, Disorders, Diseases and ...bilities, including Blood Disorders, Bone & Spinal Disorders, Brain Defects & Abnormalities, Chromosomal Disorders, Congenital ...rt Defects, Movement Disorders, Neuromuscular Disorders and Pediatric Tumors & Cancers. This carefully written directory ...s: understandable Descriptions of 15 major bodily systems; Descriptions of more than 200 Disorders and a Resources Section, ...iling National Agencies & Associations, State Associations, Online Services, Libraries & Resource Centers, Research Centers, ...oort Groups & Hotlines, Camps, Books and Periodicals. This resource will provide immediate access to information crucial to ...lies and caregivers when coping with children's illnesses.

"Recommended for public and consumer health libraries." –Library Journal

...0 pages; Softcover ISBN 1-59237-045-4, $165.00 ◆ Online Database $215.00 ◆ Online Database & Directory Combo $300.00

... preview any of our Directories Risk-Free for 30 days, call (800) 562-2139 or fax to (518) 789-0556

The Complete Directory for People with Rare Disorders, 2002/03

This outstanding reference is produced in conjunction with the National Organization for Rare Disorders to provide comprehensive and needed access to important information on over 1,000 rare disorders, including Cancers and Muscular, Genetic and Blood Disorders. An informative Disorder Description is provided for each of the 1,100 disorders (rare Cancers and Muscular, Genetic and Blood Disorders) followed by information on National and State Organizations dealing with a particular disorder, Umbrella Organizations that cover a wide range of disorders, the Publications that can be useful when researching a disorder and the Government Agencies to contact. Detailed and up-to-date listings contain mailing address, phone and fax numbers, web sites and e-m addresses along with a description. The Complete Directory for People with Rare Disorders will be an invaluable tool for the thousar of families that have been struck with a rare or "orphan" disease, who feel that they have no place to turn and will be a much-used addition to the reference collection of any public or academic library.

"Quick access to information… public libraries and hospital patient libraries will find this a use resource in directing users to support groups or agencies dealing with a rare disorder." –Boo

726 pages; Softcover ISBN 1-891482-18-1, $165.00

The Directory of Drug & Alcohol Residential Rehabilitation Facilities, 2004

This brand new directory is the first-ever resource to bring together, all in one place, data on the thousands of drug and alcohol residential rehabilitation facilities in the United States. *The Directory of Drug & Alcohol Residential Rehabilitation Facilities* covers over 1,000 facilities, with detailed contact information for each one, including mailing address, phone and fax numbers, email addresses an web sites, mission statement, type of treatment programs, cost, average length of stay, numbers of residents and counselors, accreditation, insurance plans accepted, type of environment, religious affiliation, education components and much more. It also contains a helpful chapter on General Resources that provides contact information for Associations, Print & Electronic Media, Suppo Groups and Conferences. Multiple indexes allow the user to pinpoint the facilities that meet very specific criteria. This time-saving tool is what so many counselors, parents and medical professionals have been asking for. *The Directory of Drug & Alcohol Residential Rehabilitation Facilities* will be a helpful tool in locating the right source for treatment for a wide range of individuals. This comprehensive directory will be an important acquisition for all reference collections: public and academic libraries, case managers, social workers, state agencies and many more.

"This is an excellent, much needed directory that fills an important gap…" –Boo

300 pages; Softcover ISBN 1-59237-031-4, $135.00

Sedgwick Press
Hospital & Health Plan Directories

The Directory of Hospital Personnel, 2005

The Directory of Hospital Personnel is the best resource you can have at your fingertips when researching or marketing a product or service to the hospital market. A "Who's Who" of the hospital universe, this directory puts you in touch with over 150,000 key decision-makers. With 100% verification of data you can rest assured that you will reach the right person with just one call. Every hospital in the U.S. is profiled, listed alphabetically by city within state. Whether you want to define or restructure sales territories… locate hospitals with the purchasing power to accept your proposals… keep track of important contacts or colleagues… or find information on which insurance plans are accepted, *The Directory of Hospital Personnel* gives you the information you need – easily, efficiently, effectively and accurately.

"Recommended for college, university and medical libraries." –AR

2,500 pages; Softcover ISBN 1-59237-065-9 $275.00 ◆ Online Database $545.00 ◆ Online Database & Directory Combo, $650.00

The HMO/PPO Directory, 2005

The HMO/PPO Directory is a comprehensive source that provides detailed information about Health Maintenance Organizations and Preferred Provider Organizations nationwide. This comprehensive directory details more information about more managed health c organizations than ever before. Over 1,100 HMOs, PPOs and affiliated companies are listed, arranged alphabetically by state. Detail listings include Key Contact Information, Prescription Drug Benefits, Enrollment, Geographical Areas served, Affiliated Physicians a Hospitals, Federal Qualifications, Status, Year Founded, Managed Care Partners, Employer References, Fees & Payment Informatior and more. Plus, five years of historical information is included related to Revenues, Net Income, Medical Loss Ratios, Membership Enrollment and Number of Patient Complaints. *The HMO/PPO Directory* provides the most comprehensive information on the most companies available on the market place today.

"Helpful to individuals requesting certain HMO/PPO issues such as co-payment costs, subscription costs and patient complain Individuals concerned (or those with questions) about their insurance may find this text to be of use to them." –AR

600 pages; Softcover ISBN 1-59237-057-8, $275.00 ◆ Online Database, $495.00 ◆ Online Database & Directory Combo, $600.00

To preview any of our Directories Risk-Free for 30 days, call (800) 562-2139 or fax to (518) 789-055

Grey House Publishing
Business Directories

Directory of Business Information Resources, 2005

100% verification, over 1,000 new listings and more than 12,000 updates, this 2005 edition of *The Directory of Business Information rces* is the most up-to-date source for contacts in over 98 business areas – from advertising and agriculture to utilities and esalers. This carefully researched volume details: the Associations representing each industry; the Newsletters that keep members nt; the Magazines and Journals - with their "Special Issues" - that are important to the trade, the Conventions that are "must ds," Databases, Directories and Industry Web Sites that provide access to must-have marketing resources. Includes contact s, phone & fax numbers, web sites and e-mail addresses. This one-volume resource is a gold mine of information and would be a me addition to any reference collection.

"This is a most useful and easy-to-use addition to any researcher's library." –The Information Professionals Institute

pages; Softcover ISBN 1-59237-050-0, $195.00 ◆ Online Database $495.00

ions of the World, 2005 A Political, Economic and Business Handbook

completely revised edition covers all the nations of the world in an easy-to-use, single volume. Each nation is profiled in a single er that includes Key Facts, Political & Economic Issues, a Country Profile and Business Information. In this fast-changing world, xtremely important to make sure that the most up-to-date information is included in your reference collection. This 2005 edition t the answer. Each of the 200+ country chapters have been carefully reviewed by a political expert to make sure that the text ts the most current information on Politics, Travel Advisories, Economics and more. You'll find such vital information as a try Map, Population Characteristics, Inflation, Agricultural Production, Foreign Debt, Political History, Foreign Policy, Regional urity, Economics, Trade & Tourism, Historical Profile, Political Systems, Ethnicity, Languages, Media, Climate, Hotels, Chambers mmerce, Banking, Travel Information and more. Five Regional Chapters follow the main text and include a Regional Map, an ductory Article, Key Indicators and Currencies for the Region. New for 2004, an all-inclusive CD-ROM is available as a anion to the printed text. Noted for its sophisticated, up-to-date and reliable compilation of political, economic and business nation, this brand new edition will be an important acquisition to any public, academic or special library reference collection.

"A useful addition to both general reference collections and business collections." –RUSQ

pages; Print Version Only Softcover ISBN 1-59237-051-9, $145.00 ◆ Print Version and CD-ROM $180.00

Directory of Mail Order Catalogs, 2005

shed since 1981, this 2005 edition features 100% verification of data and is the premier source of information on the mail order ng industry. Details over 12,000 consumer catalog companies with 44 different product chapters from Animals to Toys & Games. ains detailed contact information including e-mail addresses and web sites along with important business details such as employee years in business, sales volume, catalog size, number of catalogs mailed and more. Four indexes provide quick access to nation: Catalog & Company Name Index, Geographic Index, Product Index and Web Sites Index.

"This is a godsend for those looking for information." –Reference Book Review

pages; Softcover ISBN 1-59237-066-7 $250.00 ◆ Online Database (includes a free copy of the directory) $495.00

Directory of Business to Business Catalogs, 2005

completely updated 2005 *Directory of Business to Business Catalogs*, provides details on over 6,000 suppliers of everything from uters to laboratory supplies… office products to office design… marketing resources to safety equipment… landscaping to tenance suppliers… building construction and much more. Detailed entries offer mailing address, phone & fax numbers, e-mail sses, web sites, key contacts, sales volume, employee size, catalog printing information and more. Jut about every kind of product iness needs in its day-to-day operations is covered in this carefully-researched volume. Three indexes are provided for at-a-glance s to information: Catalog & Company Name Index, Geographic Index and Web Sites Index.

"An excellent choice for libraries… wishing to supplement their business supplier resources." –Booklist

ages; Softcover ISBN 1-59237-064-0, $165.00 ◆ Online Database (includes a free copy of the directory) $325.00

preview any of our Directories Risk-Free for 30 days, call (800) 562-2139 or fax to (518) 789-0556

The Directory of Venture Capital Firms, 2005

This edition has been extensively updated and broadly expanded to offer direct access to over 2,800 Domestic and International Venture Capital Firms, including address, phone & fax numbers, e-mail addresses and web sites for both primary and branch locatio Entries include details on the firm's Mission Statement, Industry Group Preferences, Geographic Preferences, Average and Minimu Investments and Investment Criteria. You'll also find details that are available nowhere else, including the Firm's Portfolio Compa and extensive information on each of the firm's Managing Partners, such as Education, Professional Background and Directorships held, along with the Partner's E-mail Address. *The Directory of Venture Capital Firms* offers five important indexes: Geographic Inde Executive Name Index, Portfolio Company Index, Industry Preference Index and College & University Index. With its comprehen coverage and detailed, extensive information on each company, *The Directory of Venture Capital Firms* is an important addition to any finance collection.

"The sheer number of listings, the descriptive information provided and the outstanding inde
make this directory a better value than its principal competitor, Pratt's Guide to Venture Capital Sour
Recommended for business collections in large public, academic and business libraries." –C

1,300 pages; Softcover ISBN 1-59237-062-4, $450.00 ◆ Online Database (includes a free copy of the directory) $889.00

Thomas Food and Beverage Market Place, 2005

Thomas Food and Beverage Market Place is bigger and better than ever with thousands of new companies, thousands of updates to existing companies and two revised and enhanced product category indexes. This comprehensive directory profiles over 18,000 Foo Beverage Manufacturers, 12,000 Equipment & Supply Companies, 2,200 Transportation & Warehouse Companies, 2,000 Brokers & Wholesalers, 8,000 Importers & Exporters, 900 Industry Resources and hundreds of Mail Order Catalogs. Listings include detailed Contact Information, Sales Volumes, Key Contacts, Brand & Product Information, Packaging Details and much more. *Thomas Foo Beverage Market Place* is available as a three-volume printed set, a subscription-based Online Database via the Internet, on CD-ROM well as mailing lists and a licensable database.

"An essential purchase for those in the food industry but will also be useful in public libraries where needed. Much of the informa
will be difficult and time consuming to locate without this handy three-volume ready-reference source." –A

8,500 pages, 3 Volume Set; Softcover ISBN 1-59237-058-6, $495.00 ◆ CD-ROM $695.00 ◆
CD-ROM & 3 Volume Set Combo $895.00 ◆ Online Database $695.00 ◆ Online Database & 3 Volume Set Combo, $895.00

The Grey House Performing Arts Directory, 2005

The Grey House Performing Arts Directory is the most comprehensive resource covering the Performing Arts. This important director provides current information on over 8,500 Dance Companies, Instrumental Music Programs, Opera Companies, Choral Groups, Theater Companies, Performing Arts Series and Performing Arts Facilities. Plus, this edition now contains a brand new section on Artist Management Groups. In addition to mailing address, phone & fax numbers, e-mail addresses and web sites, dozens of other fields of available information include mission statement, key contacts, facilities, seating capacity, season, attendance and more. This directory also provides an important Information Resources section that covers hundreds of Performing Arts Associations, Magazin Newsletters, Trade Shows, Directories, Databases and Industry Web Sites. Five indexes provide immediate access to this wealth of information: Entry Name, Executive Name, Performance Facilities, Geographic and Information Resources. *The Grey House Perform Arts Directory* pulls together thousands of Performing Arts Organizations, Facilities and Information Resources into an easy-to-use source – this kind of comprehensiveness and extensive detail is not available in any resource on the market place today.

"Immensely useful and user-friendly ... recommended for public, academic and certain special library reference collections." –Bo

1,500 pages; Softcover ISBN 1-59237-023-3, $185.00 ◆ Online Database $335.00

Research Services Directory, 2003/04 Commercial & Corporate Research Centers

This Ninth Edition provides access to well over 8,000 independent Commercial Research Firms, Corporate Research Centers and Laboratories offering contract services for hands-on, basic or applied research. *Research Services Directory* covers the thousands of typ of research companies, including Biotechnology & Pharmaceutical Developers, Consumer Product Research, Defense Contractors, Electronics & Software Engineers, Think Tanks, Forensic Investigators, Independent Commercial Laboratories, Information Broke Market & Survey Research Companies, Medical Diagnostic Facilities, Product Research & Development Firms and more. Each ent provides the company's name, mailing address, phone & fax numbers, key contacts, web site, e-mail address, as well as a company description and research and technical fields served. Four indexes provide immediate access to this wealth of information: Research Firms Index, Geographic Index, Personnel Name Index and Subject Index.

"An important source for organizations in need of information about laboratories, individuals and other facilities." –A

1,400 pages; Softcover ISBN 1-59237-003-9, $395.00 ◆ Online Database (includes a free copy of the directory) $850.00

To preview any of our Directories Risk-Free for 30 days, call (800) 562-2139 or fax to (518) 789-055

For Reference

Not to be taken from this room